English America and the
Restoration Monarchy of Charles II

J. M. Sosin

ENGLISH AMERICA

AND THE

Restoration Monarchy
of Charles II

*Transatlantic Politics,
Commerce, and Kinship*

UNIVERSITY OF NEBRASKA PRESS
Lincoln • London

Publication of this book was aided by a grant from the National Endowment for the Humanities.

Library of Congress Cataloging in Publication Data

Sosin, Jack M
  English America and the Restoration monarchy
of Charles II.

  Includes bibliographical references and index.
  1. United States—History—Colonial period, ca.
1600–1775.   2. Great Britain—History—Charles II,
1660–1685.   I. Title.
E191.S67   973.2   80–16215
ISBN 0-8032-4118-6

For Craig

Contents

A Note on Dates

ALL DATES unless otherwise indicated are in the Julian calendar, ten days behind those of the Gregorian calendar adopted by some of the states of western Europe in 1582–83. In England, where the Gregorian calendar was not to be adopted until 1752, it had become the custom from the thirteenth century to advance the number of the year on 25 March, the date of the Feast of the Annunciation. Not until 1750 did Parliament by statute provide that year numbers would change on 1 January in and after 1752 and that the day following 2 September 1752 would become September 14. In the notes to this work I have followed the practice often used by contemporaries of writing dates from 1 January to 25 March to indicate both the civil and the Julian year, as, for example, 2 February 1660/1. In France or other regions where the new style, or Gregorian, calendar was in use, this date would be written as 12 February 1661. By 1752 the discrepancy between the Julian and Gregorian calendars had increased from ten to eleven days.

English America and the
Restoration Monarchy of Charles II

Introduction

IN THE YEARS following World War II, historians of the English colonial experience in America have generally devoted themselves to monographic studies of the local scene, the province and the town—some rejecting England as an extraneous, almost alien element—or to institutional and ideological analyses of imperial government. With the exception of Lawrence Henry Gipson, whose works, begun in the interwar period, dealt with the very last stages of the first British empire, historians have eschewed the approach of an earlier generation of scholars—such men as George Louis Beer and Charles McLean Andrews—who viewed the empire from a broader perspective. But in the treatment of the "imperial" school, the center of attention was the metropolis, London, with the West Indian islands and the North American provinces relegated to the periphery.

This book, the first of a projected three-volume study of English America and the later Stuart monarchies, is an attempt to return to the older tradition, to offer an integrated, syncretic treatment, but with a difference: to picture a transatlantic community in which central and local forces, events both in England and in the American colonies, interacted. America did not develop independently of the English scene. Strong ties of commerce, kinship, and religion bound together men on both sides of the Atlantic.

In crossing the ocean to live or to work along the shores of Massachusetts or Chesapeake bays, Englishmen left behind but did not cut themselves off from kinsmen—fathers, uncles, brothers, and cousins—or from business associates or coreligionists in London, Bristol, or Norwich. No integrated or monolithic interest group existed on either side of the Atlantic. To the contrary, several diverse political, familial, religious, and economic communities in the colonies had connections in England. Englishmen had formed a web composed of these multiple strands, a web spanning the Atlantic, by the time the later Stuart rulers and their ministers sought to impose some measure of control over the foreign plantations.

1

The nexus of personal transatlantic relations blunted and often frustrated efforts by royal government either to subject the overseas colonies to tighter control or to subject the empire to rational regulation or formal institutional procedures. Despite the rise of the modern nation-state, the "absolute" monarchy, and the establishment of more efficient bureaucracies and administrative machinery (phenomena dramatically portrayed in conventional general historical treatments), national governments in the late seventeenth century did not function smoothly, efficiently, or even effectively over any great distance.

The royal administration in Whitehall was no exception. In 1660, after years of civil war and unrest, monarchy had won only by default. It had yet to find a political and religious settlement acceptable to most Englishmen. The English gentry on both sides of the Atlantic were accustomed to governing themselves in their local communities. Provincialism characterized their thinking and influenced their behavior and their reaction to Whitehall and Westminster.

The problem of governing from London was further handicapped by a haphazard, confusing administrative apparatus. The court was politically unstable, financially weak, and not blessed with qualified men knowledgeable in governing overseas possessions. It faced a vigorous populace reluctant to accept central authority, a Parliament grudging in voting money, and, in the case of many Puritans of New England, a people filled with a sense of their own importance and self-appointed mission. Information for administering government for the colonies was often lacking. Customs and Treasury officials did not keep adequate records, and since the overseas plantations originally had been private enterprises, copies of their records often had not reached government files. At times, when ministers of state left office, they did not draw a sharp distinction between state and private papers and took important documents with them. At times files were so broken that contemporaries could not reconstruct what had happened under their predecessors.

The weakness of government at Whitehall, reports of plots to overthrow the monarchy, and open opposition in Westminster by opportunistic politicians appealing to fears and prejudices over religion encouraged Puritans in America in the view that the reign of Charles II would not long survive, that they could outlast attempts to bring their commonwealth under control. While crown officials probably grossly overestimated the military strength of the New England provinces, they appreciated the actual and potential wealth accruing from the expanding overseas plantations. They were concerned that, following the hiatus of neglect under the Commonwealth and Protectorate, the colonies should no longer remain "loose and scattered" but should be brought under a "uniforme inspeccion and conduct." At best this proved but a formal goal, to be achieved, it was unrealistically concluded, merely by the crown commissioning or instructing governors for the American provinces.

Charles II himself apparently had another objective: to further liberty of religious conscience, at least for the various Dissenting Protestant sects, a goal denied him in England by a House of Commons dominated by an Anglican squirearchy resentful of the treatment afforded them by the Puritans during the rule of the Roundheads and determined to maintain their political and ecclesiastical monopoly.

Toleration, some consolidation, and a closer political tie to London were but goals. In practice it was all to work out differently, as Charles confirmed the separate existence of almost all of the disparate provinces founded through the efforts of private groups and went on to sanction still others, a result of the monarch's propensity for rewarding personal favorites and accommodating Protestant Dissenters. Six additional provinces, each diverse in its social structure, pluralistic in its ethnic and religious fabric, and bizarre in its governmental arrangements, were begun in the king's reign.

Charles II failed to curb local authority and to make the separate colonies more closely dependent on the crown of England. Indeed, the policy of granting several provincial charters, patents requiring representative assemblies, almost ensured failure. The English dominions in America became even more loose and scattered, with the explicit sanction of the crown. Hard-pressed at home, the king and his ministers of state had to hold royal expenditures in the foreign colonies to a minimum, often reducing his officers there to dependence on local leaders while seeking to increase royal revenue from expanding colonial trade as the overseas plantations prospered and their economy became integrated into the growing commerce of Europe in the latter half of the seventeenth century. And throughout the reign there existed diverse private interests in England and the colonies seeking to influence policy.

Only after twenty years and more did the ministers of the crown take steps—they were grossly inadequate—to impose some unity on the northern provinces in America. Observers and partisans caught up with the Whiggish and anti-Catholic rhetoric of Westminster and Boston then charged the men at Whitehall with a plot fundamentally to alter religious institutions and the political structure of English America as they had haphazardly developed, and to impose authoritarian rule. In reality the government of Charles and his brother reacted to disparate events in the individual American and West Indian colonies only as they occurred. Yet whatever plans ministers of state might pose, their schemes came to nothing. William Blathwayt, a man at the very center of the apparatus for administering the overseas colonies, made the most telling comment at the end of the century: whatever had been proposed had either not been implemented or had been successfully opposed by various interest groups in America and their supporters in England.

The piecemeal efforts of James II to impose a consolidated political facade on the northern American provinces soon collapsed with the overthrow of the Catholic monarch in England. In America local leaders again seized control of the governments. Yet the need more adequately to provide for the defense of the northern colonies survived the politics of the Glorious Revolution of 1688–89. At the same time, the outbreak of a major protracted conflict with France, one lasting for a generation and extending to the colonial territory of the belligerents, made it politically and financially impossible to bring about any realignment of colonial government or to restructure the provincial establishments. The American colonies remained in their "loose and scattered" condition.

The collapse of the dominion government established in America so belatedly and inadequately by James II—the governor had at his disposal only a company of troops—brought into sharper focus than ever the factionalism and inherent instability characteristic in provincial America, a factionalism brought on by the gape between social aspirations and political opportunity in the colonial scene. The almost continuous increment—either through immigration or upward social and economic mobility—of men with real or pretended claims to status disrupted government in America.

The history of the English Atlantic community is not just the story of Whitehall and Westminster or of Boston, the Chesapeake, and the other American settlements and their denizens. To neglect either side of the Atlantic is to present a one-dimensional view. The early Americans appreciated that their destinies were the result of both their own actions and those of their friends, relatives, coreligionists, and rulers in England. The synthesis of their conflicting designs is the topic of this study.

CHAPTER 1

English Colonial and Overseas Commerce
The Nexus of Kinship and Trade

MAY 29, 1660
This day came in his Majestie *Charles* the 2d to London.

It WAS A DAY of jubilation for many Englishmen disillusioned by years of religious strife, civil war, and military rule. Soldiers brandishing their swords and "shouting with unexpressable joy" escorted Charles Stuart along streets strewn with flowers and hung with tapestries, past fountains running with wine and bells ringing in towers. The windows and balconies of the houses along the way of the royal procession were set with ladies dressed in their finest and lords arrayed in velvet and cloth of gold and silver. As resplendent were the officials of the City who greeted the returned monarch, the mayor, the aldermen, and all of the Companies in their livery with chains of gold and banners flying. Myriads of people flocked into the streets. In the Strand watching the procession, John Evelyn thanked God: "All this without one drop of bloud, & by that very army, which rebell'd" against monarchy.[1]

Charles II had returned to govern a kingdom of 5–6,000,000 people with perhaps 120,000 more living across the Atlantic in the foreign plantations of New England, Maryland, Virginia, Barbados, and the Leeward Islands. While physically distant from the friends, relations, and coreligionists in the mother country, the colonists by 1660 had developed a transatlantic commercial network. This web of trade, based on kinship and service, predated the code the Parliament of England enacted to govern the trade and navigation of the kingdom and the plantations across the seas. The commerce of America had already been linked with the mother country before the government at Westminster sought by statute to channel elements of the trade of the colonies through the English metropolis.

By 1660 several factors had contributed to the formation of this network. Merchants in the colonies lacked sufficient capital and credit and the knowledge of markets to trade with distant ports hundreds and sometimes thousands of miles away. Impersonal institutions to provide them with quick, reliable information on market conditions and the worthiness of potential customers did not exist. The English, especially the London mercantile community, offered what the colonial business-man needed, but lacked: credit, marketing information, and established contacts in the ports of Europe, where for some time English merchants had traded and maintained resident factors. While the Dutch might have provided some services, the English had one further, decisive advantage. Reliable factors and correspondents were critical in an era of capricious and uncertain economic relations. Businessmen could not rely on the judgment, honesty, and financial circumstances of men situated hun-dreds of miles away about whom they knew little. The logic of the situa-tion led merchants to rely on friends and family relations or on mid-dlemen and factors recommended by someone with proven experience and judgment.

For a century the landed and merchant class had contributed financial resources for the expansion of English overseas trade and for the migrations of people to America. The urban merchants, particularly the Londoners, had provided the organization and leadership. Relatively few of the merchants were very wealthy, and the political influence of businessmen was limited. While a few obtained seats in the House of Commons and held office in the municipalities, they did not secure the chief offices of state or dictate foreign or trade policy.[2]

Merchants trading overseas to various regions and in various commodities employed different techniques and methods. Those traf-ficking to the East Indies and the Levant as well as to the Baltic operated within companies. The trade across the Atlantic and to Spain, France, and Portugal was not subject to the restrictions of corporate organizations, but lay in the hands of individual merchants who sometimes joined in partnerships, often on a family basis. A few mer-chants used the fortunes gained in foreign trade to diversify their holdings and to venture into politics and higher finance. Maurice Thompson, William Pennoyer, Martin Noell, and Thomas Povey had first become prominent in the West India trade. Noell and Povey then became active in the finances of the Cromwell administration. When Noell died during the plague in 1665, the tangled state of his affairs testified to the range of his interests as well as to the often haphazard and uncertain methods of conducting business during the era. As Pepys commented after Noell's death, "It seems nobody can make anything of his estate," whether at his demise he was "worth anything or no, he having dealt in so many things," public and private, "as nobody can understand whereabouts his estate is—which is the fate of these great dealers at everything."[3]

One of the wealthiest of the London merchants engaged in overseas trade was Alderman John Jeffreys, known as "the Great Smoker" after he lost twenty thousand pounds in Chesapeake tobacco in the Great Fire of London. Yet when he died in 1688, he left the enormous fortune of three hundred thousand pounds and his business to two nephews, John and Jeffrey Jeffreys. The Great Smoker's wealth set him apart from the several hundred other Londoners engaged in the tobacco trade. Well below the scale set by the Jeffreys were two of the merchants of the metropolis, Edward Lloyd and Richard Bennet, who had settled in Maryland and Virginia during Cromwell's rule. After the Restoration, Lloyd was counted among the two dozen or more London merchants who annually imported over one hundred thousand pounds of tobacco. Robert Bristow and John Cary had also lived for some years on the Chesapeake before moving to London, where they set themselves up as merchants in North American and West Indian commerce.

Another major transatlantic trade involving London merchants was to New England. By far the most important element of the trade there was in ship masts, knees, and planking. While it was much cheaper to import naval stores from the lands bordering the Baltic Sea, the eastland was an uncertain source, subject to interdiction in time of war by the northern powers or the closing of the sound by the Danes. The commissioners of the Royal Navy looked to New England as an alternative source, despite the prejudice against North American masts and tar as inferior. The trade in naval stores was a highly competitive business. On one occasion Sir John Hebden in submitting his estimates begged the Navy Board that his bid be kept "secret from the [other] merchants, that another may not plough with his heifer." Sir William Warren, the great merchant who maintained a large timber yard at Wapping just below London, to best a rival, resorted to bribing the clerk at the Navy Board.[4]

In the transatlantic trade in naval timber, the merchants of England operated through factors or correspondents in New England, at Boston and at Portsmouth, located at the mouth of the Piscataqua, or "Piscataway," River. Here resident merchants served as agents for the Londoners who had contracted for masts and stores with the Royal Navy. The business involved considerably more capital than the colonial merchants could raise, for the navy commissioners preferred to deal in large lots to be able to benefit from a lower price offered for purchases in volume. The London entrepreneurs provided the financing and government connections, while the men in America furnished the timber. The colonists with the best contacts in England were in a position to outdo any rivals. Both William Vaughan, who immigrated to New Hampshire, and Peter Lidget, who settled in Boston, had close connections with Josiah Child, a London magnate. In 1679, when the crown established a separate government for New Hampshire, many on the newly founded council were appointed on the recommendation of Sir William Warren. This commercial nexus was but one aspect of a more complex, far-reaching transatlantic community based on commerce, kinship, religion, and amity.

Several Anglo-Virginia connections were formed as young Englishmen from the lesser gentry took advantage of opportunities in the New World. The Ludwell brothers of Somerset, Thomas and Philip, came to Virginia about 1660 and rose quickly in local political circles, as did Nicholas Spencer, the second son of a Bedfordshire family. Some immigrants to Virginia had a mercantile background. The Carys were a London-Bristol-Virginia business family; the Lees, another. Richard Lee belonged to the cadet branch of a family of modest landowners in England who established themselves in London as merchants. He managed their trading ventures with the Chesapeake region. The pattern of sons of the gentry and merchants migrating to America was evident elsewhere. The Bulls of Kingshurst Hall were lesser gentry in Warwickshire. After the Restoration two sons migrated to Carolina, while others set up in London. Francis Champernoun, Nicholas Shapleigh, and Alexander Frost, who settled their families at the far northern edge of English settlement in Maine, also came from the gentry.

Family relations and friends in England served the colonists in their legal and business dealings. Nicholas Spencer of Virginia corresponded with "his honored friend," Gawin Corbin, a merchant at the Black Lion, on Fish Street Hill, London. In what was to prove a common arrangement, members of the Maryland council employed a London tobacco dealer, Peter Paggen, as their agent.[5] Strong ties of kinship and commerce also united England with the Puritan colonies. Several influential Londoners—Edward Hopkins, Nehemiah Bourne, and Stephen Evance—had New England backgrounds. Evance, the son of one of the signers of the town compact of New Haven, became an important financier. The Hutchinsons, a Lincolnshire family, were prominent in the early settlement of Massachusetts and Rhode Island. Richard Hutchinson became a well-to-do businessman in London; Eliakim and Elisha, merchants in the Bay Colony. Among their relatives in America were the Sanford brothers of Rhode Island. When Peleg Sanford opened a commercial correspondence with William Pate, a merchant at the Princess Arms in Gracechurch Street, London, he used Elisha Hutchinson as a reference.[6] Another prominent New England and West Indian family, the Winthrops, were related to the Downings of England. Lucy, sister of John Winthrop (the first governor of the Bay Colony) was George Downing's mother. The English representative at The Hague was thus the cousin of the future agent and governor of Connecticut, John Winthrop, Jr. When the younger Winthrop came to London in 1661, he financed his stay by borrowing money from John Harwood and the Ashurst family. Harwood, a merchant, was himself related by marriage to the Boston merchant Hezekiah Usher.

The Ashursts illustrated another connection—one based on religion—between old and New England. Henry Ashurst, a Dissenter and draper by trade, with his sons, Henry and William, were active in London politics and in an Anglo-colonial missionary society, the Corporation for Propagating the Gospel. Although Robert Boyle, a moderate Anglican, became governor of this New England company and several peers from Charles II's Privy Council were among the sponsors, the rank and file were London Dissenters, members of the livery companies of the City of London, and men who held office in the Levant, East India Company, and other overseas trading corporations.[7] Founded to further piety among the natives of North America, the society also functioned as a political agency, providing intelligence and funds for the Puritans in New England. John Knowles, John Collins, and Major Robert Thompson, the latter two London merchants, kept Governor John Endecott of Massachusetts informed of the plans of the English court regarding the Bay Colony. The Puritan regime drew funds to support the activities of its agents in London from Thompson, Henry Pelham, Nehemiah Bourne, and Alderman William Peake.[8]

In the development of the New England fishing industry, traders almost without exception relied on friends and kinsmen, merchants in England, who provided them with capital, contacts, and information concerning markets in Spain, Portugal, and the wine islands of the Atlantic—Canary, Madeira, and the Azores. Benjamin Keene, son of the Bostonian Thomas Keene, established himself in London as a merchant and became his father's correspondent. Richard Povey lived in Jamaica, his brother William in Barbados, and another brother, Thomas, conducted the family business in London. The Winthrops were to be found in Boston, New London, Hartford, and in the West Indies. Richard Hutchinson, the merchant of London, with his brothers, Samuel and Edward; his nephews, Elisha and Eliakim; and their brother-in-law, Thomas Savage, formed a family business with contacts reaching from London to Providence, Boston, and the West Indies. John Hull of Massachusetts early in his career dealt with his uncle, Thomas Parriss in London. When the elder man, a haberdasher by trade, died in 1672, a cousin, Daniel Allin, who continued the business at the Hatt in Hand within Aldgate, became Hull's correspondent. Other Londoners, "Coz" Thomas Buckham, John Ives, and Thomas Papillon, filled Hull's orders for clothes, cloth, paper, and notions for the New England market and provided him with credit. When dispatching the ketch *Seaflower,* the New Englander ordered the master to sail for London. Should an appropriate lading not be found there, he was to run over to France and take on salt and brandy. "If you shall need any money . . . you may . . . get some of our New England friends to be found for it." These friends of New England also constituted a commercial link with Englishmen residing in Spanish and Portuguese ports. William Harris, a Boston merchant, contracted for the ship *Bonaventure* to load fish for the account of Samuel Wilson of London to be delivered at Bilbao for Joseph Throckmorton, Wilson's correspondent in Spain.[9]

Although New Englanders before the Restoration had done business with Dutch and French carriers, the overwhelming bulk of New England commerce was conducted with other Englishmen, simply because commercial relations with foreigners were difficult to establish, too uncertain and too hazardous, given the lack of reliable institutional arrangements.[10] By the time the Restoration Parliament at Westminster enacted various laws to govern certain facets of overseas trade, the commercial connection between England and the colonies had already been formed. Based on kinship, this nexus did not depend upon, and thus survived beyond, the political tie between America and London.

The latter decades of the seventeenth century witnessed the integration of the economies of the English colonies in the Western Hemisphere into the commerce of northern and southern Europe. Sugar from the West Indies, fish and lumber from New England, and tobacco from the Chesapeake in a steadily increasing volume flowed into European ports.

England's foreign trade also underwent profound change. Although English adventurers during the early reign of Elizabeth had turned to the New World for profit, trade with Europe still predominated as it had in the days of the Angevin kings. The central feature of the island's overseas commerce had remained unchanged until Cromwell's time. Wool, or woolen cloth, constituted almost the whole of English exports; the greater part of England's imports consisted of wine, mostly from France, and a variety of central European manufactures brought in from the Netherlands. Traditionally her trade had flowed between London and Antwerp, the entrepôt for central Europe. But the outbreak of troubles in the Spanish Netherlands and the collapse of the old marketing arrangements through Antwerp forced English merchants, especially Londoners, to find new, direct entries to European markets.

For roughly three quarters of a century, from about 1570 to 1640, they sought to extend their trade to the major ports of Europe and the Mediterranean coast, to widen the export of woolen goods, and to find new imports. Trafficking directly to Danzig on the Baltic or Leghorn and

Smyrna in the Mediterranean called for techniques different from those employed in the well-settled trade to the nearby Netherlands, more capital, more extensive organization, and more and different types of ships. As English businessmen exported cloths directly over a wider area by longer sea routes, English factors—sons, partners, apprentices, and employees—of the merchants of London and Bristol took up residence in the ports of Spain, Portugal, France, and Italy and established the contacts needed for an extensive trading network.

This shift in English commerce was the precursor of a greater geographical reorientation in English trade. Although the traffic of the East India Company from Asia was reaching significant levels, before 1640 the American and West Indian colonies were of little commercial importance. English trade continued to be based essentially on the export of cloth to Europe, although the relative importance of various markets on the continent had changed and English merchants had established direct contact with ports along the entire littoral from Helsinki and Danzig in the eastern Baltic to Smyrna in the eastern Mediterranean.

By the time Charles II came to the throne, another change was becoming apparent. Through English ports, Europe began receiving increasingly large quantities of produce and goods from India, America, and the West Indies. By 1689 these Asian and American commodities when reshipped accounted for one-third of all English exports; by 1700, one-half. Sugar and tobacco from the West Indian and the Chesapeake plantations became available in ever-increasing quantities to more European consumers. Greatly increased production quickly brought prices down and thus widened the market, turning sugar and tobacco from semiluxury commodities to near necessities for Englishmen and many Europeans.[11]

The new Atlantic trade required capital, organization, connections, and shipping. An extensive traffic carried out over vast distances made new demands and posed new requirements. No longer would a fleet of small vessels designed for short voyages suffice. Traditionally traders had laid out their capital for brief periods of time for goods sent to markets two hundred or so miles away. The colonial trade required financial resources sufficient to send merchandise several thousand miles on voyages lasting many months, with both time and method of payment uncertain. When buying goods for export, English merchants customarily had obtained credit from their suppliers, but in marketing colonial produce they found themselves advancing funds. They had also to lay out money for building and manning the ships that crossed the Atlantic in the new trades.

Traditionally transportation, particularly in northern waters, had been dominated by large, wide-bodied cargo carriers, slow but cheap to operate. In the last years of the sixteenth century the Dutch had brought this type of vessel to great refinement in the "flyboat." This vessel, specialized in design, was not only cheaper to construct and to operate, but for its particular purpose, it was better than the vessels of the other European nations. The maritime commerce of Europe fell into two areas. For those regions exporting bulky commodities, freights ran high in comparison to costs and required many ships. These regions could best be served by vessels cheaply built and operated, constructed for carriage, and armed lightly, if at all. These regions—encompassing northern and western Europe from the Garonne to Archangel—exported wine, salt, fish, grain, timber, as well as lead, tin, iron, and copper. English-built ships were unsuited for the shallow waters of the Baltic and the carrying of bulky commodities like timber. Writing from The Hague, George Downing described them as "rather Tubs than ships, made to Looke like a Man of Warre & yet . . . by reason of their Shortness & of their forecastles & Steerage they are so lit[t]le in hold & so bigg above Water that there is noe good to be done with them in this Trade."[12] Southern Europe from the Bay of Biscay to the eastern shores of the Mediterranean, the Atlantic Islands, Guinea, and the East Indies—the regions of the so-called rich trades—for the most part shipped cargoes low in weight in proportion to their value. The trade in these regions was also more dangerous; ships ventured here at greater risk. For these rich trades English vessels, frequently larger and built to sacrifice cargo space for armament and fighting crews, could compete with the lighter and more spacious, but less well armed and manned, Dutch flyboats, vessels designed to carry the bulky but cheap commodities of the northern and eastland trades.

By the latter decades of the seventeenth century a remarkable increase in English shipping was underway. English ships built with an eye for speed and defense could operate in the more dangerous voyages. Yet the English fleet early in the seventeenth century was hardly adequate to meet the demands of the commerce of the American and West Indian trades. The initial reaction was to employ Dutch vessels, but in response to a prohibition against employing foreign ships enacted shortly after the Restoration, the English shipbuilding industry experienced rapid growth. Before 1660 the construction of vessels for the coasting trade and the fisheries had supplied the stimulus for growth in the English shipbuilding industry, but for twenty or thirty years after the Restoration large vessels constructed for the foreign trade, ships bound for Norway, the Mediterranean, the Chesapeake, and the West and East Indies, fueled the expansion. Within a short time the American and West Indian trades ranked a close second to the traffic with nearby Europe in requiring the most tonnage. The colonial transatlantic trade became the most important in the total tonnage of all overseas trades.[13]

English merchants and shipbuilders were not the only investors in the burgeoning overseas commerce. The upper classes in the countryside found speculation in overseas trade a means to improve their family fortunes. As Sir John Oglander observed, "It is impossible for a mere country gentleman ever to grow rich or raise his house. . . . By only following the plough he may keep his word and be upright, but will never increase his fortune."[14] As early as the reign of Elizabeth, the gentry had joined businessmen in the towns in joint ownership of vessels and in commercial ventures, usually through some form of corporate organization. These chartered ventures were of two types, the regulated companies, whose members trafficked independently of each other but under rules laid down by the organization, and the joint-stock company, which traded as a corporate body. Both types were restrictive in that the privilege of trading to the regions specified in the charters issued to them by the government was denied to other Englishmen.

Trade to certain regions was the preserve of several established companies, among them the Merchant Adventurers, the East India Company, the Levant Company, the Moscovy Company, the Eastland Company, and the Guinea Company. With the exception of the East India Company these organizations had seen better days. They faced strong opposition from domestic and foreign interlopers.

Unlike the East India, Russia, Levant, and Africa trades, the traffic to Spain, Portugal, France, as well as the transatlantic commerce, was not subject to the limitations of company organization, but was conducted by individuals who at times joined together in small partnerships, often on a family basis. As the century progressed, such ventures became more prevalent, and with the curtailing of the privileges of the Merchant Adventurers and the Eastland Company the only important branches still controlled by companies were the trades with the Levant and with Asia.

The individual merchant trading on his own account or in partnership became the dominant unit of overseas enterprise. The growth of commerce had increased the potential for specialization by individual traders in commodities handled and in the regions for investment. The companies since their formation in the latter half of the sixteenth century had earned the enmity of the independent traders, who feared the threat of monopoly control to the individual businessmen. Traders in the outports of Bristol, Liverpool, and Falmouth also resented London, where the chartered companies maintained their headquarters. That independent men protested against the dominance of the corporations and the metropolis, that they campaigned in public print against monopoly and employed the rhetoric of free trade did not mean that they were precursors of the later advocates of laissez faire. When John Cary, a prominent Bristol merchant and writer on commercial affairs, published pamphlets objecting to the dominance of the London business community or to the chartered companies, he was advocating measures to benefit himself and his business associates in Bristol, but not necessarily others.

Contemporary usage in England restricted the term *merchant* to wholesalers who imported and exported commodities and goods. Of these, except for the very wealthy who tended to diversify or extend their interests to several areas, the men who engaged in overseas commerce concentrated on one line of business or dealt with one geographical region. Hence contemporaries referred to a man dealing in Chesapeake tobacco as a "Virginia" merchant. They would call others West Indian, Portugal, or Straits merchants. The mercantile community of England formed not a class with unified interests, but was, rather, an occupational group divided and often at odds. Smaller merchants opposed the larger; the independents, the companies, and the residents of the outports opposed the citizens of the metropolis. And by the end of the century rival gangs of merchants competed in London.[15]

Foreign trade was a highly tentative, pragmatic business. Many voyages consisted of a series of decisions made step by step at each juncture by a single merchant or partners who instructed the masters of the oceangoing vessels. They made their decisions at times with but scanty information and in light of opportunities perhaps but dimly perceived. Traders in America had an even more limited knowledge of the distant markets. In 1675 the Massachusetts merchant, John Hull, dispatched John Harris, master of the ketch *Seaflower,* with instructions to proceed to London and there procure glass bottles, tobacco pipes, alum, copperas, nails, small rigging, or whatever he thought might have a ready sale in New England. If Harris could not procure a sufficient cargo there he was to go on to France and load salt and brandy. A few years later Hull consigned a load of codfish in the *Albemarle* with Robert Breck to be sold at Lisbon. Breck was then to proceed to Madeira, there, at his discretion, to load a cargo suitable for Barbados or Jamaica, whichever he found most appropriate.

In London Captain John Harris might have been able to obtain information about markets either at the Exchange or at a tavern or one of the newly fashionable coffee houses where men involved in New England trade congregated. Here traders met and exchanged information during the working day. The major center for commercial life had been the Royal Exchange and the streets behind it. This "old" exchange burned down in 1666 during the great fire and was not rebuilt for several years. Merchants seeking news about distant markets or ship captains looking for a cargo would also congregate at the "Jamaica" or the "Virginia" coffee house to learn news about a particular market or region. In a vast oceanic trading world, one without electronic communications and refined institutional facilities for determining market conditions and credit ratings, those doing business had to rely on connections with proven reliability in various ports and on agents, friends, or relatives. These personal connections determined the configurations of English overseas commerce. Even as late as the eighteenth century, in a trade as advanced and highly developed as the Anglo-Dutch one, firms linked by blood, marriage, religion, or, at the very least, personal acquaintance handled transactions.[16]

English merchants resident in foreign ports but related to traders for whom they acted in England facilitated buying and selling goods abroad. At Bordeaux—a major wine exporting center, but destined to develop into an entrepôt for the produce of the French Antilles—Huguenot and foreign merchants of the international community dominated. The Dutch and English were especially prominent there. Although the French monarchy later excluded foreigners from the carrying trade between French ports and the French Antilles, they continued to play their traditional role in reexporting colonial produce. In the ports of Spain, Portugal, and Italy, the family and personal connections of English merchants took up residence. John Banks consigned his goods in the Leghorn trade to Giles Lycott and Walwin Gascoigne and other men whose reliability long acquaintance had confirmed for him. At Cadiz and Lisbon he established his apprentices as his representatives. Merchant families in Bristol, England's second port, followed the same procedure. William Colston, Sir Thomas Earle, and George Lane consigned goods to their sons stationed at Marseilles, Lisbon and Bilbao. Both Bristol and London men also maintained relatives in the Atlantic islands, the West Indies, and America.

Such ties with the major ports of England were critical for the expanding commerce of the transatlantic plantations. When the Virginia planter Nicholas Spencer drew bills of credit to clear his debts, he employed as his banker his friend Gawin Corbin.[17] Others might not be so wise. At times John Hull of Massachusetts sent off business letters to persons he did not know, informing them that he had taken the liberty of consigning to them goods—sugar, tobacco, logwood, beaver skins—to be sold for his account, the proceeds used to buy commodities he ordered. Months could pass and the returns not arrive. Most members of the New England trading community appreciated that their commercial ventures were best conducted through relatives or friends of long standing. The Hutchinsons, the Winthrops, the Sanfords, and others established partnerships across the ocean, linking Salem, Boston, Newport, and a small district in London about Cheapside, Cornhill, and Leadenhall Streets. Many of the original New England merchants had once been tradesmen and shipkeepers in this district. The small business community of New Haven was composed almost entirely of former residents of Coleman Street, linked to Cheapside and Cornhill by the Old Jewry.[18] These connections formed during the second third of the seventeenth century, rather than parliamentary legislation, determined the configuration of colonial commerce.

The pattern of overseas commerce developed in the seventeenth century was a multilateral one, linking the ports of western Europe with the slaving stations of West Africa, the fisheries of Newfoundland, the agricultural townships of New England, and the farms and plantations of the Chesapeake and the West Indies.

The forests of New England were rich in timber, and until the middle of the nineteenth century, wood was the principal material for the construction of bulk containers and ships. The greater accessibility to markets of the huge forested region on the southern shore of the Baltic gave northern Europeans a great advantage over New Englanders in the mast trade, for the cost of timber on the stump was a small matter; the determining factor generally was the delivered price. American timber, some three thousand miles away, was at a disadvantage except when war threatened to cut off essential masts and stores. But New Englanders were well situated to supply the islands of the Atlantic, southern Europe, and especially the West Indies with lumber for hogsheads and barrels as well as with fish, livestock, and foodstuffs. During the first decade of large scale Puritan migration (1630–40) new arrivals in New England, until they were able to plant and to harvest a crop, created a heavy demand for grains, dried vegetables, and meat. But with the decline in migration after the defeat of the Royalists in England, the local demand for produce slackened, and prices dropped. The need for clothing and hardware, a demand inadequately financed local industries could not meet, continued unabated. To pay for continued needed imports from England the colonists had to find new markets for the surplus of their farms, the cod from the sea, and the lumber from the forests. Through English merchants and their correspondents the New Englanders found these markets in the wine islands of the Atlantic, and in France, Spain, and Portugal. The trade with these regions stimulated the construction of small oceangoing vessels in New England. These ships took off fish and timber and took on cargoes of fruit, salt, and wine as well as bills of exchange from English merchants located in the ports of southern Europe, bills drawn upon their business connections in London and Bristol.

By the middle of the seventeenth century, the West Indies offered another market. Driven from Brazil by the Portuguese, the Dutch had introduced to the English of Barbados the planting of sugar cane. Quickly, the English turned from the cultivation of tobacco, indigo, cotton wool, and cacao to the more profitable money crop, sugar. The planters of the Leeward Islands and Jamaica a generation later followed suit. The West Indians, committed to sugar cultivation, became dependent on outside sources for foodstuffs and provisions to feed the growing labor population and for lumber for casks and hogsheads to ship the growing volume of sugar to market. Initially the Irish shipped large quantities of beef and butter to the Antilles, but the New England colonies soon gained the bulk of the provision trade. Staves of white and red oak, valueless in the wine trade because of their porousness, were suitable for casks to ship sugar. The New Englanders brought in large quantities of pork, beef, butter, cheese, flour, biscuit, peas, and grain to Barbados and the other islands as the sugar revolution took hold and spread. The economy of northern America complemented that of the West Indies.[19]

The planters in the islands soon confronted marketing and pricing problems. As the volume of sugar increased, as the planters stepped up production with little or no recognition of market demand, the price they received fell. After 1670, when the French on Martinique and Guadeloupe entered the field, prices fell even more.[20]

Initially the West Indian planters blamed declining prices on an exclusion of the Dutch from the carrying trade of the English colonies and an arbitrary marketing system. The first settlers in the islands had relied on the fortuitous arrival of a ship from Europe with provisions and goods to be bartered for their produce. A more regular system developed when London merchants sent ships with goods to an agent or factor resident in the West Indies who would sell these locally and purchase returns. This suited the planters during the early years; by selling their produce on the island they did not make demands on their limited financial resources to pay the cost of freight and customs. Merchants or shopkeepers resident in the islands handled the goods of their principals in England, collected debts, and made up return cargoes. Another method, the consignment, or commission, system, became dominant. The planter shipped his produce on his own account to a merchant or agent in London or Bristol. For a fee the consignee saw to the ultimate disposal of the sugar in the English market.

This system reached its full flowering in the eighteenth century with great commission houses dominating the traffic, but it existed on a much smaller scale by the end of the third quarter of the seventeenth century. The consignee of a West Indian planter was responsible for unloading the casks of sugar from the ships, seeing them through customs, storing, and finally selling them. From the gross proceeds he deducted his commission for these services. The net proceeds then went to the credit of the planter to be used either to purchase goods from the consignee or to cover any bills of credit the planter might draw. The English merchant functioned as a selling and buying agent and as a banker for the planter. Even before the close of the seventeenth century there were indications that he was more and that his relation with the planter was something more than a business one. Social ties had developed in a system so reliant on mutual trust.[21]

Many of the same techniques in pricing and marketing emerged in the Chesapeake tobacco trade during this century. In addition geography imposed a pattern of commercial dispersion on the planters of Maryland and Virginia. The four great tributaries of the Chesapeake Bay, extending into the interior and accessible for great distances to most oceangoing vessels, meant that it was unnecessary to develop a single entrepôt to discharge cargo and to load tobacco. Two principal varieties were grown. The region between the James and York rivers produced sweet-scented tobacco, distinguished by its round leaf, fine fibers, and mild flavor. It commanded a premium in the English market. Oronoco, coarser, bulkier, and stronger in flavor, was raised throughout Virginia and Maryland. Europeans had initially welcomed the exotic American plant as a valuable drug, but as the habit of smoking spread, it met condemnation. King James I wrote a *Counterblaste to Tobacco*, although neither he nor his successors went as far as to make the use of tobacco a punishable offense, as did the authorities in the Swiss cantons, Turkey, Persia, and Russia. The monarchies of western Europe valued the revenue to be collected from tobacco. Indeed, the governments of England and France went to far as to prohibit domestic planting in order to derive the maximum yield from duties on tobacco imported from the Western Hemisphere. These restrictions were not entirely effective until very late in the seventeenth century.

Demand by Europeans grew strongly, and production increased even more strongly, especially in the Chesapeake region, as hundreds of immigrants to Maryland and Virginia staked their hopes on the one staple they seemingly could sell to Europeans. As they increased production, they met falling prices. Many of the planters failed to recognize or would not accept the nature of the problem. It was easier to blame the English middleman who, presumably, had been given a monopoly of the market when Parliament required the shipment of tobacco only in English vessels. It was one of those colonial products to be shipped and landed in England before carried elsewhere to Europe.

Legally, Chesapeake tobacco after 1660 could not be sent *directly* to other European markets. Governor Sir William Berkeley, a long-time resident of Virginia, reflected the frustration of many of the planters when he complained publicly in England of the low price offered for tobacco there. Forty thousand souls in the Chesapeake region were being impoverished "to enrich little more than forty merchants, who being the only buyers" of the crop "give us what they please . . . and after it is here [in England] sell how they please, and indeed have forty thousand Servants thus at cheap rates."[22] The governor, perhaps understandably, greatly understated the number of merchants engaged in the tobacco traffic and incorrectly attributed to them collusive practices in depressing prices. The tobacco trade was much more complex than he and some Virginia planters admitted.

During the seventeenth century profound changes occurred not only in the plantation economy of the Chesapeake but also in the pattern of consumption by Europeans. Around 1615–20, when shippers imported about fifty thousand pounds of tobacco annually into England, tobacco was a luxury commodity; its high price restricted consumption to the wealthy classes. But as the volume of production increased, prices dropped. The very cheapness of tobacco broadened the market. What had been a luxury available only to the wealthy came within reach of the middle class and by the end of the century became a solace to all classes. As prices dropped, the smoking habit spread, and a larger market was opened not only in England but also on the continent. By the end of the century the English consumed roughly thirteen million pounds each year and reshipped a further twenty-five million pounds to Europe. Yet for the planters on the Chesapeake the years following the Restoration generally were years of great economic difficulty. The days when their product fetched luxury prices were gone, as glut forced prices lower.

The low price of Chesapeake tobacco when exported from England, however, made it more competitive in the European markets. Holland was the great center in Europe where buyers throughout the continent could have their orders filled, not only for Chesapeake leaf but also for the tobacco of the Portuguese and Spanish colonies as well as for tobacco grown in Europe. Here the Dutch mixed Chesapeake leaf with inferior tobaccos in order to satisfy the less discriminate markets. Only when the price of English colonial tobacco fell drastically did it compete with the cheap, coarser tobacco grown in Europe for local consumption.

A free, open market in Europe for Chesapeake tobacco did not exist. The colonial powers of western Europe protected the economies of their own colonies; consequently Spain and Portugal and, to a lesser extent, France relied on their own plantations in the Western Hemisphere for tobacco. Markets in central Europe, those that lay inland from Holland up the German rivers and could not be reached directly from America or England, were left to the middlemen of Amsterdam, Bremen, and Hamburg. The north of Europe—Norway, Denmark, Sweden, and the Baltic littoral (the eastland, as it was called)—never became a major market for English tobacco, as the English merchants could not overcome their competitors from the Netherlands. The Dutch extensively cultivated tobacco in the United Provinces, mixing this domestic leaf with the tobaccos imported via England or directly from America. On the great exchange at Amsterdam, "Amersfoort," or "Inland," tobacco held its own not only against the more expensive Virginia leaf and the exotic "Varinas Canaster" from Venezuela—the luxury tobacco of the period—but against the cheaper competing leaf grown in Germany and elsewhere in Europe. By mixing leafs and using cheaper tobacco, the Dutch maintained a strong competitive price advantage over the English.[23] The Dutch would not have been able to maintain this advantage if they had relied solely on English tobacco, even if imported directly from the Chesapeake. Tobacco grown in Holland and Germany was cheaper than American leaf.

Merchants based in America or in England faced another obstacle in marketing English tobacco. With the exception of the United Provinces there was no free trade in tobacco. Legislation to grant the plantations of the colonial nations of Europe a monopoly in the metropolis, Dutch competition, and fiscal restrictions made it impossible to deal in tobacco solely on economic considerations. European governments did not allow unlimited or unfettered traffic, but heavily taxed or severely limited the amount imported, often by granting monopolies to special groups, like, for example, the Farmers General in France or the Tobacco Company in Sweden. Individual merchants could not trade freely under these circumstances. Governmental intervention was needed. France was perhaps the largest potential market for Chesapeake leaf. For fiscal considerations the French monarchy in 1676 restricted the growth of tobacco in France. Two years before, it granted a monopoly for the sale of tobacco to the tax farmers. The policy they set limited the quality and quantity available to French consumers. One Englishman accustomed to the better Chesapeake leaf wrote to a friend while visiting Paris, "I heartily wishe your Lordship some of the good wine I dayly drinke. . . . but I confess . . . a man cannot gett a pipe of good tobacco for love nor money."[24]

Monopoly sanctioned by government existed elsewhere. Private traders and shippers—even the more substantial among them—had difficulty in dealing with the Tobacco Company, granted a monopoly at Stockholm by the Swedish crown.[25] Although the combined pressure of the English and Dutch governments was able to eliminate in 1685 the last monopoly in Sweden and to throw open the trade of the Swedish dominions to all, the Dutch for some years were able to control the greater part of the traffic. The most realistic prospects for the Chesapeake tobacco trade would lie in a superior American leaf at a price low enough to compete with the inferior European tobacco and, in addition, political pressure by the English crown to allow Chesapeake tobacco to enter the tightly controlled ports of Europe.

Few, if any, of the planters and tradesmen in the infant colonies in America during these years had the requisite economic resources, knowledge of markets, and political influence necessary to do without either Dutch or English middlemen in the tobacco trade. Initially the trade was carried out in a haphazard manner. An English merchant might himself venture forth with a vessel loaded with goods he thought might be in demand in the colonies, or he would authorize the master of a vessel to peddle his merchandise in exchange for tobacco bought on the spot or later sold on consignment in London. The merchant was ignorant of conditions in the colonies, while the planter knew little of the markets in England and Europe. These difficulties were to some extent mitigated when merchants migrated to the Chesapeake or established factors or agents there, relatives or planters to act as intermediaries.

In time two methods of marketing tobacco developed. The merchants of the outports of England seemed to favor direct purchase. They or their factors would buy tobacco in the colony; ownership was there transferred, and the cost of transporting and the risk of marketing was borne by the English owner. Under the consignment system the planter retained ownership, but shipped his crop to a merchant who supervised the unloading, paid the customs, saw to the storing of the tobacco, and then sold it at the best price prevailing in the market. For these services he received a commission, a percentage of the gross sale. In addition, he might attend to other needs of the planter: providing freight and insurance or supervising the purchase and shipment of goods ordered by the planter. For these tasks too he deducted a commission.[26] The planter bore the risk and expense of transporting and marketing, but the merchant provided the financing. Many of the larger planters consigned not only their own crop but also the tobacco grown by their neighbors. Under consignment the most important benefits the planter received were the full market price for his crop in England and credit.

Considerable understanding—knowledge the planter did not necessarily have—of rapidly fluctuating markets in England and Europe was necessary. The planter needed to trust the merchant to obtain for him the best possible price, and in turn the merchant hoped that the tobacco shipped him would cover the cost of goods ordered by the planter. The system rested on mutual trust.

With the great distances involved and the lack of knowledge under which the principals operated, misunderstandings were inevitable. Planters complained of the careless way their crop was loaded or unloaded and of the commissions charged by the merchants. Since these were levied against all charges and included the fixed costs of freight, insurance, wharfage, porterage, lighterage, storage, and, especially, customs duties, they varied little whether the price the planter received for his crop was high or low. Controversies arose also over the cost and quality of goods ordered by the planter. If the price was more than he expected or the quality less (regardless of the imprecision of his specifications), he might blame the commission agent. It was not unusual for a dissatisfied planter to transfer his business to another merchant, one recommended by a neighbor, or to send small consignments to a number of English merchants. William Fitzhugh commonly did both. The planter in turn might be careless in overextending his account, in ordering extravagantly, or in drawing bills of credit against the proceeds of future shipments.

But both planters and merchants might benefit from the system. For the merchant who managed properly it returned profits; for the planter it provided essential marketing and credit facilities, services not available in the underdeveloped economy of the Chesapeake for several generations to come. The consignment system worked best when based on the friendship and trust of men on both sides of the Atlantic. For good reason Nicholas Spencer of Virginia dealt with his honored friend, Gawin Corbin.

An alternative procedure to the consignment system was the direct purchase of tobacco in Virginia and Maryland. The planter sold tobacco in the colony to a shipmaster, agent, or partner of an English merchant who assumed the responsibility, the risk, and the cost of shipping. The planter knew the price he was getting, but it might not be as high as what he might realize if he retained title until the crop was sold in England.[27]

Despite the charge by Sir William Berkeley—and it may have been merely an assumption on his part—that English merchants acted in collusion to restrict prices in the tobacco trade, there was competition among traders, between London and the outports as well as between the larger and smaller merchants. In marketing a perishable crop subject to seasonal variations in price, traders operating with limited capital were anxious to get their ships out and back as quickly as possible. At the outset of each season the first ships to return would benefit from peak prices. Those vessels arriving later, and particularly during a season of good crops, would find the market glutted and potential buyers so well supplied as to be unwilling to take on additional stocks except at low, bargain prices. During the seventeenth century ships engaged in the bulk trade to the West Indies and the Chesapeake rarely made more than one round trip a year. The time spent in arranging for a cargo, returning to England, refitting, and collecting returns in the home port was insufficient to allow more than one voyage. When vessels left English ports for American waters, the size of the crop to be returned was not accurately known. Fluctuations in the size of the crop were reflected not so much in the number and size of vessels dispatched as in the difficulties shipmasters encountered in getting a cargo. A poor crop meant only partially filled holds, much time spent in searching for cargoes, and low freight earnings, while a good harvest resulted in fully loaded ships, a shorter turnaround time, and high freight rates. More efficient use of shipping and a more refined marketing system was a long century off.[28]

In time the English maritime industry benefited greatly by the policy the English government adopted to enhance its finances and to increase the naval power of the state. It sought to achieve these goals by regulating certain sectors of overseas commerce. For the Dutch, such manipulation was unnecessary. Their shipping was already predominant in the carrying trade of northern Europe; Amsterdam was already an entrepôt, financially preeminent. The rulers of the Netherlands could opt for freedom of trade in view of their superior economic position. For them the fiscal needs of the state did not take precedence over their advanced trading positions. In England and France this was not the case. And in London the lessons of a monarchy once overthrown because of taxes imposed on a stiff-necked people were not to be lost on officials who saw in channeling foreign trade a less direct, less irritating means of meeting the fiscal needs of the government.

The general configuration of American commerce was already set by the time Charles II arrived in London, its pattern fixed by the economic shortcomings of the colonists, the more advanced position of the English merchants, and the personal relations linking the colonial and metropolitan communities. This economic configuration the government of England did not basically alter when it sought to channel colonial commerce and to derive revenue from overseas trade in an effort to meet political needs at home. Although monarchy was restored, neither the political nor the religious tensions that had brought on the Civil War and brought down the Protectorate had been resolved. The old animosities remained, potentially as dangerous as before. Attempts by the king and the men who had brought about the Restoration to strengthen the monarchy, to reduce tensions, and to resolve conflicts directly involved America in England's religious and political controversies. American society itself experienced the same maladies.

CHAPTER 2

The Restoration
The Political and Religious Settlement

ON THAT MEMORABLE DAY in May 1660, John Evelyn, watching the procession of Charles II in London, saw the restoration of monarchy as the Lord's doing.[1] More realistically, monarchy had won by default. Its victory was uncertain, based on a tenuous, undefined accommodation with dissident elements of the Protectorate who had attempted unsuccessfully to govern England since the death of Oliver Cromwell two years before.

Following the victory of the Puritans in the Civil War, the various Protestant sects had been unable to agree on a national religious settlement even when Parliament had been purged of some dissident elements. The "Rump" had proved incapable. Toleration, limited as it was under the Cromwellian protectorate, had come, not from conviction, but from necessity. Moderate Presbyterians and Independents viewed Roman Catholics (Papists) as well as radical Protestant sectaries with great suspicion. They condemned these extreme Protestants as "scum," "infectious as the plague," as seditious malcontents contemptuous of all authority and bent on disturbing the peace of their neighbors while pursuing their own self-appointed mission.

Religious toleration had seemed to spawn new varieties of bizarre and insolent delinquents. One group in particular had offended public opinion: George Fox's Society of Friends, or "quakers in the sight of the Lord." At first more radical than temperate, driven by a compulsion to change the world, and affecting to despise constituted authority, both political and clerical, the Quakers preached to their resentful, often hostile fellows their doctrine of the inner light, a notion based on emotion rather than reason, one appealing more to the unlettered than to the conventionally learned.[2]

There had been little agreement either on religion or on the structure of the government as opponents of Richard Cromwell had contended with one another in Parliament and the republicans had intrigued with factions in the army. It was soon clear that if anarchy was to be avoided, a choice had to be made between military dictatorship and a restored monarchy. Conservative parliamentarians and moderate Presbyterians were now alienated from the revolutionary cause, and the officers no longer commanded an army worthy of the name. General George Monck's force in Scotland was the exception. Monck moved his units south.

When the general entered London, public feeling was clearly with him. On his march he had received a series of addresses asking for either the admission of the excluded members or the summoning of a free parliament. On 11 February 1660 Monck demanded the issuing of writs for elections and the fixing of a day for the dissolution of the Rump. Londoners seemed to go mad with joy. Evelyn recorded that "many thousands of rumps" of meat were "roasted publiquely in the streets at Bonfires this night." Ringing bells testified to the "universal jubilee." Samuel Pepys, hurrying home that same night from Cheapside, noted the fires burning and the bells ringing in all the churches. "The common joy . . . was everywhere to be seen!"[3]

Clearly out of favor, many of the Puritan old guard simply stopped attending at Westminister. Moderate Presbyterians, some of them well affected toward royal government, dominated both Parliament and the new Council of State. The enthusiasm greeting the readmission of the excluded members seemed a prelude to something more. On 16 March 1660 the Long Parliament dissolved itself. Monck, secretly in communication with the exiled Charles, advised him to issue a formal declaration offering general pardon for offences committed against the monarchy and liberty to tender religious consciences. Charles accepted a draft drawn up by his advisor, Edward Hyde, with such conditions. In England elections for the meeting of a new parliament went overwhelmingly against the republicans. Signs of a jubilant royalism were evident in London: pictures of the exiled Charles displayed in windows of houses and the royal arms shown in churches and on ships.

During the elections the Independents and the Presbyterians had revived their old animosities. Unable to reconcile their differences, they helped to ensure the eventual triumph of the men who had followed the executed archbishop William Laud. The Laudian Anglicans now appeared openly for the king. By the end of April not only the House of Commons but also the House of Lords were meeting as of old. The Presbyterians had failed to obtain the exclusion of the Royalist Cavaliers who now dominated the important committee on privileges and elections. Monck apparently had consented to the admission of all members without regard to their qualifications. The more rigorous Puritans now appreciated that he had come down on the side of men who would accept the return of monarchy on the least restrictive terms.

On 1 May 1660 the members of Parliament listened to a reading of

Charles's conciliatory Declaration of Breda, inspired by Monck and Hyde. Charles promised the Commons of England he would submit himself and all things to them. That same day the City of London issued its own declaration disclaiming any other government than that of the traditional monarchy and Parliament. At Westminster both houses joined in a resolution that according to the fundamental laws, England yet again was and ought to be governed by King, Lords, and Commons. That night once more bonfires blazed and bells rang as Londoners sank to their knees in the streets "drinking of the King's health." According to one of the regicides, a man who had signed the warrant condemning Charles I to death, God's people lamented over the great profaneness with which the common folk expressed themselves. Some of the diehard Puritans thought it significant that many dogs ran wild in the streets and died suddenly. That day Colonel William Goffe—he was to be proscribed for his role in the death of the late king—attended service at a "good Minister[']s" church. A broom was stuck up near the pulpit; the congregation took it as a sign that the minister "should shortly be swept away from them."[4]

Charles landed at Dover on 25 May and entered London four days later. Not all rejoiced, not all accepted the restored monarchy and the repudiation of the Puritan experiment in government by self-conceived saints. Even before the call went across the Channel for the king, General John Lambert had escaped from the Tower to lead a band of diehards. The "fanatics," as such men were called, were put down late in April. But from time to time unstable minds, compelled by what they conceived as religious visions, rose in arms to challenge the Restoration political and ecclesiastical settlement. Particularly disturbing were the rumored activities of former soldiers, Protestant sectaries, and the Fifth Monarchy men, so called because of their belief that, the four great kingdoms of antiquity—Assyrian, Persian, Macedonian, and Roman—having passed away, it was their duty according to the mystical chapters in the book of Revelation to institute the millennium, the new kingdom. In December 1660 authorities uncovered a plot organized by Major General Richard Overton to burn the palace at Whitehall and kill the king and Monck. A sensational outbreak occurred the following month. Thomas Venner, a sometime wine cooper of Salem and Boston in New England, led a band of fifty or so religious fanatics who worshipped at a conventicle off Coleman Street, in London. On the night of 6 January 1661, stirred to a frenzy, they burst out of their meetinghouse in Swann Alley armed to conquer the world in the name of Christ. Venner had promised his followers that if they fought valiantly enough, King Jesus himself would join them. The fanatics threw London into an uproar. They managed to kill several innocent people before they were cornered and captured.[5] Puritan extremists rose again near Leeds in 1663. Forewarned, the government suppressed them. Rumors continued to circulate of plans to overthrow the government.

Some men who had served the Cromwellian regime were more moderate, were willing to come to an accommodation with the monarchy. Monck, the man perhaps most instrumental in restoring the king, accepted a peerage as duke of Albemarle and took high office. Edward Montague had clandestinely turned Royalist in 1659 and helped to bring the fleet into line. Raised to the peerage as earl of Sandwich, he continued in office under Charles II. Among the Presbyterian lords who had worked secretly to bring about the restoration of the monarchy was Thomas Belasyse, Viscount Fauconberg. The Restoration House of Lords included a small group of peers who constituted a Puritan block: William Fiennes, Viscount Saye and Sele; William Russell, fifth earl of Bedford; Arthur Annesley, earl of Anglesey; Denzil Holles, Baron Holles; William, Baron Paget; and John, Baron Robartes. The Puritan earl of Manchester became lord chamberlain under Charles II; Anthony Ashley Cooper, chancellor of the Exchequer. (Ashley Cooper went far, later as Baron Ashley and still later as first earl of Shaftesbury.) Annesley, George Downing, and Holles also made the transition and served the new government on the Privy Council and on commissions and councils for regulating the overseas plantations and foreign commerce. Among the financiers and advisers to the Cromwellian regime were Martin Noell and Thomas Povey. The latter became treasurer to the duke of York (the king's brother) and a member of the royal commission for Tangier. Noell, a merchant trading to the West Indies, had been a member of the Cromwellian Council of Trade and Foreign Plantations. Although Noell had been a personal friend of Cromwell, Charles II named him to boards advising the crown on overseas commerce and colonies and in 1662 awarded him a knighthood. Pepys, the able naval administrator, wondered on hearing the news, but yet, on reflection, added: "He is certainly a very useful man."[6]

Joining the Cromwellians and moderates who made their peace with the new government were Royalists of the old school, men like Edward Hyde and Edward Nicholas. Hyde, created earl of Clarendon, became lord chancellor, while Nicholas joined Sir William Morrice as one of the two principal secretaries of state. Charles II seemed deliberately to have sought to avoid putting himself completely into the hands of any one group. In 1660 several distinct elements formed the king's council. One component consisted of old Anglican Cavaliers, Clarendon (chancellor); Thomas Wriothesley, earl of Southampton (treasurer); the duke of

Ormonde (lord steward and lord lieutenant of Ireland), and Edward Nicholas (a principal secretary of state). Among the Presbyterian-Puritan contingent were Anglesey, Manchester, and Viscount Saye and Sele, an old opponent of the king's father and grandfather, as lord privy seal. When Saye and Sele retired in 1661, the king raised the Presbyterian Robartes to the peerage. Albemarle, Ashley Cooper, Holles, and Sandwich were among the old Commonwealth-Protectorate servants.

The nobles held the principal offices of state. Whatever part financiers and merchants had played during the previous regime, their role in the restored monarchy was minimal. They held few important posts in national administration. In England and in the United Provinces of the Netherlands—the most commercially developed of the western European states—merchants were able to control some municipalities, but they did not dictate foreign policy or dominate the central government. Moreover, a class of nascent civil servants "for whom political values meant more than the huckstering of traders" was rising. Sir William Coventry once implored a colleague to warn the king, "If he once admit a merchant to sit" as a navy commissioner, "the reputation of that office is lost."[7]

The conduct of public affairs fell to those in the king's favor, men such as Clarendon, Henry Bennet, and Sir Henry Coventry, who had proved their loyalty in exile, or those like Sandwich and George Downing, men with ability who had something to offer. Initially Clarendon had great power. Although Charles did not favor him as a personal companion, at first he could not do without him. Necessity and some sense of gratitude in the king for the chancellor's prior service sustained Clarendon for some years, but as early as 1663 the royal favor was fading, and rivals were attempting to dislodge Clarendon.

The administrative center of the nation was a large sprawling, undistinguished jumble of courts, galleries, and suites, a rambling village on the edge of London, the palace of Whitehall. It was the social as well as the political heart of the kingdom. Crowded in among Charing Cross, the city of Westminster, the Thames River, and Saint James's Park, it was cluttered with the residence of the sovereign and his queen, the London houses of the grandees, the apartments of the royal mistresses, and many of the public offices. Here men competed fiercely for honor and profit, for place and influence. Some had seen the old order collapse and had shared the bitterness of exile with Charles. They now expected to enjoy their rightful places. But new men had arisen, courtiers who expected to join the governing elite. England did not lack ruthless men who aspired to high position.

Courtiers constantly battled for advancement. Ministers were the chief contenders, and each candidate had a coterie of followers whose political fortunes rose or fell with those of their chief. Alliances were tenuous, short-lived; all ministries were composites of these temporary coalitions, constantly threatened and at times disrupted by intrigue and maneuver. Rivals waited to exploit any weakness, to use any issue (particularly religion) to unseat incumbents.

At a lower level there developed a small core of quasi-professional administrators, men such as Samuel Pepys at the Navy Board, Henry Guy at the Treasury, and after 1675, William Blathwayt at the Plantation Office. They were men of business, more hard working and more knowledgeable than their masters. They might add some coherence in the administration of affairs, if not in policy. Possessing little political weight in their own right, they sought to survive when one court favorite gave way to another in a department of state.

The early years of the reign were characterized by instability and uncertainty at the uppermost level of government. In 1660 Clarendon enjoyed the greatest influence and power among the king's ministers. Other men soon challenged him, chief among them George Villiers, duke of Buckingham, Sir Henry Bennet (later earl of Arlington) and Ashley Cooper (later earl of Shaftesbury). A common enmity for Clarendon united them in opposition. Another faction in the court consisted of the men associated with the king's brother, James, duke of York. Appointed lord high admiral, James gathered around him a naval interest: Sir George Carteret, Lord John Berkeley, and Sir William Coventry.

An open attack on Clarendon—he dominated the discussion of colonial affairs during these early years—began as early as 1662, but the old Royalists did not lose out until 1667. When Southampton died, Charles entrusted the Treasury to a commission. Charges were then brought against Clarendon in Parliament, among them that he had attempted to introduce arbitrary government on the model of the French regime.[8] The charge became a standard one for politicians. In the face of growing resentment in Parliament, Charles abandoned his old servant.

The next six years witnessed government by cabal, but from the beginning Ashley, who was later to lead the first organized opposition to the Stuart brothers, despite his talent for administration and finance, never enjoyed the king's confidence. At first Charles relied on Arlington and John Maitland, duke of Lauderdale, and then on Clifford. The king used Ashley and Buckingham, a dangerous game to play with a man of Ashley's temperament. The vehemence of his later opposition came in great measure from "the bitterness of a self-confident and self-important politician who realizes that he has been had."[9]

To a rake like John Wilmot, earl of Rochester, the three preoccupations of the age were women, politics, and drink, but the scene at Whitehall, particularly at the council board, often disgusted Samuel

Pepys, John Evelyn, and John Povey, serious, hardworking administrators. The king's government was ill suited to rule effectively either at home or in the plantations overseas. Vicious backbiting, unprincipled attacks in an effort to discredit ministers, made capable men reluctant to accept high office. Sir William Coventry hesitated to act alone in office: "Whosoever did do anything singly are now in danger, however honest and painful they were." At the council board he was the only man who spoke his mind clearly, the others sitting silent and "having nothing said to them" were not "taken notice of." Robartes, the Presbyterian who held the privy seal, was "a very sober man," but he often failed to attend to public affairs, and when he did, according to Clarendon, he found more ways "to obstruct and puzzle business . . . than any man in that office had ever done before."

Charles II himself probably had much more ability than most of his servants, but had little stomach for sustained work. It was openly bantered about that the lord chancellor repeatedly remonstrated with him and that he was "a lazy person and not fit to govern." At the Royal Exchange merchants and men of business accused the king of looking only to his "lusts and ease," of sacrificing trade and the interests of his kingdom to "his own pleasures." Officials of the navy were particularly distressed at the inability of the administration to act, particularly after the humiliating raid in 1667 by the Dutch against English installations and shipping in the Thames River. John Povey complained bitterly: no council, no money, and a lazy king who followed "the women as much as he ever did." A paymaster confided to a colleague that matters at court had never been as bad "for gaming, swearing, whoring, and drinking." According to John Evelyn, a member of the Council on Foreign Plantations, the king would not gainsay anything relating to his pleasures.

At times Charles II demonstrated great perception, yet he gave the impression of having his father's fault: he seemed to doubt his own judgment and seemed easily swayed from his opinions. The king regularly attended sessions of the full council, but without his presence to give direction, meetings of the committees were often chaotic. Pepys attended a session held during the Second Dutch War. He left a damning account: "But Lord, how they meet; never sit down—one comes, now another goes, then comes another—one complaining that nothing is down, another swearing that he hath been there these two hours and nobody came." At last Anglesey stood up: " 'I think we must be forced to get the King to come to every committee, for I do not see that we do anything at any time but when he is here.' "

Such a government inspired little confidence, leading one observer to declare that he expected the nation "will fall back to a commonwealth."[10]

Gross inefficiency in the court, coupled with sporadic plots to overthrow the monarchy, may well have encouraged Puritans in old as well as New England in the view that the reign of Charles Stuart would not long endure. In Massachusetts Bay, the focal point of royal policy for English America during these years, reports of the scene in London might well encourage commonwealthmen that they need not heed commands from England, that they would outlast Charles II just as their fathers had survived his.

The task of governing England and the possessions overseas was a formidable one even for able ministers dedicated to their duty. The English on both sides of the Atlantic were tough people, difficult to discipline and accustomed to governing themselves in their local communities. A resentment against outside interference characterized the thinking and influenced the behavior of the gentry in the counties and in the colonies across the Atlantic. A recurring problem facing governments during the seventeenth century lay in balancing the relations between local power and the centralized monarchy. While the quasi-civil servants under Charles II—Pepys, William Blathwayt at the Plantation Office, or Sir Leoline Jenkins—might, in time, see a model of efficiency and centralized administration in the techniques employed by Louis XIV and Colbert in France, for all the vaunted authoritarianism of the French monarchy, the strong traditions there of local independence, rights, and privileges persisted. In the more remote corners of France, absolutism may merely have tempered disobedience.[11] In England and across the Atlantic in the distant plantations it was no less so.

Compounding the problem of reconciling national with local interests and of ordering government was the anachronistic administrative and financial system the Restoration monarchy inherited. Certain elements of the machinery of government dated from the Middle Ages, when the crown paid for essential services of government from its semiprivate, hereditary income. This source was now grossly inadequate. Nor had Cromwell's government been able to meet expenses, despite introducing a new excise along with increasing traditional customs duties on imports. In the years after 1660 the court faced factious opposition in Parliament, whose members voted money grudgingly for the king's service. Their appropriations were nearly always inadequate, particularly in time of war. Officials both high and low charged with the responsibility of paying for vital services faced the burden of delayed payments, uncertain credit, and exorbitant interest charges. Salaries were kept low to ease the cost to government. They had been fixed before inflation in the sixteenth century distorted prices. For almost all public officials, from the highest to mere doorkeepers and room sweepers, the incidental profits to be derived from their posts—fees, gratuities, and douceurs— were essential to supplement their incomes. The system was an open invitation for abuse and corruption for men whose salaries were inadequate and often years in arrears.[12]

Of great concern immediately on the return of Charles to England was the settlement of the church, a matter that had frustrated as well the various Puritan elements from the outset of the Long Parliament through the fall of the Protectorate. What had emerged from the deliberations in Parliament during the Commonwealth had been a state-imposed form of Presbyterianism, but one the other Protestant sects, particularly the Independents, had contested. The chaotic situation prevailing after the death of Oliver Cromwell increasingly disturbed the moderates among the Presbyterians and the Anglicans, inclining them toward a possible reconciliation in the form of a modified Presbyterian establishment.

The alliance of the moderates and the Royalists had made possible the restoration of the monarchy in 1660, but the specific religious settlement was still uncertain. The Presbyterians were divided and faced strong opposition from the other sects, particularly the Baptists and Friends. The Presbyterians and Independents (Congregationalists) had been unable to cooperate during the elections for Parliament in 1661; both suffered losses at the polls. At best they had 10 percent of the seats in the House of Commons.

The Anglicans were also disunited. They could not agree on matters of doctrine, liturgy, structuring the national church to comprehend the bulk of the Dissenters, or on toleration for those left outside the ecclesiastical order. When the Commonwealth and Protectorate governments had restricted Anglican worship, the bulk of the clergy had remained quiet, but a minority, young and gifted followers of the late archbishop William Laud, had remained active. Ejected from their livings, they made a conscious effort to introduce members of their party into the homes of the nobility and gentry as tutors and chaplains. They inculcated the principles of orthodox Anglicanism into the minds of the generation of young squires who dominated the Restoration Parliament.[13]

The composition of the House of Commons was critical. In the Declaration of Breda, Charles had favored liberty of tender conscience—no man ought to be called into question in matters of religion if he did not disturb the peace—but he had also pledged to accept the settlement of the church as determined by Parliament. After Charles returned to London, spokesmen for the various sects met to consider the religious establishment. Clarendon had suggested a clause to allow the members of the various denominations to meet as long as they did not disturb the peace, but one prominent Dissenting minister, Richard Baxter, opposed this concession, as allowing liberty to the Catholics.[14] Some clerics hoped that the Anglicans and Presbyterians might work out a compromise at a synod, the Savoy conference, to revise the prayer book so as to make it acceptable to most worshipers, to restore unity, and to devise a formula for a comprehensive Anglican Church. But the elections of 1661 strengthened the position of the Church of England men. The victorious Cavaliers required all members of the Commons to accept the Sacrament according to the Anglican rite. The rigid Anglicans dominating in Parliament and in the church convocation undermined the policy of toleration enunciated by the king and dashed the hopes of the Presbyterians. In revising the Book of Common Prayer, the convocation paid little heed to the points the Presbyterian divines had raised at the Savoy conference.[15]

The Anglicans won out in the Commons, and in 1662 Parliament passed the Act of Uniformity, ejecting Nonconformist ministers from their livings. The Cavaliers took retribution on the Puritans who, during the Commonwealth, had ejected orthodox Anglican clergymen and banished Royalists to a distance of five miles from Oxford. By the Act of Uniformity the Cavalier Parliament required everyone holding ecclesiastical office to declare his consent to the provisions of the Book of Common Prayer. The House of Commons had rejected a provision Clarendon had brought into the Lords to allow the king to dispense with the act for any peaceable and pious minister.

Although Charles II accepted these stringent provisions in 1662, the lord chancellor hinted strongly that the king was not surrendering his policy and that the monarch would find some means to keep the Presbyterians within the church by his prerogative power in matters of religion. When the bishops and the crown law officers opposed a plan for the king to suspend the Act of Uniformity, Charles II turned to another prerogative formula: royal dispensation from the law for Nonconformist ministers. But the Nonconformists were divided on the proposal for liberty of conscience for all peaceable Dissenters, including Catholics. Congregationalists welcomed the measure. Major Robert Thompson, the prominent Puritan merchant, told Pepys that the Independents "are very well contented that if the king thinks it good, the papists may have the same liberty with them." In contrast, the Presbyterians could not bring themselves to allow freedom for Catholics, whatever the cost to themselves, and shied away from a general toleration. Robartes and Ashley, in promoting a bill to give the king the power to dispense with the Act of Uniformity, received little support. The Anglicans insisted on nothing less than conformity. On 23 February 1663 the Commons resolved that no indulgence be granted. Charles had to drop the issue.[16]

Events outside Parliament and the court may have increased the difficulties of broadening the church so as to bring about a comprehensive religious establishment acceptable to a wider section of Protestant opinion and to win toleration for those persons remaining outside the national church. Early in 1661 the Fifth Monarchists under Thomas Venner had taken up arms in London. Continued agitation by religious extremists led some men to think of Dissenters as people threatening the security of government and disturbing their neighbors' peace. Solomon Eccles, a Quaker, was perhaps extraordinary. He ran through Westminster Hall with only a cloth tied about his private parts and with a chafing dish filled with burning brimstone on his head, crying out to startled onlookers: "Repent! Repent!"

The behavior of many of the early Quakers offended contemporaries. They were known variously as Children of Light, then Truth's Friends, or Friends of Truth. A witty Derbyshire justice had nicknamed them "Quakers" when George Fox, their founder, had bade the whole of the magisterial bench to tremble at the name of the Lord. A strong, hysterical element was present in the conduct of many of these Friends, who based their beliefs and actions on personal revelation. Early in the king's reign they replaced the Fifth Monarchy men as a cause of civil disturbance. Later the Quakers adopted a more decorous stance. Also offensive to the civil authorities was the refusal of the Friends to swear oaths in testifying. As William Penn explained, they could not swear, because "all Oaths are Grounded on falseness" and where there was no untruth there "was no need of an Oath." To swear was to reproach one's own honesty. Nor would the Friends "dare make so bold with God as to summon" him in every controversy. It was "below his Majesty." Indeed, Christ had forbidden it.[17] Not until 1666 did George Fox begin a long canvas of England and Ireland to promote group discipline among the Quakers through a system of meetings designed to inculcate proper conduct and to define membership in the society as well as to provide mutual aid. He and his allies transformed the movement. In time, spontaneity and self-expression became less characteristic of Quakerism than sobriety and group discipline.

Rumors repeatedly circulated of republican Dissenters who refused to accept the restoration of monarchy and who purportedly planned armed rebellion. Early in 1663 the government intercepted a letter to John Davenport, the Congregationalist minister at New Haven in New England, detailing the suffering of "God's people" under the Act of Uniformity and decrying the displacement of hundreds of Puritan ministers by ignorant, scandalous, and unworthy priests. John Baker, a soldier who had served Cromwell, informed the authorities of a plot to kill the king. Rumor also had it that the regicides who had escaped from

England were plotting to overthrow the government. Dissenters at Leiden and Arnhem aimed to arm the English insurrectionists with weapons imported from Holland and New England.[18]

The response at Westminster further prejudiced the cause of religious toleration. In the summer of 1663 the House of Commons pressed for a bill against conventicles, unauthorized religious meetings such as Venner's. The parliamentary session had ended before the measure could pass. But when the king, seeking to placate Anglican opinion, addressed Parliament on 27 July, he promised that he would take care that neither Papists nor Dissenters would be allowed to endanger the peace and that appropriate measures would be introduced. In May 1664 Parliament passed the Conventicle Bill. Any adult attending a religious meeting not in accordance with the Church of England with more than four persons present in addition to the members of the household was liable to punishment. In the following year, when the king proposed that all Nonconformists, Protestant and Catholic, be permitted freedom to worship and to avail themselves of the royal dispensing power, the Anglicans in the House of Commons reacted harshly by imposing the Five Mile Bill. It required Dissenting ministers to swear not to take up arms against or endeavor to alter the government of either church or state and prohibited ejected ministers from coming within five miles of any place where they had once held a living unless they so swore. Despite protests, the measure passed the Lords.

Thus were completed the Restoration penal laws commonly misnamed the Clarendon Code. The king and the lord chancellor had to accept these harsh measures to gain the support of the Anglican members of Parliament for the administration's pressing fiscal needs.

In 1670, when Charles II freed himself temporarily of his dependence on Parliament by concluding a secret agreement, the Treaty of Dover, with Louis XIV of France, he could then venture once more to test the limits of royal prerogative in favor of religious toleration. That he intended to bring England to Catholicism is highly doubtful. The king ordered the release of George Fox from prison and no longer called to council table Sheldon, the archbishop of Canterbury, who for months had upbraided the monarch for his loose living. In the council he seemed to give his favor to the lords sympathizing with the Presbyterians. The administration pressed for a comprehension bill, but rejecting the measure, the Royalist Anglicans in the House of Commons in 1670 passed a new Conventicle Bill. Having once tried to shield Dissenters, the court now prosecuted them under the act, possibly to convince them to appreciate and to accept the benefits of toleration. The Presbyterians still refused to cooperate in any toleration benefiting Catholics.

Ashley and others at court urged the king to exercise the royal prerogative. By the provisions of a declaration issued on 15 March 1672 Charles II declared that the forcible measures employed over the past years had not resolved the religious issue. He went on to assure Anglicans that tithes and benefices would continue to be reserved for the orthodox clergy. The Church of England would remain as established by the law of Parliament, but the penal acts relating to religion must be suspended and Dissenting congregations allowed to worship openly in meeting places under ministers licensed by government. Catholics would not be allowed the same freedom. In London they could attend mass either in the household of a Catholic peer or in the chapels maintained by the representatives of Catholic sovereigns of Europe.

Convinced that it was hopeless to expect anything of Parliament, Protestant Dissenters now availed themselves of the royal indulgence. In response to their applications the government granted over fifteen hundred licenses to preachers. Some Anglicans, perceiving a threat to their church from two fronts, favored an accommodation with the Presbyterians against the sectaries and the Catholics, an accommodation made easier by the death or retirement by 1673 of some of the older Cavaliers who had suffered sequestration under Puritan rule. But sufficient resistance from the Anglicans in the House of Commons remained. Charles II did not press the issue. In 1673 he accepted a Test Act. In addition to subscribing to the oaths of supremacy and allegiance, recognizing the monarch as head of the church, all officeholders had to declare against the Catholic doctrine of transubstantiation and to receive Holy Communion according to the Anglican rite. The Test Act confined office to Anglicans, although in later years other Protestants by conforming occasionally qualified. In forcing the king to accept the measure and to exclude Catholics, the Anglicans in Parliament compelled Charles to abandon the policy of toleration. The king's brother had to resign the Admiralty and Clifford the Treasury. It meant also the end of the cabal. Shaftesbury, deprived of his offices, went into opposition.[19]

For a dozen years following the restoration of the monarchy, the Anglicans had dominated the House of Commons. In later years the more moderate among them would prefer a policy of comprehension rather than toleration of Dissenters outside the establishment, since comprehension held out the possibility of an almost inclusive national church, while toleration made permanent the existing divisions among English Protestants. They might be willing to allow a limited freedom to those few people who would still accept no compromise with Anglicanism. Yet subsequent attempts at comprehension and toleration involved as well the issue of Popery, the king's Catholic brother, and the struggle to control the succession to the throne, the seat of power. For men consumed by ambition—Shaftesbury knew few equals in this respect—religion during the succeeding decade served as a political weapon.

During the first half of his reign Charles II sought to dampen the fires of religious controversy, but the implacable opposition of the staunch Anglicans who dominated the Cavalier House of Commons frustrated comprehension and toleration. Rigid Anglicans and strict Presbyterians both refused to compromise. While some Anglicans held that within the traditional limits of the national church a wide range of belief and practice was possible, the Laudians rejected comprehension. The conservative Presbyterians, for their part, refused to have anything to do with episcopacy. Charles II, limited in his freedom of action by his dependence on parliamentary grants, had accepted the national church as narrowly prescribed by the Act of Uniformity and acquiesced in the exclusion of Catholics and Protestant Dissenters from civil and ecclesiastical office. But outside the realm, across the Atlantic, the penal laws did not extend.

In the American colonies the king had more freedom to act. During his reign he issued half a dozen charters and concessions for the establishment of new colonies; in all, a provision for liberty of tender conscience for all of his peaceable subjects appeared. And for those provinces already established in New England, the king urged on the Puritan governments a similar policy.[20] Charles insisted on liberty of conscience in America. Moreover, the plantations seemed an appropriate place for Dissenters once the Anglican-dominated Parliament forced the king to accept the Act of Uniformity and subsequent penal laws. "And because we are willing to give all possible encouragement" to persons of different persuasions to transport themselves to America, Charles informed Governor Sir William Berkeley of Virginia, "you are not to suffer any man to be molested, or disquieted in the exercise of his religion," provided he was quiet, peaceable, and not giving "therein offence or scandal." But Berkeley himself must profess the Protestant religion as it was established in England and recommend it to settlers in his government "as far as it may consist with the peace and quiet of our said Colony." Similar instructions relating to liberty of conscience went to the Puritan authorities of Massachusetts Bay. But officials there were not initially to extend this indulgence to Quakers, persons whose principles were inconsistent with any kind of government. The activities of the Friends at times offended the king. On one occasion he was so incensed by "the more than ordinary insolence of Quakers and other sectaries" that he ordered those convicted of breaking the penal acts to be sent off to the plantations.[21]

But where in the colonies to send the Quakers? As early as the winter of 1661 Quaker leaders were contemplating establishing their own community along the Susquehanna River, but hesitated, in view of the animus held against them by Maryland officials who had resented the role a prominent Quaker, William Fuller, had played in an attempt to overthrow the government of the Catholic proprietor. In New England the situation for Quakers was perilous. Having been expelled from the Bay Colony, some Friends seeking martyrdom had returned and had been executed. At the time of the Restoration Quakers were under sentence of death in neighboring New Plymouth. Appeals—part of the long catalogue of complaints against the Puritan governments of New England—were carried back to London and placed by Quaker leaders before the king in council. After a committee appointed to consider affairs in New England had reported on the matter, Charles II ordered the governors of the New England provinces not to allow the execution of Friends or other persons under sentence of death for disturbing the religious peace but to send them to England together with the charges against them.[22]

Yet in view of the stringent penalties forced on the administration by the terms of the Conventicle Act of 1664, the court was forced to transport offenders to the plantations. The government seems to have made an effort to protect those deported from hostile authorities in New England and Anglican Royalists in Virginia who had suffered during the interregnum. Quakers confined in Newgate in London and the jail in Hertford were ordered deported to Jamaica, Barbados, and Nevis, but not to the Old Dominion or to New England.[23] Presumably they would bear the heat of the tropics better than the wrath of the Puritans and Anglicans in America.

CHAPTER 3

Trade, Plantations, and Customs
The Administrative Framework

THE RESTORATION of monarchy in 1660 brought back rule by the king and the men he selected as his servants. For a generation to come the administration of government lay with the committees of Charles's Privy Council. Late in the century the council gave way in importance to individual executive departments and to a cabinet council. In the interval the business of governing the overseas plantations suffered from a confusing arrangement of overlapping boards and committees. This situation reflected a continuous struggle for power among the many men and interests to whom Charles II owed his restoration and reflected as well the yet ill-defined and unstructured nature of monarchical and imperial government.

The machinery for dealing with overseas trade and the colonies especially suffered from these defects. In response to the pleas of various merchants and others concerned with America, the king on 4 July 1660 appointed a committee of ten councilors to meet every Monday and Thursday to hear matters relating to the foreign plantations. The membership of this body, reflecting the various interests in the government, included the "Puritan lords": Manchester, Viscount Saye and Sele, Lord Robartes, Denzil Holles, Arthur Annesley (later Lord Anglesey), Southampton, Clarendon, Anthony Ashley Cooper, and the two principal secretaries of state, Sir Edward Nicholas and Sir William Morrice.

To widen support and to demonstrate concern for the varied trading interests, a few months later the crown established two advisory councils, one for trade and another for foreign plantations. Notices went out to the various chartered companies and to individuals involved in overseas trade to submit names of four individuals to represent each of the various geographical areas of foreign commerce.[1] Nominations came in from the principal trading organizations as well as from the merchants trading to Spain, Portugal, and France. In addition, merchants trafficking to the West Indies named Thomas Kendall, William Bunkley, John Colleton, and James Daix, while those trading to the Chesapeake

39

designated Edward Digges, William Allen, John Jeffreys, and Thomas Colclough. The administration added several prominent spokesmen from the gentry as well as a few officeholders. The more than sixty men named in the commission for trade issued on 7 November 1660 were drawn from several categories, including persons thought to be well versed in foreign affairs and merchants nominated by the various commercial and trading interests.[2]

The newly formed Council of Trade had a wide mandate: to investigate all aspects of English foreign and domestic trade and to suggest specific ways to improve the export of English commodities; to regulate the fisheries, not only in home waters but off Newfoundland and New England as well; and to inquire into the balance of exports and imports, the stock of bullion, and the shipping and trade with the foreign plantations.

The questions raised before the new council indicated a certain prejudice as to what the crown considered desirable. How could foreign trade be managed so that the English might sell more than they bought and the stock of money and coin thus be preserved and increased? How were the fisheries to be improved and regulated to the greatest advantage of English navigation (shipping) and the exclusion of foreign vessels? How were the manufactures of England to be increased to the greater employment of the king's subjects and to the better advantage of the public? How were the increase and security of English navigation to be provided? What was the condition of the colonies, their trade, and their navigation? How could they be utilized—by encouragement or by restraint?

Some flexibility was evident in the thinking within court circles. It might be advantageous to establish free ports, facilities open to ships of the European nations for depositing goods on payment of some slight customs duty. It might even be "more conducive" to the public good "to have a free and universal open trade" in all ports or for all commodities, domestic and foreign, as some men proposed. It might be proper to consider how far the Dutch had become the richest and most powerful nation in Christendom. While dominating the shipping of the English plantations, the Dutch did not suffer the vessels of their European rivals to trade or be employed in any of their own colonies.[3]

The privy councilors appointed to the new board showed no great zeal in attending to their duties. Delay and inefficiency also limited attempts by the Council of Trade to gather information on trade and general economic conditions. On 13 December it called for a proclamation inviting concerned persons to petition or to otherwise offer information. Three weeks later the proclamation, although approved by the Privy Council, still had not been issued. Not until January 1661 was the council able to begin serious consideration of the matters within its jurisdiction, when it debated the question of free ports and how to make English shipping competitive with Dutch navigation.[4]

In addition to a Council of Trade, the crown created a parallel advisory Council of Foreign Plantations with forty-eight members. Higher officers of state, minor officials, and merchants representing various trades sat on this board. Twenty-eight men were common to the Council of Trade and the Council of Foreign Plantations, although more merchants trading to the American and West Indian colonies were named to the latter than to the former. Philip Frowde served as clerk of the new body, one dominated by Lord Chancellor Clarendon and the principal ministers, any five of whom were to constitute a quorum. The commission issued on 1 December 1660 laid out the formal reason for the additional council. The king's subjects in the distant colonies through great industry had much enlarged their power and wealth; they had become a great and numerous people whose extensive trade and commerce employed and increased the navigation of the kingdom, provided produce for the mother country, and took off the manufactures of England as well as increasing the treasure of the Exchequer by the payment of customs duties. Consequently the foreign plantations should no longer remain in a "loose and scattered" condition, but ought to be brought together under a "uniforme inspeccion and conduct" so that the crown might secure and benefit from them. The Council of Foreign Plantations began functioning early in January 1661, initially at the Inner Court of Wards, at about the same time as the companion Council for Trade.[5]

The administration had created an unwieldy, overlapping apparatus for dealing with overseas trade and colonies. While the large membership and representative nature of these advisory boards perhaps facilitated the gathering of information and gratified the sense of importance of various groups, the system was cumbersome. Clarendon, most influential during these early years, for one, was dissatisfied with the arrangement. The Council of Trade became a debating society of merchants with diverse and, at times, conflicting interests. For the privy councilors it was not worth attending the deliberations of such a body. As for colonial matters, the real work was done by a committee of the Privy Council rather than by the Council of Foreign Plantations. Although both advisory boards continued in nominal existence until 1667, in practice they ceased functioning sometime before their recorded sessions came to an end in 1664.

Control had already passed to the Privy Council, acting through a standing committee for foreign plantations and other committees appointed ad hoc to deal with specific matters, such as the affairs of New

England.[6] The standing group, consisting of major officers of state, had been reorganized; it met at least once every week at the council chamber at Whitehall.[7]

The fall of Clarendon in 1667 brought about changes in the personnel of the Privy Council and a realignment of its committees. To consolidate conciliar control and enhance authority, Charles II organized the Privy Council on a more systematic basis with four standing committees: one each for naval and military matters; foreign relations; complaints and grievances; and trade and plantations. The two secretaries of state as well as the Duke of York sat on all four of the committees. Certain ministers exercised control on the committee for the colonies, for although three councilors might constitute a quorum, the lord president, the lord keeper, or one of the two principal secretaries of state had to be present at their meetings.

The Committee for Trade and Plantations, presided over by the lord privy seal, was at the center of colonial administration. It was to receive all communications from the governors overseas and to report directly to the full council. But as an instrument for supervising affairs in America and the West Indies, it was severely handicapped for its jurisdiction, and thus attention also extended to the affairs of Scotland, Ireland, and the Channel Islands (Jersey and Guernsey).[8]

Since the concerns of the various committees of the Privy Council ranged so widely, some ministers gave thought to creating particular agencies to advise in the specific areas of trade and the overseas colonies. The councils for trade and for foreign plantations established in 1660 were now moribund. In August 1668 Ashley met with Benjamin Worsley, a doctor of medicine long interested in commerce. He had served on Cromwell's Council of Trade and claimed to have authored the Commonwealth Act of Navigation. In a long memorandum, Worsley drew Ashley's attention to certain problems with colonial trade. Although the privy councilors for some months had been considering the feasibility of reviving the old commissions,[9] the boards established in 1668 probably reflected the ideas of Ashley and Worsley. They seemed to have learned little from previous experience.

The new Council of Trade commissioned in October 1668 was another large, unwieldy group consisting initially of forty-two and later forty-eight members. They had authority to investigate a broad range of economic matters: the state of commerce, the execution of the acts of navigation, the plantation trade, the export of wool, the decline of the fisheries, and the usefulness of the merchant companies. Those appointed to the new commission included ministers of state and courtiers, merchants like Josiah Child and Thomas Papillon, and men experienced in government and administration like Worsley and George Downing.[10]

The mercantile composition of the new council caused some comment. John Nicholas, son of a former secretary of state, complained that "the Merchants are most of them [religious] Phanatiques" who thought that the only way to increase and encourage the nation's trade was to grant "a Tolleration of Religion to all perswasions." Nicholas presumed that the sentiments of the majority of the members were known to the administration before they were named to the commission. Rumor at Whitehall had it that the duke of York was displeased with the councilors, especially Josiah Child, to whom, out of a personal animus, he would hardly speak.[11]

The new Council of Trade accomplished little before it was assimilated into still another advisory body, another of Ashley's schemes. This was a revived, but select, Council of Foreign Plantations. Rather than a large amorphous body of forty or so individuals with little time to devote to their task, the new organization, commissioned in July 1960, contained a nucleus of ten salaried members under the presidency of Edward Montague, earl of Sandwich. It had its own secretary, Henry Slingsby, and an advisor, Benjamin Worsley. Arlington, Ashley, and a few other ministers of state attended as members ex officio. Sandwich, like Ashley a former official in the Puritan government, had been instrumental in restoring the monarchy and had long been interested in overseas commerce. Having served on Cromwell's Commission for Trade and on the Restoration Committee for Foreign Plantations as well as on a committee of the House of Lords studying the decay of trade, he had more than fifteen years of administrative experience in colonial and commercial matters. The other commissioners were not noteworthy. Among the men added to the commission the next year, but not on a salaried basis, were two men with decided interests in North America, Thomas, Lord Culpeper; and Sir George Carteret.

The circumstances under which the councilors for foreign plantations began their labors were not auspicious. John Evelyn, a member of the board, recorded that Charles II proposed that each commissioner contribute twenty pounds toward the construction of a new chamber and conveniences in Whitehall, where the king might himself come and sit among them and hear their debates, the money to be reimbursed to them out of the contingency funds set aside for their salaries. The commissioners agreed, but evidently nothing came of the request, for the commission the next year met in King Street near Whitehall at the rented house of Barbara Villiers, countess of Castlemain, then mistress of the king.[12]

Another reorganization came in 1672 with the death of Sandwich in a naval engagement against the Dutch. The two boards were amalgamated into one, the Council of Trade and Foreign Plantations. Its membership was largely a continuation of the more successful Plantation Board, with Ashley, now made earl of Shaftesbury, as president, and Culpeper as vice president. Worsley, formerly a consultant to Ashley, now became the council's secretary. A year later he resigned, declining to comply with the provisions of the Test Act of 1673. Shaftesbury's private secretary, John Locke, succeeded him.[13]

Shaftesbury, now lord chancellor, was seemingly at the height of his power. But his glory, unlike his ambition, was short-lived. Charles had never trusted him and now excluded him from the inner secrets of the court. The passage of the Test Act required every officeholder to take the sacrament of Holy Communion according to the rites of the Church of England. Clifford, a Catholic, refused to comply and gave up the Treasury. Charles then turned to Thomas Osborne, who had begun his climb as an obscure Yorkshire baronet. Created earl of Danby, as lord treasurer he sought to lessen the king's financial dependence on both Parliament and the secret subsidies from Louis XIV by exploiting every resource for revenue and by economizing on expenditures, including those for colonial administration. As a creation of Shaftesbury, the expensive Council for Trade and Foreign Plantations was doubly vulnerable.[14]

What was to take the place of the tainted board? Among the various proposals Danby received was one entitled "An overture for the Better Regulation of the Forreign Plantations." Thomas Povey probably was the author. It proposed vesting plenary power solely with the king in council, with officers appointed from the Privy Council to sit regularly before the meetings of the full council. A model for such a body already existed in the committee empowered to deal with admiralty affairs and with Tangier, the North African city acquired by Charles on his marriage to the Portuguese princess.[15] An industrious secretary was needed to correspond with public officers in the plantations. He ought to be an ordinary (that is, permanent) clerk of the Privy Council.[16]

The crown adopted the substance of this proposal. In abolishing the advisory Board of Trade and Plantations, the king and Danby might also have responded to the need to reduce financial outlays. The salaried commissioners of trade and plantations drew a total of eight thousand pounds a year.[17] At the end of 1674 Charles revoked the commission for trade and plantations and the following March entrusted the conduct of colonial affairs to a committee of the Privy Council consisting of the principal officers of state. Immediate supervision fell to nine councilors headed by the lord privy seal, with any five members—later reduced to three—to constitute a quorum. This inner group included Sir George Carteret; Arthur Annesley, earl of Anglesey; John Robartes, now earl of Radnor; William, earl of Craven; and John Egerton, earl of

Bridgewater. The committee had its own secretary, a regular clerk of the council, in attendance.

The Lords of Trade, as they were called, within a short time sent out to the governors of the colonies circular letters requesting information on the state of each province.[18] A "Plantation Office" now came into being, with an official responsible for corresponding and for maintaining records. On the annulment of Shaftesbury's advisory board, its books and papers had been turned over to Sir Robert Southwell, who for ten years had served as an "ordinary," or regular clerk, of the Privy Council. William Blathwayt assisted him in managing the Plantation Office.[19]

Initially at the Restoration, the crown had sought to utilize large advisory bodies of men drawn from various segments of the commercial and political world in administering overseas trade and the foreign possessions. Such bodies had served to bring in various shades of opinion, but the influence of the merchants and amateurs—if they had had any influence at all—was greatly reduced by 1676, when the professional politicians, supported by a small core of administrative assistants, prevailed.

After fifteen years some measure of stability, expertise, and direction came to the administration of colonial affairs.

Other departments of state involved with overseas commerce also underwent an uncertain history. Throughout the early decades of the seventeenth century the financial needs of the crown and the means government employed to raise money from its subjects had been central issues. They had been crucial to the dispute between the sovereign and Parliament, a conflict leading to rebellion and civil war. The Commonwealth and Protectorate governments too had experienced great difficulties with fiscal problems. Clumsiness and waste characterized all seventeenth century financial administrations. In the face of the growing needs of national government, the Parliamentary regime during the Civil War had instituted new measures for raising revenue, including direct monetary assessments on the counties. In addition to continuing traditional taxes such as import duties, it had imposed an excise, a tax used successfully by the Dutch republic. Although later a tax on commodities manufactured or sold within the country, initially the excise differed from customs not so much in the nature of the articles taxed as in the method of collection.

During the interregnum it had been thought more advantageous for the government to farm out, or to sell, the right to collect customs to private individuals in return for a fixed sum. The state immediately gained much-needed cash, while the syndicate of "farmers" retained any excess money it garnered. Yet, despite the expedients and innovations employed by the Protectorate, there was a large, constant gap—nearly a million pounds a year—between the income of government and its expenditures. Cromwell had been forced to resort at first to concealed and then, finally, to open borrowing.

At the Restoration some attempt was made to overhaul and reform finances. Ancient feudal duties and contentious charges such as ship money were thought politically inexpedient, but the excise introduced during the interregnum was retained. The settlement of the customs revenue in 1660 was one facet of a larger policy involving trade as well. Imports into England were subject to three types of duties: tunnage, a definite rate levied on each tun of wine imported; poundage, a shilling in the pound on imports whose value was listed in a Book of Rates; and additional duties. By an act (12 Charles 2, c. 4) passed on 28 July 1660, additional duties were imposed on imported wines, linens, wrought iron, silks, and tobacco, among other items. An Act to Encourage Shipping (12 Charles 2, c. 18), passed some weeks later on 13 September, listed, or enumerated, certain produce of the colonies, among them sugar and tobacco, requiring that they be carried from the plantations first to some English port, where duties would be paid. They would then be eligible for shipment elsewhere.

Direct collection of the customs through officials appointed by the state was initially attempted in 1660, but the restored monarchy also considered farming, an easy, even advantageous, technique. The government might realize increased yields from competitive bidding by rival groups of financiers. Regular, fixed payments of rent by the farmers also offered certainty of income for the crown.

At first, changes in the rates set by the Act of Tunnage and Poundage, as well as unsettled conditions of trade, made it difficult to estimate the value of the customs. Consequently, potential bidders for the customs farms were not inclined to bid. The estimated returns from customs valued for the general revenue settlement in 1660 at £400,000 was highly conjectural; it fell short by over £100,000 during the first years of the new reign. There was no alternative but to continue direct collections by officials appointed by the crown until 1662, when the government negotiated a contract with a syndicate of financiers who rented the customs collections, paying an annual sum to the government of £390,000. But the outbreak of war with the Dutch in 1664 and the ravages of the plague, with resultant losses in trade, meant that the farmers could not meet their annual rent. The contract was renegotiated in 1667, but the system continued to be unsatisfactory.

The sale of crown lands in 1670 temporarily strengthened the government's financial position and enabled the crown the next year to return to a system of direct collection by its own officers. Under the supervision of the Treasury, a Board of Customs Commissioners in London appointed collectors in all ports, with responsibility for receiving duties and returning money and accounts to London. Parliament in 1662 provided Customs officials in England with various legal safeguards against harassment and prosecutions for actions performed in the line of duty.

The Restoration Treasury under the earl of Southampton had been little more than an agency for routine administration, with only limited initiative in handling problems in revenue. With the death of the timid, ineffectual Southampton and the close of the Second Dutch War in 1667, control passed to more tough-minded, able, and energetic commissioners. Ashley, Sir Thomas Clifford, Sir William Coventry, and Sir John Duncombe extended the jurisdiction of the Treasury.

At the lower levels, the machinery for collection of money continued to be inadequate, marred by inefficiency and corruption. In general there was an unwillingness to pay taxes, in part a reaction to the upheavals and financial exaction imposed during the Civil War, when the populace was heavily overtaxed. During the reign of Charles II, Englishmen may have been the most delinquent taxpayers in Europe. Merchants and shippers in the colonies were no exception. Few men appreciated that the king and his officers could not finance even ordinary services from the personal revenue of the crown and that expenses had to be met by taxation. A large standing army and prerogative courts would have been useful in collecting taxes, but neither was possible, given the experience of Charles I and the political circumstances making possible the Restoration.

The monetary grants Parliament grudgingly gave the king—grants members thought wildly extravagant—were, in fact, nearly always inadequate in the face of the growth of governmental services and necessary expenditures. During the first twelve years of the reign the ordinary revenue was some 25 percent below the annual sum the parliamentary leaders had estimated as requisite to maintain the government. In time of war, the gap between expenditures and supply was much greater. The loss of revenue from the disruption of trade during the Third Dutch War and increased expenses meant the crown operated with a still larger deficit. Despite the payments made to Charles II by Louis XIV under the secret terms of the Treaty of Dover of 1670 and the business acumen and efficiency of Danby and Laurence Hyde (later earl of Rochester) who succeeded him at the Treasury, the debt at the time Charles died was more than a million and a half pounds. In order to pay off the dead king's debts and to restore the Navy and Ordinance, suffering from deterioration due to financial stringencies, additional customs were granted, especially on sugar and tobacco, for eight years.

Greatly expanded trade was essential for financing the crown. This expansion assumed the proportions of a major boom. By the end of the 1680s the total revenue from overseas commerce came to nearly a million pounds annually.[20] The channeling of overseas trade—particularly, enumerated commodities from the transatlantic colonies to English ports—was of prime concern to the financial well-being of the English crown. As the earl of Nottingham noted with satisfaction on one occasion later in the century, the arrival of the Barbados and Virginia fleets with sugar and tobacco would pay to the king's treasury at least three hundred thousand pounds in customs. Revenue from foreign commerce increased as the volume of overseas trade swelled. It had another advantage, particularly in an age when taxpayers were not apathetic. The burden did not fall directly on the consumer and landowner. Indirect taxes were less visible and thus politically less offensive. During the Second Dutch War one observer had reported the reaction to a proposal in the House of Commons for raising three hundred thousand pounds to outfit the fleet. "We are all against a land tax, & excise, though the best and more equal assessment under heaven[,] we will by no means hear of."[21]

Revenue from foreign trade, including some produce from the overseas colonies, was essential to the Restoration monarchy. A legislative code for trade and navigation could best secure the crown's vested financial interest.

CHAPTER 4

The Restoration Navigation Code

THE EARLIER Stuart governments, like their Tudor and medieval predecessors, routinely had taxed foreign trade and manipulated the course of overseas commerce by various statutes, edicts, and impositions. The Restoration monarchy and its successors employed similar regulations. In time these came to be known conveniently, if not altogether accurately, as the "navigation laws," or the "acts of trade." They did not make up a comprehensive system. There was no continuity of purpose or clarity of logic linking the various statutes enacted from mid-seventeenth to mid-eighteenth century. A governor in the colonies charged with enforcing the various acts, upon reading his instructions, observed perceptively that the laws were far from clear; indeed, they were "dark and difficult," enacted at different times and "penned by different persons who seem not to have had the same view of things." Statutes to encourage shipping, to regulate trade, to raise revenue, or to encourage the production of specific staples were not all of one piece.

Enactment of these laws on trade was not merely an attempt to implement a comprehensive set of related ideas, the doctrine of mercantilism. Stuart officials were not impelled by the force of these ideas to translate them into a legislative code. The various views expressed in miscellaneous pamphlets and publications themselves were not a reflection of mercantilist theory, for a good deal of mercantilist writing consisted of special pleading for private economic interests. While statutes for regulating the overseas trade of the nation were at times couched in language similar to the rhetoric employed by publicists, these laws were less the result of the influence of special commercial interests or the implementation of the theories of writers than they were efforts to meet the needs of the state for naval power and revenue.

Mercantilist theorists posited a closed imperial trading system and envisaged separate, distinct roles for the economies of the metropolis and the overseas colonies. The latter were to trade only within the empire and to provide raw materials not available to the mother country and were by no means to compete with her function of manufacturing. The laws enacted by the English parliament over the course of a century, roughly from 1650 to 1750, well after the postulates of mercantilism had been laid down, never imposed this role on the colonies.

The acts of trade and navigation represented attempts by government over a number of years to solve particular problems. Revenue from customs duties helped to meet the financial needs of government, and the growth of English shipping raised the potential resources for the Royal Navy and enlarged the available pool of mariners. During the Protectorate era, officials had kept fiscal interests in the forefront in considering commercial policy for the country. How would a particular measure affect national revenue? A secondary consideration was shipping. Would legislation directly or indirectly improve the size, availability, and efficiency of the navy?

The interests of the crown might coincide with those of certain subjects. Legislation designed to enhance the potential naval power of the state by restricting the commerce of the nation to English carriers would eliminate foreign competitors to English shipowners. But for the English business community, for those men engaged in producing, selling, and carrying goods, there was no identity of interest.[1] Governmental action favorable to one group might not serve the needs of others.

In the months following the Restoration, the crown received numerous petitions from various and, at times, opposing interest groups pleading their case and requesting remedies for their specific economic grievances. In the newer, expanding trades, competition was intense, as the number of men engaged in commerce increased. With the boom in tobacco imports the number of London traders dealing in tobacco tripled. At least 250 Londoners were involved in the traffic by the middle of the century. Scores of others did business in Bristol, Liverpool, and the other outports.[2]

The merchants engaged in foreign trade could not agree among themselves or with the government on how this overseas commerce should be organized. Was it to be open to all Englishmen, or limited to merchants already established? Companies dominated by Londoners in some instances had managed to secure privileges in certain markets. They wished to exclude outsiders or to impose irksome restrictions. Bristol merchants had for some time contended with the London vintners (over the wine trade), with the Levant Company, with the African traders, and with the Hamburg Company.[3] Generally, businessmen in the outports were wary of the Londoners. In the last years of the century, the Merchant Venturers of Bristol, learning that the House of Commons was considering establishing a new council or commission for trade, wrote their members that the trading cities ought to be represented by men acquainted with their needs rather than by "Courtiers" inexperienced in trade or Londoners who would endeavor to monopolize.

While Londoners themselves did not present a common front, they feared outsiders. Richard Chiverton, governor of the Fellowship of the Eastland Merchants, defended their right to seize a cargo of iron imported from Sweden and to fine an interloper, as justified by the crown's charter. In 1660 English shipmasters and mariners petitioning the House of Commons protested foreigners resident in England, especially Frenchmen who threatened to engross the trade across the Channel. They requested either "stinting" the number of foreigners or incorporating the English merchants trading to France—the latter they conceived to be the "speediest and most effectual means." The Common Council of London went so far as to petition that the trade in all foreign commodities be reserved for merchants in regulated companies.[4] Among those seeking a charter to preserve a monopoly were merchants importing wine from the Canary Islands. Despite the efforts of this Canary "gang," in September 1667 the crown called in its charter and threw open the trade to all Englishmen.

Dissension also marked the organization and governance of the Newfoundland fisheries. Merchants of Dartmouth, Totnes, Plymouth, and Barnstable complained of the numerous mariners who went out to the fishing banks as private passengers on vessels bound for Newfoundland, leaving ships from the outports regularly engaged in the fishery short of seamen. The gentry and traders of the smaller western towns feared also the dominance of merchants in Bristol and London.[5]

More complex and hazardous was the trade to the west coast of Africa and to the Caribbean. Despite opposition in the House of Commons against monopoly charters earlier in the seventeenth century, Rowland Wilson, Maurice Thompson, John Wood, and Thomas Walter had formed the Guinea Company, a venture with limited capital, but had been unable to maintain even a precarious hold with one factory or station in Africa. In this region, as elsewhere, monopoly organization stirred opposition from individual merchants, both Londoners and provincials.[6] Some merchants involved in the African traffic, Maurice Thompson, Martin Noell, and Thomas Povey among them, were also concerned in trade with the West Indian islands. They too had sought a monopoly to exclude English as well as foreign rivals in the commerce of the islands. Trade to the West Indies and to the American colonies at the time of the Restoration was still open to all Englishmen. While merchants in England might agree on the need to exclude foreign businessmen and shipping from the commerce of the plantations, they resisted the attempt of Thompson. Noell, and Povey to limit the trade to a chartered company. In the islands, the planters, for their part, insisted that the trade be free, that is, open to ships of all nations.[7]

Among the various organizations, individuals, regional spokesmen, and commercial interests there was little agreement on the conduct and organization of English overseas trade. The crown had its own needs: the well-being of the nation through a strong economy, the development of English naval power through an expansion of the nation's shipping, and an enhancement of the government's financial position by taxes on foreign trade, a potentially attractive source of revenue which would not evoke in the minds of the king's subjects the harsh exactions of the Commonwealth and Protectorate. In 1660 the government of Charles II could look to numerous precedents in the regulations adopted over the previous century to meet specific needs. Some of these enactments might yet be appropriate to meet comparable problems now confronting the state.

With the establishment of plantations in America, James I and his ministers had acted quickly to tap a new source of revenue. In 1621 they required all tobacco grown in Virginia and Bermuda first to be shipped to England, landed, and have duties be paid before being transshipped for sale elsewhere in Europe. To increase the yield from imported tobacco, planting in England was prohibited. Under Charles I the government had not attempted to limit the sale of Chesapeake tobacco to England and had not sought to prevent colonial tobacco from entering the European market. By an order in council in 1631, half of the duties imposed on the importation of colonial tobacco landed in England were drawn back on export. For the early Stuarts, revenue was the important consideration. Their regulations had not established a closed system wherein the colonists were restricted ultimately to trading with the mother country and foreigners were prohibited from obtaining commodities grown in the English colonies. On 24 October 1621, the Privy Council had ordered that all tobacco and other commodities from Virginia "shall not be carried into any forraine partes untill the same have first been landed here and his Majesties Customes paid therefore." Again, in 1628, the Privy Council emphasized that by allowing ships laded with tobacco to proceed immediately, that is, directly to foreign ports, "his majestie looseth the Customs and duties thereupon due." No shipmaster was to sail his vessel from the colony without giving bond to the colonial governor to proceed directly to some English port.[8] The fiscal motive for routing plantation tobacco through English ports and restraining the growing of tobacco at home was also clear in the practices adopted by the Protectorate government in continuing the regulations laid down by the earlier Stuart kings. An ordinance passed in April 1652 again prohibited planting in Gloucestershire and Worcestershire.

Some men had argued that the English ought to imitate the Dutch, who, by lowering duties, had created an entrepôt at Amsterdam. The city had outstripped the other ports of northern Europe as a center for maritime trade. They favored the creation of free ports in England, where commodities destined for transshipment would be deposited in warehouses and then reshipped within six months on payment of a small composition fee. Such a system had been established at Dover in 1634, when the disruption of trade during the Thirty Years' War had necessitated rerouting commodities destined for the Spanish Netherlands. With Dutch shipping hindered during the conflict, English navigation had been able to dominate the carrying trade between Flemish and southern European ports, but with the conclusion of hostilities in 1648, Dutch vessels regained their superior position in northern European waters.[9]

The passage of English shipping through the Danish Sound was then threatened by an agreement between Denmark and the United Provinces. The Commonwealth government attempted to negotiate with the Dutch, stressing in the instructions to the English envoys the need for English vessels to have access into the Baltic to obtain naval stores. This trade had allowed the employment of a great number of ships and, because of the short voyages involved, had provided a pool of available seamen. When the Dutch rejected the English demand that they cancel the treaty with the Danes, the English retaliated in 1651 with an "act for the increase of shipping and encouragement of navigation." On scores of occasions, dating back to the Middle Ages, English governments had enacted laws relating to shipping. As recently as 1645 Parliament had decreed that only vessels English-owned and manned could bring in whale oil and fins from Greenland waters. And to prevent Royalists from benefiting from commerce with the colonies, Parliament in 1650 had restricted trade with the plantations to ships licensed by Parliament or the Council of State.

The Act for the Increase of Shipping, passed the year following the collapse of the negotiations with the Dutch, was avowedly a measure for the promotion of English navigation, not necessarily a statute to advance English trade. By its provisions, no commodities from Asia, Africa, or America were to be carried into England, Ireland, or any possessions of England except in ships belonging to English subjects. Products of Europe could be imported into England, Ireland, or any English possession only in ships belonging to Englishmen or subjects of the country or place where the goods were produced or usually first shipped. The act sought to eliminate Dutch carriers between northern Europe and England, Africa, America, and Asia.[10] Benjamin Worsley, then secretary to the Council of State, in a pamphlet entitled *The Advocate* put forth the government's case.[11] What the Dutch gained in trade and navigation, others, including England, lost. And the consequence of a reduction in trade was a loss of power. *The Advocate* was concerned with the need to increase the power and security of the state.

Yet, at mid-seventeenth century, the English shipping industry was inadequate to meet the obligations the act imposed on it, particularly in carrying bulky naval stores from the Baltic. Moreover, wartime hazards limited the ability of English vessels to service the colonies across the Atlantic. Since the foreign plantations could not be provisioned without the aid of Dutch shipping, the Protectorate government had instituted a piecemeal system of licensing foreign shipping and had not rigidly enforced the Act of Navigation. Some confusion resulted, as traders and governmental officials were unsure how to interpret and enforce the law.

When Charles II came to the throne, the royal government was in a position to employ the provisions of the Protectorate ordinance with other precedents to meet its needs. The queries posed during the succeeding months to the various councils and committees dealing with overseas plantations and trade indicated the priorities of the king and his ministers. Which branches of foreign commerce were to be reserved, regulated by charter, and which were to remain open to all Englishmen? How was the trade of the nation to be managed so that the wealth and navigation of the kingdom increased and its people were employed? How was the store of coin and bullion to be preserved and augmented? In 1660, as in the decade before, a strong merchant navy meant potential sea power; and the need for revenue was as pressing as ever. Indirect taxes, the revenue derived from overseas commerce, had an appeal to a government conscious of its tenuous political position. As John Nicholas reported the prejudices of the Commons later in the decade over the means to raise three hundred thousand pounds for outfitting the fleet, "We are all against a land tax, & Excise, though the best and most equal assessment under heaven we will by no means hear of." In addition to providing revenue, colonial produce when reexported would help redress an unfavorable balance of trade. As the volume of sugar and tobacco reshipped from England increased, less bullion would be needed to pay for imports from Europe.[12]

Within weeks of the return of the king, the government acted when, in the House of Commons, a large committee undertook to consider ways of encouraging the navigation of English ships. The members included George Downing, Sir John Shaw (a commissioner of customs), Anthony Ashley Cooper, and Edward Deering (a navy commissioner). Downing and Shaw were managers of the bill for the encouraging and the increase of shipping and navigation. Given the large, unwieldy membership of the committee and the speed with which it brought in a bill, it probably worked from a prepared draft.[13]

On September 4, during the third reading of the bill, an important clause was added, one introducing the principle of enumeration, a measure linked with the reorganization of the royal revenues. The Act for the Encouraging and Increase of Shipping (12 Charles 2 c. 12) provided that no goods were to be imported or exported from any English possessions in Africa, Asia, or America except in English, English colonial, or Irish ships. Only subjects of the king of England were allowed as merchants or factors in the colonies. Goods of foreign origin brought into England or Ireland had to be carried in English vessels or those of the country of origin or the usual first port of lading. Certain products of Asia, Africa, and American colonies (sugar, cotton wool, indigo, ginger, tobacco, fustic, or other woods used for dyeing), except when shipped to another English colony, had to be carried to some port in England, Ireland, or to Berwick on Tweed. Shipmasters bound for the colonies had to give bond with English customs officials that in case they loaded any of these enumerated commodities, they would carry them back to an English or Irish port. The captains of vessels legally permitted in the plantation trade who arrived in a colony without offering proof of having given such assurance had to take out a bond to return to England or Ireland on loading enumerated goods.

As Pepys, the secretary to the Navy Board, realized, the law aimed to further the growth and development of English shipping. "Had not foreigners built as good ships as we, as well as cheaper," there would have been no need for the statute.[14] The law gave English and English colonial shipping a monopoly, excluded Dutch vessels from the colonial carrying trade, and aided the balance of payments by eliminating the freight charges paid to Dutch carriers. By requiring that enumerated products be landed first in some English port and by excluding foreign ships from the ports of the English colonies, the statute aimed to transfer from the United Provinces to England the center for distributing the plantation trade to Europe. London and the outports would be the entrepôt for tobacco, sugar and the other designated products.[15] The requirement that enumerated products be landed in England before shipment to Europe enabled the government to collect customs and excise, particularly from sugar and tobacco. The duty on the latter, in 1660, came to twopence per pound. To gain full benefit, customs officials were ordered to dispatch officers to the colonies to supervise the execution of the law, and Parliament, in December 1660, passed another act (12 Charles 2 c. 34) prohibiting planting of tobacco in England. The government encountered great resistance to this ban, but stressed that the great quantities of tobacco grown in the western counties greatly prejudiced the foreign plantations as well as the royal customs and hindered the navigation of the kingdom. Significantly, it left supervision of the prohibition against domestic planting to the surveyor general of the Customs.[16]

The fiscal needs of the crown, not fostering a monopoly in marketing tobacco for merchants in England, concerned the government. Shipping intelligence indicated that it was both legally and commercially feasible to carry Chesapeake tobacco and West Indian sugar to European markets via English ports. John Lucas of Topsham brought his vessel, laden with Virginia tobacco, into Falmouth, where he entered his cargo before proceeding to Amsterdam. A Bristol ship, the *Samuel and Mary,* also landed Chesapeake tobacco at Falmouth before continuing to Holland. Colonial vessels participated in this trade. The *Diligence,* from the Piscataqua River in New England, laden with Virginia tobacco, cleared Lyme as required by the act of Parliament and proceeded to Amsterdam. The *Rebecca,* of New York, made her landfall at Falmouth before going on to Holland with tobacco.[17] Such traffic in colonial produce to European ports did not raise the ire of royal officials. Only in cases such as the *Hannah and Katherine,* of Boston (New England), was the crown concerned. After entering Weymouth, her master refused to pay customs on Virginia tobacco and sailed without license "to the great dimunition of our revenue."[18]

Sugar and tobacco, considered by European governments to be luxuries, were appropriate items for taxation. In addition to the statute to encourage shipping, the convention Parliament passed a Tunnage and Poundage Act (12 Charles 2, c. 4) to lay the foundation for customs revenue for the Restoration government. Import duties on enumerated products of the English plantations were lower than those imposed on produce from the foreign colonies.[19] Spanish tobacco rated at ten shillings per pound (an arbitrary and not a market value) paid sixpence duty; English tobacco valued at one shilling eightpence per pound returned one penny. In addition to this subsidy of one penny, an additional one penny was imposed on English colonial tobacco. This was a specific duty added to the Book of Rates in lieu of the excise levied during the interregnum. In order not to burden commerce unduly, a portion of the duties was rebated when colonial tobacco was reexported within a specified time.

Fiscal considerations had led the government to require that shippers land tobacco at some English port where duties would be collected. Consequently, it viewed locally grown tobacco as a threat to revenue from overseas sources. But the administration, politically weak, was all too aware of the experience of its predecessor and of the sensitivity of the landowning classes; they controlled law enforcement in the counties. Royal cavalry riding down tobacco plants would have been a vivid reminder of Cromwell's troopers collecting arbitrary exactions. The laxness of the government in London in stamping out tobacco planting in the western counties may have reflected its hesitance to use methods reminiscent of the hated Protectorate. Some tobacco could be grown locally for medical purposes, the plant being thought to have therapeutic effects. In 1665 no tobacconist had died of the plague. Samuel Pepys, passing several doors in Drury Lane marked with a red cross and the plea, "Lord, have mercy upon us," was reminded of the widely held belief in tobacco and purchased some to relieve his fear of contagion. Despite a fine of five pounds imposed for each offense, the law against planting tobacco met with little support among local officials in the west and with open resistance by rioters. For more than twenty years the repeated orders of the Privy Council found little compliance.[20]

Smuggling of imported tobacco also drained revenue. In an attempt to combat evasion of duties, Parliament, in 1662, passed an act "to prevent Fraudes and Concealments of His Majestyes Customes and Subsidyes." The statute allowed customs officials armed with warrants or writs of assistance, under specified procedures, to search for smuggled goods. The new law also clarified some ambiguities in the Act of 1660 to Encourage Shipping. Subjects residing in the English colonies were considered as Englishmen in fulfilling the requirement that the master and three-quarters of the mariners of ships engaged in the carrying trade be English. Foreign ships were not qualified unless purchased by Englishmen and registered before 1 October 1662.[21]

In the West Indian and American colonies and in some commercial circles in England, there was strong reaction to the requirement that sugar and tobacco be landed first in a English port, where a duty was to be paid, before they could be sent to a European market. John Bland, a merchant of London with interests in Virginia, printed a remonstrance setting forth the grievances of the planters of the Chesapeake: by barring the Dutch from trading, the Act for Encouraging Navigation would prove destructive to the trade of the tobacco plantations. The law met resistance. The Council for Foreign Plantations learned of violations of the act through a clandestine traffic in tobacco from the Chesapeake to New Netherlands and New England. The king's envoy at The Hague, Sir George Downing, also reported that English ships loaded in Barbados had arrived in Holland without touching in England.

A major problem in the West Indies was the difficulty in getting the planters, English merchants, factors, and shippers to agree on a price for sugar to be carried off by the English. Some Barbadians apparently were turning to the Dutch. In the spring of 1663, the crown made clear its displeasure to the governor, Lord Willoughby: the royal revenue was diminished by ships of foreign nations coming to the island without having paid any duties on the goods they brought in. Willoughby was now required to collect the same customs on these commodities as required when they were imported into England and to persuade the provincial council and assembly to agree on a procedure for fixing reasonable prices on sugar. These the crown would then recommend "to a body of good and substantial merchants" so that "the whole growth of sugars shall be taken off" the island at agreed-upon prices.[22] Royal officials also learned from shipmasters and merchants trading to Virginia, Maryland, and New England of a traffic being conducted to Dutch, Spanish, Italian, and other European ports. In North America the governors were neglecting to examine English vessels arriving at the plantations to determine whether they were qualified under the Act to Encourage Navigation or whether their masters had given bond to return enumerated commodities to England. A circular letter to the governors was ordered sent requiring them to enforce the navigation code.[23]

As the king and his ministers attempted to close off the Dutch carrying trade and the consequent drain on customs revenue, Parliament was taking up complaints against the role of foreign merchants in the commerce of the kingdom. Within a few months after the Restoration, various tradesmen, shopkeepers, and artificers in and about London had petitioned the king against the importation of foreign woolens, laces, ribbons, and silks by alien merchants in London. English factors residing in Italian, Spanish, French, German, and Portuguese ports may well have provoked similar resentment among the tradesmen of Europe. But the English Privy Council had given little satisfaction to the complaints of the Londoners. At best, a committee of the council advised that a voluntary program—wearing only apparel of English manufacture—be adopted.[24] The Londoners took their case to Parliament when the House of Commons resolved to appoint a large committee to bring in a "sumptuary" bill to prevent encroachments on trade by Jews, Frenchmen, and other foreigners. Attendance might have been poor, for, twelve days later, another twenty men were added, among them Sir George Downing, Sir John Shaw, and William Coventry. The committee, with added administrative weight and experience, was now empowered to receive proposals and to prepare a measure for regaining and advancing trade.

This broad mandate opened the way for various interest groups to register their complaints and to propose remedies. On 7 April, Sir Robert Atkyns reported from the committee various proposals to be included in a bill. These included a prohibition against carrying European commodities (wine from the western isles in the Atlantic and salt for the fisheries of Newfoundland were exempted) to any English colony in Asia, Africa (Tangier excepted), or America except from England and in

English ships as manned and defined by the Act to Encourage Shipping and the Act to Prevent Frauds in the Customs. England thus was designated the entrepôt through which goods destined for the colonies first had to pass.

While the bill was before the Commons, amendments reflecting the interests of various groups were added. Irish ports presumably were no longer to be eligible to receive enumerated products directly from the colonies. Limitations were imposed on the importation into England of Irish and Scottish cattle, but servants, horses, and provisions from Ireland and Scotland were among the foreign commodities allowed to pass directly to the plantations.

Under the provisions of the bill, it would no longer be possible to evade the Act for Encouraging Shipping by sending goods (except those specifically exempted) directly from Europe to the colonies even in English vessels.[25] According to the language employed in the Act for the Encouragement of Trade, commonly called the Staple Act (15 Charles 2, c. 7), as it related to the colonies, Parliament intended to maintain a closer connection with the foreign plantations, to keep them more firmly dependent and more beneficial to the mother country through the greater employment of English shipping and seamen and the sale of English commodities, and to make England a staple not only for the commodities of the plantations but also for the manufactures of foreign nations. It was the practice of foreign states, so the explanation ran, to keep the trade of their own plantations to themselves.

As Sir George Downing, stationed at The Hague, viewed the Act for the Encouragement of Trade, it would disrupt the commercial correspondence between Dutch Jews and the West Indian islands and hinder the sale of Dutch manufactures across the Atlantic. The traffic could not bear the cost of first shipping goods from Holland to England, where customs would be collected, and then transporting them to the colonies. Consequently, colonial customers would favor the cheaper English manufacturers. Downing's expectation that the cost of trans-shipping European goods to America through the English entrepôt would be prohibitive was not to be borne out. In the years to come, European manufactures, in significant volume, passed legally through London and Bristol to the English colonies in North America. The Staple Act of 1663 did not create a monopoly in the colonies for the merchants and manufacturers of England.[26]

The attempt by parliamentary statutes to channel the trade in specified commodities from the colonies through English ports and in English (and English colonial) carriers provoked great resentment among Charles II's subjects in the kingdom of Scotland. They sent two delegates, the earl of Glencairn and the earl of Rothes, south to London to request the king to intervene, to allow the Scots the same privileges in the plantation trade his English subjects enjoyed.

English customs officials reacted strongly, however, condemning the proposal as prejudicial to the king's revenue and the English, by whose efforts and money the colonies had been planted. If the Scots were allowed into the colonial trade, the government of England would lose revenue, since there would be no way to enforce the terms of the bonds the Scots posted to return enumerated produce directly to England. Moreover, the proposal would nullify the very essence of the Act to Encourage Navigation. The carrying trade to the plantations employed annually more than two hundred ships; it bred an abundance of sailors; and it returned in customs four times more than the East Indies ever had. To allow even a few Scottish vessels into the trade would result in the loss of twenty thousand pounds in customs a year. Lord Treasurer Southampton and the other privy councilors at Whitehall added another objection: only the English Parliament could grant the dispensation asked by Charles's subjects in the northern kingdom.

Finding no immediate relief at Westminster, the Scots exerted economic pressure by imposing heavy duties on English salt, coal, cattle, and grain imported into the northern kingdom. English merchants distressed by this retaliatory legislation petitioned the House of Commons, but to no avail. A committee of the Commons merely referred the matter to the king's ministers. Inasmuch as the English exported to the Scots more than they imported from their northern neighbors, the Council of Trade recommended making some slight concessions in the Act to Encourage Navigation, but not to allow Scottish vessels to engage in the plantation trade.[27]

The outbreak of war with the Dutch in 1664 prevented any quick resolution of the dispute, but following the cessation of hostilities, the Scots reopened the issue. Hoping to win some concessions, Lauderdale and his friends pushed for a conference between commissioners from the two kingdoms. In view of the precarious political state in 1667, the king referred the appointment of commissioners to discuss terms with the Scots to Parliament, where, in debates at Westminster, Sir George Downing warned the Commons to take no action which might damage the customs and reduce the income of the government. Downing was among the English commissioners appointed to deal with the Scots, along with Buckingham, a member of the ministerial ring, and Richard Temple, a leading parliamentarian. Among the Scots, Lauderdale and his friends, Tweeddale and Moray, dominated.[28]

The English commissioners faced two problems: how to protect home industries, and how to preserve the integrity of the navigation code in the face of the demand by the Scots that in foreign trade they be treated as the king's English, Welsh, and Irish subjects. The Scots insisted that this latter issue be given priority in the talks. They were willing to give assurances that enumerated produce of the colonies carried by Scottish ships would be brought first to England (except for the small quantities carried directly to Scotland and consumed there) before being carried to Europe. The English, for their part, insisted that although the legislatures of the respective kingdoms were under one monarch, each was yet free to make such laws regarding trade and commerce as it thought fit. Moreover, some of the English plantations and colonies, those in the East Indies and Africa, belonged to particular companies of Englishmen. Not even other Englishmen had the right to trade there. As to the colonies in America, individual Scots might settle there, but Scottish vessels must not have liberty to bring into England commodities of foreign growth or manufacture. It would be too great a blow to the navigation of England. She must preserve enough ships and seamen for the naval service.

The Scots refused to accept any distinction between the king's subjects in England and those in Scotland. Citing the opinion of Chief Justice Edward Coke in Calvin's Case (1606) that all persons born in Scotland, Ireland, or the Channel Islands of Jersey and Guernsey were subjects and enjoyed the same privileges as those born in England, the Scots demanded equal right in the colonial trade. They went on to cite the role played by the Scots in the settlement of the West Indies. Again they offered to have their ships engaged in the carrying trade from the plantations return enumerated products to English ports. Rather than calling merely for privileges for six years, the Scots now demanded entry on a permanent basis into the colonial trade. Insisting on equality with the English, the Scots received nothing. Negotiations broke down later that year.[29]

Except for an occasional concession in extraordinary circumstances,[30] Scottish trade to the colonies, until the Act of Union between the two countries in 1707 created the United Kingdom of Great Britain, consisted of illicit ventures. In time of war, when the Dutch and the French interdicted English shipping, Scottish carriers were particularly welcome in the American colonies. As press gangs caught up seamen from the merchant navy and enemy privateers hindered the sailing of merchantmen from English ports across the Atlantic, the Scots took up the slack.

During the early years when the Restoration code regulating trade with the colonies was being laid down, two consistent goals were evident: employing English ships and mariners, and providing revenue for the crown by channeling European trade with the colonies through English ports. They remained objects of concern. Establishing a monopoly for the merchants of the mother country did not appear to rank high in the minds of governmental officials. For example, the instructions to the Council of Trade created in 1668 required the commissioners to consider creating a free port for storing foreign goods for a limited time, on payment of a small composition fee. The privilege of importing might be so regulated that all merchants, "strangers and foreigners as well as natives," might be encouraged and the revenue accruing to the crown not prejudiced.[32]

The requirements of English trade and the fiscal needs of the English state came into conflict when war imposed extraordinary burdens on the Treasury. In 1668 members of the House of Commons took up means to raise a supply of over three hundred thousand pounds for the fleet. They divided sharply; some favored customs duties levied at the ports as recommended originally by the committee on supply; others advocated excise duties imposed at the retail level. Additional customs duties, it was argued, burdened the merchant, discouraged imports, and encouraged smuggling, thus prejudicing not only the yield from any new supply but also the revenue from the customs duties already voted. The committee had initially reported in favor of additional taxes on linen, wine, brandy, and tobacco to be imposed at the ports of entry. Sir William Coventry protested the additional burden on tobacco, as did Sir Thomas Clifford. The higher rates would result in lower imports, thus endangering the yield of one hundred thousand pounds annually from imported leaf. Sir John Knight, a merchant of Bristol, supported these arguments. Inasmuch as tobacco was grown in the plantations by natives of England, "it was in a manner a home commodity." Parliament might destroy the trade in tobacco by excessive taxes, thus encouraging the Dutch to expand production in their own plantations. The Commons took no further action on tobacco at this time, but the issue came up again in March 1670 when some members voiced concern over the balance of trade and the state of domestic manufactures.

Again a conflict between revenue and commerce ensued. Supporters of each aligned themselves with the court and the country factions in the Commons. For months they engaged in a running controversy on proposals to restrict the importation of luxuries and to compensate for the ensuing drop in revenue by imposing additional taxes on tobacco and sugar imported from the colonies and by enforcing the ban on planting tobacco in England. In November 1670, John Jones spoke up for the tobacco retailers, whose position was threatened by the proposal to increase the taxes on tobacco. Under the current tax burden their profit was small enough; the local seller, if fortunate, realized only a farthing in the pound.[33] Sir John Knight of Bristol claimed tobacco shipments returned one-third of the customs receipts of England and engaged half the six thousand tons of the shipping in the port of Bristol. An additional duty would ruin both the navigation of the kingdom and the revenue of the king. Indeed, the current rate ought to be lowered. Sir William Thompson sided with Knight. The Dutch had lowered their duties on tobacco; for the English to raise their rate would lead to increased smuggling and a drop in receipts.

These arguments were to no avail. The committee for supply recommended an additional duty of threepence per pound on English colonial tobacco to be paid by the first buyer and further taxes on sugar. The debate on the additional impositions on sugar from the English islands was particularly sharp. It continued on 4 January 1670/1, when the excise levy was broached. Arguing that the English plantations could not bear further taxes on their produce, spokesmen for the West Indian planters objected strenuously. They suggested the example of the French ought to be followed: a higher duty on foreign sugar.

The planters of Barbados had formed a lobby in London—Sir Peter Colleton and other property owners of the islands then resident in London—to protest against any new impositions and to obtain freedom for the Scots to trade to the islands. The merchants trading to Virginia, also opposed to further duties on tobacco, employed a counsel, Robert Efley, to present their case. But they offered nothing which every member of the Commons had not already known and which had not been repeated over and over. On 24 March 1670/1, the Commons passed a bill for additional impositions.[34] But the Virginia lobby received another chance when the Barbadians presented a petition to the House of Lords on 29 March 1671, objecting to the imposition of additional duties on sugar. The merchants importing tobacco joined them. The testimony of customs officials several days later further strengthened the case of the colonial producers. Heavier duties would encourage smuggling and lessen the revenue. Shipping interests also petitioned for a reduction in the proposed increase in the duty on sugar. But at this point both houses of Parliament became embroiled in a constitutional argument over the right of the Lords to amend a money bill; there the matter stood when the king prorogued Parliament.[35]

As the needs of the crown for revenue mounted, however, it was to the growing volume of tobacco and sugar imports that the government looked. (Additional duties were to come in the first year of the reign of James II.)

Despite differences in opinion regarding customs and excise, Parliament remained committed to the navigation code. It passed a law for preventing the planting of tobacco in England and for regulating the plantation trade (22/23 Charles 2, c. 26). The act confirmed a previous ban on domestic planting of tobacco and called for governors in the colonies to take oaths to enforce the provisions of the navigation code.

The passage of this act also offered an opportunity to define more clearly the position of Irish shipping and ports in the carrying trade with the overseas plantations. By the Act to Encourage Shipping, passed in 1660, Irish ports had been eligible to receive enumerated products shipped directly from the colonies. While it had been intended three years later, by the Act for the Encouragement of Trade, to rescind this privilege, the governing clause of the Staple Act was ambiguously worded. The statute to regulate the plantation trade enacted in 1671 now excluded Irish ports for a period of nine years as ports for landing enumerated products. Merchants in Cork, Galway, Dublin, and Belfast now depended on Bristol and the western outports of England for tobacco and sugar. The new law also jeopardized a considerable export trade in Irish beef, butter, tallow, and other provisions for the West Indies. A long, drawn-out battle ensured pitting the lord lieutenant and the customs establishment in Ireland against its counterpart in London. In successfully urging the rigid enforcement of the ban on direct Irish trade to the plantations in enumerated produce, the English commissioners emphasized that the measure was intended to make England the staple, the entrepôt for the commodities of the colonies sold to other countries.[36]

The last of the laws making up the Restoration navigation code came in 1673 during hearings held to investigate a decline in English trade with Russia, the eastern Baltic, and Greenland. On 13 February, the House of Commons had appointed a committee of inquiry and declared any member of the Commons who sat for a port town or on the Council of Trade or the royal commission for customs eligible to attend. George Downing, John Jones of London, and Sir John Knight, the Bristol merchant, were among the twenty members designated by name to the committee.

During the deliberations held that day a motion was made to look into the condition of the trade to Virginia and the other plantations. Merchants trading to the Chesapeake had complained that while they were required by law to return tobacco to English ports for the payment of duties before reexport, some New England carriers were taking enumerated commodities duty-free from the Chesapeake to a colonial port and then directly to Ireland or to Europe. After some debate the house referred the matter to the committee appointed that day to consider the Greenland and eastland trade. As a result of the committee's recommendations, the House of Commons, contrary to the wishes of the Eastland Company, threw open the Baltic and Greenland trades and further qualified the provisions for carrying enumerated produce from the colonies.[37] The measure did not go as far as some had suggested: to limit the lading of tobacco to specified locations and to prohibit carrying tobacco from one colony to another.[38]

The Act for the Encouragement of the Greenland and Eastland Trades and for the Better Securing the Plantation Trade (25 Charles 2, c. 7) first summarized the basic law to encourage shipping and navigation. It permitted the carriage of certain specified commodities from one colony to another without the payment of customs. Some colonists, not content with obtaining sugar, tobacco, or other products for their own use free of the taxes paid by English subjects when those commodities were imported into England, had carried them to Europe, thus diminishing the royal revenue and the trade and navigation of the kingdom. Parliament now required that if any ship legally qualified to trade entered a colonial port to take on enumerated goods without having given bond to return those articles first to some English port, a tax was to be paid at the port of lading. The duty to be paid in the plantation on tobacco was less than that imposed when carried directly to England. Under the rate set in 1660, colonial tobacco paid twopence (one penny subsidy and one penny additional duty) when entering England; by the new Plantation Duty Act, tobacco exported from one colony to another on a ship for which bond had not been given to return her cargo of enumerated produce to England paid only one penny per pound. Whatever else, the act ensured that colonial consumers would not enjoy tax-free tobacco while their English counterparts absorbed the cost of the import duty.

The provisions of this law caused great confusion even among officials in England. Could colonial carriers pay the duty of one penny per pound in some American port and then proceed directly to Europe, thus escaping the obligation to land their tobacco in England where another penny was due? That seemed to be the interpretation of some shippers, especially in New England. Some provincials assumed that the law would impose a system of double taxation if they were required to pay a tax on leaving an American port and then another if they carried their cargo to England.

The confusion among highly placed English officials over the meaning of the Act for Securing the Plantation Trade may well have reflected the fact that the measure had not originated in a department of state. It was, rather, a hurried, somewhat ill-thought-out reaction in the House of Commons to the complaints of English merchants that rivals were undercutting them, avoiding the payment of any tax simply by carrying enumerated commodities from one colony to another and then sailing directly for an Irish or European port. The highest legal officers, the keeper of the Great Seal and the attorney general, could not agree what exactly was due in customs on tobacco brought into Ireland and England. Customs officials themselves were confused and turned for direction to the Treasury. The earl of Danby, for his part, saw the imposition of a duty in the plantations by the act of 1673 as a device rather "to turn the course of Trade than to raise any considerable revenue to His Majesty."

The Committee for Trade and Plantations was forced to ask Sir William Jones, the attorney general, for clarification. If a ship took on enumerated goods in a colonial port, declared for another colony, and paid the plantation duty, was it then exempt from giving bond to return to England and free to carry those goods wherever the master pleased? The attorney general, in his reply, drew a distinction between English ships leaving the mother country without giving bond to return enumerated produce directly to England, and ships arriving in a provincial port from some other colony. In the case of the former, no duties were required to be paid in the colony, only a bond to return the cargo to some English port. But vessels coming from any place other than England (presumably another colony) must pay the duty on any enumerated item and give bond to carry it to some English plantation or to England.[39]

As the Commissioners of Customs were to interpret the law, the act of 1673 did not repeal the provisions of the Act for Encouraging Navigation and Shipping that required tobacco, sugar, or any other enumerated commodity to be carried to an English port before shipped to European markets. This interpretation became the accepted view.[40]

Whatever had been the intention of the members of Parliament in posing the plantation duties, crown officials interpreted and enforced the act as aiming not so much to raise revenue locally in America or to exclude colonial trade with Europe as to channel enumerated plantation products to England, where they would be taxed before being sold or reexported.[41] Ships entering from the colonies, paying the required customs, and then proceeding to foreign ports were not molested. It was the revenue collected in London and the English outports on colonial commerce that mattered.

Circumstances, particularly during the first years under the navigation code, at times made it difficult for shippers fully to comply with the requirements of the laws. As a result, the crown had to grant limited dispensations or to suspend temporarily the provisions of the code. In 1664, English forces had taken over the Dutch settlements in the lower Hudson and Delaware estuaries. As a condition of the capitulation, the Dutch had received permission for several vessels to sail directly from the Netherlands.[42] Permission was given for foreign ships to bring in the great quantities of timber necessary to rebuild London after the Great Fire and for the employment of foreign seamen when plague struck the crews of English merchantmen. War with the Dutch and French imposed much the greatest burden on the English merchant fleet, as normal shipping patterns were disrupted. At times not enough vessels from England were able to reach the plantations and to service adequately the commercial needs of the overseas colonies. The temptation was strong to avoid vulnerable English shipping and to employ Scottish or neutral vessels or to bypass the exposed English outports and to sail directly from the colonies to European harbors in violation of the navigation code in peacetime or under ordinary circumstances.

Parliamentary statute restricted the carrying trade between the colonies, England, and Europe to ships owned and manned by Englishmen or English colonists. Certain colonial products—the more important at this time were sugar and tobacco—when exported from the plantations had to be carried to England, where duties were paid, before being reexported to Europe. Merchandise from Europe (with some exceptions), if imported into the colonies, had to come, after being landed in some English port, in ships qualified under the navigation code. Execution of this code lay with customs officials and governors in the colonies appointed by the crown.

Protests later arose that the Restoration statutes on trade and shipping imposed an awkward, artificial, or heavy burden on the overseas trade of the infant American settlements. As late as 1675 it was clear that some officials in America, even the governors entrusted with the responsibility by the crown, were not complying with the requirements of these statutes.[43] Merchants in the mother country complained that New Englanders imported goods directly from Europe, avoided customs duties, and sold in the colonies at rates cheaper than the English traders could afford. Massachusetts shippers, for their part, charged that the requirement to carry tobacco and sugar to England before shipping to a market in Europe imposed an uneconomical burden, as did the requirement that European goods must be transshipped from England to America. As one American observer put it: the entrepôt requirements of the navigation code imposed the cost of running a double venture, paying double freight and wages in addition to the costs "that doth arise by the loading and unlading" of goods. Irish shippers remonstrated that "to return thither again from the Plantations, and to unload in England did not allow them to quit costs."[44] Spokesmen for the planters on the Chesapeake and in the West Indies complained that by the exclusion of the Dutch from the direct trade in sugar and tobacco

English merchants were granted a monopoly. Protected by parliamentary statute, they could fix prices for produce raised in the colonies and for manufactures sent across the Atlantic. That was the planters' explanation for the decline in prices received for colonial produce.

Did the navigation and fiscal programs adopted by the Restoration government divert the colonial trade into artificial economic channels and impose substantial hardships? Or were these complaints unfounded? Did New Englanders and others in bypassing the English entrepôt attempt to squeeze added profits by evading customs? Englishmen on both sides of the Atlantic during these years commonly evaded paying taxes.[45]

In answering these queries and in assessing the impact of the navigation code an examination into the actual conduct of Anglo-colonial overseas trade proves revealing.

In the transatlantic commerce with the American and West Indian colonies, English colonial as well as English carriers benefited by the exclusion of Dutch rivals. Moreover, the entrepôt provisions of the navigation code seem not to have excluded European goods from the colonies or to have given English merchants an artificially protected monopoly in America. For years European drygoods, textiles, draperies, clothing, and haberdashery imported into New York, for example, did pass legally through London and Bristol.[46] And as shipping intelligence from the English ports confirmed, colonial shipmasters did find it economically feasible to carry sugar, tobacco, and other enumerated produce to European ports after fulfilling the requirements of the navigation code by stopping at some English port.[47] The merchants of New England had already established a pattern of trade to England and Europe employing their friends and relations in London as commercial agents.[48]

The bulk of the trade carried on by the New Englanders during the middle decades of the century was conducted *within* the navigation code. Fish, provisions, and lumber, the major exports of the northern colonies, were not among colonial products enumerated. Nothing in the laws restricted New Englanders from exporting these commodities to the West Indies, the Atlantic islands, and Europe. The ban on foreign shipping from the carrying trade eliminated Dutch rivals. Since the New Englanders had already established the practice of ordering manufactures through friends and relatives among the merchants of the mother country, the provisions of the Act for the Encouragement of Trade and the Staple Act of 1663, prohibiting the direct importation of European goods to the colonies, were of slight consequence.

American trade to Europe conducted independently of English connections was marginal. Masters of New England ships carrying timber and fish to the islands of the Atlantic and the Iberian Peninsula often had to exchange their bulky wares for smaller cargoes of wine and fruit or simply for specie and bills of exchange drawn on London to pay for English manufactures. Occasionally, it was tempting to put into some port to pick up a load of French brandy or lace to run across the Atlantic.

In the trade to the Antilles, New England timber-carriers found it difficult to return from the West Indies with a full cargo of molasses, cotton wool, and sugar. Seeking to make the return voyage as profitable as possible, New England shipmasters stopped along the Chesapeake Bay or Albemarle Sound for some tobacco.

The nature of the New England carrying fleet during these years did not make the colonial vessels serious competition for English freighters. Their share in the tobacco trade was petty, carried out for the most part in ketches, barks, and other small vessels navigating along the smaller creeks and inlets. They were too limited in number and small in size to take off more than a trifling portion of the bulk of tobacco which moved in legal channels from the Chesapeake. It is highly improbable that a direct, and hence illegal, trade in tobacco and sugar at this time was ever as large as some merchants in England and some customs officials in America, perhaps for political reasons, claimed. Economic considerations alone limited the participation of the New Englanders in a direct trade with Europe, and the majority of the complaints registered by the most zealous of English customs officers in the colonies against New England merchants involved minor, technical transgressions.[49]

The need for far-flung correspondents and reliable business connections limited the ability of the New Englanders to play a role in overseas trade independent of English merchants. Without institutional mechanisms in international trade, personal connections and family and religious ties formed the nexus of the English transatlantic trading world more than did legislative codes.

For some planters, whose horizons did not go much beyond their immediate environment, it was easier to blame the navigation code for their economic difficulties. Initially, the harshest complaints against the carrying provisions came from spokesmen for the planters of the West Indies and the Chesapeake. To the Barbadians it appeared the Act of 1660 for the Encouraging of Shipping had caused a sharp drop, a 20 percent decline, in the price of sugar by limiting the sale to one market, England. As English subjects they were willing that only English ships be allowed in the trade to the islands, but they demanded that they have access to a wider market, to be allowed to send their produce to any friendly nation. What was difficult for the Barbadians to accept or to appreciate was that they no longer enjoyed a dominant position as producers. With every passing year, the expansion of sugar production on new plantations in the Antilles increased supplies and lowered prices in Europe. Moreover, the European market was not as open as the planters thought, for the French, Spanish, and Portuguese governments adopted a protectionist policy favoring their own colonies.

Tobacco producers in America subject to much the same economic situation registered similar complaints against the navigation code. The years down to the last decade of the seventeenth century witnessed expanding production on the Chesapeake, declining prices, and growing markets in the British Isles and elsewhere in Europe as the tobacco habit spread. To win entry into these markets, English tobacco had to be priced low, but as was the case with sugar, English tobacco was not admitted in all areas of Europe. Under the navigation code the planters in the English colonies had a near monopoly in England, the most fully developed market for tobacco in Europe. Tobacco was already established as a commodity of common use in England, but not in France, where the level of consumption was much lower. The French could satisfy their needs with tobacco grown in the metropolis or in the French Antilles. The Portuguese and the Spanish also relied on their overseas colonies. During these years the crowns of Spain, Portugal, and France adopted preferential tariffs favoring tobacco produced in their own plantations over the leaf exported from the English Chesapeake.[50] At best, Virginia and Maryland tobacco would have to compete in a limited market in northern Europe against inferior but lower priced tobacco grown in Germany and the United Provinces of the Netherlands.

For the planters and farmers about the Chesapeake Bay a more immediate and superficially plausible cause to explain the drop in prices came to mind: the enumeration of tobacco and the carrying provisions of the Act to Encourage Navigation. Shortly after the statute went into effect, the General Assembly of Virginia requested Governor William Berkeley to travel to England, there to plead for the repeal of the onerous law. In both public and private pronouncements, Berkeley, while in London, charged that the forty thousand settlers in the Chesapeake plantations were being impoverished to enrich little more than forty merchants in the mother country "who being the only buyers of our tobacco give us what they please for it and after it is here sell how they please, and indeed have forty thousand Servants in us at cheap rates." John Bland, a Londoner with a plantation in Virginia, made similar charges in his "Humble Remonstrance."[51] But there was no real contemporary evidence to support their contention that so few English merchants controlled the tobacco trade—indeed, many more were involved than Berkeley thought—or that they conspired to keep prices low.

During the seventeenth century the trade was much more diversified than later. Some English merchants in the outports, James Twyfort of Bristol, for example, through agents in the colonies purchased tobacco in America and assumed the risk themselves in shipping and marketing in Europe.[52] Some Londoners, Thomas Sands and Peter Paggen, for example, preferred to purchase for themselves and to take title to tobacco in the colonies, where they offered the planter a specific price at the time of sale.

In such transactions, local market conditions on the Chesapeake determined the price that factors, merchants, and shipmasters paid for their cargoes. Robert Anderson, who combined the trades of merchant and planter in Virginia, once complained to a correspondent that the "market has so Rul'd heare with us that I have been forc'd to give a great prise for the Tob^{co}." In explaining to John Page, a London merchant, why he had been unable to purchase tobacco for him at the rate of twelve shillings and sixpence per hundredweight, Anderson remonstrated that Bristol merchants operating in Virginia had offered fourteen shillings. With the arrival of more ships in Chesapeake waters, the price locally had risen to twopence per pound.[53] Another planter-trader in Virginia, William Fitzhugh, explained in 1685 that he was shipping no tobacco that year on consignment for sale in England, since "it gave too good a market here."

Fitzhugh was representative of the larger planters who purchased the crops of their smaller neighbors and then either sold locally to some representative of an English merchant at a known price or gambled and shipped large consignments across the Atlantic to be sold for them by some English middleman. The requirement to ship tobacco through some English port did not deter Fitzhugh from proposing to enter into a "speedy Dutch Trade" with the English merchant, Thomas Clayton. He asked Clayton to send over a ship to load two hundred hogsheads of tobacco to be dispatched by late October, "by that means [to] have the first & choice of the Crops here, and the first & best of the Dutch Market there."

The larger planters who chose to send their tobacco to the European market by consignment were able to pick and choose the merchants with whom they dealt. Among Fitzhugh's correspondents in Bristol and London were Thomas Clayton, John Taylor, John Cooper, Sir John Hudlestone, Cornelius Sergeant, George Mason, Henry Hartwell, Sir William Dains, and Richard Gotley (or Gostley). Fitzhugh often shopped about for consignment agents to act for him, dispatching small lots of a few hogsheads. At times, the men he selected were not personally known to him, but had been recommended by some friend or neighbor. Robert Anderson also consigned shipments of tobacco to London on the basis of recommendations of friends or neighbors in Virginia.[54] From these consignment merchants, the planters or local traders in the Chesapeake would order hardware and clothing, to be purchased with the proceeds earned by the sale of their tobacco. Fitzhugh asked James Bligh to make up a return cargo, relying on the discretion and judgment of the London merchant.[55] With such vague instructions much would depend on the mutual trust and confidence of both parties. Not surprisingly, confusion, dissatisfaction arose at times.

A variety of factors—size of crop, the availability of shipping (particularly in time of war), market information (often dated)—would influence the prices planters received either on the Chesapeake or in the English market. While drought, heavy rains, or frustrated, desperate men cutting down plants in the fields might at times reduce the size of crop, above all, the general pattern was for increased production and depressed prices in the years following the restoration of the king.

Even as Governor William Berkeley was protesting in London the presumed effects of the Restoration navigation code, it was clear to him and to others that there were alternatives: limitation of production and diversification by the cultivation of other staples: silk, flax, and hemp. But limiting production required the cooperation of the governments of Virginia and Maryland, the crown, and the English merchants. Diversification would entail capital investment, and, in Berkeley's view, the wealthier planters in Virginia still were concerned mainly with realizing immediate returns and then retiring to England.[56]

What was not appreciated in the Chesapeake region until much later was the opportunity the revolution in sugar cultivation in the Antilles offered as a market for foodstuffs and livestock when the West Indian planters committed their resources to the most valuable cash crop and drew upon the outside world for provisions. By mid-seventeenth century, Virginians were producing sufficient foodstuffs for their own consumption; all that was required was a greater emphasis on grain, beef, and pork. William Byrd had already realized the opportunity and had developed connections with Barbados, but few of the leading planters perceived the opportunity for diversification until much later.[57] In the interval, other Englishmen, one or two hundred miles to the north along the Delaware and Hudson rivers, in colonies recently come into English hands, planted flourishing agricultural settlements and established a prosperous provision trade with the sugar islands.

At the Restoration the royal administration and Parliament had to solve a variety of economic problems and the demands of several, at times conflicting, commercial interest groups. Drawing on discrete past practices rather than on mercantilist theory, they placed on the statute rolls a navigation code excluding foreign vessels from the colonial carrying trade and channelling the marketing of certain products of the overseas plantations through English ports. These requirements produced essential revenue for the crown and enhanced the potential naval power of the state; they were intended to serve the needs of government, not necessarily to further the interests of particular economic groups. The great bulk of American commerce flowed legally within the parameters of the navigation code. Despite smuggling in England and in the colonies and protests on both sides of the Atlantic, the various acts of trade did not impose an artificial pattern on colonial commerce. Private men, relatives, friends, and business associates had already established the commercial nexus between America and England and other overseas markets before the enactment of the navigation laws. But in time of economic strain, dislocation, or changing commercial conditions and when confronted by competition or little understood commercial forces, planters on the Chesapeake found it easy to blame a complex and prolix series of statutes enacted by a distant legislature at Westminster.

CHAPTER 5

Early Problems, 1660–62
The Legacy of Weakness and Neglect

In the months following the return of Charles II, he and his chief ministers of state were presented with a variety of complaints and grievances concerning the colonies in America, most of them the result of the ignorance, weakness, and neglect of earlier administrations.

At the time Englishmen first founded settlements in America, little was known of the region. Consequently the early Stuart kings had issued grants with conflicting or overlapping boundaries. Further to add to the confusion, religious animosities had become prevalent among the settlers. Only three of the colonies in existence in 1660 had received sanction from the crown, but as a result of personal rivalries and religious animosities other communities outside Massachusetts, Virginia, and Maryland had been formed. From the perspective of Whitehall the American settlement seemed loose and scattered.

A generation before, crown officials had thought to act, but they had proved too weak. Domestic affairs had intervened. War, first with the Scots and then with the Parliamentary forces, occupied the resources of the crown. Under Cromwell the Commonwealth had imposed some control over the Chesapeake colonies, but the Puritans at Westminster, whether by design or neglect, had allowed the Puritans in New England to remain virtually independent. After the Restoration, complaints involving the situation in New England predominated among the grievances relating to the American colonies. Over a period of several months the king, Clarendon, and the other key ministers had to become familiar, if not expert, with what had occurred over the past forty years with the claims, the grants, the grievances of the various contending groups in America. They had to satisfy Quakers, Anglicans, Dissenters, land speculators, and merchants, protect the position of the crown, and yet not antagonize unduly the singular-minded rulers of the most populous and most powerful of the colonies, the Puritan Bay.

The Puritan commonwealth of Massachusetts exemplified the problem the monarchy faced: confusing charters, religious antagonism, resentment over the restoration of monarchy, and determined conduct based on the premise that the reign of Charles II would not long endure.

Monarchical government under Charles II hardly seemed qualified to preside over the most dynamic empire of the early modern era. It was politically unstable, financially weak, and not blessed with men knowledgeable in the task of governing overseas colonies.

The overlapping boards and agencies established in the months following the return of the king were an initial source of difficulty. The cumbersome councils on foreign trade and on plantations did not function smoothly, and without the personal attention of the king to give direction, the committees of the Privy Council accomplished little. Not until 1668, following the fall of Clarendon, was the council to be reorganized on a regular and systematic basis. But continued friction and internal rivalries would hamper effective administration. After more than a quarter century one veteran bureaucrat would comment sarcastically that the goals of securing the colonies and rendering them more useful to the mother country had been commonplaces "that have entertain'd us these many years but the means which are very plain have always been opposed or not prosecuted."

Government often lacked sufficient information to make timely judgments. Recognizing the problem of communicating across the ocean, the Council for Trade and Plantations recommended to governors that they and their provincial councils appoint knowledgeable men who would take up residence in London or who might travel to the metropolis from time to time "to represent and agitate such things as may tend to be to the advantage" of the crown and the particular province concerned.[1] But no such agencies were established on a systematic basis during these years. Communications remained slow and haphazard and information incomplete. Even a proposal made by Captain Silas Taylor in 1667 to establish a regular packet boat service with the colonies came to nothing.

Travel across the Atlantic by sailing ship in the seventeenth century was slow and at times hazardous. A normal crossing involved six, eight, or ten weeks. Secretaries of state often had to rely on merchant shipping that sailed on a seasonal schedule. In February 1683 one official in Whitehall urged a governor in Virginia to write promptly, "this being the last ship bound for your parts till August next." Months might pass before officials in Whitehall received critical information. One governor at New York—not yet the busy port it later became—apologized for not maintaining a more frequent correspondence with ministers in London. The secretary of state must understand "how slow our Conveighance [*sic*] is [,] like the production of Elephants once almost in two years."

The uncertainty of vessels from England touching at convenient ports often led letters "to become abortive."[2]

Most detrimental to effective administration under the Stuart monarchs was the financial weakness of the crown and the shortsighted insistence that administration of the overseas possessions be financed from revenues raised in the colonies. Charles's reign began in debt and ended in greater debt. With Parliament's appropriations inadequate and the machinery for public credit rudimentary at best, the crown was forced to borrow money at exorbitant rates. It was tempting to pass on to others costs and charges. The auditor general of the plantation revenue later complained to a crown official in Virginia, "You cannot but know under how many keys our Excheq[ue]r here is kept."[3] The unwillingness to finance crown officials in America compromised their ability to implement policy from Whitehall and rendered the civil and puny military establishments there vulnerable to political pressures exerted by the colonists.

In administering the foreign plantations, men at Whitehall faced a wide range of problems, among them the conflicting claims of individuals and governments in America, where discord and animosity, the legacy of the previous Stuart monarchs, prevailed.

In the initial stages of English colonization of North America and the West Indies the English government had played no role beyond granting through charters to individuals and corporations the right to govern and to hold land. In the years between 1606 and 1633, charters had been issued initially to the Virginia (then a term for North America) companies of London and Plymouth, the Council of Plymouth, and the Governor and Company of the Massachusetts Bay, as well as to George Calvert, Baron Baltimore of Ireland, to establish colonies across the Atlantic. These grants at times overlapped and conflicted one with another. The financial collapse of the Virginia Company of London had induced the crown to take over supervision of the government of the Jamestown settlements in 1624, but subsequent attempts by Charles I and his ministers to bring the tough-minded Puritan dissenters of the Bay Colony under the crown were aborted with the outbreak of war with the Scots in 1639 and the Civil War in England shortly after.

During the intervening years until the Restoration in 1660, dissension, often on religious grounds, had marred relations among the English colonists in America—among the Anglicans, Puritans and Catholics settled on the Chesapeake and among the Puritan and Anglican villages in New England. These conflicts had led some groups to break away, to form their own communities, to confederate, and then to establish separate provincial governments. Control over islands in the Carribbean too was disputed between Francis, Lord Willoughby; the earl of Carlisle;

and the earl of Kinnoul, the heirs to the proprietary charter; and a group of planters headed by John Colleton, who sought to have Barbados placed under direct control.[4] One of the first items of business when Charles II returned to Whitehall was to require the attorney general to review all of the patents for lands and territories in America to certify their legality and prepare a breviate of the powers granted by these charters. But royal officials experienced great difficulty in reducing the colonies to some order. Provincialism and social mobility even more evident in America than in England hindered any attempt to impose a hierarchial government.

By 1660 some seventy-five thousand Englishmen were settled in North America: of them there were about twenty-five thousand in towns and villages in New England on or near the coast from the eastern end of Long Island north and east to the Kennebec River in Maine and another forty thousand on farms and plantations about the Chesapeake Bay. About five thousand Dutch and Swedes resided in villages on Long Island, Manhattan, and along the Hudson and lower Delaware rivers.

The political horizon of the great bulk of colonists across the Atlantic was no broader than that of the gentry of England whom they sought to emulate. Although the colonists had crossed the Atlantic, they brought with them to America the strong sense of localism tenaciously held by Englishmen, a resentment against outside interference. They gave their loyalty to the immediate community; they retained their traditional values.

Customarily, political leadership was identified with social status, but economic opportunity and social mobility had their impact. Political contests in the English counties were struggles among local leaders for prestige and influence. The sons of the lesser gentry who crossed the Atlantic and the men who rose from the lower orders continued in the belief that social prestige must be recognized by the exercise of political power. The scene in America was characterized by greater economic opportunity, social mobility, and more fragmented political authority.

From the outset, distinctions in status stemming from family, wealth, and education were present in the new English communities. In the New England towns they were one basis for the distribution of common lands. Elsewhere too men distinguished between "ye meaner sort of people" and those "of note." In Virginia a well-to-do planter would refer to the small farmers as "our wild Rabble." Giles Bland, son of an English merchant and landowner, when he insulted a member of the Virginia council, was not content merely to call him "son of a whore," "Puppy," and "coward," but added that he was a "mechanic fellow."[5] Manual labor lowered social status.

As evidenced by the careers of several of the more prominent planters, in the developing society men could rise by their abilities and fortune's smile. Freshly attained wealth or even a marriage to a wealthy, newly made widow conferred privileges. The continuous migration from England of young merchants and the sons of the lesser gentry, men lured by economic opportunity, increased the number of persons with claims to political power and office, if for no other reason than as a mark of social status. The expansion of the area of settlement, and with it the creation of additional towns and counties, for a time provided them with the marks of esteem: commissions as justices of the peace, as clerks, and as officers in the militia and seats in the elected local assemblies. But the higher offices in the provincial governments, those above the county level, were limited in number. Lord Chesterfield's somewhat cynical but apt analysis of the problem ministers of state later faced with members of the English House of Commons and their followers might well have applied in America: the greatest difficulty was "to find pasture enough for the beasts they must feed."[6] Social mobility and economic opportunity created more aspirants for the higher positions of political power than could be accommodated.

In the colonies, political power was fragmented among several institutions. Men might seek to enhance the elected assemblies, claiming for themselves in that body the same rights and powers contested during the seventeenth century by men in the English House of Commons. They might attempt to better their position through the patronage and authority of a governor and council appointed either in the name of the crown or a proprietor. And if denied gratification on the local political scene, an aspiring politician could always appeal to Whitehall and Westminster to reverse an unfavorable decision. The American scene was characterized by instability and friction brought on not only by the pursuit of economic advantage but also by the disparity between social status and political power at the upper levels and competition between those who held power and those who aspired to it as a mark of recognition, as a symbol of having arrived. That men resorted commonly to the rhetoric of liberty or the rights of Englishmen or preached the virtues of prerogative government often indicated no more than that they needed to appear high-minded even while pursuing their own interests. Anti-Popery at times served the same purpose.

The attempt by the government of Charles II at Whitehall to bring the colonists to acknowledge dependence on the crown added but one more dimension to the political scene; created yet another avenue for those seeking honor, recognition, and profit; and posed a threat to those who based their power on the sanctions of a local authority—in the Puritan commonwealths of New England, for example, on the General

Court. As one observer of the Pennsylvania scene was to advise the proprietor: "It will be greatly to thy Interest to have the chief of those concerned in thy Affairs in Posts of Hon[ou]r in the Gov[ern]m[en]t for it will . . . shew thy Strength at home." In Virginia, Nicholas Spencer, a councilor and customs collector, had won high office under the aged governor, Sir William Berkeley, but fearing what might happen under a successor when Berkeley died, Spencer wrote his brother in England to obtain confirmation of his posts from Whitehall. The salary from his collectorship was not so much to be valued as the "many advantages it gives me otherways."[7] Politics, the quest for status and office, was a passion with seventeenth-century colonists. William Penn once described America as "this licentious wilderness" and the Friends there as filled with a sense of their own importance. He enjoined them, "Be not so *governmentish,* so noisy and open in your dissatisfactions," avoid "factions & partys, whisperings and reportings, & all animositys."[8]

The focus of Restoration colonial policy for America was New England, and particularly the Puritan commonwealth of Massachusetts Bay. Confused and conflicting claims to territory had marred early settlement by the English in this region. In 1606 James I had granted to a group of investors from the environs of Plymouth a charter to hold land and to govern. The earliest ventures undertaken by the Plymouth organization to establish a settlement in Maine had failed, and in 1620 the group was reorganized as the Council of Plymouth, or Council of New England. While this company had authority from the crown to establish government, it was doubtful whether it legally could delegate such sovereign power to other parties. Nonetheless, within the next fifteen years, under the leadership of Sir Ferdinando Gorges and Robert Rich, second earl of Warwick, the members of the Council of New England issued grants to a number of individuals and groups for settlements. Among the first to receive such a patent were the Pilgrims, or Separatists, who had founded New Plymouth. Their grant furnished the title to the lands of the community but conferred no legal jurisdiction. The right to exercise governmental powers for the initial settlement and the nine other communities founded thereafter rested on no more secure foundation than usage and practice.

In succeeding years, the English-based Council of Plymouth issued several more patents, among them a grant to an Anglican sea captain, John Mason, for the area covering Cape Ann and adjoining territories; another grant to Ferdinando Gorges and Mason for the land between the Merrimack and Kennebec rivers, one the two men then divided between themsleves; and still another grant in 1628 to the New England Company. The following year this last group received from Charles I a charter incorporating the members as a joint-stock company—the Massachusetts Bay Company—with title to the soil and royal sanction to govern. The territory assigned to the Massachusetts Bay Company overlapped a portion of the previous grant made in 1620 by the crown to the Council of Plymouth. The northern limits of the new colony were to run three miles north of the Merrimack River.

Puritans won control of the Massachusetts Bay Company. Once settled in America, they disregarded the grants Gorges and Captain John Mason received from the Council of Plymouth and set their northern limits at the upper source of the Merrimack.

Warwick, as president of the Council of Plymouth, further confused matters in 1632 by making out another deed for lands in southern New England to several of his friends, Puritan lords, and gentlemen. This Warwick "patent" the full Council of New England never approved. The grant was also marred by the vague description of the boundaries. They began at the Narragansett Bay (or River, as it was also called) and extended forty leagues along the coast southwest or west toward Virginia and across to the Pacific Ocean. Eight months after initiating this ambiguous grant, Warwick lost the presidency of the Council of Plymouth. The organization soon ceased to function after it had divided the remainder of the region, initially granted to it by James I, among its eight members, including the earl of Hamilton and William Alexander, earl of Stirling.

Mason and Gorges, to protect their claims against Massachusetts Bay, had turned to the crown for confirmation of their grants. Mason was still negotiating for a royal charter when he died, but Sir Ferdinando Gorges, a staunch opponent of the Puritans, had initiated proceedings to have the crown by writ of quo warranto vacate the Massachusetts charter. Charles I then undertook legal action, and in 1639 Gorges obtained royal confirmation of his patent from the Council of New England in the form of a charter for the province of Maine. But the outbreak of the war with the Scots and the civil strife in England prevented Charles I and Gorges from pursuing the issue in America. With the Puritans emerging victorious over the Royalists in England, the authorities in the Bay Colony established their jurisdiction over the infant fishing and farming communities in northern New England.

Before the outbreak of the English Civil War, other Dissenting Protestants, some from England and others from the Bay Colony, had established settlements in southern New England. Three towns were formed by the followers of the Reverend Thomas Hooker along the lower Connecticut River, others at Saybrook, New Haven, and on Long

Island Sound under the Reverend John Davenport, and still others under the leadership of Anne Hutchinson and Roger Williams about Narragansett Bay and on Rhode Island.

The townsmen of Windsor, Hartford, Wethersfield, and Saybrook, confederated as the colony of Connecticut, had based their title to the land and authority to govern on a patent from Warwick made in 1632. But there was nothing to show by what right the earl had made the grant. At best the document was only a deed for land, not a grant of government. But the authorities in Connecticut acted as if it were. The leaders in the confederated New Haven towns along the coast to the southwest thought to use the same Warwick grant—dubious as it was—as the basis for their provincial government. Officials of Connecticut and New Haven had commissioned agents to cross the Atlantic to obtain a patent from the Puritan Parliament then engaged in war against the king. They hoped to repeat the successful approach employed by agents of the dissident settlers from the villages of Rhode Island and Narragansett Bay.

The townsmen of Providence and Portsmouth, in an effort to strengthen their position against Massachusetts Bay, had dispatched Roger Williams to England to obtain from Parliament legal sanction for their lands and government. By the patent issued by a parliamentary commission in 1644, the townsmen of Providence, Portsmouth, and Warwick had authority to govern themselves in civil concerns. In 1652 the Council of State confirmed the parliamentary patent for Rhode Island, but apparently nothing came of the request of the New Haven confederation for a comparable grant from the Protectorate authorities.[9]

By 1660 some twenty-five thousand English men, women, and children—some were Anglicans, but most were Dissenters who had fled the efforts of Charles I and his archbishop, William Laud, to enforce conformity with the Church of England—lived in about sixty villages in New England under several separate jurisdictions, some tenuous and conflicting.

The collapse of the Protectorate and the restoration of monarchy nullified, or at least brought into question, several of the patents by which these colonies were governed, and presented an opportunity for the descendants of John Mason and Sir Ferdinando Gorges to put forth their claims to the region north of the lower reaches of the Merrimack and for the heirs of the earl of Stirling and the earl of Hamilton to demand Long Island and territory in southern New England.

Whatever their legal status, five distinct provincial governments— Massachusetts Bay, New Plymouth, New Haven, Rhode Island, and Connecticut—were actually administering authority over the New England towns. Of these colonial regimes only the corporation of the

Governor and Company of the Massachusetts Bay had any sanction from the crown. Its charter, granted by Charles I in 1629, although threatened in the years immediately preceding the outbreak of the Puritan Civil War, had not been vacated. It served as the institutional model for the other New England provinces so that the governmental forms, if not the substance, of these Dissenter regimes were all similar.

The charter granted in 1629 by Charles I to the governor and members of the Massachusetts Bay provided for a typical joint-stock company with powers vested in a general court elected by the freemen, that is, the members of the corporation. The governing body met quarterly, at three of the sessions to frame bylaws and in May to elect a governor, deputy governor, and assistants (or magistrates). Despite attempts by the first governor, the elder John Winthrop, and his assistants to preempt legislative authority in violation of the requirements of the royal patent to the company,[10] the terms of this charter became the institutional and legal framework for the Puritan effort to establish a community serving a particular religious vision.

The representatives or deputies from the towns, along with other officials at the provincial level, were to be chosen by the freemen of the corporation and, along with them, exercised legislative power. By a law enacted in 1634, membership in the corporation, or freeman-ship was restricted to those who were members of the established Congregationalist churches in the towns. And the practice soon developed to accept into full communion only those who were visible saints, those whose psychological makeup enabled them to give com-pelling evidence of God's saving grace. John Cotton, a leading Puritan divine in Boston, insisted that evidence of redemption from candidates was essential before they could be admitted to full communion in the churches. John Davenport supported this view. Others had disagreed. Thomas Hooker, like Cotton a strong personality, the spiritual leader who led many families on an exodus out of the Bay Colony, held that prospective members of the congregations should be accepted with only slight signs of the stirring of grace in their souls.

Given the peculiar psychological bent, the religious mentality of many of the first generation of Puritan migrants to the Bay, and the early flight from the colony of dissidents to form new settlements in Rhode Island and the lower Connecticut River valley, the Bay Colony enjoyed a high degree of religious uniformity during the second decade of set-tlement. The exodus by families who followed William Coddington, Anne Hutchinson, and Roger Williams to the shores of the Nar-rangansett Bay and Thomas Hooker to the lower Connecticut Valley may well have drawn off from the towns in the Massachusetts Bay men who could not have qualified for full membership in the churches.

Because of this exodus and the mentality of many of the initial immigrants to Massachusetts, a majority of the adult males who remained in the villages of Massachusetts had the psychological disposition to enable them to testify to an experience of saving grace and thus to qualify for full communion in the established Congregational church. Among the first generation, roughly half of the adult men had offered proof of regeneracy, that they were visible saints. To them went freemanship and the right to elect deputies to the General Court and to hold provincial office.

But this peculiar mentality was not always transmitted from the "saints" to their offspring. The platform devised at Cambridge in 1648 at a meeting of elders and ministers allowed certain privileges of church membership to the descendants of the godly elect, but these rights had no bearing on the religious qualification for freemanship. While a later concession in 1657 confirmed partial membership to children of church members, it did not allow these offspring full communion or the vote in church affairs. In 1660 the General Court reiterated that full communion remained the qualification for the provincial franchise.[11] In dealing with the children of those who had failed to achieve visible saintliness, a synod in 1662 recommended, not full, but halfway membership.

With the failure of many of the second and third generations to achieve full church membership and with the increase in numbers in the general population of the colony, the proportion of the male adults eligible to vote decreased considerably. By the last third of the century perhaps one in three men in the colony as a whole—and in the new towns further removed from Boston, fewer still—could vote.

Although there was nothing in the legislation of the Bay Colony relating directly to property qualifications for the provincial franchise, in practice those who had the franchise and especially the men they elected as deputies, governors, and magistrates owned property. Contemporary views did not demonstrate that there was any intention to create a wide suffrage or to eliminate social differences. Henry Ireton, during the army debates conducted at Putney outside London, had probably expressed the views of most Puritans when he denied that every man be considered equal with a voice in selecting representatives to govern the English nation. Such a contention could only be based on "an absolute natural Right, and you must deny all Civil Right." Ireton denied that there was any such thing as a natural right. In choosing those who "shall determine what lawes wee shall be rul'd by heere, noe person hath a right to this, that hath not a permanent fixed interest in this kingdome."[12] The saints in Puritan Massachusetts Bay did not repudiate the notion that those with a material stake in society would determine the rules governing it, but they explicitly added a further qualification. Those men able to relate the experience of saving grace would have a voice in determining the governance of an orthodox society whose function was to honor God's word as the saints perceived it. Generally, the men who were full members of the church were men of means. This was especially the case with the men elected to provincial office.[13]

Dissenters in the other colonies established in New England appropriated the form and structure of the government of the Bay Colony, a joint-stock company, but they did not necessarily adopt the same religious essentials for political participation. Theophilus Eaton and John Davenport, the leaders of the New Haven communities, had closely followed the Massachusetts precedent when they adopted the Fundamental Agreement, the basic code for the federation of towns known as the New Haven Colony. In these communities on the north shore of Long Island Sound it became customary for the freemen to continue magistrates in office and to advance them along a prescribed order of precedence. The franchise was restricted to those of orthodox religion. John Davenport fully sided with the ministers of the Bay Colony in upholding the religious establishment.

New Plymouth had been the first of the Dissenting communities in New England. Here too the authorities used the term *freeman* to designate citizens, including those with the right to vote for provincial officials, but they did not at first make requirements explicit. After 1658 they enacted statutes to exclude those who did not worship in the orthodox manner. Proof of spiritual regeneration was not required for freemanship, however. In 1657 the provincial general court required the towns to select four men to set rates for the support of ministers and took steps to regulate more strictly the conduct of persons on the Sabbath and to ensure a closer supervision of religion in new communities. Committed to defend the established Congregationalist churches and to sustain organized religion, the authorities of New Plymouth also tightened the requirements for participation in political life. Apparently the disruptive tactics of newly arrived Quakers led to a rethinking of the basis for citizenship.[14]

Of all the orthodox Congregationalist colonies or those accepted into the United Colonies, or the Confederation of New England, Connecticut had perhaps the most permissive franchise. In the Fundamental Orders adopted shortly after the river towns were founded, the settlers of Connecticut subscribed to a frame of government generally similar to that in the royal charter for the Bay Colony. The General Court was composed of magistrates, deputies from the towns, a governor, and a lieutenant governor. While Massachusetts law had distinguished between inhabitants admitted to reside in the towns and freemen, reserving to the latter the choice of deputies and magistrates to the General Court, in Connecticut the admitted inhabitants voted not only for local officials but also for deputies from the towns to the assembly at Hartford. Those selected for provincial office, however, came from the ranks of the freemen. As was the case in the neighboring colonies, those provincial officials were regularly returned to office.

Shortly before the restoration of the monarchy in England, the regime at Hartford raised the requirements, defining freemanship more precisely: adult householders, men having held office or possessing a personal estate worth thirty pounds and presenting a certificate of good behavior attested by the deputies of their town, were eligible. Church membership was not essential for freemanship in the initial years, although there was a close correlation between membership in the churches and officeholding. The presence of Quakers in the colony in the late 1650s had led the General Court to insist that a certificate of peaceable and honest conduct be in evidence. In 1658 it passed two orders. No persons were to embody themselves as a church without the consent of the provincial government and the approval of neighboring congregations; and the consent of both was needed to settle any separate ministers in a town.

In Connecticut the Friends and those Dissenters inclined toward Presbyterianism challenged the control of the Congregationalists by questioning the rite of baptism, church discipline, and the authority of the ministers. As power slipped from the clergy to the brethren in the churches, the inhabitants in the town meetings challenged the authority of both.

In the Connecticut towns, as elsewhere, a problem had arisen over the offspring of saints, who had been baptized in infancy but were barred from full communion. The supporters of the halfway convenant, recommended by a synod in 1662, proposed a special category for them and to allow their children to be baptized. Men who were not full members of the churches used this convenant as a lever to challenge the authority of the religious bodies by having it imposed by the town meeting.[15] These disputes over church organization and the authority of ministers and elders may well have reflected a struggle for influence between strong-willed men seeking to assert themselves.

No less strong-willed and contentious were the leaders of the settlements about the Narragansett Bay. Other controversies, not the role of the state in supporting an ecclesiastical order, disrupted the relations of the inhabitants of Rhode Island. William Coddington, Roger Williams, Anne Hutchinson, and the other founders objecting to the particular church establishment in Puritan Massachusetts and branded as heretics had fled the Bay Colony. With their supporters they founded the villages of Newport, Portsmouth, and Providence. Warwick was later added to the confederation of Rhode Island. "Rogues' Island," as the orthodox Puritans called it, was a haven for Quakers from the other New England colonies.

After some difficult years the townsmen of Rhode Island had agreed to appeal to the government in England. In 1644 they had received a patent from the Long Parliament allowing them to create a civil government, not an easy task for the highly eccentric Rhode Islanders. The collapse of the Protectorate government and the restoration of the monarchy in 1660 invalidated the patent on which the provincial regime based its legitimacy. Moreover, pressure from the more populous Puritan colonies, added to internal bickering, posed a serious threat. Roger Williams's strongest opponent at Providence was a contentious malcontent, William Harris. He launched a series of law suits over land, litigation which kept the towns and the province in turmoil for over a generation. The basis of the dispute over this "Pawtuxet Purchase" lay in the vagueness of the early memoranda recording acquisitions of land obtained from neighboring Indians. Harris's suits against the towns of Warwick and Providence rent the colony. The townsmen of Warwick were against him; those of Newport and Portsmouth were sympathetic, while the men of Providence were divided.[16]

Controversies also sprang up over the jurisdiction of lands west of the Narrangansett Bay. Various speculators—a few from Rhode Island and others from Massachusetts, Connecticut, and New Plymouth—had made questionable purchases in the region from the Narrangansett Indians. Newport men had acquired deeds from the natives to the region between Weekapaug Inlet and the Pawcatuck River in the southwestern corner of the province, a region claimed by Massachusetts as bounty from the Pequot war of 1637.

A group of Massachusetts merchants and speculators headed by Major Humphrey Atherton posed the most serious threat to the claims of Rhode Island to this Narrangansett country. In violation of the law of Rhode Island the "Atherton Associates" secured a deed for land from local sachems and then went on to extort the title to the whole of the Narrangansett country from the Indians who were accused of warring against white settlers in eastern Connecticut. As an indemnity the commissioners of the United Colonies—Rhode Island was not a member of the Confederation of New England—imposed a fine of 595 fathoms of wampum to be paid to Connecticut within four months. The Atherton Associates claimed their territory. Officials of Rhode Island refused to recognize the validity of the transaction. If the self-styled proprietors of the Narrangansett country wished to secure their claim, their only recourse was to eliminate Rhode Island, to push for an extension of the boundary of Connecticut east to the Narragansett Bay.[17]

English colonists also disputed with each other the jurisdiction over the scattered towns and villages in northern New England. Four towns between the Merrimack and the Piscataqua fell within the region once called Laconia, later New Hampshire. Extending further east and north along the coast in the region known as Maine were the towns of Kittery, York, and Saco, and beyond the Kennebec River in the area named Pemaquid were yet smaller villages, inhabited for the most part by fishermen and fugitives settled there, so it was thought, to avoid justice elsewhere. It was said of them that "as many men may share in a Woman, as they do in a Boat, And some have done so."[18]

Diverse elements had founded the villages of New Hampshire. Edward Hilton and his followers, in conjunction with fishermen from the West Country of England, had settled Dover (initially Hilton's Point). The inhabitants of Strawberry Bank (Portsmouth) had come directly from England in a project undertaken by John Mason, Ferdinando Gorges, and several London merchants organized as the Laconia Company to exploit the fisheries and the fur trade. These early arrivals were Royalist in their political leanings and Anglican in their religious persuasion. Fugitives banished from Massachusetts had established Exeter in 1638. Initially these settlers had come from East Anglia, as had the founders of Hampton who had accepted the orthodox Massachusetts way.

With the death of John Mason, the demise of the Council of Plymouth, and the outbreak of the Civil War in England, no effective authority served to unite the diverse villages. The Anglican inhabitants on the lower Piscataqua, the older planters (as they were to be called), were a majority in Portsmouth, at least as late as 1660. They established rudimentary institutions to meet their needs, including an Anglican parish church. There was little resistance, however, when the stronger, more populous Bay Colony to the south extended its jurisdiction. The Puritan officials, perhaps out of necessity, extended lenient terms to the settlers about the Piscataqua. The men of Hampton, Portsmouth, and Dover, but apparently not Exeter, *then* qualified as freemen were permitted to select representatives, or deputies, to the General Court meeting in Boston and to vote in the nomination of assistants.[19] Church membership as a requirement for freemenship was waived for those settlers who already had the franchise, but not necessarily for later applicants. At Dover, a faction favorably inclined to the Bay Colony received strong backing from the Puritan authorities. Here the Boston regime located the agencies for the administration of justice.

During the years following the annexation by Massachusetts, new elements entered the Portsmouth area to challenge the Anglican old planter element for control: Joshua Moody (or Moodey), a young

Puritan graduate of Harvard College; and merchants associated with the Bay Colony. They consolidated their power by controlling the region's imports and exports as well as the timber trade. These merchants became the nucleus of a faction supporting the jurisdiction of Boston. Prominent among them were Richard, John, and Robert Cutts (sons of a Bristol merchant); Elias Stileman, who had resided in London before moving to Salem and then to Portsmouth; and the London merchant, Bryan Pendleton, who had helped develop Watertown and Sudbury before moving to Ipswich and then to Portsmouth. Richard Martin, another merchant, had also lived in Boston for a time. These men later joined Moody in forming the first Puritan church in Portsmouth.

The rise of a merchant faction oriented toward rule by the Bay Colony inclined the old planters of Portsmouth to question the jurisdiction of Massachusetts and to view the royal government as a potential curb on the Puritans.

The restoration of the monarchy in 1660 also led to a revival of the claims of the Mason family. These pretensions exacerbated relations between the crown and the settlers in New Hampshire for over a generation. John Mason, the original patentee, had received a total of four grants of land in New England, but the crown had not confirmed the patent issued to him in 1635 by the Council of Plymouth when he died later that year. When Charles II returned to London, Mason's heir, his grandson Robert Tufton Mason, petitioned the king to clear his "inheritance" in New England of Puritan encroachment.[20]

The status of Maine was somewhat different, but equally confused. Before the outbreak of the Civil War, Charles I had confirmed the region to Sir Ferdinando Gorges, but with the collapse of royal authority and the death of Gorges in 1647, Edward Godfrey had attempted to form an independent union of towns between the Piscataqua and the Kennebec. Several of the leading settlers in Kittery and Agamenticus (York) favored the association, but a majority of the inhabitants at Wells refused to take part. Settlers at Cape Porpoise (Kennebunkport), Saco (Biddeford), and other communities beyond the Kennebec remained outside the union formed by Godfrey. Given the precarious position of these scattered settlements, the preponderance of the Bay Colony, and the victory in England of the Puritans under Cromwell, the authorities in Boston had in 1652 been able to impose their jurisdiction. Godfrey had left for London, where for some years he sought unsuccessfully to have the Cromwells intercede on his behalf. This was the situation when Charles II returned to London. Godfrey then took his case to the king, complaining not only of the usurpation of the Puritan Bay but also of the "grandees" who served the Gorges interest.[21]

The agents of the Gorges family in 1661 took the initiative in America. At a meeting in Wells, they resolved to proclaim the king in Maine and to collect the arrears in rent due to the proprietor. Each of the towns would elect a trustee to meet with the others at Wells to enact laws for the province. In the interval, Francis Champernoun, Henry Jocelyn, Nicholas Shapleigh, and Robert Jordan would govern. The Bay Colony was not without its supporters in these eastern towns. The leader of the group favoring Massachusetts was Bryan Pendleton, a trader of means and an opponent of both the Gorges interest and the royal government. At Wells and York, the spokesmen of the Bay Colony argued that the claims and pretensions of the Gorges family were immaterial. The great body of the settlers in Maine, wearied of years of confusion and anarchy, had applied to the regime at Boston. It had subsequently been discovered, so the spokesmen for Massachusetts argued, that the boundary line stipulated in the patent to the Bay Colony took in the greater part of Maine. Yet the Puritan authorities were uncertain enough of their claims to offer through Daniel Gookin of Cambridge to buy out the claims of Gorges.[22]

There were other putative proprietors with claims to lands in New England and the northern frontiers: Thomas Crown put in for Nova Scotia, and the Hamilton and Stirling heirs for territory in southern New England and Long Island. In addition, the status of each of the governments of New Plymouth, Rhode Island, Connecticut, and New Haven was questionable; all exercised jurisdiction without benefit of any sanction from the crown of England.

Within the Bay Colony were certain dissident elements, men also willing to take their complaints to the royal government in London. At the least, they were amenable to the argument that Puritan Massachusetts could not remain outside the larger political community. Some merchants—they did not necessarily share the values of the saints—were dissatisfied with the limited position they enjoyed in the councils of government in Boston. Among the later arrivals who found themselves alienated was the Royalist Thomas Breedon, an agent for another Royalist, Colonel Thomas Temple, who was seeking to control the trade of Nova Scotia. Also associated with Temple were the Bostonians Hezekiah Usher and Samuel Shrimpton. Another late arrival in Boston with ambitions was Richard Wharton. In 1659 he married Bethis, daughter of William Tyng, a prosperous merchant. The Tyngs, through marriage, were also related to the Ushers and Dudleys. Peter Lidget came to Boston from Barbados. A partner of Thomas Deane and a man of some standing in the London business community, he was a correspondent for Londoners who traded with New England.

By the standards of the society of the mother country, such men ought to have held important office in America, but in Massachusetts the governor and magistrates, as well as the deputies from the towns to the General Court, were elected by the freemen of the villages, those who had been admitted to full church membership after successfully relating the experience of saving grace. For such men living in the relative isolation of the rural towns of Puritan Massachusetts, Wharton and worldly merchants like him hardly merited consideration as rulers of a biblical commonwealth. Some of these merchants, dissatisfied with their status in the government of the Bay Colony, looked to London.[23]

The flight of other dissidents had not brought tranquility to the Bay Colony. By the second decade of settlement, deputies in the General Court from Essex and Norfolk counties challenged the domination of Suffolk and Middlesex. This sectional rivalry became muted in the face of the threat from religious dissenters such as Samuel Gorton and Robert Child, who sought to take their complaints of disenfranchisement on religious grounds to England. By mid-seventeenth century, the ecclesiastical officials had carefully defined Congregationalist church policy, and the General Court had legislated to ensure that the government of the colony remained in the hands of the saints.[24] While a degree of religious conformity had been achieved by the exodus of some families who could not adhere to the system, Anglicans, Presbyterians, Baptists, and other Dissenters from Congregational orthodoxy continued to be a problem. A few Quakers, psychologically compelled to seek martyrdom, persisted in returning to suffer whippings and mutilation. Finally, the authorities executed three of their sect. Two members of the Society of Friends, William Robinson and Marmaduke Stevenson, bitterly condemned the Puritan rulers: "You be a stif[f] necked people, got[t]en up high in your own wisdome."[25]

With the return of Charles II to England, the Friends took their case against the Puritan regime in Boston to Whitehall, and in 1661 George Bishop published a graphic account of the persecution of the Quakers, *New-England Judged.* From London, Robert Boyle, a moderate Anglican and president of the New England Company, a society generally sympathetic to the orthodox Puritans, warned a New England divine, John Eliot, of the ill effects of the "great severity" the Bay Colony had shown to Dissenters. This behavior seemed to be all the more strange and all the less defensible on the part of people who had left England and crossed the ocean that they might there enjoy the liberty to worship according to their own consciences. More than others, the New Englanders ought to allow their brethren a share in what was professed to be the right of all men.

As the number of dissidents increased, the problem of religious nonconformity in Massachusetts grew more pressing. In 1665 Thomas Gould and his friends formed a Baptist church in Charlestown. When they later moved to Boston, Gould and four others were tried, convicted, and disenfranchised, a prelude to further penalties.[26]

In London the outcries of the Friends swelled the chorus of grievances against New England, especially against the Bay Colony. Robert Mason and Ferdinando Gorges petitioned the crown to protect their rights to New Hampshire and Maine, while the surviving English investors in an ironworks erected in Massachusetts complained that Puritan authorities had unfairly seized their property for alleged debt and imprisoned their agents, John Gifford and William Avery. All attempts to seek justice in the Massachusetts courts had failed. Gifford was one of thirteen self-styled "sufferers" who petitioned the crown on behalf of "thousands" in New England. They claimed that "multitudes" of the king's subjects there had been unjustly and grievously oppressed through the tyranny of those in power in the Bay Colony, contrary not only to the laws of Massachusetts but also to the statutes of England. The king's subjects had suffered imprisonment, fines, whippings, and banishment, all at the hands of officials who had assumed the privileges of a free state and made and broke laws at their own pleasure.

One of these petitioners, Archibald Henderson, related that he had stopped off in Boston on a journey from Barbados. Ignorant of the usage and the laws of the Bay Colony—in several particulars they were contrary to the laws of England—one Saturday evening he had taken a stroll in the streets of the town half an hour after sunset. Later that night a constable had entered his lodgings, seized him by the hair, and dragged him off to jail. Denied relief by Governor John Endecott, Henderson had been prosecuted by the then attorney general of the colony, John Leverett.[27]

Other men submitted evidence calculated to bring Massachusetts Bay into disrepute. John Crown testified that he had been in Boston soon after the king's restoration. There he witnessed the arrival of two regicides who had fled England. The authorities had conducted Edward Whalley and William Goffe to the home of the governor, John Endecott, who purportedly had embraced them, bade them welcome, and announced that he wished more such good men as they would come over from England. When two young Royalist agents, the merchants Thomas Kellond and Thomas Kirke, arrived to apprehend and return the regicides, Whalley and Goffe were no longer in Boston. The royalist messengers then traveled to Hartford where Governor John Winthrop, Jr. informed them that the two regicides had departed for New Haven.

There the deputy governor, William Leete, claimed he had not seen the two fugitives in nine weeks. The New Haven minister, John Davenport, had harbored them in his home. Frustrated, Kellond and Kirke gave up their mission and took ship at New Amsterdam for England. Tradition had it that Goffe and Whalley lived out their lives in New England under assumed names. The royal authorities had been unable to apprehend them so Davenport speculated, because of God's overruling providence.[28]

Some detractors of Massachusetts thought otherwise in relating the situation to the crown officials in Whitehall. The most persistent critics of the Puritan commonwealth were Thomas Breedon and Samuel Maverick. Breedon, a Royalist associated with Thomas Temple, and a small number of Boston merchants were attempting to reassert English control over Nova Scotia, territory then held by the French. Breedon had been in Boston when Whalley and Goffe, under the assumed names of "Richardson" and "Stevenson" had arrived. When he had commanded them to appear before the governor, Breedon was labeled a malignant malcontent. The marshal-general of the colony abused Breedon and, "grinning" in his face, taunted him to speak against Whalley and Goffe, "if ye dare, if ye dare, if ye dare."

In relating the incident, Breedon drew the attention of officials in London to the distinction drawn in the province between the freemen and other subjects. Appealing obviously to the prejudices of his audience in Whitehall, he compared the distinction in the Bay Colony to the division between Roundheads and Cavaliers in England. The king's ministers might then judge how difficult it was to reconcile independency in religion with monarchy in government. The men deprived of the franchise in the colony supported the king, he claimed. But the Puritan authorities, looking upon themselves as a free state, neglected to proclaim the monarch or to take an oath of allegiance to him. They required residents in the province to take an oath of fidelity to them. Two-thirds of the militia in Massachusetts Bay not qualified as freemen would welcome a governor commissioned by the crown. They would have the king proclaimed and then live under the laws of England but for the statutes of the Puritan state, laws decreeing death to those who would endeavor to change or alter the code or the frame of government. Men who were openly in the king's interest, the Puritan authorities thereby considered guilty. Goffe and Whalley had been assiduous in fomenting the rumor that the restored monarchy would not long survive and that a change in government was imminent in London.[29]

Samuel Maverick was an even more outspoken and persistent critic of the orthodox order in Massachusetts. One of a number of Anglican merchants who had settled in Boston, he had been an associate of Doctor

Robert Child and the Presbyterians who had remonstrated against the religious qualification for freemanship and the franchise. For this affront and for daring to take their complaint to England, they had been fined. Maverick had moved to New Netherlands, but with the Restoration he took up the cause against Puritan orthodoxy before the Council for Foreign Plantations and Lord Chancellor Clarendon.

Maverick's indictment was broad and far-ranging. The settlers in New England were a great and considerable people, but the sooner they were reduced to obedience, the better. The regime at New Plymouth, despite its pretensions, had no valid claim to govern, while the governments of Connecticut and New Haven were in a state of confusion. Order would come only by the king's taking authority into his own hands. As for Massachusetts, the nonfreemen, a majority of the populace, would welcome royal government. Yet, care must be taken to grant the inhabitants liberty of conscience and to burden them as little as possible by taxes. Child and the remonstrators had been punished for threatening the state merely for wishing to have a body of laws as near as possible to those of England, for advocating that the vote be given the body of freeholders, and for asking that persons with a competent knowledge of the Christian faith and inoffensive in their conduct and speech be admitted to the sacraments and have their children baptized. As for liberty of conscience, the ostensible motive for the Puritans settling in New England, they had yet to allow it to any men who differed from them ever so little.

Reducing the Bay Colony to obedience would prove difficult, if not undertaken quickly, Maverick warned.[30]

The agent for the Bay in London, Captain John Leverett, had kept his constituents in America informed of the events leading up to the restoration of the monarch and of the charges levied against the Puritan commonwealth in New England. Leverett, for his part, had solicited the aid of the Puritan lords on the king's council, Viscount Saye and Sele and the earl of Manchester. Both peers had promised to use their influence so that nothing would be done on these complaints until the Puritan colony had an opportunity to be heard.

In Boston, Governor John Endecott, on learning of the return of Charles II, had assembled the magistrates and deputies of the General Court. They adopted addresses to the king and to both houses of Parliament asking for a hearing before any action was taken on complaints made against them, and for a continuation of the civil and religious liberties granted them under the royal charter of 1629. The provincial officials dispatched these petitions to Leverett or, in his absence, to Henry Ashurst and Richard Saltonstall, two Dissenter merchants, to be used at Whitehall and Westminster. The agents must cultivate as much influence as possible, and if questioned as to what privileges the Bay government desired, they must respond, those already granted by the charter and currently enjoyed in both matters of church and commonwealth without any other power being imposed over them. And infringement would destroy the goals of the first settlers in establishing their colony in New England. To allow appeals from Massachusetts in any case, civil or criminal, was an intolerable, unsupportable burden, one rendering the Puritan authorities ineffective and bringing them into contempt. The General Court asked that no action be taken against them on any charge until they had an opportunity to reply. They would send a full answer in due course. Saltonstall and Ashurst must make it clear to the king's ministers that the Puritan government had not empowered them to answer for the authorities in Boston. The agents were to act only in a private capacity.

Thus the Puritan rulers inaugurated the systematic pattern of evasion and procrastination they would follow for more than two decades. Daniel Denison, a magistrate, had scoffed at the regime in London and taunted the Quakers: "You will go to England to complain this year, the next year they will send to see if it be true, and by the next year the government in England will be changed."[31]

Aware perhaps of the anxiety created in the minds of the Puritans by the restoration of the monarchy, Charles II sent word to the Bay Colony shortly after he took up residence in Whitehall that he would encourage and protect all of his subjects in New England. He would ensure that they would partake equally in his promise of liberty and toleration for tender consciences as expressed in his declaration on religion.[32]

Early in 1661 the Council for Foreign Plantations began to take into consideration the problems of New England and in a matter of weeks had before it the myriad complaints of those with grievances against the Puritan commonwealth. The issue was not long in doubt: the testimony of Breedon and Robert Mason, among others, as well as the information that Whalley and Goffe had been entertained in the Puritan colonies, was decisive. The authorities of Massachusetts were judged to have invaded the rights of their neighbors and to have transgressed on the grants and powers derived from Charles I. They had enacted laws repugnant to the statutes of England as related to life and property and had imposed unreasonable and unequal penalties in matters of conscience and religious worship. When called upon to answer these charges and complaints, Leverett had replied that his agency had expired and that he had no instructions from the authorities in Boston or further information to offer.

The king's councilors then concluded that the officials in Massachusetts had deliberately withdrawn all means of corresponding and of having their actions in England judged, expecting that no action would be taken against them while they were in no position to make known their defense. They recommended dispatching a letter requiring them to offer an account of their actions. An English colony "ought not, and cannot Subsist, but by Submission to, and a protection from" the king and his government.

On 11 May 1661 the Privy Council delegated to a select committee, a body including Clarendon, Lord Treasurer Southampton, Albemarle, and the Puritan lords, Holles, Anglesey, and Saye and Sele, the task of framing appropriate orders from the king to the governor of New England, as Massachusetts was commonly called.[33] Of special concern was the plight of the Quakers in New England, the Friends in England having presented a vivid account of their suffering in the Puritan colonies. A separate circular went out that summer to Endecott of Massachusetts and the governors of the other colonies in New England requiring that any Quakers there condemned to death, sentenced to corporal punishment, or imprisoned be sent back to England, where the charges against them would be heard and the cases decided according to English law and by the nature of their offenses.

Despite the arguments of Maverick that quick action be taken, Denison's prediction, in part, was borne out: the Bay Colony was to have an opportunity to present a defense.

Notwithstanding the bold face the leaders in Massachusetts had put on, they differed among themselves as to the best manner of dealing with the threat presented by the complaints against the Puritan regime and the challenge from the government in Whitehall. A small group of young merchants, Thomas Breedon, Thomas Kellond, and Thomas Deane among them, openly welcomed the intervention of the royal government. Recent arrivals in Boston, they had no sympathy for the religious ideals of the biblical commonwealth. They were men outside the church and without a voice in government. But the Anglican merchants were few in number. There were other men, more numerous, who shared the vision of the saints yet saw the need for some accommodation. They included the ministers John Norton, John Wilson, and Charles Chauncey; the magistrate, Simon Bradstreet, and deputies to the General Court, Edward Johnson and Thomas Clarke. Prominent men, loyal to the government under the charter, they yet questioned the wisdom of adopting an inflexible posture toward the English crown. They received support from townsmen in Boston, Dedham, Hadley, Northampton, Salem, Charlestown, and Roxbury. Opposed to the Royalists and the moderates were the men of the commonwealth faction headed by Governor John Endecott, Deputy Governor Richard Bellingham, and the magistrates Daniel Gookin and Thomas Danforth and including inhabitants from every walk of life—farmers, merchants, artisans—all united in the belief that the province must remain a biblical commonwealth recognizing no other authority than the government as established under the charter. For them the religious goals for the initial settlement of Massachusetts made self-government under the patent mandatory. The less numerous but no less notable moderates saw a danger in rigidly insisting on independence. Extreme pronouncements and manifestos and a blatant disregard for the government in England might endanger essential institutions and practices in Massachusetts.

In the spring of 1661 the commonwealthmen predominated among the deputies in the towns. In June they adopted a strongly worded declaration written by the spokesmen for the more orthodox, a statement arguing for the independence of Massachusetts. Its citizens owed allegiance only to the charter and the government formed under it; the king of England had only a titular claim over them. The deputies conceived the charter of 1629 (under God) to be the first and main foundation of their civil polity, and the governor, assistants, and deputies as having full power to rule without conceding appeals to any other authority.

Some token of respect seemed advisable to soften the impression this created. On 1 August 1661 Endecott in the name of the corporation signed a letter to the king, ". . . may New England, under your royall protection, be permitted still to sing the Lord['s] song in this strange land." At the same time, the governor wrote Clarendon requesting that he use his influence to offset the baseless and unjust complaints of their adversaries in London.[34] Endecott and his colleagues made one concession to royal sensibilities. On 27 November 1661, the General Court adopted an order suspending until further notice corporal punishment for Quakers, although it affirmed that much chastisement had been necessary for the preservation of religion, order, and peace against a restless, impetuous, and disruptive people. In transmitting a copy of this order to London, the provincial secretary, Edward Rawson, assured the king's secretary of state that the Friends were "men of such turbulence as renders them not only disturbers of the peace, but professed enemies to all established Governments and the truth."[35]

In the face of the intransigence shown by the commonwealthmen controlling the Chamber of Deputies, the moderates who enjoyed a bare majority among the magistrates held a special meeting with a group of ministers who urged that envoys be sent to London to clarify, perhaps to soften, the harsh position taken by the lower house of the General Court. After some wrangling between the deputies and magistrates, the choice fell on Simon Bradstreet, a senior magistrate on the board of assistants, and the Reverend John Norton, minister of the First Church of Boston and a leading divine in the colony. Both men were apprehensive about their mission. They were particularly concerned that they might be held responsible in London for the inflexible position adopted by the commonwealthmen in the General Court.[36]

With the journey of Bradstreet and Norton was inaugurated a systematic pattern of evasion and procrastination and a protracted contest between the court at Whitehall and the commonwealth regime at Boston. For the former, no colony should exist but by submission to the crown, no matter how lenient the conditions granted; for the latter, obedience must be only to God's will, as perceived by his servants. Thus was set one of the central issues about which all English policy for America for the next generation revolved.

Bradstreet and Norton were not the only emissaries from New England to depart for London. The need to gain support among the New Englanders for the crown in its attempt to bring the Bay Colony to accept royal supervision was to work to the advantage of the agents from Connecticut and Rhode Island seeking confirmation of their political and ecclesiastical institutions as well as protection from their more powerful neighbor.

CHAPTER 6

New England and the Crown, 1662–73
Years of Indecision

FOR A DOZEN YEARS royal officials wrestled with the problem of the obstreperous Puritans of the Bay Colony, vainly attempting, so it proved, to induce them to accept some supervision from London. Conscious of their own weakness and misinformed as to the strength of the commonwealth, they looked for support elsewhere in New England, sought to assure potential allies there of their commitment to religious toleration and to a high degree of self-rule. As a result they responded favorably to the provincial regimes already established and functioning in New England, but, ironically, they failed over these years to bring Massachusetts into line.

In contrast to the commonwealthmen of Massachusetts who remained steadfast in their refusal to acknowledge the authority of the crown over the Bay Colony, officials of the confederated towns of Connecticut, New Plymouth, and Rhode Island did not hesitate to come to terms with the royal government. They took advantage of the political change in England to place their governments on a more sound legal basis. In March 1661 the General Assembly at Hartford commissioned Governor John Winthrop, Jr., to carry out an embassy to London. The younger Winthrop was well connected in England. His uncle George Downing represented the monarch at The Hague, and his brother-in-law had commanded a unit in the army of George Monck, the force which had played a key role in the Restoration. Winthrop's eldest son, Fitz-john, had been an officer in Colonel Robert Reade's regiment. The governor of Connecticut himself had come to the attention of Charles even before the young monarch had returned to England. In April 1660 Charles had written Winthrop of his appreciation of the good offices he had done. Charles Stuart seemed to have been under some obligation, however slight, to Winthrop.[1]

Winthrop's charge was to obtain from the crown confirmation of the patent supposedly issued thirty years before by the earl of Warwick for the right to govern the territory of Connecticut. While the General Assembly implored the monarch to accept the colony into his empire and pledged the submission and allegiance of the inhabitants to the king's "sacred" majesty, it sought rights and privileges from the crown as full as those stipulated in the charter to Massachusetts, as well as the territory east from New Plymouth, along the coast to the Delaware Bay. The territorial ambitions of the Connecticut officials thus brought them into direct conflict with Rhode Island and the confederate towns of New Haven as well as the Dutch on Long Island, Manhattan, and along the Hudson and Delaware valleys.

Winthrop's mission posed no threat to the towns of new Plymouth. On learning of the intended journey to London, Governor William Prence wrote to his colleague requesting that he submit to the king a petition from New Plymouth as well. The Plymouth men in their application to the crown sought a confirmation of their religious and civil liberties and of a patent they alleged James I had granted to them.[2]

Some of the younger settlers of New Haven were not averse to joining the nearby Connecticut towns with their somewhat more liberal franchise. But among the older, rigorous Puritans was one of the founders of New Haven, John Davenport. He had been a friend of Hugh Peter and Henry Vane, men condemned for their part in the execution of Charles I. Another close friend of Davenport then living in London was William Hooke, his former colleague in the church in New Haven. Hooke's brother-in-law was the fugitive regicide, Edward Whalley. Evidence later reached the royal authorities implicating the New Haven divine in the successful escape of the regicides in New England. An influential minister in New England, Davenport strongly urged the commonwealthmen in the Bay Colony to resist recognizing any appeals to England. He preferred matters to remain as they were, hoping that the Puritan lords in London, Saye and Sele and Manchester, might stay any action against New Haven. The aged minister denounced Governor William Leete for his willingness to cooperate with the Connecticut agency in London. On learning of Winthrop's mission Leete suggested Winthrop might serve as a common agent to obtain one charter for the two colonies. Leete may have had in mind a federal union under a common patent from the crown.[3]

Winthrop did little for the towns on the north shore of Long Island Sound. By the time Leete wrote his colleague, the governor of Connecticut had already departed from New Amsterdam on a Dutch ship. He arrived in London on 12 September 1661 and took up lodgings in Coleman Street at the home of William Whiting, a merchant and son of the former treasurer of Connecticut. Next door was the church John Davenport had once served.

Before Winthrop took up residence in London, another colonist, a mysterious figure from the New England villages located in the disputed region between Connecticut and New Netherlands, had crossed the Atlantic. A supple, unscrupulous man, John Scott had joined with Simon Bradstreet, Daniel Denison, Amos Richardson, Edward Hutchinson, and the other Atherton Associates in contesting with Rhode Island for possession of the Narragansett country. He had arrived in London shortly before Winthrop, also a member of the group, to lobby for the Massachusetts syndicate. Through Thomas Chiffinch, a backstairs courtier and procurer at Whitehall, Scott obtained an introduction to Joseph Williamson, then secretary to Sir Henry Bennet.

In December 1661 Winthrop, following the instructions given him at Hartford, approached the aged Puritan nobleman, Lord Saye and Sele, seeking to verify the patent issued by the earl of Warwick almost thirty years before to the founders of Connecticut. But Saye and Sele, old, infirm, and suffering from gout, was of little help. He could hardly remember the names of the men who had been associated with him in the Connecticut venture and could only give Winthrop a letter of introduction to another Puritan survivor, the earl of Manchester. But fortunately for Winthrop, through the efforts of Robert Boyle he received an invitation to meet Clarendon, then the dominant figure among the king's ministers.[4]

Both Winthrop and Scott shared a common goal: to circumvent the claims of Rhode Island to the Narragansett country by extending the eastern boundary of Connecticut to the Narrangansett Bay. The Rhode Islanders were not quiescent; Samuel Gorton, John Wicks, and Randall Holden of Warwick bitterly protested against the Atherton Associates, arguing that the men from Massachusetts could not have been ignorant that the lands in question had been previously ceded to them by the chief sachem of the Narragansetts. The Warwick men too took their claims to the earl of Clarendon.[5]

Winthrop's major adversary in London was Doctor John Clarke. English-born, Clarke had lived in Rhode Island for a while and had accompanied Roger Williams on a mission for the confederated towns to London, where he had remained for some years acting as agent for the colony. When the General Court in Providence had learned of the return of Charles II, it commissioned Clarke to secure a charter confirming Rhode Island's privileges and protecting the colony against encroachments from its neighbors. Late in January 1661 Clarke presented a petition to the crown reciting the situation of the Rhode Islanders, recounting the difficulties they had encountered with their neighbors, and requesting that they might have the protection of the royal government to live quietly with freedom of concience in religious worship.

Wiinthrop later claimed that he did not learn of Clarke's mission until some months later. At best he would recognize Clarke as the representative of a few private persons rather than the government of Rhode Island.[6] Whatever the status of Clarke, Winthrop acted swiftly and, apparently, decisively. He simply ignored Clarke and applied directly to the crown for a charter, since there was little hope Saye and Sele or Manchester would provide him with evidence sufficient to validate the Warwick patent.

From the minutes taken by Sir Edward Nicholas, a principal secretary of state, it was clear that crown officials appreciated that both Connecticut and Rhode Island desired charters and that New Plymouth and New Haven as separate jurisdictions were united with Massachusetts and Connecticut in the Confederation of New England. In the ensuing contest for recognition from the crown, the five colonies fared differently. New Haven as a political entity went out of existence. New Plymouth continued its apparently inoffensive status without benefit of a royal patent, while Connecticut and Rhode Island received charters confirming existing political and ecclesiastical institutions. The ministers of the crown, unsure of their ability to deal with the more powerful Bay Colony, may have been seeking support in southern New England as a makeweight against Boston.

Concessions to Connecticut came swiftly. On 28 February 1661/2, the Privy Council authorized a warrant for a charter for Connecticut with the men named in the petition presented by Winthrop to be confirmed as the assistants of the corporation.[7] The territory Winthrop had specified for the grant included the towns within New Haven on the west and the territory east to the Narragansett Bay, thus covering the region desired by the Atherton Associates. In nominating the men to be included in the charter as members of the corporation, Winthrop had inserted the names of the more prominent English planters on Long Island, thus seeking to ensure their support against Dutch, New Haven, or any other English claimants.

The patent incorporating the English colony of Connecticut was completed by 23 April. All of the king's English subjects there were to enjoy the liberties of natural subjects and to take the oaths of supremacy and obedience. The charter provided for the annual election of a governor, a deputy, and twelve assistants chosen from the body of the freemen. Twice yearly or more often as required, the assistants and freemen (not exceeding two from each town) were to meet as a general assembly. This body had power to erect courts and to make laws not contrary to those of England. Its jurisdiction extended north to Massachusetts, east to the Narragansett River (commonly called the Narrangansett Bay), and south and west to the South Sea (presumably the Pacific Ocean). The grant was liberal in its territorial as well as its political and religious provisions.

John Clarke pressed the case for Rhode Island. On 14 May he formally requested the crown to issue a charter for the Providence regime and to review the proposed grant to Connecticut, inasmuch as the charter issued to the government at Hartford threatened to swallow half of its eastern neighbor. For a time it seemed the issue between Clarke and Winthrop might go to the law courts, but during the summer of 1662 the two agents met several times in the presence of Lord Chancellor Clarendon, with Robert Boyle and Thomas Temple attempting to mediate between them. Winthrop, refusing to have his charter altered, sent a copy to Connecticut and wrote to the Atherton Associates to prompt them to send further evidence of their claim to be used against Clarke and the Rhode Islanders.

By the end of the summer John Clarke had won at least one point. Clarendon announced that a patent of incorporation would be issued for Rhode Island. But the king had resolved to send commissioners to New England to settle the respective interests of the several colonies.[8] Winthrop and Clarke would make a last effort to resolve the differences between Connecticut and Rhode Island when John Scott returned from New England on a mission to the Atherton Associates.

Winthrop faced another immediate challenge. The New Haven men, dissatisfied with events in London, had made known their grievances to their friends in the capital, Major Robert Thompson, the Dissenter merchant, and William Hooke, a former colleague of John Davenport and at one time chaplain to Oliver Cromwell. In a meeting held on 2 March 1662/3 with Winthrop, Thompson and Hooke argued the case for New Haven's enjoying its liberties in church and commonwealth. According to Hooke, Winthrop maintained that it was not his intention that New Haven be denied; Leete had asked him to include the New Haven towns in any grant Connecticut obtained. At Hooke's insistence, Winthrop wrote Acting Governor John Mason and the assistants at Hartford requesting that they suspend any action in assuming control over the New Haven towns until his return.[9]

The following month Winthrop and Clarke attempted to clarify the provisions of the grant establishing the eastern boundary of Connecticut at the Narragansett River (or Bay). Both men agreed to abide by the decision of arbiters: Thompson, Captain Richard Deane, John Brookhaven, William Brereton, and Doctor Benjamin Worsley. On 7 April the arbiters seemingly decided in favor of Rhode Island, but actually resolved nothing. In order to adhere to the language of the charter granted to Connecticut in 1662, they ruled that the boundary designated in the patent be retained, but the name "Narragansett" be applied to the Pawcatuck River. Secondly, the inhabitants and proprietors of the

Narragansett country should be free to choose whether Connecticut or Rhode Island would have jurisdiction over the disputed region.[10] Inasmuch as Rhode Island had already denied the claims of the Atherton Associates, they could be expected to vote for Connecticut.

The passage of the charter for Rhode Island then proceeded quickly. A warrant was issued on 26 June, and the charter sealed some days later on 8 July 1663. On the assumption that both parties had agreed to the decision of the coadjutators of 7 April, the officials drafting the charter for Rhode Island specified the western border of the new province, and hence the eastern boundary of neighboring Connecticut, as the channel of the Pawcatuck River. It was expected that Winthrop and the Connecticut authorities would abide by the decision reached by the arbiters and formally accepted by the Connecticut agent and governor. The provisions of the Rhode Island patent did not *explicitly* repeal the provision of the grant to Connecticut the previous year establishing the boundary at the Narragansett River (Bay). The charter for Rhode Island also specified the northeastern boundary of the colony as the upper reaches of the Narragansett Bay up to Pawtucket Falls. This was the most western line of New Plymouth, thus implicitly recognizing the existence of that colony. But to add to the confusion, the crown issued no formal instrument for government to the Plymouth regime as it had in response to the petitions of Clarke and Winthrop.

The form of government stipulated for the corporation of the Governor and Company of Rhode Island and Providence Plantations resembled that allowed Connecticut the previous year and followed existing practices in the colony. Until elections were held, Benedict Arnold, William Brenton, and their assistants continued as governor and deputy governor and magistrates. Thereafter, the freemen of the towns annually were to elect officials. Deputies from the villages and assistants sitting as the General Assembly would admit freemen to the corporation and enact laws—statutes not repugnant to the laws of England. The charter further provided for appeals from the colony to the crown. As requested in the petition Clarke had presented, the crown stipulated that persons who did not disturb the peace were not to be molested or called into question for religious reasons.

Winthrop had sailed for New England shortly after signing the agreement of 7 April, but Scott remained in London to continue the struggle for the Atherton Associates against Clarke and the Rhode Islanders. On 21 June 1663 Joseph Williamson drafted a letter for the king addressed to the governors of Massachusetts, New Plymouth, Connecticut, and, ironically, New Haven, asking that they see that justice was done for the Atherton Associates. The royal letter explicitly recognized the legality of their title from the Indians and condemned the resistance offered to them by the Rhode Island settlers in the Narragansett country.[11]

In responding indiscriminately to various pressure groups and in failing to delineate clearly the boundaries of the new corporations in New England, the ministers of state had further confused the situation in America. Despite the language Clarke had inserted in the charter for Rhode Island, the royal letter of 21 June 1663 seemed to confirm the view adopted by the assembly at Hartford that Connecticut had jurisdiction over the Narragansett country.

The authorities of Rhode Island had requested that no action be taken in America until Winthrop returned, but seizing on the procedure stipulated in the agreement accepted by Clarke and Winthrop in London, twenty of the Atherton Associates in July 1663 gathered at Richard Smith's trading house in the disputed region and voted to accept the jurisdiction of Connecticut. The magistrates at Hartford quickly accepted their decision and appointed officials for the settlement they now named Wickford. When Clarke sent over a copy of the new charter for Rhode Island, officials at Providence set up a rival town, Westerly. The controversy continued for many years, at times threatening to erupt into violence.

Dissension was evident elsewhere in southern New England. Despite a common religious faith, the prospect of material gain and competition for prestige and office led strong-minded men to clash. In securing the charter for Connecticut in 1662, Winthrop had intended that it embrace the towns settled by Englishmen on the eastern end of Long Island and on the mainland as far west as the Hudson River. At New Haven, where opinion was divided, the authorities initially resisted annexation.

Ignoring all, Connecticut officials moved ahead. In October 1663 the General Court authorized the local magistrates at Southampton and Easthampton on Long Island to exercise authority over Southall (a New Haven dependency). Dissatisfied minorities in Guilford and Stamford, responding to the claims of Connecticut, turned to the authorities at Hartford for protection. Only the townsmen of New Haven, Milford, and Bramford remained loyal to the old federation. Finally, in 1664, when the settlers learned that the king had granted the area contested with the Dutch, New Netherlands, to the duke of York as a proprietary province, they agreed to accept Connecticut rule. Not all men accepted annexation by Connecticut, where the franchise was more liberal and church membership was not an explicit requisite for voting.[12] John Davenport moved to Boston, where he joined those who resisted the adoption of the halfway convenant for church membership and supported the commonwealthmen in repudiating any dependency on the English crown.

What the ministers of state in England would have required of Massachusetts was evident in the charters granted to Connecticut and Rhode Island. These sanctioned existing political and ecclesiastical institutions, freedom of conscience for Protestants, and virtual self-government under a general assembly elected by the freemen of the corporations. Only the provision that the General Assembly could not pass laws contrary to those of England and that appeals could be taken from provincial courts to Westminster limited the will of the government elected by the freemen. Yet the charters themselves contained no mechanism for implementing these limitations.

Despite the broad concessions granted by the crown to Connecticut and Rhode Island, the men controlling Massachusetts Bay refused any accommodation. Although adherents of the more moderate view, Simon Bradstreet (a senior member of the board of magistrates) and John Norton (minister of the First Church in Boston) had been named to represent the colony before the royal government, the uncompromising deputies in Boston had allowed them no latitude to negotiate. The crown of England had only a titular, nominal claim to the soil in Massachusetts; the inhabitants of the colony owed allegiance to the charter granted by Charles I in 1629 and to the government formed under it. This patent, under God, they conceived was the foundation of the civil polity. Officials under the charter had full power and authority to govern all inhabitants in the Bay without allowing any appeal. Bradstreet and Norton had hesitated to undertake a mission to defend such propositions, but when the majority of the General Court refused to modify them, they left Boston in February 1662 to cross the Atlantic.[13] Their journey proved fruitless, but enlightening.

The Massachusetts cause received another blow in London by the report submitted by the Doctors' Commons, the authorities on civil law, in response to the complaints made by Robert Mason, self-styled proprietor of New Hampshire, and Edward Godfrey of Maine. Massachusetts stood accused of unlawfully extending its jurisdiction, encroaching on the inheritance of Mason and Gorges, and compelling subjects to submit to an arbitrary government, one declared by the officials in Boston to be independent of the crown. These officials had endeavored to model Massachusetts as a free state, one with no connection with England.[14] Shortly after the lawyers issued this report, the Privy Council began hearings on New England late in February 1662.

In the weeks to follow, John Winthrop and John Clarke won liberal terms for the charters incorporating the sister colonies Connecticut and

Rhode Island, but Simon Bradstreet and John Norton could do little in arguing the case for Massachusetts, restricted as they were by the uncompromising instructions of the General Court.

Charles II declared himself ready to renew the charter granted by his father so that the inhabitants of Massachusetts might freely enjoy their liberties and privileges, but in turn the officials of the province must meet certain conditions. Justice must be administered in the name of the king and oaths of allegiance taken to him. Inasmuch as the colonists saw the principal purpose of the charter to be liberty of conscience, the king required that those desiring to perform their religious devotions according to the Anglican Book of Common Prayer should not be denied or made to suffer any prejudice thereby. All persons of good and honest lives ought to be admitted to the sacrament of the Lord's Supper, and their children baptized.

Charles and his ministers insisted on one fundamental political alteration in the province. While the institutions were to remain as set out in the charter of 1629—possibly the number of assistants might be increased later—all freeholders of competent estates orthodox in religion and not vicious in conversation had to have a choice in the election of officials. Under the current statutes in the Bay Colony, the General Court admitted to freemanship only full church members, those able to recount the experience of saving grace.

These terms were embodied in a letter signed by the king on 28 June 1662 to be delivered by Bradstreet and Norton to the General Court at Boston and published along with the king's assurance to the inhabitants that he was ready to receive any address and would advance their interests and their trade with his utmost endeavors. The agents had won a respite for the Puritan regime. Indeed, the long-time opponent of the commonwealthmen in Boston, Samuel Maverick, charged that Norton and Bradstreet shortly before departing London had openly boasted that by the assistance of some great persons (probably the Presbyterian lords on the Privy Council) they had obtained what they had come for, time. He remonstrated with Clarendon that the rulers of the Bay still styled themselves a state and commonwealth, that they had vowed they would never recognize the sovereignty of the king until there was no way of avoiding it.[15]

In the interval the Privy Council resumed consideration of colonial problems late in the summer of 1662. On 25 September, when a committee agreed to a patent of incorporation for the Rhode Island towns, Clarendon announced that the king intended to send over commissioners to settle disputes in New England. That the choice of men for this task lay with the duke of York might have indicated that at this early date the court had in mind combining the commission to investigate the northern colonies with a naval expedition to take over the Dutch settlements on Long Island and in the Hudson valley.[16]

By this time Bradstreet and Norton had returned to Boston to be vilified by the commonwealthmen who held them responsible for the terms of the royal letter. They were accused in carrying the king's message of laying the foundation of the colony's ruin. Norton did not survive long; he died within a year. The moderates were hampered in their efforts to defend the agents by rumors about the contents of the royal letter, spread by the commonwealth faction, who refused to allow the document to be made public. Instead, they circulated the story that a governor and an Anglican bishop were to be sent over from England and that the militia would be used to overturn the government.

The General Court had taken no action to meet the terms specified in the royal letter by March 1663, when some of the younger merchants and others who had not been made freemen offered their votes in the nominations for the board of magistrates. In May, when villagers from Woburn complained of the refusal to publish the king's message and the prohibition of all but full church members from voting, the House of Deputies, where the commonwealthmen predominated, blocked any investigation. Hoping to avoid a direct confrontation with the dominant group but convinced nonetheless that the king's injunction had to be taken into account, a number of magistrates suggested that the matter be presented to delegates of both houses and to elders of the churches for consideration. A committee was formed, but took no action.[17]

Suspicion in Boston centered on Samuel Maverick, then in London soliciting for an appointment to the crown commission for North America. To offset the arguments of the commonwealthmen against him, Maverick presented to Clarendon testimonials from New England. In response to the apprehension expressed in New England, the king himself declared at a session of the Privy Council that he intended to preserve the charter of Massachusetts and to send over commissioners to reconcile differences among the settlers.

The problem assumed wider dimensions late in 1663, when John Scott returned to England. He had been active in America stirring up the villagers in the English towns on Long Island to contest Dutch rule. Earlier that year the Council of Foreign Plantations had taken up his complaint that the Dutch were intruding on the English domain. Some on the council saw in the Dutch presence a threat to the Act of Navigation and a drain on the royal customs. Scott and Maverick were asked to advise the council on various aspects of the problem, including the strength of the Dutch and means necessary to expel them. In

December Scott informed Joseph Williamson that the English townsmen on Long Island were ready to support the king's interest against the Dutch.[18]

The ministers of the crown now determined to act. In January 1664 several of the duke of York's associates at the Admiralty, Lord John Berkeley, Sir George Carteret, and Sir William Coventry, reported that the Dutch were weak and the English in the Connecticut and New Haven towns inclined to aid the attempt by the crown to take New Netherlands. By February plans were under way to outfit an English expedition under Colonel Richard Nicolls and to award the territory to be won from the Dutch to the king's brother as a proprietary colony. But the land granted the duke included not only the region held or claimed by the Hollanders but also lands then under uncertain jurisdiction—Pemaquid lying between the Saint Croix and Nova Scotia, Long Island, and neighboring Martha's Vineyard, Nantucket, and Block Island—as well as the mainland west of the Connecticut River. The grant conflicted directly with the claims of Massachusetts Bay and Connecticut, the successor to New Haven under the charter secured by Winthrop in 1662.

The mission to subdue the Dutch settlements on the Hudson and Delaware compromised any success commissioners sent out from England might have in reconciling the New Englanders to the royal government or imposing the will of the crown by force. Colonel Richard Nicolls had only four companies of soldiers. Equally prejudicial to the royal service in New England were the personalities of the men named to the commission. Ability, tact, and discretion would be requisite for a most delicate task. One of the commissioners, Samuel Maverick, according to Secretary Williamson, was debauched, idle, and prejudiced against the Bay Colony. Of all men he was the least suited to this mission. Sir Robert Carr, an obscure knight, was "weak," as was Colonel George Cartwright, an officer of little merit or competence.[19] Nicolls, who had just turned forty, was an experienced army officer, having served in the entourage of the duke of York. A Royalist, he was moderate in his views, intelligent, and able. But fully occupied by the task of governing at Manhattan, he would not be able to restrain his colleagues or to help win over the commonwealthmen in Massachusetts.

The officers of state in Whitehall who drafted the instructions for the commission to reconcile the New Englanders with royal government were themselves weak and uncertain of their tactics.

Thomas Povey thought it essential to establish the sovereignty of the king and the property of his subjects. The royal arms ought to be displayed in the local courts, vice admiralty jurisdiction established, customs duties collected according to English law, and the acts of trade and navigation enforced. Local statutes contrary to the laws of England must be abolished, liberty of conscience allowed, and some favor shown to the Church of England. These were the conditions essential for the crown when issuing a charter confirming the liberties of the colonies.

A basis of support must be established locally before confronting the regime in Boston. Both Robert Mason and Ferdinando Gorges might surrender to the crown their claims to New Hampshire and Maine, where presumably men of means were inclined to the king, and the generality as well disposed as could be expected. The royal commissioners could first establish themselves on the Piscataqua and win over the local populace by confirming their land titles and offering the advantages of improved trade. As to the Bay Colony, if the commissioners did not "intermeddle" with the government or religious establishment, the stiff, factious party would then find it difficult to stir up the populace. By "insinuation" rather than by "force" the commissioners and supporters of the crown would prevail.

Lord Chancellor Clarendon, perhaps the most influential of the ministers in determining the course the crown took, also appreciated the weakness of the government. He had grave misgivings about the impression a failure to reduce New Netherlands might create in the minds of the officials in Boston.[20]

On leaving England for the mission to America, the royal commissioners carried a set of public instructions intended to be shown to skeptical opponents of royal government. In addition they had private instructions stressing that they were to conduct themselves judiciously, to win over the principal men, and to induce them to renew their patent, but to accept such alterations as might appear necessary. The charter issued in 1629 remained the keystone of royal policy, yet it needed revision.

The ministers of state in London, then and later, when seeking to bring the foreign plantations into a greater dependence on the crown, had great faith—and it was to be entirely misplaced—in the ability of a governor appointed by the crown to influence events in an American colony. The royal commissioners were now apprised that a governor ought to hold office for a limited period, from three to five years. From a list of three nominees submitted by the voters the king could select a successor to serve another term. The commissioners were also to examine local laws for any "indecent" expressions or language contrary to the dignity of the crown or repugnant to the laws and customs of England. Such statutes must be repealed and justice administered in the name of the king.

As to liberty of conscience—a goal expressly stipulated in the charters sought by the New Englanders and one approved by Charles II himself—the king was determined that this freedom be observed. The commissioners themselves and all men who associated with them must be careful not to do or say anything to give any person the impression that the crown proposed to make any alteration in ecclesiastical government or to introduce any other form of worship than that the New Englanders had chosen. Yet the colonists ought not to deny liberty of conscience to others. It was essential the commissioners not antagonize the Puritans. They might take with them their own chaplain to perform devotions according to the Church of England, but he was not to wear the surplice. This ecclesiastical vestment, not having been seen in New England, might give offense.

The mission of the commissioners was to unite and to reconcile people of different judgments and practices, at least in matters concerning their peace, their prosperity, and their submission to the king and his government. Their private instructions expressly cautioned them to beware of factious persons, to avoid partisanship, and to proceed cautiously. They must not propose any alteration in religion or government, unless raised first in the elected assembly. But to promote the selection of deputies from the towns best disposed to royal government, they must encourage potential candidates. There were two immediate objectives: placing the militia of the Bay Colony under an officer recommended by the king (Colonel George Cartwright) and electing Nicolls governor.

In these instructions the men in Whitehall engaged in much wishful thinking and self-deception, but given the weakness of the royal government, they could do little else. The open instructions to the commissioners and the letters they carried to the governors of the individual New England provinces contained tactful and mollifying words, designed to dispel anxieties. They sounded one sarcastic note relating to Massachusetts: it was scandalous that any man should be barred the exercise of religion according to the laws and customs of England by those who had been granted liberty of conscience by the crown to profess what religion they themselves pleased. Consequently, inhabitants in the Bay Colony who desired to use the Book of Common Prayer should be permitted to do so without incurring any penalty or reproach. Men of good and honest conversation ought to enjoy all privileges, civil and ecclesiastical; differences in religious views ought not to lessen the colonists' mercy one to another, "since charity is a fundament to all religion."[21]

Thus equipped with orders, suggestions, and platitudes, the royal commissioners departed on their mission: the subjugation of New Netherlands for the duke of York and the submission of Massachusetts to his brother, Charles II. With four companies of soldiers in four vessels, they departed in mid-May, intending to land first at Long Island

But the small fleet encountered crosswinds and bad weather and after ten weeks the vessels lost contact with each other. Two of the ships, with Carr and Maverick aboard, put into the Piscataqua, and the others carrying Nicolls and Cartwright anchored off an island in the approaches to Massachusetts Bay. Some days passed before the two parties were reunited.

In the interval, Nicolls and Cartwright sampled the atmosphere in Boston. They received a chilling reception. With the election of Francis Willoughby and William Saltonstall, the commonwealth party controlled the board of assistants. Having learned that the king's ships were on the seas, the General Court had ordered that on their arrival only a limited number of officers and soldiers, unarmed, could come ashore to refresh themselves. They must behave in an orderly manner and not give offense to the people and the laws of Massachusetts.

Several days passed after Nicolls and Cartwright arrived in Boston without any provincial official acknowledging them; at the Sunday services the governor ignored them. To Nicolls the behavior of the Puritan officials seemed calculated to prevent the commissioners from taking any action, since it was known they intended to proceed against New Netherlands as soon as the other two ships arrived from the Piscataqua. Finally, when Daniel Denison and William Hawthorne of the board of magistrates presented themselves, the commissioners delivered the royal letters. More than a dozen merchants in a body also came "to pay a civility" to the king's agents. Two years before, on the arrival of Charles II's orders, these merchants had petitioned unsuccessfully to be made freemen. Cartwright and Nicolls now suggested that they apply again, and if refused once more, they were at liberty to appeal for redress to the commissioners. "I never saw people kept under such a slavery as many are under this Government." Nicolls reported.[22]

More pressing matters elsewhere required the presence of the commissioners, and Governor John Winthrop of Connecticut was more accommodating than his counterpart in Massachusetts. He agreed to meet Nicolls and his force at the western end of Long Island for a campaign against New Netherlands. The next month Nicolls and Winthrop, after raising the English inhabitants on Long Island, secured the surrender of Governor Peter Stuyvesant at New Amsterdam. By the end of August, Nicolls was occupied at Manhattan with the administration of the duke of York's colony, while Carr led a small force against the Dutch on the Delaware.

Toward the end of 1664 Cartwright and Maverick went up to Boston, taking up residence at the home of Captain Thomas Breedon, a Royalist sympathizer. They accomplished little. Cartwright suffered from gout, and Maverick spent much of his time visiting acquaintances. Not until the following May did the full commission assemble to get down to the business of the Bay Colony.

In the interval the Puritan officials made only one concession, a slight one to satisfy the Royalist merchants who had hitherto been denied the provincial franchise. The General Court now passed a new election law, one the Chamber of Deputies had previously rejected. In addition to those adult males who were in full communion with some established church, other men were granted the vote: those who were orthodox in religion and not vicious in their lives, as evidenced by a certificate from the minister of the town where they lived, and were freeholders with property assessed in a single county rate to the value of ten shillings. Very few men had sufficient property to so qualify. The concession did nothing to lessen the power of the commonwealth party, whose strength was based on the full church members in the towns. The very wealthiest men who did not enjoy full church membership could now enter political life. But most men, as before, still had to seek the franchise through the sacrament of the Lord's Supper administered only to full church members.[23]

The Puritan government took the offensive, appointing a committee to draft a petition for the recall of the royal commission. On 6 September 1664 the board of magistrates issued a proclamation, a virtual declaration of independence placing the province in a state of martial law, making it a crime to criticize the action of a duly qualified court, and decreeing the death penalty for anyone seeking to alter or subvert the form of the government. To the secretary of state in London, the Puritan authorities bitterly complained of the royal commissioners, one of them, Maverick, "our known and professed enemy," being empowered to hear and determine complaints against them. Rather than being governed by men of their own choosing and laws of their own making as was the fundamental privilege by their charter, "wee are like to be subjected to the arbitrary powers of strangers, proceeding not by any established laws, but by their oune discretions." Misrepresentations of great divisions and discontent in Massachusetts had misled the king. It now "plainly appears that the body of this people are unanimously" satisfied in the present government and reject change. "Wee suppose ther is no government under Heaven wherein some discontented persons may not be found . . . yet thro the favour of God, there are but a few amon[g]st us that are malcontent & fewer that have cause to be so."[24]

Governor John Endecott pursued the case against the royal commission in a private letter to the lord chancellor. Clarendon had sought to assure the Puritans of his concern for their welfare. The commission was utterly inconsistent with the privileges and the charter the king had granted—a patent he had promised in his letters not to violate. Endecott, "being now full of days" and expecting daily to pass from this stage into another world, entreated Clarendon to intercede with the king in behalf of this "poor people." The inhabitants of the Bay Colony, "God[']s people heare," are "deare to mee, and I dare not neglect my duty to them, whereby I am bound to seeke their welfare."[25]

While Puritan officials sought the recall of the royal agents, the commissioners by their ineptness weakened their own position. When Carr, off on an expedition against the scattered Dutch villages on the Delaware, failed to return, Nicolls set out to investigate. He reported his wayward lieutenant on the Delaware determined to "set up his roost with the booty" taken from the small Dutch garrison and "to look no further" after the service of the crown. On his return to Manhattan the governor found the garrison had mutinied and imprisoned Cartwright, his second in command. Forced to borrow money to supply the soldiers, Nicolls was fully occupied in New York with settling the claims of the English inhabitants for their lands and resolving a dispute with Connecticut over boundaries. Carr finally arrived in Boston in February 1665, but then set about traveling. Cartwright and Maverick spent a frustrating winter in New England.

The commissioners were the subject of widespread gossip and slander. One report circulating in Boston had it that Carr "kept a naughty woman" and that Cartwright was a Papist. It was further bandied about that the commissioners were set on demanding high rents for improved land, that they intended to infringe on the discipline of the established Congregationalist churches by compelling baptism of children, and that they would alter the form of government by admitting appeals from the judgments of the provincial government. In the face of sustained opposition Cartwright recommended to Nicolls that they ought first to settle with the other New England colonies, especially Connecticut, since Governor John Winthrop had proved more friendly than the Bostonians. A successful tour in Connecticut, Rhode Island, and New Plymouth by the commission might induce the authorities of the Bay Colony to adopt a more reasonable stance. Maverick thought it essential in dealing with Massachusetts that all men eligible to be freemen appear before the elections set for May 1665.[26]

From London Clarendon attempted to guide the actions of the royal commission. He regretted that Nicolls was not at Boston, but crown officials feared an attack on New York by a powerful squadron sent from the United Provinces. The inhabitants of the Bay Colony were a "froward and a peevish people and not well affected to Government," the lord chancellor admitted, but he rejected the "peevish" complaints of Endecott that the issuance of the royal commission dissolved the charter, stripped away privileges, and left the settlers subject to the unlimited, arbitrary power of the king's agents. Yet from the distant vantage of Whitehall, Clarendon conjectured that if handled discreetly, the commonwealthmen might be brought over. A "humorous People," the men and women of Massachusetts had to be handled with "greate dexterity." By dividing them "[you] *will govern* them."

In an official answer dated 25 February 1665 to the petition from Massachusetts asking for recall of the royal commission, the king, Clarendon, and the other ministers emphasized the distinction between the people and the rulers of the Bay. A few persons too long in power had instilled unfounded, unwarranted apprehensions in the minds of the king's subjects. How else but by a royal commission could the complaints made in the various colonies against the encroachments of the Boston regime and the grievances of men in Massachusetts of injustice be ascertained? Once again Charles II assured the colonists of the full and peaceable enjoyment of their privileges and liberties granted in the patent, but he could not accept the contention that by granting the charter "he hath parted with his Souvraigne power over his Subjects there." Clarendon also sought to assure the Puritans when he conferred in London with persons whose judgment the commonwealthmen might trust: the lord chamberlain; Robert Boyle, president of the society for disseminating the gospel among the Indians in New England; and Ashurst, the Dissenter merchant. Boyle himself assured Endecott, as he had Governor Winthrop before, of the good intentions of the king and the lord chancellor. Clarendon had repeated the pledge he had authorized Boyle to make to the friends of New England. Boyle seemed struck by the concern manifested by the ministers of state, especially in the matter of liberty of conscience. He warned the commonwealth officials: their friends in London would be much discouraged if they persisted in their unwarranted demands and charges.[27]

To gain as much support as possible in the other New England colonies, Cartwright, Maverick and Carr, early in 1665 before confronting the commonwealth men in Boston, undertook a cursory tour of New Plymouth, Rhode Island, and Connecticut. They stopped first in New Plymouth, where Governor Thomas Prence and the General Court, seizing upon a suggestion from the king that he would preserve the liberties and privileges of the colony, presented the commissioners with a petition for a charter. The royal agents countered with a proposal that the colony allow the crown to appoint a governor from among three men nominated by the freemen. If they had succeeded in this, it might have set an example to be used elsewhere. But they did not press the issue and in their report to Whitehall found little to complain about in the conduct of the authorities of New Plymouth. They then hurried on to Rhode

Island, where again they found much to reassure them. Hard-pressed to defend the boundaries of the province against the claims of the United Colonies, the Rhode Island officials made a great demonstration of their loyalty and obedience. All who so desired were admitted as freemen; all who lived civilly, even Quakers and "Generalists," had liberty to worship. Governor Benedict Arnold and his deputy, William Brenton, were eager to have the commissioners decide boundary disputes and to affirm Rhode Island's claim to the Narrangansett region. Despite the intervention of Governor John Winthrop of Connecticut with Nicolls in New York, the commission placed the area they now named "the King's Province" *temporarily* under the jurisdiction of Rhode Island magistrates pending further word from England.[28]

Frustrated in their quest for the Narrangansett country, Connecticut officials prevailed with the commissioners against the claims of the heirs to the earl of Hamilton to a portion of southern New England called New Cambridge. Carr, Cartwright, and Maverick quickly dismissed the contentions of the Scottish family. They could find no agents, servants, or planters sent out by the lords Hamilton. Even before setting out on their visitation the royal commissioners had reached an accommodation with the regime at Hartford over the boundary with New York. Connecticut, excluded from the offshore islands (including Long Island), retained the mainland as far west as the Mamaroneck River.

The tour of inspection of Connecticut by Carr, Cartwright, and Maverick was cursory, to say the least. Crossing over from Rhode Island, they held a brief inquiry at New London on 25 March 1665. As was the case with New Plymouth and Rhode Island, they found little to fault. The General Assembly promised to require oaths of allegiance to the king and pledged not to base the franchise on religious qualifications and to allow freedom of worship. They would hinder no person from partaking of the sacraments and using the Book of Common Prayer, provided he did not oppose the public maintenance of ministers of God. No doubt the authorities promised much to get rid of the commissioners as quickly as possible. Religious nonconformity and disputes in the churches were already matters of public concern in the towns, and in practice, if not in law, there was a close connection between church membership and officeholding in Connecticut.[29]

The stage was now set for the confrontation between the royal commission and the Puritan officials of Massachusetts. Maverick, Carr, and Cartwright, now joined by Nicolls, moved on to Boston. Their headquarters was the house of Thomas Breedon, one of the merchants sympathetic to the Royalist and Anglican cause.

The commonwealthmen had not been idle over the winter months. Through speeches and petitions they sought to bolster support and to incite opposition against the commission. They did not have it all their own way, however. An official warning from Whitehall that unless the government proved less refractory, there might be a change in the corporation had strengthened the determination of the moderates: the best way to protect the province was to reach some accommodation with the crown. Men from a number of towns—Boston, Northampton, Hadley, and Dedham—sent in petitions to the General Court warning against further antagonizing Charles II. Two weeks before the annual elections the Reverend Charles Chauncey delivered a paper to the board of magistrates calling on the government to adopt a more conciliatory attitude. John Endecott had died earlier that year, but the new governor elected in May, Richard Bellingham, the last of the original patentees of 1629, was as committed to the commonwealth view as his predecessor.[30]

Nicolls and his colleagues arrived in Boston on 1 May 1665. Distressed by the malicious reports circulating against them, Nicolls wanted to clear the air by addressing the General Court. He was refused permission. The commissioners then insisted that they were competent to hear complaints and appeals from individuals charging the Bay Colony with violations of the charter. This the magistrates refused to consider: it would usurp the authority of the General Court. When the agents demanded to know if the government of Massachusetts recognized their authority as representatives of the crown, the moderates at best could devise an ambiguous reply, while Bellingham and the commonwealthmen fell back on a literal interpretation of the charter. Charles I had given them so much power in their patent that he had reserved none for himself and his successors, not even authority to call them to account for any transgressions against the grant. The commissioners responded that the king in issuing their commission was merely extending his courts of Chancery and King's Bench to America for the benefit of his subjects there. The talks now broke down.

Bellingham, Thomas Danforth, John Leverett, and Daniel Gookin then set down the position of the commonwealthmen in a formal declaration adopted on 23 May 1665 by the General Court and published the next day. The government of the Bay Colony insisted that it was only maintaining the king's authority according to the rules and prescriptions of the charter. It went on to declare in the name of the king and by the authority vested in the royal patent that in observing a duty to God and the king and the trust committed to the deputies and magistrates by the inhabitants of the colony it could not consent to or approve of the proceedings of the commission. Nicolls and his colleagues retorted that the officials of the Bay Colony were misusing the power granted in the patent to controvert the sovereignty of the king. They would take the issue to Charles II.[31]

There was little they could do, for the government in England was in no position to antagonize the Puritan regimes. Learning that a strong Dutch fleet was operating in American waters, Nicolls hurried back to Manhattan. On 23 June he sent Governor John Winthrop copies of a letter from the king calling on the New England colonies to join in defense of New York. Another threat loomed later that year following an English declaration of war on France. The governor of Canada invaded the Indian country to the north with a force of several hundred men. Nicolls wrote repeatedly to his neighbors in Connecticut, pointing out the common danger and the need for cooperation.[32]

Following Nicolls's hurried departure from Boston, the other commissioners set out to investigate conditions in the villages along the Piscataqua and in Maine, where, despite orders from London, the Puritan regime in Boston had refused to relinquish control. The authorities of the Bay Colony appointed Samuel Symonds and Thomas Danforth to hold court for what they termed the county of York and to set aside any proceedings undertaken by the royal commission. They must not allow complaints against the Bay government. Undeterred, Maverick, Carr, and Cartwright traveled north and east, stopping off at Salem and Ipswich, where the moderate leaders received them in their homes. Maverick remained some days at Portsmouth, while Carr and Cartwright went on to Hampton. They reported the villagers eager to be free of Massachusetts. Crossing the river to Kittery and York, they commissioned various local men to administer justice. From Kittery they issued a notice to the inhabitants of the New Hampshire villages to attend a meeting to be held at Portsmouth.[33]

Sentiment in the towns was divided. Opponents of the Bay Colony were unevenly distributed, but those most hostile to Massachusetts were concentrated in Portsmouth, the largest of the settlements and hitherto the center of Anglicanism. In contrast, Hampton warmly supported the Boston regime. Hampton had been settled under Boston authority by people from Massachusetts whose land titles derived from the Bay Colony. In Dover, Major Richard Waldron, a noted merchant and Indian fighter, dominated; he lent his prestige to the Boston cause.

In Portsmouth, by far the largest town, opposition to the old Anglican planters centered on a clique of five or six merchants closely associated with the Boston community and with the Reverend Joshua Moody. They dominated economic life. Those among the original settlers who possessed the franchise when the authorities of Massachusetts assumed control of the government in 1641 had been allowed to vote, but men who later came of age had to qualify by church membership. The group wishing to separate from Massachusetts consisted of moderates, such as Henry Sherburne, a member of the Anglican chapel who had lost local office to the Puritan merchants, and the younger tradesmen and shipmasters who had been excluded from the coasting trade in lumber by the older merchants linked with Boston.

Disturbed by the call of the royal commissioners for a meeting of the Piscataqua inhabitants, the selectmen at Portsmouth sent off a hurried message to Boston. Bellingham and the magistrates quickly assured them that the claim of the royal commissioners to present a letter from the king to the townsmen "cannot but be accounted a figg-leafe by all." Neither the selectmen or any of the inhabitants were to treat with any but officials from Massachusetts.

Numbers of villagers gathered at Dover, however. The question was soon raised: Who would have liberty to vote? The reply, "All and everyone," disturbed the Puritan selectmen; this liberty, they complained, "wee fear will be improved by our Inhabitants in future meetings to our disturbance." Abraham Corbett, a tavernkeeper and ferryman, produced a petition calling for independence from Massachusetts and union with Maine as a single royal colony. Some settlers signed the document; others, a petition favoring the existing government. The Portsmouth selectmen claimed that the populace supported the Massachusetts government by a ratio of five to one but feared the royal commissioners, who were secretly "seducing the Ignorant and ill affected."[34]

The commissioners did little to consolidate the position of the opponents of Massachusetts. Colonel Richard Nicolls, appointed by the putative proprietor of New Hampshire, Robert Mason, as his agent, was occupied in New York. The other commissioners did not long remain on the Piscataqua.

Cartwright was to cross over to England with the findings and recommendations of the commission. Some strong measures were needed immediately: a forfeiture of the Bay charter and a show of force against those men who had openly declared against the king's authority. They must not be allowed to escape punishment. The commissioners entered a severe indictment against the commonwealth faction. The reform of the election law was but a sham. So high were the property qualifications imposed on those men unable to qualify by full church membership that scarce three men out of a hundred could benefit. Only members of the established churches were admitted to communion or allowed to have their children baptized, yet all persons were compelled to attend sermons on penalty of five shillings fine. The authorities had even fined Christians for observing Christmas. They claimed by their charter to be under obligation to the monarchs of England "but by civility" and had long since styled themselves a commonwealth, a free state. By procrastinating and writing occasionally to various officials in Whitehall, they intended to spin out the years.[35]

Governor Richard Bellingham and the commonwealthmen in the General Court denied all. The best defense was an offense. The Royalists, so they claimed, had undermined the unity of New England, "the wall & bulworke, under God, against the heathen." The king must not be overly hasty in accepting their judgments. Many of the persons complaining to the commissioners were Indians, Quakers, libertines, and malefactors, as all knowledgeable men in New England appreciated. The General Court was always ready to give a "rationall account" of all its actions.[36] Another year would pass before this letter was received, answered, and a reply sent out and received in Boston.

In the interval, the commonwealthmen acted swiftly and decisively to strengthen their hold. With the royal commissioners dispersed, there was no one to rally the dissidents in the Piscataqua and Maine villages. The Puritan merchants sponsored a petition disavowing secession and pledging support for the Boston regime. Philip Chasey of Oyster River, a supporter of Robert Mason, later testified that Richard Waldron threatened him with a taunt: "You are one of these that petitioned for kingly government, You shall have a king, and I will be your king." The General Court at Boston ordered enforced all fines imposed for profaning the Sabbath, neglecting God's public worship, and reproaching the laws and authority established by the charter. In the spring of 1666 Abraham Corbett, the Kittery travernkeeper, was found guilty of sedition, fined £100, and banned from holding public office and retailing beverages. The justices appointed in the name of the king, Henry Jocelyn, Francis Champernoun, and Edward Risworth, appealed in vain to Nicolls in New York.[37] The governor at Manhattan and Maverick were already planning to return to England.

Providence—whether in the form of the Puritan's Jehovah, fire, plague, or the Dutch fleet—was with the commonwealthmen. The ministers of state at Whitehall were occupied with other—to them, more pressing—matters. Rather than using force against the Bay Colony, the crown was constrained by its weakness to ask for military assistance from the New Englanders against the Dutch and the French in the Western Hemisphere. It was in no position to support any moderates in New England who might have been inclined to accept a larger role by the government of England. The king recalled the royal commission— ostensibly to present a more detailed account—and commanded the governor and assistants to dispatch delegates, preferably Bellingham and the more outspoken commonwealthmen among them, to London to explain their resistance. But at the same time, he reiterated his pledge not to infringe on the charter.

Clarendon did not know what to make of the demeanor of the Bay officials, but he was certain that if they did not obey this order, the court would give them cause to repent it.[38] It was an empty threat.

Maverick delivered the king's letter to Bellingham in Boston, but it was more than five weeks before he could prevail on the aged Puritan governor to call a meeting of the board of assistants. Many men in the colony thought the commonwealthmen had gone too far in their affronts to the government in London. Petitions arrived at the General Court from Boston, Salem, Ipswich, and Newbury requesting that agents be dispatched to London as ordered. More than one hundred men, styling themselves principal inhabitants of Boston, directly challenged the interpretation of the commonwealthmen of the charter. The patent could never be construed to divest the sovereign of power over his natural subjects. Acknowledging the zeal of the ruling group to uphold the liberties of the province, these dissidents remained convinced that in a matter of so great concern, touching the honor of God, the credit of religion, and their own persons and estates, no faction ought to follow a course so potentially dangerous. They threatened to take their case to London. For their presumption the General Court voted their petition as scandalous and labeled them betrayers of the liberties of the country, ill affected to the government, and, as such, ineligible to hold office.[39]

Four of the magistrates—they included members of the Atherton Associates—favored complying with the royal order, but Bellingham and his deputy, Willoughby, controlled both houses of the General Court. The assistants and deputies met during the second week in September 1666. Six ministers joined them to debate "the duty we owe to his majesty." Simon Bradstreet spoke for the moderates. He granted Bellingham's point that legal process in a course of law, that is, a writ from an English court, did not reach them in an ordinary cause, but the king's prerogative gave him the power to command their presence "which before God and men we are to obey." Joseph Dudley supported him: "The king's commands pass anywhere; Ireland, Calais, & c. although ordinary process [writs] from judges and officers pass not." In rebuttal Willoughby stressed a danger: the king might easily repudiate any pledge he now made. The commonwealthmen must "as well consider God's displeasure as the king's, the interest of ourselves and God's things, as [well as] his majesty's prerogative; for our liberties are of concernment." To this Dudley replied that prerogative was as necessary as law for the good of the whole community. While power might in the hands of weak men be abused, the right to exercise it could not be denied on that account. To refuse to answer the king's officers in America was to deny the king's jurisdiction.

The arguments of the moderates counted for little. The commonwealthmen prevailed in the reply to Whitehall voted on 17 September. They had given their reasons the previous year why they could not submit to the royal commissioners and had nothing more to add. The moderates continued to protest, fearing the loss of all if the royal courts at Westminster issued a writ of quo warranto against the charter.[40]

The obstreperous officials of Massachusetts appeared so contemptuous of the royal authority that Nicolls in New York was moved to redundancy. By "their false Sophistry" they had construed the king's letter to mean whatever they wished. The situation was critical, for "the Ey[e]s" of all in the other colonies are "bent upon this Strange Deportment" of the Bostonians. Yet he counseled that to use force would be unwise. "It might easily frighten the innocent as well as the nocent." A temporary embargo on trade until those responsible were delivered up would better serve the king's cause. In a flight of wishful thinking Nicolls speculated that the numerous, well-affected people in Massachusetts and the other colonies would give up the ringleaders of the commonwealth faction. Maverick was then planning to leave for London to provide fuller details on the situation, while Nicolls himself only awaited instructions from the duke of York to depart for England.

Thus ended the royal commission for New England. It had accomplished little. With the departure of the crown's agents there was no one to rally opposition to commonwealthmen in Boston.

Bellingham, Willoughby, and Thomas Danforth had fended off the challenge to their claim that the charter, once issued, had established an autonomous government. One royal official in America, Governor Sir William Berkeley of Virginia, reported that the New Englanders, confident of their ultimate victory, were openly predicting civil war would break out in the mother country. In 1667 it was clear that officials in Whitehall felt themselves too weak to provoke a test of strength. They held vastly exaggerated notions of the number and armament of the New England militia.[41]

The Puritan regime in Boston moved decisively in 1668 to strengthen its position in northern New England. Peter Ware and Francis Raynes, acting for Richard Waldron, circulated a petition in Maine calling for the return of Massachusetts authority. In May the General Court authorized the provincial major general, John Leverett, Waldron, and others, with a troop of horsemen to settle a government in what was termed Yorkshire. The officers from Boston turned out the justices appointed by the royal agents by citing the freely given consent of the inhabitants of Maine, the boundaries of the charter of 1629, and the discord fomented by those who pretended to support the king's interests. In the New Hampshire villages, with the prosecution of Abraham Corbett and the defection by Henry Sherburne from the old planter faction, Richard Waldron, the Cutts brothers, and Elias Stileman reasserted Puritan authority.

Nicholas Shapleigh, a Quaker, along with the justices in Maine displaced by Massachusetts, urged Robert Mason to unite his province

with the territory north and east of the Piscataqua and to seek an order
from the king securing the northern regions from Massachusetts.[42] It was
Ferdinando Gorges, the heir to the proprietary of Maine, who took the
initiative in 1670 with the formation at Whitehall of the select Council
for Plantations. The president of the new board saw in the proposal to
unite the two proprietaries, as supported in testimony by Nicolls,
Nathaniel Phillips (a justice appointed by the royal commissioners in
1665), and John Archdale (an agent in the employ of Gorges), a means of
checking the power and influence of Massachusetts.

But decisions were not easily arrived at or carried out in Whitehall during these years. According to Evelyn, a member of the Council
for Foreign Plantations, while the board was concerned with various
colonial affairs, "most we insisted on, was to know in what condition
New England was." Massachusetts, "rich and strong," appeared to be
very independent, able to contest with all the other colonies of New
England, and "altogether breaking from all dependence of this nation."
Some councilors favored sending the authorities in Boston "a menacing
letter," but those who "better understood" the "touchy and peevish"
humor of the Puritan officials were utterly opposed to such a tactic.
More information was needed. They agreed to send off a letter, provided
it was conciliatory in tone, since the commonwealthmen were on the
very brink of openly renouncing any dependence on England.

Both Cartwright and others pressed for the use of force, but Sandwich, the president of the council, hesitated; it was already too late to use
force or to issue preemptory orders. Massachusetts was too strong. A
numerous militia in the colony precluded reducing the Bay. The only
feasible alternative to restrain a province seemingly determined on independence was to check its growth by supporting the territorial claims
of the duke of York and the other New England colonies. Rhode Island
must be encouraged and Maine and New Hampshire united as one royal
colony under conditions "by noe meanes greevous to the Inhabitants."
On 3 July 1671 Sandwich presented this program to a full meeting of the
Council of Foreign Plantations, with many of the lords of the Privy
Council in attendance. Mason and Gorges asked that a commission be
sent to require Massachusetts to confine itself to its charter limits.

Debate centered on whether or not the authorities in Boston were
capable of resisting the crown and establishing themselves as an independent state. Late that summer the board finally agreed to dispatch
the commission, but not until the following spring. It was then too late in
the season for ships to depart.[43]

Little was done that winter. Toward the end of January 1672, with
the season now approaching to dispatch ships to reach the New England
ports by the spring, the council moved the king that commissioners be

selected. But in February Lord Richard Gorges brought in an account of the military force allegedly available to Massachusetts, fifteen thousand men of whom about six thousand were members of the established Congregational churches.[44]

Time and circumstances again worked in favor of the common-wealthmen. In 1672 England was once more at war with the United Provinces of the Netherlands, and the next year the fall of the cabal disrupted the court at Whitehall. The selection of prudent, discreet commissioners who would not offend the sensibilities of the men of Massachusetts would have to wait. Over the course of a dozen years, little had been done to extend royal influence in Massachusetts. For the moderates in the colony, whatever else may have led them to differ with commonwealthmen, inaction by the crown had given the lie to their argument that the colony had to make some concessions. The common-wealthmen had been proven correct. Dilitory tactics and time favored the status quo.

Animosities and tensions in New England continued to disrupt the Puritan communities. Proportionally fewer men were able to recount the necessary experience of saving grace to win membership in the churches, and consequently the relative size of the electorate in the Bay Colony continued to fall. Friction over religion continued. Baptists, refusing to attend Congregational meetings, sought to form their own churches. When several residents of Boston and Charles Town, among them Samuel Shrimpton and John Usher, petitioned on their behalf, they were fined and forced to make public apology.

During these years three of the towns in New Hampshire—Hampton, Dover, and Portsmouth—returned deputies to the General Court at Boston. The election of Richard Waldron, Elias Stileman, Peter Coffin, and Richard Martin signified the victory of the Boston-oriented faction in the Piscataqua towns. They had joined with the Reverend Joshua Moody to form the first Puritan church in Portsmouth, had displaced the old Anglican planters, and were transforming the New Hampshire villages into Puritan communities.

While the power of orthodox Congregationalism was being more firmly entrenched in northern New England, the authority of the ministers was being challenged in the towns in the lower Connecticut valley. There were those who favored accepting into the churches all persons of honest and godly conversation who had a competent knowledge of Christian doctrine and going beyond the halfway convenant to extend baptism to all children and rights in full communion when they were grown. John Davenport, before moving from New Haven to Boston, had argued strenuously against the covenant, and in his zeal he had railed against the government of England both in church and state.

From Manhattan Richard Nicolls had protested against such seditious discourse: no charter privileged men to speak treason. It was to be hoped that the clergy of Connecticut would not come out against general baptism, since it was an element of liberty of conscience. Those men who had been denied membership in the Congregational churches used the halfway covenant to dilute ecclesiastical authority and to narrow the gap between church and community.[45]

Connecticut continued to dispute with neighboring Rhode Island over the Narragansett country. On 23 June 1671 at a meeting held at the house of one of the Atherton partners, Captain William Hudson, commissioners appointed by Connecticut rejected the claims of the Rhode Islanders and declared the contested region to be part of their province.[46] Rhode Island set up a rival jurisdiction. In this dispute Connecticut had the support of Massachusetts and New Plymouth. Confronted by this united opposition in New England, the Rhode Islanders appealed to the king, reminding him that his commissioners had given them authority over the Narragansett country.

Occupied by the war with the Dutch and the French and the internal political crisis, the court in Whitehall did nothing. After a dozen years, New England remained in a loose and scattered condition.

CHAPTER 7

The New Proprietaries, 1663-73

DURING THE YEARS following the Restoration, the English crown exercised little control over the squabbling, petty jurisdictions in New England. Charles II compounded the problem of governing the foreign plantations by allowing still more diverse colonies, provinces not subject to the immediate supervision of the crown, to be formed. The origin of four additional colonies—North and South Carolina, New York, and New Jersey—diverse in their social structure and bizarre in their governmental arrangement, was laid during these years, the result of the king's propensity for rewarding personal favorites—particularly a small coterie associated with his brother, James, duke of York—by granting them special proprietary rights in America. The decision seemed immediately attractive: it offered an opportunity to displace foreign powers and to allow the English to preempt portions of North America claimed by the Dutch and Spaniards. Whatever else the king and his advisers hoped to achieve in Puritan New England, religious toleration for Englishmen in the colonies who did not abuse liberty of conscience to disrupt the peace of the community remained a goal, as evidenced by the charters Charles granted to these proprietors.

Despite precarious early beginnings, the Jerseys and the Carolinas survived as colonies. Their early history was traumatic, marred by an impractical—in the case of the Jerseys, a grotesque—division of governmental authority and seemingly irrepressible conflict among settlers with diverse ethnic backgrounds and religious loyalties.

The vast area stretching south from Virginia to Spanish Florida had attracted the attention of various groups of Englishmen. By 1660 Virginians had settled in the Chowan region and along the streams flowing into Albemarle Sound. This area was then considered part of Virginia. In 1662 the provincial council at Jamestown appointed Samuel Stephens commander of what it called the southern plantation. New Englanders had also viewed the region as a site for potential settlement. But of the various English groups, the most influential were the English planters from Barbados, where the introduction of sugar cane a

generation before was bringing about a social and economic trans-
formation, a preponderance of black slaves in the labor force, and the
domination of the wealthier planters, who alone commanded sufficient
capital or credit for extensive cultivation. The employment of black
slaves on a large scale and the consolidation of estates led to an exodus of
whites from the island, not only former owners of small plots but also
former servants who had completed their time and found land in Barbados difficult to acquire. Confronted with competition from the
Leeward Islands and Jamaica and faced with the prospect of reduced
profits from sugar cultivation, some landed Barbadians also sought to
move.

A number of planters looked to the mainland. A group organized by
John Vassall arrived at Cape Fear in the spring of 1663. Another party
led by Sir John Yeamans, eldest son of Nathaniel Yeamans, an alderman
of Bristol who had been executed by the Parliamentarians during the
Civil War, proposed to settle two colonies, one at Cape Fear and another
at Port Royal Sound. Especially active in formulating plans to settle the
Carolina coastline were Sir John Colleton and his son, Peter. The elder
Colleton, a Royalist officer, had withdrawn to Barbados following the
victory of the Roundheads in the Civil War. With the Restoration he
returned to London, where he and Sir William Berkeley of Virginia
formed a group to promote English colonization of the region north of
Spanish Florida.

Colleton and Berkeley managed to interest several courtiers involved
during the decade in various marginal overseas promotions. Anthony
Ashley Cooper, Baron Ashley and later first earl of Shaftesbury, was a
key figure in these ventures. Also brought into the Carolina promotion
were two associates of the royal duke, Lord John Berkeley (brother of
the governor of Virginia) and Sir George Carteret, treasurer of the navy.
To give added political weight other prominent figures at court were
added: the earl of Craven, the duke of Albemarle, and Clarendon (the
lord chancellor and James Stuart's father-in-law). Carolina was not the
only colonizing venture to attract the prospective proprietors. Carteret
and Lord John Berkeley in 1664 received from the duke of York a
portion of the former Dutch holdings in North America, a region they
called New Jersey.

As early as 1662 the prospective investors began to solicit settlers
from England for a proposed colony in Carolina. But not until 24 March
1663 did the crown issue a charter to the eight proprietors. By the terms
of this patent Charles II continued the liberal conditions, especially
relating to religion, that he had offered to the corporations in New
England. Except in emergencies, the proprietors of Carolina had to
formulate laws with the approbation of the freemen or their deputies.
Within this prescription wide latitude might exist, and while the

proprietors might establish the Church of England, the proprietors had liberty to grant dispensations to those who for conscience' sake could not conform to the ritual and doctrine of the established church.

An immediate obstacle to religious toleration had first to be removed. For some who had indicated a willingness to settle—they were probably New Englanders—liberty of conscience seemed to be jeopardized by the existence of a previous patent covering the territory in question. Prospective immigrants negotiating with the new proprietary board made it explicit that they would not move to Carolina without an assurance of liberty of conscience, a dubious condition should any previous patents to the area prove valid. As Sir John Colleton emphasized to Albemarle, it was essential to remove this obstacle.[1]

In the summer of 1663, after the Privy Council had verified the patent against the claim of any previous grants, Colonel Thomas Modyford and Peter Colleton, representatives of more than two hundred gentlemen of Barbados, presented to Albemarle proposals for moving to Carolina.[2] Apprehensive over reports of New Englanders said to be considering settlement in the Cape Fear region, these planters expected to have the sole power of electing all delegates and officers, of making laws, and of governing themselves according to the charter granted by the king. In transmitting this proposal Modyford and Colleton made it clear to their cousin, Albemarle, that in their view the adventurers ought to be content to enact bylaws rather than general statutes and to select municipal or county officials rather than governors.

Within a few days the proprietors issued "A Declaration and Proposals" to the Barbadians. They could settle on the Charles (Cape Fear) River, but before setting out, they were to nominate thirteen men. From this group the proprietors would commission one as governor and six others as councilors. The freeholders of the settlement would choose deputies, two from each parish, to enact laws, regulations not repugnant to the laws of England, to be presented within one year to the proprietors for ratification and to be in force until the proprietary board repealed them or they expired. The declaration further provided for freedom of religious conscience.[3] Both Albemarle and Lord Chancellor Clarendon wrote to Governor Willoughby of Barbados and to Peter Colleton and Modyford asking that they promote the Carolina plantation among prospective adventurers in the West Indies. In addressing themselves specifically to the Barbadians the proprietors pledged that, if other ways of framing the government were preferable and did not limit the powers the proprietors had reserved to themselves, Colleton and Modyford might conclude an agreement with prospective emigrants.[4]

For the planters already seated on the Chowan River, the proprietors empowered one of their own number, Sir William Berkeley, who had returned to America to resume the governorship of Virginia, to appoint a governor to exercise authority and, with the consent of a majority of the freemen there, to enact laws. At this early stage the proprietors had in mind compact settlements, with the acreage held by an individual limited to the amount of land a man could clear and work. They were willing to allow up to five years before the payment of a halfpenny per acre rent was due.[5]

In America, Berkeley appointed as governor for the Albemarle settlements William Drummond, a Scottish-born attorney who had recently arrived in Virginia. During his term, early in 1665, the proprietary board in London altered the administrative structure of Carolina. Peter Carteret, a near relative and deputy of Sir George Carteret, was appointed deputy governor and sent to the Albemarle settlements with instructions that the region be administered as the county of Albemarle. The Cape Fear area under Sir John Yeamans was designated the county of Clarendon, the territory to the south as Craven County. The proprietors had also concluded an agreement with William Yeamans, the spokesman for a group of Barbadians who proposed to settle on Cape Fear. This codicil incorporated a document known as the Concessions and Agreement and consigned great powers to the elected deputies of the freemen in the proposed settlement. Anticipating that New Englanders who would not submit to the discipline of the Church of England might constitute a majority of the population, the proprietary board endeavored to comprehend all interests.[6]

Some doubt then arose as to the validity of the proprietary title of Albemarle, the initial grant from Charles II having been issued before the Privy Council declared all previous patents to be vacated and void. It was now also apparent that the Chowan settlements designated by the proprietors as part of Albemarle County lay to the north of the line of 36° north latitude, the northern boundary specified in the initial charter. The crown remedied both defects in a new patent issued on 30 June 1665, setting the limits of Carolina at 36°30′ N and 29° N. As before, the king required the proprietors to make laws with the advice, consent, and approbation of the freemen through their elected deputies, provided such laws were reasonable and, as near as might be convenient, agreeable to the laws and customs of England. Churches could be erected according to the ecclesiastical code of England, but no person was to be called into question for any difference in opinion or practice in matters concerning religion, provided he did not disturb the peace or abuse this liberty by licentiousness, notwithstanding any law, usage, or custom of the realm of England to the contrary.[7] This was a direct repudiation of the religious code imposed *within* the realm by the Cavalier Parliament.

The early pronouncements of the Carolina proprietors indicated they planned to see established compact, yet widely separated, settlements—plantations to provide them income from quitrents. Limited by the conditions of the royal charter and cognizant of conditions in Barbados and New England, the proprietors by these early arrangements allowed the settlers some voice in the nomination of officials and in the determination of the laws governing their lives. Evidently expecting a substantial migration from New England, they had been especially solicitous of the rights of Dissenters to enjoy freedom of conscience.

The conditions on landholding set out by the proprietors raised doubt, at least in the mind of one man familiar with the situation in America and the aspirations of the planters, Thomas Woodward, the proprietary surveyor appointed for Albemarle County. It might be more profitable for the proprietors to permit planters to take up what tracts of land they pleased at a low rent rather than restrict them to small holdings at a high fee. Woodward's assessment proved correct.[8] The West Indian adventurers at this stage failed to migrate in sufficient numbers, and the New Englanders did not respond to the proprietary offers.

The proposed settlements at Cape Fear (Clarendon County) and Port Royal Sound (Craven County) never prospered. When war with the French broke out in the West Indies in January 1666, ships and men needed to hold the Caribbean for the English could not be spared for Carolina. By the fall of 1667 a settlement founded two years before at Cape Fear by Sir John Yeamans had broken up; the few plantations on the Chowan River in the county of Albemarle remained the only settlements within the proprietary jurisdiction. In October 1667 the board in London attempted to tighten control by new instructions sent to Governor Samuel Stephens.[9] As time later proved, however, geography and population tied Albemarle to Virginia, a colony over which the proprietors had no control.

Aside from formulating regulations for the distribution of land and setting out the structure of government within the limits prescribed by the two royal charters, the eight proprietors had done little to aid in establishing settlements. They had relied almost exclusively on the resources of the "adventurers" from the West Indies. Financial contributions by the proprietors had been small. During the first three years of the venture each member had contributed only £75, and of the £600 expended, half had gone for fees to process the two charters, the remainder to the purchase of arms and ammunition.[10]

During the last years of the decade the proprietary board might well have collapsed and the Carolina project been abandoned. Sir John Colleton was dead and Clarendon exiled. Albemarle, less active in these years, died in 1670. Carteret was over seventy years of age, and the Berkeley brothers were both over sixty. Sir William was fully occupied with his government in Virginia. Sir Peter Colleton had succeeded his father, however, and Ashley in 1670 at forty-nine years of age was vigorous. He and John Locke, whom he persuaded to become secretary of the proprietary board, now took a leading role in forming a program for Carolina.

The proprietors now determined to invest more heavily in new settlements and to recruit colonists for the southern reaches of Carolina. Menaced by the Dutch, the English planters of Surinam offered to emigrate to the region of Port Royal if offered transportation for themselves and their slaves. A month after the memorial of the Surinam planters reached London, six of the proprietors and their representatives met and pledged to make specific payments over the next five years "for the speedy set[tle]ment" of Carolina. Any proprietor failing to contribute his allotment would forfeit his share to the others.[11]

Two months later Ashley and Locke produced a new frame of government for the colony, the Fundamental Constitutions. They sought to place the burden of colonization on wealthy investors who would recruit and transport the bulk of the laborers. As an inducement, they would receive land and broad social and political privileges. The royal charter of 1665 constrained the proprietors to govern with the advice, consent, and approbation of the majority of the freeholders or their deputies. Within this limitation the Fundamental Constitutions provided for representation by social classes or estates, a medieval arrangement. To avoid arriving at decisions by mere numbers, three distinct social groups were recognized: the proprietors and their deputies in the colony, a provincial nobility consisting of landgraves and caciques (or cassiques), and the commonality (freemen) and tenants. The proprietors themselves each occupied a key executive office.[12]

The colony was to be divided into counties of 480,000 acres, or 750 square miles. Each county contained eight seignories of 12,000 acres, one for each of the proprietary shares. One-fifth of each county was to be divided into eight baronies for the hereditary provincial nobility. The remaining three-fifths, including manors of not less than 3,000 and not more than 12,000 acres, was reserved for the commonality. Quitrents, a penny per acre annually, were due after 1689.

Governmental arrangements under the Fundamental Constitutions were awkward. They provided for eight supreme courts with carefully defined jurisdictions for each of the eight offices held by the proprietors. They (or their appointed deputies) and forty-two councilors who sat with them on these courts were to constitute a grand council to prepare all matters put before a legislature. The parliament included the eight proprietary deputies, the hereditary nobility (three from each county), and four freemen (each holding at least five hundred acres of land) from each county, elected by freemen possessing a minimum of fifty acres of land.

Public worship of God was required, although any seven or more persons could band together for worship or could form a church, provided they did not abuse others of different religious persuasion.

The proprietors never posed these articles as final organic law, but seemed rather to have held them out as a prospectus for potential investors in the colony, setting out in greater detail the generalities contained in the charters. At best the various versions of the Fundamental Constitutions—there were to be five editions in all—represented a goal toward which the proprietary board in London strove unsuccessfully for three decades. More often the proprietors relied on the various instructions issued by the board to appointed governors. As matters went, each proprietor regularly named a deputy in the colony. At least twenty-six landgraves were created, beginning in 1671, and thirteen caciques, the first in 1678. They sat with the governor's council.[13]

While the proprietors in promulgating the Fundamental Constitutions hoped to induce men of wealth to invest in and promote migration to Carolina, they themselves took steps to subsidize colonization rather than, as before, relying exclusively on the initiative of Barbadian adventurers or New England Dissenters. In 1669 Ashley and his colleagues outfitted three ships, *Carolina, Port Royal,* and *Albemarle,* with about 140 crewmen and passengers, mostly servants, and supplied them at a charge of almost three thousand pounds with provisions, clothing, tools, arms, and articles for the Indian trade. It was hoped families from Barbados, Virginia, England, and Ireland would join these initial adventurers. The small fleet under the command of Joseph West left the Downs at the end of August 1669 for Kinsale. Through Robert Southwell, Ashley sought to recruit servants in Ireland, but the projected colony in Carolina held no attractions for the Irish peasants. They had been so terrified by the ill treatment their countrymen had received in the Caribbean, where they had been sent as convicts, that they would not believe they might expect better elsewhere. With enough work at home to sustain them, they were loath to leave the smoke of their rough cabins.[14]

After several weeks at Kinsale, West sailed for the West Indies, carrying with him a blank commission and instructions for the governor of the proposed settlement at Port Royal Sound, Sir John Yeamans. Inasmuch as there would not be a sufficient number of eligible men to put into effect the Fundamental Constitutions, Yeamans as soon as possible was to summon the freemen at Port Royal to elect five persons to be joined with the five deputies of the proprietors to serve on the council. At some appropriate time the governor would call on the freeholders to elect twenty men to join with the proprietary deputies to frame laws. As commercial agent for the board in London, West was to lay out proprietary estates to be planted with sugar cane, ginger, Indian corn, peas, turnips, carrots, potatoes, and vines for grapes and to call on Thomas Jordan and Richard Bennett in Virginia for livestock and Thomas Colleton in Barbados for ginger roots and cotton and indigo seed.[15]

Little of this ambitious program was realized.

The *Port Royal* and the *Albemarle* were cast away before reaching their destination. The largest vessel, the *Carolina,* reached Barbados early in November. Some islanders, responding to Sir John Yeamans's appeal, answered the call for adventurers. But Yeamans himself accompanied the expedition only as far as Bermuda. He then declined to serve and selected as governor an old Puritan of nearly eighty years, William Sayle. At the end of March 1670 the expedition reached the mainland, where Sayle and his followers decided against Port Royal as unsuitable and instead selected a neck of land, Albemarle Point, about twenty-five miles up the Ashley River for their settlement, Charles Town.[16]

By the end of June, with only a few weeks' store of provisions left and with no word having come of a ship dispatched to Virginia, the colonists had to send to Bermuda for supplies. There were other difficulties. Livestock imported from Virginia was expensive, the price for hogs being three times what it was in England.

By September the aged Puritan governor and his council wrote back to London that the infant settlement needed stores of every type and especially an able minister "by whose meanes corrupted youth might be very much reclaimed, and the people instructed in the true religion, and that the Sabboth and service of Almighty God be not neglected." Joseph Dalton, appointed provincial secretary, found it difficult to perform the duties of his office, particularly registering land grants, having little in the way of paper or entry books. Most had been lost or damaged in the voyage across the Atlantic.[17] In Barbados many planters who were otherwise inclined to partake in the Carolina venture were discouraged by the provisions in the Fundamental Constitutions for granting lands. They regarded the undertaking as too uncertain under these conditions.

From the outset, friction characterized the government of the settlement at Albemarle Point. Only a few months after Yeamans had penned in William Sayle's name in the governor's commission, he was forced to admit that Sayle, although the ablest man he could find, was hardly adequate for the task. Henry Brayne, charged by Sir Peter Colleton to secure livestock and provisions for the settlement, went much further. He offered to pawn his life that Sayle was one of the most unfit men in the world for the position—indeed, that the governor was "crazy." Only three or four of the councilors—Joseph West, Stephen Bull, William Scrivenor, Robert Dunn (or Donne), and secretary Joseph

Dalton—had any competence. Some others, although honest men, knew nothing of plantations. Florence O'Sullivan, the surveyor general, was actually dishonest. Stephen Bull joined in the complaints against O'Sullivan, a contentious, troublesome Irishman who extracted high fees for his services. Bull was somewhat more charitable toward the old governor, implying that fever and ague may have been responsible for Sayle's acting so contrary to the commission issued by the proprietors. Whatever the case, the aged governor was not expected to live long.[18]

Sayle died on 4 March 1670/1 after designating Joseph West as his successor. But West was uneasy in his administration. He and the councilors feared Yeamans might take it upon himself to come to the colony and assume the governorship. Almost immediately they had to contend with two troublesome, disruptive spirits in the infant settlement, William Owen and William Scrivenor, Lord Berkeley's deputy. Sayle and the council had decided against calling an election for a parliament on the grounds that there were then not enough freemen in the settlement to meet the requirement in the proprietary instructions for twenty elected members. Owen, an Anglican who possibly resented the Dissenter Sayle, then conducted his own canvass. But too few men were returned. Owen himself attempted to make good the deficiency by naming Michael Moran, an Irish indentured laborer, and Richard Crossley, a servant dismissed by his master for idleness.

Not until the arrival of two ships with additional settlers was it possible to hold a proper election. Owen, with the support of Scrivenor, then agitated among the new arrivals, arguing that since there was no provincial seal in the colony, the settlers' lands and improvements could not be assured unless a parliament was chosen to secure their rights. Owen's bid collapsed when West promised to hold elections. Scrivenor and Owen, sensing that they would lose popular support, attempted to backtrack, but the council, condemning their behavior in inciting the settlers as sedition and mutiny, suspended Scrivenor and ruled Owen incapable of holding public office.[19]

From London, Ashley sought to placate the various contentious personalities in the colony. In the spring of 1671 he, Craven, Colleton, and Carteret issued another set of "Carolina Instructions." To put matters in the infant colony on a more stable basis, the governor was to summon the freeholders to elect representatives. With the proprietary deputies these delegates would make laws. The provincial parliament was also to select five persons who with the five deputies and five of the oldest nobles in the colony would form a grand council. In these instructions the proprietors laid down stringent regulations for land to be laid out systematically in townships. Ashley in his correspondence to the various leaders in the colony held up the model of compact settlement in

New England for the Carolinians to follow, as against the haphazard, diffuse pattern of planting employed in Virginia. The New England way was the more conducive for the protection of the inhabitants.[20]

In the summer of 1671, Yeamans arrived in the colony with about fifty immigrants from Barbados. He quickly assumed leadership of an Anglican faction. As a landgrave, he held the highest rank of anyone in the settlement—he also owned a good proportion of the livestock—and by the terms of the Fundamental Constitutions, the senior noble, provided none of the proprietors was resident in the colony, became the deputy of the palatine. Despite these qualifications, West, who had been selected to act as governor following the death of Sayle, refused to surrender his post until specific instructions arrived from London. He argued that the Fundamental Constitutions had never been made fully operative. A bitter factional struggle broke out; it carried over into the election for members of the provincial parliament.

Later that year, on learning that Yeamans had arrived in Carolina, the proprietors repudiated the action of the council at Albemarle Point in choosing West to succeed Sayle and named Sir John as governor. He had been their original choice when they had sent out the founding fleet in 1669, and his rank as landgrave gave him added weight. The proprietors were relying on firmness by Yeamans to maintain order. He must take the initiative and draft whatever bills he deemed proper for the plantations. The elected body could only debate what the council proposed to them.

While Ashley was concerned over the undue influence of the wealthy Barbadians, he was forced to acknowledge that their arrival had materially benefited the infant settlement. In an apparent bid for the support of the newcomers he designated one of their number, Maurice Matthews, as his deputy in place of Stephen Bull, an English immigrant.[21] Ashley urged moderation on the governor, counseling Yeamans not to "revenge yourself on any who have spoke their apprehensions with that freedom which must be allowed men in a country wherein they are not designed to be oppressed and where they may justly expect . . . equal justice and protection." Yet he chided the Barbadian for having been too forward in "grasping" at power on his arrival and subsequently endeavoring to diminish the authority of the proprietary deputies, an open reference to Yeamans's forming a clique of Barbadian Anglicans.

To Ashley, a man who would become notorious in London within a few years for his factional political behavior, the solution for Carolina was simple: Yeamans had but to direct the administration of his government "wholly to the impartial prosperity of the whole plantation and all the planters" in order to remove the jealousies some settlers entertained. Nonetheless, Ashley sought to limit the power of the governor vis à vis the proprietary deputies. What distinguished the governor from the other proprietary representatives, he wrote his own agent, Maurice Matthews, was precedence rather than overruling power. Yeamans had no more freedom than any other man on the council to deviate from the rules the palatine expected his deputy to follow.[22] Ignoring no faction, Ashley sent a conciliatory message to the deposed "Governor" West and the other councilors calling on them to set aside their jealousies and unite for the common good. In order that animosities might not continue to disrupt the infant settlement, Ashley would endeavor to find a disinterested governor, but in the meantime West and his colleagues must adhere to proprietary regulations. The deputies represented the proprietors and ought not consequently to lessen their rights by making themselves "cyphers" by submitting tamely to the will of a governor.[23] Ashley was seeking to prevent one group or faction from dominating in the colony.

As a result of the tactics Ashley adopted, power in the infant colony was divided and fragmented. Strong-willed men seeking to assert themselves by opposing local authority could easily find some legal sanction or justification for their position.

During the first three years almost five hundred souls—over three hundred men—had arrived at the settlement on the Ashley River. Of these about 10 percent had died. Another two hundred or so came during the remaining years of the decade. The West Indians—and particularly the Barbadians—constituted the dominant element. A significant number of them were younger sons of families of means. In the main they were Church of England men. Settling together along Goose Creek, a branch of the Cooper River, they formed a dominant party challenging the authority of the proprietary board in London. To offset the dominance of the West Indians, the proprietors sought to induce other ethnic and religious elements—English Dissenters, Scots, and French Huguenots—to emigrate to the colony. As a consequence, ethnic and religious diversity complicated further the problem of governing the province, a colony already made unstable by the clash of personalities, the complicated governmental arrangement adopted by the proprietary board, and the division of political authority.

Throughout these years the government of Charles II had played almost no role. The monarch had sanctioned the broad outlines for government in the charters, had required freedom of conscience and the consent of the settlers to the laws governing them, but otherwise had left responsibility for the infant province to the proprietors in London. Even when the crown sought to bring the Carolina plantations into the royal customs system, it relied on proprietary officials. For men of a generation familiar with the deposition and execution of a king, proprietary government three thousand miles away might safely be ignored if their interests so dictated.

Respect for proprietary authority was no more evident to the north in the county of Albemarle among the three thousand settlers living on isolated, often marginal farms in the districts of Perquimids, Pasquotank, Currituck, and Chowan. The majority of the farmers and certainly the more prominent of the leaders had come from Virginia, under whose jurisdiction the scattered plantations had initially fallen. These planters had tolerated a succession of governors. Samuel Stephens had first commanded under the authority of the Old Dominion; following the initial royal grant of 1663, Sir William Berkeley administered the region apparently as part of Virginia until the proprietary board in London named another Virginian, William Drummond, as governor and register. When Drummond gave up the post in 1667 to return to Jamestown, Stephens resumed the governorship. This was the situation in the summer of 1669 when the proprietors sent out the complex, but incomplete, Fundamental Constitutions. During the latter years of the decade the planters had suffered from the effects of drought and hurricanes.

The imposition of proprietary regulations further exacerbated the situation. Discontent and factional opposition were soon evident. In neighboring Virginia, a more generous system of land tenure prevailed; there the crown demanded of landholders only a farthing per acre in quitrents; in proprietary Carolina the rate was one halfpenny.[24] Governor Stephens had died shortly before the orders for revising the government under the Fundamental Constitutions arrived in Albemarle. His widow, Frances Culpeper, soon after married Sir William Berkeley, one of the Carolina proprietors and the governor of nearby Virginia. Berkeley evidently had not thought much of Stephens. "He had not that fullness of understanding w[hi]ch men bred in Europe have." Nonetheless, Berkeley made clear to the assemblymen of Albemarle his displeasure that the planters should have opposed Stephens rather than maintain peace and uphold the authority of the governor. Without these no colony "can long subsist." Some bolder souls reportedly had been so presumptuous as to have drawn their swords against Stephens, an offense meriting capital punishment if committed elsewhere. As a proprietor, Berkeley would not have the council select as an interim governor anyone who had set so ill an example in offering indignities and violence to Stephens.[25] This threat led the concilors in Albemarle to accept Peter Carteret, the deputy and secretary, as governor.

Among the more prominent members of the provincial board a few had qualifications to lead. John Jenkins, a landowner in Virginia and a licensed trader, had moved to Albemarle about 1658 and had later become the deputy for the earl of Craven. John Harvey had come also from Virginia, as had Richard Foster, a burgess in Jamestown. John Willoughby—he may have been related to the governor of Barbados— was Ashley's deputy on the council.

Communications between the isolated Albemarle colony and England broke down. After two years had passed, in April 1672 the leading lights decided to send Carteret and John Harvey on a mission to London.[26] As testimony to the qualifications of some of the councilors, three of them had to place a mark rather than sign their names to the instructions to Carteret and Harvey. The two emissaries were ordered to secure a reduction in the quitrents and an alteration in the limitation on the amount of land an individual planter might secure. Existing conditions supposedly discouraged planters in Virginia from migrating. The councilors also sought the elimination of the duty of two shillings imposed by the government of the Old Dominion on every hogshead of tobacco shipped from Albemarle through her northern neighbor. They further objected to a clause in the Fundamental Constitutions prohibiting the representatives of the freemen from initiating legislation.[27]

Before leaving Albemarle, Peter Carteret commissioned Jenkins as his deputy with authority to exercise the powers he himself held by virtue of his commission from the proprietary board. Under the Fundamental Constitutions all deputations would expire after four years.

By July 1672 Harvey and Carteret were in New York. At this point Harvey abandoned the mission, while Carteret took ship for London. When he arrived, he found the proprietors and an agent for Sir William Berkeley engaged in negotiations for the transfer of the Albemarle region to the governor of Virginia as his share of the original proprietary grant. Although never completed, these negotiations dragged on for several years. Some doubt had arisen as to the validity of the proprietors' title to Albemarle, since the area had been included in Virginia before the second charter was issued in 1665. Inasmuch as the proprietors probably expected to transfer the settlements on the Chowan to the governor at Jamestown, they failed to renew their deputations to their officials in Albemarle county or to appoint new deputies.

By the fall of 1674 the proprietary commissions sent out four years earlier had expired. Technically the region was without government sanctioned from England.[28] Elements dissatisfied with proprietary rule could with impunity now challenge the right of those men exercising power.

Two of the Carolina proprietors, Sir George Carteret and Lord Berkeley, were involved in another colonial venture to the north, one growing out of an attempt by Charles II and his ministers in 1664 to eject the Dutch from their holdings in North America. The machinations of the adventurer from Long Island, John Scott, and the rivalry between the Puritans of New England and officials of the Dutch West India trading company at New Netherlands also contributed to still another bizarre experiment in proprietary colonization.

A proprietary was considered a species of property, to be alienated, bought and sold, and divided. In the case of the territory known as New Jersey, the logic of the proprietary colony was carried to an absurd conclusion. The division of the property and the government into first two and ultimately more than one hundred shares, with some proprietors residing in America and others in England and Scotland, produced a preposterous situation.

Scattered between the English colonies on the Chesapeake and the Puritan commonwealths in New England was a mixed, heterogeneous population composed of a few thousand Dutchmen, Swedes, Finns, and Englishmen. By 1664 a handful of small settlements located on the lower Delaware were all that remained of an abortive experiment in colonization by the kingdom of Sweden. It had fallen victim to the more numerous Dutch based on the lower Hudson valley. But New Netherlands, an outpost of the Dutch West India Company, was in turn hard-pressed by the aggressive Puritans of Connecticut and New Haven, bent on annexing Long Island and the Hudson and Delaware valleys.

Weakly supported by the government of the United Provinces of the Netherlands and the Dutch West India Company, the director at New Amsterdam had negotiated with commissioners of the United Colonies of New England a temporary line of demarcation between the English and the Dutch towns on Long Island and the mainland. Repudiating this agreement, by 1663 officials of Connecticut were attempting to extend their jurisdiction. John Scott, possibly aware that the English crown planned to send out a military expedition to take over New Netherlands, had also stirred up the villagers against Dutch rule.[29] The authorities at Hartford moved quickly. Following elections held in May 1664, the General Assembly accepted deputies from Hempstead, Jamaica, Newtown, and Flushing and declared Long Island to be one of the off-shore, adjoining isles granted to Connecticut by the royal patent obtained by Governor John Winthrop from the king in 1662. Even before the forces sent from England under Colonel Richard Nicolls were actually in possession, Charles II in February 1664 had decided to grant the territory disputed with the Dutch to his brother, James, duke of York, as a proprietary colony.[30]

The charter issued to the duke on 22 March 1663/4 was ambiguous, even tortured in the language used to delineate the territory it conferred and singular in the political system it created. The grant encompassed a conglomerate of territories: Pemaquid (the region far to the north and east between the Saint Croix and the Kennebec rivers); various islands off southern New England (Block Island, Manhattan, Martha's Vineyard, Nantucket, and Long Island); and, on the mainland, all of the territory from the Connecticut River west to the Delaware. The patent conflicted with the claims of Massachusetts in northern New England, claims the crown had not recognized, but also directly contravened the charter granted but two years before to Connecticut. By the patent issued to the duke of York the corporation of Connecticut lost all of the territory on the mainland west of the Connecticut River as well as Long Island, an area officials in Hartford had claimed from the Dutch. These boundary provisions in the charter granted James may have been the result of carelessness, indifference, or even monumental ignorance on the part of officials in Whitehall, but more probably they may have reflected the need, as perceived by the ministers, to establish through the charter to the royal duke a full title to all territory disputed with the Dutch and the French.[31] Any discrepancies with the boundaries of other English colonies they might later settle with the provincial regimes.

James himself further confused matters. Shortly after Richard Nicolls and the other royal commissioners departed for America, the royal duke without informing his deputy granted away much of the land he had received from his brother, the territory between the Atlantic and the Delaware River, to two courtiers, Lord Berkeley and Sir George Carteret. Both men the previous year had been recipients of the royal largesse as members of the Carolina proprietary board. In 1662 Berkeley had purchased for the sum of £3,500 a portion of the lands on Long Island claimed by the earl of Stirling by virtue of a patent issued to his grandfather thirty-one years before by the defunct Council of Plymouth. Failing to win the king's confirmation of this purchase, Berkeley came to an understanding with James, who promised to pay Stirling the purchase price.[32] The duke, perhaps in an attempt to compensate Berkeley and his associate, on 24 June granted them the territory east of the Delaware River, the region to be known as New Jersey. Both parties assumed—and it was a dubious assumption—that with the grant went the right to govern the property.

Thus was created yet another proprietary arrangement—a system of government and landholding ill suited for stability. In New Jersey it was to lead to a bizarre, even grotesque situation.

In contrast to the other charters issued during this decade, the grant to the duke of York imposed no requirement that the proprietor allow the inhabitants of the colony any voice in formulating the laws under which they lived. The proprietor and the officials he appointed were not required to call an assembly elected by the freeholders. They were, however, limited by two other stipulations: the crown reserved the right to hear and determine appeals from the courts in New York and specified that the laws of the colony could not be contrary to the laws of England.[33] In issuing this grant Charles II and his advisers departed from a condition previously contained in the charters to Connecticut, Rhode Island, and Carolina and the formula to be incorporated almost two decades later in the charter granted to William Penn in 1681. They may have thought that since a substantial proportion of the populace of the colony was Dutch and consequently potentially subversive in view of the war with the United Provinces, to govern with the consent of an elected assembly was impractical.

Nicolls carried out the "conquest" of New Amsterdam with little difficulty. Despite the frigid reception the royal commissioners received in Boston, Governor John Winthrop and the authorities at Hartford amply supported the English expedition against New Netherlands. Governor Peter Stuyvesant was in no position to resist and accepted the terms of a capitulation arranged on 27 August 1664 at Manhattan. After receiving a promise of free trade with the Netherlands, the Dutch capitulated two days later. New Netherlands became New York. But for how long? Nicolls remained at Manhattan to establish proprietary rule, while Maverick and Cartwright set off to tour the New England colonies and Carr went off with a small force to reduce the Dutch on the Delaware.

The charter granted to James had included the lands to the east of the river, but for the territory along the western shore, where the Dutch and Swedish settlements—New Amstell, Fort Altena and Hoerenkill (Harlot's Creek)—were located, there were other claimants. Townsmen from New Haven had purchased lands from the local Indians. The proprietor of Maryland also had an interest inasmuch as under the terms of the charter granted to the baron Baltimore in 1632 the northern boundary of his colony was set at 40° north latitude. When Carr set off to take possession of the region, he carried instructions to hold the lands then occupied by the Dutch for the king of England. Local magistrates were placed in office subject to the authority of Nicolls at Manhattan. Technically his commission as governor of the duke of York's province did not extend to the settlements on the western shore of the Delaware Bay.[34]

From Manhattan Nicolls sought to justify to Clarendon the reduction of the settlements on the Delaware by Carr despite their not being included specifically in the duke's patent. The king's instructions were that no foreigners should be allowed to usurp the dominion of his territories. Moreover, if left unchecked, the Dutch on the Delaware might have become as great a threat as their compatriots at New Amsterdam. He urged Clarendon not to allow the Delaware villages to pass to Maryland. Indeed, he suggested that Baltimore had forfeited the patent to his own colony by allowing trade with the Dutch in violation of the acts of Parliament.

Nicolls's position in New York was precarious. While he was absent to inspect the situation on the Delaware, the soldiers of the garrison at New York, short of provisions and money, had mutinied. As Nicolls saw it, the needs of the duke's government and the garrison at New York must be met if they were to maintain themselves among the Dutch populace. A regular trade with England in appropriate merchandise was also essential to prevent Dutch merchants from Amsterdam dominating the commerce of the province. Nicolls feared the Dutch West India Company and the United Provinces would seek to recapture their lost colony. Of more immediate concern was the situation he found on Long Island. Despite all that he and Clarendon had been told in London— probably by John Scott—there were but fifteen "poor" villages scattered over an island 120 miles in length.

Nicolls had yet to settle with commissioners from Connecticut the conflict over boundaries, to verify land titles in the towns, and to establish laws for the polyglot population of the duke's province. The governor well realized his own limitation in such matters. Appreciating that "a good Lawyer will not leave Westminster Hall and his Golden fees for a little Poltry and Corne," he urged the lord chancellor to send out someone knowledgeable in the laws of England. In the interval he sent out requests to the governments of the other English colonies for transcripts of their legal codes. Thomas Ludwell, secretary of Virginia, in dispatching copies of the statutes of Virginia, warned, however, that some peculiar to the Old Dominion would not be appropriate for New York.[35]

Little material support for Nicolls came from London. Clarendon warned him that a squadron had left the Netherlands to raid the English colonies. The enemy might be expected to strike Barbados and then Virginia before reaching New York. The proprietor had himself spoken with several merchants in London who had promised to send a ship or two with supplies. Until they arrived, the royal duke depended on Nicolls to keep up the spirits and courage of the soldiers and the devotion of the people of the colony.[36]

In view of the war with Holland and the massing of a French force in Canada to invade the country of the Iroquois Indians of New York, Nicolls was dependent on the military support of the New England colonies, particularly Connecticut. It was best that he adopt a conciliatory stance in the negotiations with officials from Hartford over the boundaries between Connecticut and New York. Governor John Winthrop along with Nathan Gould (or Gold) and two of the leading residents of the towns on the eastern end of Long Island, John Howell of Southampton and John Young of Southold, met with Nicolls and his colleagues. The Connecticut men gave up their claim to the offshore islands. The commissioners for the duke, for their part, did not press for the Connecticut River as the eastern boundary of New York. Both sides then agreed that the line between the two colonies on the mainland should run along the Mamaroneck River about thirteen miles east of Westchester and then northward.[37] By these terms the five New Haven towns fell within the jurisdiction of Connecticut.

The agreement did not prove satisfactory to all parties. From London the duke of York looked upon this arrangement as only temporary. He later ignored it, instructing his deputies in America to press for all of the land east to the Connecticut River as specified in the charter from his brother. Others closer to the scene were also dissatisfied with the settlement. Howell and Young refused to sign, and Thomas Pell, the principal land speculator of Westchester, whose titles from the local Indians Nicolls regarded with skepticism, condemned the Connecticut representatives for having violated the terms of their charter. He threatened to appeal to the commissioners of the United Colonies, the Confederation of New England.[38]

The antagonism of the settlers in the English villages made governing difficult for Nicolls. Political practices on Long Island and in the colony in general varied. The greater part of Long Island east from Oyster Bay had once come within the jurisdiction of New Haven and Connecticut. In the towns located in this region the laws and procedures of the Puritan commonwealths had prevailed. Initially Nicolls attempted to placate the disgruntled leaders of these villages, men resentful over the failure to include them in Connecticut. He confirmed the local magistrates in office and promised fair treatment, equal to what was accorded in New England, with no taxes other than those already imposed by Connecticut and New Haven. In February 1665 he requested the townsmen who were rateable in the villages on Long Island and the English in Westchester to elect delegates to attend a meeting at Hempstead, where they could present all the records relating to town boundaries. This was a sensitive issue.

At the sessions held at Hempstead late in February 1665, thirty-four delegates—only nine of them Dutch—attended. Taking the initiative, the proprietary governor presented a frame of government and a code of civil and criminal law borrowed in part from those codes prevailing in the other colonies, particularly the New England provinces. An English lawyer, Mathias Nicolls—no relation to the governor—may well have had a hand in compiling this code, commonly known as the Duke's Laws. There was no provision for an elected assembly representing the freeholders in the towns. None was required in the charter issued by Charles II to his brother. The appointed governor, council, and local magistrates would administer law; rateables in each town would select a constable, and overseers would govern the villages. Although the proprietor had ordered religious liberty for all Christians, under the code promulgated by Nicolls each town was given the power to levy taxes for the support of a minister acceptable to the majority of ratepayers. This followed the procedure employed in the nearby Puritan provinces. To win support among the residents of the English towns, Nicolls used his power of patronage, appointing to office men from these communities.

The governor also had to provide local government for the Dutch. By the terms of the surrender negotiated with Stuyvesant, Nicolls had promised to continue in office for a time the officials in New Amsterdam. On 13 June 1665 on orders from the proprietor but over the objection of the burgomaster, Oloff van Cortlandt, Nicolls dissolved the old government and incorporated all of Manhattan as an English municipality. Instead of a burgomaster with four schepens and a schout nominated by the council and appointed by the director general of the province, New York City would have a mayor, five aldermen, and a sheriff named by the duke's governor. Nicolls chose the first set of municipal officers without calling on the incumbent Dutch officers for their nominations. Under Stuyvesant only one Englishman had sat on the municipal board; under Nicolls, initially four Englishmen and three Dutchmen held office, but the important posts went to the English.

The locus of power under the duke's regime was New York City, where under Nicolls and his successor after 1667, Colonel Francis Lovelace, a close connection existed between the provincial council and the municipality. The council with few exceptions reflected the dominance of the merchants of the city. Most influential were Mathias Nicolls, the lawyer appointed secretary of the province; Thomas Delaval, a customs official now raised to the post of receiver general; and Cornelius Steenwick, one of the few substantial merchants among the

Dutch inhabitants. Inasmuch as England and the United Provinces were at war three times within the third quarter of the seventeenth century, the relegation of the Dutch in New York to a lesser role during the administrations of Nicolls and Lovelace was not strange. The English mercantile community in the city during this decade was also prominent, given the failure of New Amsterdam to develop under the Dutch West India Company. The earliest adventurers in the Dutch town had sought profits from the West India trade rather than develop local resources, while officials of the company had viewed the colony merely as an outpost for plundering the Spanish empire. For them New Netherlands had been a place to make a modest fortune before returning to Europe.

The restrictive practices of the Dutch West India Company in Amsterdam had forced out of the transatlantic traffic the traders in the colony; consequently, New Netherlands had failed to develop a sizable class of substantial merchants. There were a few well-to-do Dutch families, the Cortlandts, the Philipses, and the Schuylers. These families along with the family of Stephen Delancey, a Huguenot refugee who arrived from London some years later, were to intermarry and form an elite among the Dutch, but one not divorced from the more recently arrived English.

For some years after the English conquest, Manhattan remained a commercial backwater, giving little promise of the great economic expansion it enjoyed in future decades. Dominated by Boston shipping, it was the home port of relatively few oceangoing vessels. While the Dutch merchants of New Netherlands had begun an export trade in flour, demand had suffered because of uneven quality.[39]

The tradesmen and merchants of the city were often at odds with the settlers elsewhere in the province because of economic and ethnic differences. While the Dutch were in the majority both in New York and Albany, the residents in the northern town made their living primarily from farming and the trade with the Indians in furs. In many sections of Long Island where the English dominated, the townsmen engaged in farming and whaling. They held economic and political grievances against the port and the provincial government centered at New York. The city retained the trading privileges and monopoly rights granted to New Amsterdam during the Dutch regime. It was the staple for the entire province. Goods brought into and shipped from the colony went through this one port.

Opposition to the provincial administration imposed by the proprietary duke was strongest in the Long Island towns previously under the jurisdiction of Connecticut and New Haven. The villagers objected to the oaths required by the proprietor, the failure to grant rights fully equal to those enjoyed in the local communities in New

England as Nicolls had once promised, and continued taxation by a provincial government in which the townsmen had no voice. In the spring of 1668 violence flared up in Southampton, Southhold, Easthampton, and other villages. The governor fined some of the offenders, removed constables and undersheriffs who had refused to carry out his orders, and through the court of assizes threatened action against towns whose patents the provincial government had not confirmed. The threat seemed effective, as one by one the towns acquiesced and submitted their patents for confirmation.[40]

During these critical years Nicolls had little support from England. He found himself unable to pay the soldiers of the garrison holding New York or the proprietary officials. Salaries alone came to two thousand pounds. The sum of one thousand pounds granted each year by the royal treasury for the troops was inadequate and payment irregular. Nicolls received little from the duke, who expected to realize profits from his proprietary. The governor contracted over eight thousand pounds in debts to administer the province by the time James yielded to his request to be relieved of his burden. His successor, who arrived in New York in March 1668 was Colonel Francis Lovelace. The new governor too was often left to his own resources. Two and a half years after he arrived in the colony he was forced to apologize to Williamson in Whitehall for not maintaining a frequent correspondence. The uncertainty of ships from England touching at New York made corresponding with royal or proprietary officials uncertain. When Nicolls left New York in August 1668, he sailed for England in a Dutch vessel![41]

Lovelace faced a chronic problem in meeting expenses. When the court of assizes in November 1669 issued a warrant to the sheriffs to levy a rate of one penny in the pound on all assessed property, the townsmen on Long Island protested sharply. Their complaints included economic matters, chiefly the prices set by merchants of the metropolis for produce and for imports as well as the monopoly granted New York City as the port facility of the province. They also demanded an assembly, a call Lovelace had no authority to meet, and reiterated this demand in 1670 when the court of assizes—attended by only a few justices—ordered a levy to raise money to repair Fort James. The townsmen protested against their loss of liberties and the taxes imposed without the consent of elected deputies, rhetorical protests now standard in English politics. Not only was the fort of no use to them, they claimed in a more pragmatic note, but they were unable to pay because of the high prices merchants of New York City were charging. Contending that their deeds had been invalidated and their titles to lands threatened, some of the eastern towns asked to be annexed to Connecticut or formed as a separate, free corporation.

The favored position enjoyed by New York City only heightened tensions. Nicolls and Lovelace—and Edmund Andros, who succeeded them—sought to stimulate the commercial development of the colony and thus to increase the revenue derived from duties on imports. Upgrading the quality of its agricultural exports—pork, beef, and flour—would stimulate demand in the West Indian markets. To ensure standards, regulations were issued for the slaughter of cattle and hogs, the packing of meat, and the milling of wheat. Butchers, millers, and packers in the city were licensed and their operations inspected. While these and other regulations ultimately enhanced the reputation of produce from the colony and stimulated the provincial export trade, initially they appeared to confer what some considered unfair privileges on the merchants and processors of New York City.[42]

There was little support among the English towns in the province when the proprietary government came under direct threat from outside forces. After only two years, Lovelace, in the face of the problems confronting him, had desired leave to return to England. There were rumors too, according to the Calvert family, that James, dissatisfied with the burden and expense of the colony, was unhappy and might be willing to sell the proprietary.[43]

For some time the proprietor of Maryland had been disputing with the governors of New York over the conquered territories on the lower Delaware River. Lovelace had incorporated the settlement at Newcastle as a bailiwick and had erected courts at Schuylkill and Upland (Chester), but these jurisdictions were challenged by officials of Maryland. Pending a final decision in London, and it did not come until 1685, the disputed region remained under the duke's officers at New York.[44]

At the outset of English rule at Manhattan the governor of New York had assumed that his jurisdiction extended to all the territory from New York Bay and the Hudson River west to the Delaware, the area subsequently to be known as New Jersey. By the grant from the sovereign, James possessed the property in the soil and the authority to make laws. In an effort to build up the English population, following the capitulation of the Dutch authorities at New Amsterdam, Governor Richard Nicolls had encouraged settlers, mainly from eastern Long Island and New England, to take up lands across the bay south and west of New York City. John Bayley and five associates received a grant for what later became Elizabethtown. The associates then disposed of a portion of their grant; one section went to men from Massachusetts who founded Woodbridge, the other to four New Hampshire colonists who established Piscataway. Nicolls also granted the Navesink, or Monmouth Patent, to a group of Baptists and Quakers from New England. They founded Middletown and Shrewsbury. Settlers from New Haven moved in to found Newark Township north of Elizabeth; and the Barbadians, William Sandford, John Berry, John Palmer, and Lewis Morris, purchased additional tracts of land. The patents issued by Nicolls, the governor of New York, had allowed a period of grace before quitrents were due. The amount of rent was not stipulated. Presumably it was to be negotiated later.

Unknown to Nicolls in New York, even before the expedition he had led against the Dutch had arrived in America, the duke of York on 24 June 1664 had turned over a portion of his proprietary—an area bounded by the Atlantic and the Hudson on the east and south, the Delaware River on the west—to his associates, Lord Berkeley and Sir George Carteret. Not until 29 November 1664 did James write to inform Nicolls in New York of the transfer. By the time the governor received the news, he had already disposed of some lands in New Jersey. The document from James granting "New Jersey" could convey only the title to the land. Charles II was the sovereign, and his brother had no right to delegate the power to rule, the prerogative of the sovereign. The deed from James could not empower Berkeley and Carteret to exercise governmental authority.[45]

Hoping for income from this windfall, Carteret and Berkeley sought to attract settlers to move to what they considered as their separate proprietary colony. On 10 February 1664/5, they issued "The Concessions and Agreement of the Lords Proprietors" of New Jersey, promising that all freemen sworn as subjects of the English king would not be disturbed in religion, provided they behaved peaceably and did not abuse this privilege by licentious behavior or breach of the peace. Under these proprietary concessions the freemen would elect twelve deputies to join with a governor and councilors appointed by the proprietors to form a general assembly empowered to pass laws.

Philip Carteret, a twenty-six year old cousin of the proprietor, received a commission as governor. The young Carteret arrived in New York Bay on 29 July 1665 accompanied by two assistants, John Bollan, designated secretary and register, and Robert Vauquellin, surveyor general of New Jersey. It was Bollan who showed Nicolls, the duke's governor at New York, a letter from Berkeley and Carteret announcing the grant from James. Nicolls was dismayed. The duke had granted away, he complained in writing home, an area of land more extensive and valuable than that he had retained. Moreover, the grant was prejudicial to New York. According to Nicolls's sources, John Scott, holding the duke responsible for his failure to obtain a grant and the governorship of Long Island, had contrived to bring Berkeley and Carteret into the scheme to limit the duke's territory in America. Nicolls proposed that Berkeley and Carteret be forced to give up New Jersey and accept an award of one hundred thousand acres of land on the lower Delaware. Nothing came of Nicolls's suggestion.[46] He left America; Philip Carteret remained.

The governor of New Jersey faced stiff opposition from the deputies elected from Middletown and Shrewsbury. Claiming the privileges in the town grants made them by Nicolls, they declined to take the oath of allegiance to the proprietary government, and the settlers in the various villages refused to pay taxes. The affairs of the proprietary government reached a crisis in the spring of 1672 over the refusal of the New Englanders in Elizabethtown to pay rents. The arrival of Captain James Carteret, the heir of the proprietor, gave the dissidents an opportunity to wrap their opposition to Governor Philip Carteret in the cloak of legality. Deputies from several of the towns met at Elizabeth on 4 May 1672 and elected James Carteret president of New Jersey. Issuing warrants in the name of the king, he denied the authority of his cousin at Bergen. Philip Carteret with the support of his councilors denounced these proceedings and took the issue to London.[47]

Their mission was successful. Sir George repudiated the actions of his son, and Charles II and his brother supported the proprietors against the claims of the dissident deputies at Elizabethtown that they were immune from the authority of the proprietary regime. To Governor Lovelace of New York James remonstrated that his grant to Carteret and Berkeley predated the patents issued by Nicolls to the New Englanders; consequently, "they are void in law." In a letter to John Berry, the deputy governor appointed by Philip Carteret, Charles II referred to New Jersey as a province "we have granted" to Sir George Carteret and Berkeley, the absolute proprietors. In fact, Charles II had not granted New Jersey to the two courtiers, but in this letter ordered Berry to call on all persons in the name of the king to obey the government established by them.

The proprietors then moved swiftly to consolidate their position by issuing a supplemental declaration. The governor and council might admit freemen to the colony, but no man was eligible to vote or to sit in the assembly who did not hold lands by patent from the proprietors. While they would not recognize title to property by virtue of any patent issued by Nicolls, the governor of New York, they were ready to hear the complaints of the townsmen if they sent over an agent to London.[48]

By 1672 there was a more immediate threat to proprietary, indeed, to English, rule on the Hudson and the Delaware. War—the third with the Dutch republic in twenty years—had broken out. Two squadrons of ships under Cornelis Evertsen and Jacob Binkes had left the Netherlands to cross the Atlantic. After raiding in the West Indies and along the Chesapeake, the Dutch men-of-war arrived off New York late in August and anchored off Sandy Hook. Dutch farmers who came out to meet the ships complained of abuses under the English and asked to be taken under the government of the States General of the Netherlands. Lovelace was not present, they informed the Dutch commander. He was off in Connecticut conferring with Governor John Winthrop. Moreover, Fort James was poorly garrisoned and ill equipped to defend the town: only sixty men and six guns.

When Evertsen landed six hundred troops, all but a few of the inhabitants of the town remained neutral. Having received word of the Dutch force, Lovelace hurried back to New York. On reaching Long Island he tried to turn out the militia of the English towns, but none answered his call. On 2 August the duke's officials surrendered on condition that the small garrison in the fort be allowed to leave. The conquerors then brought all of the territory inhabited by the Dutch on the mainland, Long Island, and the Delaware under their control.[49]

The corporate Puritan colonies of New England then intervened, not to assert the rights of the English king or his brother, but to press their own claims. The officials of Connecticut again asserted their right to the towns on the eastern end of Long Island, and the General Court of Massachusetts ordered its territory extended west to the Hudson River.

Proprietary government had few supporters among the English colonists; it had done little to strengthen the English dominion in America. Commanding no respect from the colonists and inspiring little awe, it further compounded the difficulties facing the royal authorities in bringing order to the nascent American settlements. The proprietaries founded in the decade after 1660 had been the result of the proclivity of Charles II to oblige individual favorites at the expense of rational administration. Once more in his reign, in 1681, the king followed his personal inclinations and granted to William Penn a charter for a proprietary colony. It was the last issued. A year later the Lords of Trade would recommend strongly that no such patents be granted. Later, early in the next century, the successors to the Lords of Trade were to launch an attack in Parliament against proprietaries and the corporate provinces, chartered colonies not under the immediate control of the crown. The immediate effect of the new proprietaries was further to fragment the English settlements and to increase the number of diverse ethnic and religious groups resident there as Scots, Quakers, French Huguenots, Baptists, and Welshmen responded to the opportunity to buy land and to enjoy religious toleration.

CHAPTER 8

The Chesapeake Colonies, 1660–74

THE CAROLINAS and the Jerseys were the latest of the English colonies in America, those on the Chesapeake among the earliest. But more than a generation of settlement had not appreciably fostered greater maturity or stability or lessened tensions in the Chesapeake plantations. Virginia, a royal colony, and Maryland, a proprietary province, suffered from problems inherent in their different political institutions, but in addition they also felt the effects of common, chronic economic maladies.

Nowhere in the English colonies in America were the weakness and instability of proprietary government more clearly revealed than in Maryland, one of the three provinces in North America sanctioned by the crown before the outbreak of the English Civil War. The founding of Maryland was the result of protracted efforts of Sir George Calvert, a servant of the early Stuart kings and a convert to the Church of Rome, to establish a haven for Roman Catholic gentlemen in America. He died before his vision was realized, but by royal patent on 20 June 1632, his son, Cecilius Calvert (1605–75), the second Baron Baltimore in the kingdom of Ireland, became the lord of a new province on the Chesapeake. The proprietor never visited, much less resided in, the colony, but lived instead in England. To manage the proprietary venture on the Chesapeake, Baltimore employed his relations as well as a small group of men, a trusted inner circle, who benefited from the salaries and fees accruing to them from the offices in the province awarded by their distant lord.

Religious tensions in England and rivalries on the Chesapeake disrupted the government established by the Calverts. Following the Roundhead victory in the Civil War, in 1651 the Council of State responded favorably to the pleas of William Claiborne and Richard Bennett to head an expedition to force the colonists in the Chesapeake provinces to accept the authority of the Puritan regime at Westminster. They reorganized government in the two colonies. In Virginia the royal governor, William Berkeley, retired to private life, with Bennett succeeding him and Claiborne next in authority. In neighboring Maryland, the Protestant governor, William Stone, had supported the Parliamentary cause, but Bennett and Claiborne overthrew his administration in the summer of 1654, appointing in his place a refugee from Virginia, William Fuller. A Puritan-dominated assembly in Maryland repealed the act granting toleration to Trinitarians, a statute enacted in 1649 during the proprietary regime. The Dissenters who had earlier fled to Maryland to escape persecution in Anglican Virginia turned on their benefactors. Armed conflict broke out; both sides then appealed to Cromwell.

After years of wrangling, a compromise had been effected through the efforts of an agent for Virginia, Edward Digges. The Dissenters of Maryland submitted to the authority of Baltimore, who in turn pardoned them for offenses they had committed. Baltimore then appointed, as his lieutenant in Maryland, Josias Fendall, a Protestant who had acted as the proprietor's representative in concluding the agreement.

The lord proprietor did not enjoy his province undisturbed for very long. In March 1659/60, with the complicity of a councilor, Thomas Gerrard, and a faction in the lower house of the assembly led by William Fuller, Fendall denounced the proprietor and agreed to govern under a commission from the local representatives. The Protestants, dominating the lower house, demanded that it be recognized as the highest court, independent of any other authority in the province. By this time Charles II had returned to Whitehall. In July orders were dispatched instructing the authorities in neighboring Virginia and all shipmasters trading to Maryland to aid in restoring Baltimore's authority.[1] The proprietor's half brother, Philip, already in the colony, was named governor. In November he proclaimed the king.

The dissident leaders were obliged to accept the restoration of both the monarch and the proprietor. Fendall, Gerrard, and Fuller were initially banished and their estates confiscated. But the proprietary regime later remitted these sentences and merely banned the rebels from holding office.[2]

Baltimore remained in England, ruling his proprietary through his immediate family in Maryland, with his son Charles Calvert as governor, and his brother Philip Calvert as chancellor, secretary, and receiver general. Close associates of the Calverts were named to the council. Despite the functioning of a lower house of assembly and country courts, power in Maryland lay with the proprietary family and a closed circle of their friends centered around Saint Mary's, the provincial capital. They determined all judicial and administrative appointments, controlled the distribution of land, rendered final decision in all judicial questions, and could block any measure passed in the lower house.

In the generation following the Restoration, the proprietor exhibited flagrant favoritism toward his relatives and fellow religionists among the gentry. Most of the men appointed to the council were (as far as their religion is known) Catholics. Fifteen of the twenty-five men Baltimore named to the council were related by blood and marriage to the proprietor's family. They occupied the highest places, while their friends and relatives held first claim to lesser posts in the counties. Some Protestants, William Digges, William Stevens, and Henry Taylor, entered the privileged circle, but they were particular friends of the Calverts or had married Calvert women. An advantageous marriage, a blood connection, and wealth could aid an aspiring planter, but the most important factor in elevating an ambitious man was appointment to office. Planters desiring the mark of distinction—ambitious settlers occupying lesser posts in the counties—bitterly resented the concentration of prestigious and lucrative positions in the small minority of Catholics, friends, and relatives of the proprietor.[3]

Upward social mobility within the colony and continued emigration of men to the Chesapeake from the ranks of the lesser gentry of England provided sufficient numbers of planters and traders to challenge the domination of the clique associated with the Calverts.

The population of Maryland grew rapidly in the middle years of the seventeenth century. One contemporary source placed it at about six thousand in 1663, nine thousand in 1667, and about fifteen thousand by 1675.[4] Before 1650 a few planters of means had dominated the government and economy of the province; the vast majority of people were servants, free laborers, sharecroppers, and tenants. Relatively few independent landowners were to be found. But for twenty years, beginning just before mid-century, the composition of the immigrants arriving in Maryland changed. While servants remained an important element— they now constituted about half of the total of those who arrived—there was an increase in the number of lesser gentry and merchants, persons with enough capital to establish plantations as soon as they arrived. The class of independent landowner in Maryland increased significantly.

The burgeoning population and the expansion of the settled area necessitated the creation of seven new units of local governments. Each of the new counties required sheriffs, burgesses, justices of the peace, and officers of the militia. The earliest arrivals had an advantage in securing these positions, posts which in England conferred status on the holders. In Baltimore, Dorchester, Somerset, and Cecil—new counties with a few hundred settlers each—some commoners would make the transition to the gentry class simply by filling local offices. Of the six men appointed justices of the peace when Charles County was erected in 1658, four had been servants, one could not write his name, and another was an obscure planter. Of the twelve other individuals named to the county court over the next three years, four had been servants, four others were illiterate, while three others were no more than small farmers. Only one, Thomas Stone, the son of a merchant and former governor, had the wealth, education, and status usually associated with such office. Four of the five men initially serving as sheriff were former servants. In Somerset County, of the two dozen men serving on the county court as sheriffs or assemblymen from 1665 to 1673, four could not write their names. None was wellborn or sharply distinguished from the mass of small farmers.[5]

At the upper levels of the social scale in frontier Maryland were men who could challenge the Calverts and their relations and friends. William Stone, Edward Lloyd, Robert Slye, and William Stevens had begun their careers on the Chesapeake as independent traders or factors for a family enterprise. By investing in land, practicing law, loaning money, or trading goods for tobacco, they had enlarged their fortunes. By English standards their wealth was not great, but a personal estate of fifteen hundred pounds was enough to set a man close to the top in Maryland. The small but significant change in the composition of the immigrant group at mid-seventeenth century and the progress made by former servants swelled the ranks of the independent planters, a group previously unimportant in the colony.

What had attracted the newcomers and what had made it possible for some poor men, assuming they managed to escape early death, as many did not, to establish themselves as landowners was the relatively high price tobacco commanded. Merchants seeking to increase tobacco production made credit for establishing new farms readily available. Easy credit, rising tobacco prices (at least up to about 1660), the low cost of land, and a rising demand made Maryland an attractive country for poor men and a colony of opportunity for the middle class. All free men, whether or not they owned land or headed a household, were allowed to vote during these years.

Two developments substantially altered political and economic conditions in Maryland.

Shortly after returning from a trip to England, where he had reported to the proprietor, Charles Calvert issued an order from this father to the sheriffs of the counties restricting the franchise to those with either fifty acres of land or a visible estate of forty pounds sterling. Men with short-term leaseholds could no longer vote for the burgesses returned from the counties. Political participation at the lower level was limited. In addition the economic circumstances which had allowed some men to rise to the status of independent landowner were changing. The rising flood of tobacco produced on the Chesapeake caused a drastic fall in prices and undermined the mechanism spurring economic growth.[6] To deal effectively with this problem required not only an appreciation of the nature of the difficulty but also cooperation by the planters and the proprietor, as well as by the settlers and government of nearby Virginia.

Maryland's neighbor on the Chesapeake also experienced political turmoil during the Civil War and the unsettled times following the execution of Charles I. Its governor had been William Berkeley, sent out to the colony by the king in 1641. In England the year before, Berkeley, a staunch Royalist, had charged that according to General Alexander Leslie, commander of the Scottish forces invading England, certain English peers had invited and encouraged the Scots to attack. The nobles had bluntly warned the king that if Berkeley were not able to make good his accusation, they would deal sharply with him.[7] Sent out of harm's way to Virginia, Berkeley remained a devout Royalist. Just as some Puritan divines saw in an Indian uprising in New England the Lord's wrath at his chosen people for having strayed, so Berkeley in later years on receiving news of the Great Fire of London concluded that "the cause of this Judgment was the anger of God for the murther of the blessed Martir the king."[8] In view of the execution of some of the king's supporters and Charles I himself, it was not surprising that after attempting to hold Virginia for the royal cause, Berkeley had decided to remain in the colony once the Commonwealth had been established in England.

During these years the gentry of the province had greatly expanded the jurisdiction of the county courts and their control over the membership of these boards and other key offices in the counties. Samuel Matthews, a local planter serving as governor, died at the close of 1659. By the following March, when the assembly met at Jamestown, the Protectorate government of Richard Cromwell in London had collapsed. Berkeley agreed to serve until a lawful commission should arrive from England. Less than three weeks following the return of Charles II to Whitehall, a royal warrant was issued for Berkeley to govern the Old Dominion.[9] Within a short time Berkeley left the Chesapeake for London on a mission on behalf of the assembly. As a consequence much of the Restoration political and religious settlement in Virginia was the work of local political leaders. They pushed through several acts for suppressing the contentious Quakers and the other more obstreperous Dissenters and for punishing individuals who disturbed divine service.

Across the Atlantic, Berkeley pleaded the colony's case against the act recently passed by the English Parliament prohibiting foreign ships from taking off colonial produce and requiring that tobacco be carried directly to England. Whatever else he was, Berkeley had become a leading planter in Virginia, a man with ideas and aims not greatly different from those of the other prominent men of the colony. In arguing their case in London, he attributed the low price recently received for tobacco to the system of marketing imposed by the new law.[10] Berkeley left London in 1662, having failed in his quest to modify the carrying code enacted by the Restoration Parliament.

The return of the royal governor to Virginia did not basically alter the political settlement of the colony as established during his absence in England.

In these years Virginia was primarily a colony of small farmers, many of them working the soil themselves. Some employed one or two white servants, but 60 or 65 percent of the planters had no slaves or indentured servants. Like Maryland, Virginia experienced a great increase in population, a rise brought on by a massive influx of rural poor from England. The importation of blacks had been negligible.[11] In roughly twenty years after 1640 the population had grown from about eight thousand inhabitants to about thirty-three thousand.

In response to the influx of people, local administration of government had grown. Between 1634 and 1668 the number of counties rose from eight to twenty as the area of settlement expanded from the region about Jamestown across the Chesapeake to the eastern shore and up the rivers toward the fall line. During the years when the colony consisted of only eight counties clustered about Jamestown, the governor, his council, and the elected burgesses had dealt with local affairs, but with the increase in the county units the General Assembly divided responsibility with the local boards. These county courts became important agencies of government concerned with administering of justice and implementing and enforcing statutes enacted by the General Assembly at Jamestown. The governor and his council now sat as an appellate court.

By 1660 it had become customary to regard the county court as a springboard for higher office. For the next fifteen years almost all men who sat in the House of Burgesses were at the same time local magistrates. The pool of qualified men was not large enough to fill the new posts created by the formation of almost a dozen new counties during these years, so that new arrivals in the colony might not, if they were competent, have to wait long before winning local appointment. But between 1668 and 1691, an interval when no new counties were established, the number of positions remained fixed, and competition for them intensified.

The House of Burgesses, consisting of the elected representatives from the counties, had yet to become an important body. It did not meet regularly, nor did it often initiate legislation. Laws dealing with overall provincial matters often merely paraphrased the instructions the crown sent to Governor Berkeley. Where statutes concerned local rather than colony-wide affairs, the impetus came from the justices on the county boards. In 1670 the right to vote was restricted to freeholders, thus disqualifiying those freemen who did not hold property, persons thought to have little concern in the country who had disrupted previous polls.[12]

At the apex of the political system were the councilors appointed in the name of the crown, usually at the recommendation of the royal governor. During Berkeley's second term of office forty-four men sat on the council. All possessed large tracts of land—the average in excess of seven thousand acres—most had considerable personal property, and half of them resided in the three counties adjacent to the provincial capital. The other twenty-two lived in thirteen of the remaining seventeen counties. The districts on the frontier and on the eastern shore were underrepresented. Kinship, friendship, and wealth were the keys to membership on the council, but almost all of the appointees had served an apprenticeship as county justices. Colonel Nicholas Spencer of Bedfordshire, England had come to the colony shortly before the Restoration as a merchant and settled in Westmoreland. By the favor of the governor's brother he became collector of the lower precinct of the Potomac River. Spencer felt confident of the governor's support as long as Berkeley lived, but as the governor was "ancient," the collector sought to secure his position in England should a successor, possibly Sir Henry Chicheley, put all places of profit up for sale.[13]

As the Royalist governor grew older, he seemed to have relied more heavily on his close friends, Philip and Thomas Ludwell, former neighbors from Somerset, England. When Berkeley died, Philip Ludwell married his widow, Frances Culpeper, the daughter of a Royalist who had lost his estate in the service of Charles I. Her cousin by marriage was the merchant-planter William Byrd.

Rivalry for influence, place, and profit marred the later years of Berkeley's second term, a situation exacerbated by the governor's excessive reliance on his close personal friends. Competition for certain offices—secretary, auditor, treasurer—especially prized for the fees accruing to the holders was strong.[14] At times Virginians had to contend with candidates in England.

The men associated with the governor in Virginia included the more recent arrivals. Younger sons of English mercantile families and the lesser gentry, they joined but did not displace the self-made men of lower origins who had risen during the formative decades of the colony. The newer arrivals rose to the top rather quickly in some cases. They often married the widows, daughters, and sisters of the leaders who had emerged earlier. Political power during Berkeley's second administration was divided between two centers, the governor's circle at Jamestown and the county courts, where the more substantial gentry dominated, controlling the selection of the burgesses and determining the appointment of justices and sheriffs by their nominations to the governor.

In continuing a system of plural officeholding at the local level, Berkeley was seeking not so much to reward friends or to bribe or corrupt critics as to follow a practice instituted by the local gentry. During the middle decades of the seventeenth century there had been ample opportunity for political advancement for the more successful of the established families and the newly arrived men of substance, but with the slackening of immigration there was no need to create new counties and offices for another twenty years. Continued upward mobility heightened competition as opportunities for political advancement narrowed. Factionalism and rivalry among families and cliques intensified.[15]

Calamities, both natural and man-made, further threatened the social and political fabric of Restoration Virginia. Storms and drought might destroy the planters' crops. Undesirable immigrants—contentious servants, convicts, "Newgaters"—might disrupt the peace of the community. Marauding Indians on the frontier and Dutch raiders on the Chesapeake coast were also a menace, not to be easily disposed of by legally barring them, as was the case with undesirable servants. During the Second Dutch war, fearing raids by a fleet then operating in the West Indies, Berkeley and his advisors had planned for a fort to be constructed some fifty miles up the James River, where the provincial government was located and the inhabitants sufficiently numerous to defend the position. One hundred thousand pounds of tobacco had been levied and workmen hired for the task when orders arrived from London to locate the fortification at Point Comfort on the coast. Berkeley and Ludwell protested that a post situated there would be difficult to man, ineffective; the approaches were so wide that guns would not be able to cover them. Virginia simply could not afford the expense of further fortifications unless higher duties were imposed on tobacco, "this vile weed." Two years later, when a fleet of five Dutch men-of-war sailed up the James, burned the king's frigate, and sank or carried off twenty English merchantmen, Berkeley was so discouraged he considered giving up his government.

To meet the cost of defense his administration ordered that all merchants and shipmasters before clearing their vessels give security by bills of exchange drawn on their correspondents in England to pay a duty of two shillings for every hogshead of tobacco carried out of the colony. The provincial regime even impressed carpenters from the merchantmen to cut timber for fortifications. Above all, the colony lacked large guns and ammunition.[16]

The financial resources of Virginia were further imperiled by the claims of a group of English proprietors who had benefited by the casual

largesse of Charles Stuart during his years of exile. Hoping to compensate loyal adherents for the loss of their forfeited estates and to
furnish them with a refuge in America, the prince while in exile in France
had granted what he thought was an unsettled portion of Virginia between the Rappahannock and the Potomac rivers to several followers,
including John and Thomas Culpeper, Sir John (later Baron) Berkeley,
and Henry, Lord Jermyn (later earl of Saint Albans).

The grantees had proprietary, but not governmental, rights in the
region to be known as the Northern Neck. They could sell or lease lands,
and they, not the crown or the government of Virginia, received rents
and other lawful reservations. The proprietors initially intended to divide
their holdings,[17] but the "unhappy" times of the Commonwealth and
Protectorate prevented them from exploiting the grant. Following the
Restoration, despite a royal letter directing officials of Virginia to aid the
assignees in securing their rights to the property, Sir William and the
councilors of Virginia simply suspended execution of the patent: Virginia
had already lost territory by the charter issued to Baltimore thirty years
before. His proprietary had become a haven for runaway servants, and
the same fate might befall the Northern Neck. Moreover, the king had
been misinformed, the Virginians argued: the territory had already been
settled before Charles had issued his grant to the Royalist courtiers.[18]

In the face of mounting difficulties, the governor seemed resolved to
solicit his own recall. Although the councilors supported Berkeley and
besought the king to continue the governor in office, Thomas Ludwell
was writing Arlington seeking the post should Sir William return to
England. It fell to Berkeley's cousin, Henry Norwood, to defend him at
Whitehall. The complaints against the governor centered on the raising
of two million pounds of tobacco for building forts, his failure to
prevent incursions by hostile savages, and his licensing favorites in the
Indian trade. Other charges related to alleged injustices prevailing in the
provincial courts, Berkeley's reputed greed and weakness, and the excessive influence of the councilors in the assembly.[19] These charges were
repeated against Berkeley and his colleagues in later years.

On the immediate issue of the Northern Neck, Berkeley and the
councilors at Jamestown lost out to the superior influence of the Royalist
courtiers. Saint Albans and the other assignees in May 1669 surrendered
their claim, but received a new patent, one recognizing the rights of
persons who had taken up land in the Northern Neck before 1661. The
next year the crown ordered the government of Virginia to assist the
proprietors in securing their dues.[20]

Worse news was to follow. Working through Arlington, a principal
secretary of state, Thomas, the second Lord Culpeper and eldest son of
an original proprietor and now a member of the Council for Foreign

Plantations, prevailed on the king to grant to Arlington and himself the rents from the soil and the regalities from the whole of Virginia for a period of thirty-one years. This lease was allegedly in compensation for a debt of twelve thousand pounds Charles owed to the deceased John, Lord Culpeper.

In an effort to block the grant the General Assembly of Virginia undertook to finance three agents in London, Francis Moryson, Thomas Ludwell, and Robert Smith. Sir William's brother-in-law, Alexander Culpeper, sounded out Arlington on possible terms for negotiation, but the talks broke down. The three agents from Virginia then took the issue to the king in council for what turned out to be a long suit, to be protracted over the course of three years. To finance the activities of the provincial lobbyists in London, the Virginia assembly imposed a tax of fifty pounds of tobacco per poll in the colony above all other taxes and laid additional charges on every legal action tried in the colonial courts.[21] This imposition figured prominently among the complaints against Berkeley's administration.

The meager financial resources of the provincial government, already strained, were thus diverted from the defense of the colony at a time when the planters of Virginia faced chronic economic depression and mounting debts.

From the start of tobacco cultivation in Virginia by Europeans down to the outbreak of the great wars with France in 1689, the marketing of Chesapeake tobacco was characterized by burgeoning production and expanding markets in the British Isles and in Europe as the habit of smoking spread. But as production outstripped demand and as new centers for the growth of cheap tobacco developed, prices fell,[22] a common phenomenon for commodities initially articles of luxury consumption once production is greatly expanded in response to high prices.

While some Chesapeake leaf was cheaper than the higher quality tobacco from the Spanish and Portuguese colonies, it was more expensive than the inferior tobacco grown in the Netherlands, Germany, Turkey, and Russia. Not all Chesapeake tobacco brought the same price or sold in the same markets. Sweet-scented, a bright, nutmeg-colored leaf, was smoked by the more discerning in England, while the best of the oronoco, tobacco almost gold in color but coarse and strong in flavor, was sent to Holland for distribution. The dark, inferior oronoco, unfit for the more discriminating markets, was sold to the Irish, the West Countrymen of England, or to the Barbadians. For fiscal and other reasons of state many of the European governments, the French monarchy included, restricted the importation of foreign tobacco, thus limiting the market open to Chesapeake leaf.[23]

Uncertain freights, especially in time of war, presented the planter with another problem. Sir William Berkeley in 1664 sounded out a correspondent in New York with a proposal to load a ship with tobacco, "for so few merchants are arrived hear that it is thought the warr is already begun." Merchantmen sailed from the English ports in early autumn and, because of the long delays in finding and loading cargoes among the rivers and creeks of the Chesapeake Bay, did not return to England until late the following spring. A reduction of the prolonged turnabout time for ships, standardized sizes for hogsheads, and tighter packing of tobacco would have reduced freight rates. These improvements did not come until the eighteenth century.[24]

The tobacco trade suffered from primitive marketing and pricing mechanisms. The most substantial of the tobacco producers purchased the crops of their smaller neighbors. Shipmasters or supercargoes who arrived each year spent the winter touring the Chesapeake region contracting for, collecting, and at times buying up cargoes. Some merchants in England maintained agents or partners—they could be planters—in the colony to purchase cargoes for them. Some planters preferred to sell their crops locally at prices known at the time of sale; others chose to retain title and to ship tobacco to England on consignment to some merchant, thus gambling on a higher price in Europe. Competition on the Chesapeake between Bristol men or buyers from the other outports and Londoners also influenced prices. Those planters with sufficient resources to enable them to choose among these alternatives were well aware that timing and the quality as well as the amount of tobacco produced in any one season would all bear on the prices they received. As Robert Anderson noted, when news reached England of "the shortness of our crop it must doubtless r[a]ise the tobacco to a good price." Abundant crops in excess of demand would have the opposite effect and, unfortunately for the planters, this was more often the case.[25]

For some planters on the Chesapeake it was easier to explain declining prices by the restrictions in marketing imposed by the Act of 1660 for Encouraging and Increasing Shipping. Many Virginians assumed that the exclusion of the Dutch gave a limited number of English middlemen an opportunity to depress prices arbitrarily and to impose excessive charges for various services. For a time during the unusual circumstances of the troubled and unsettled decade of the 1650s, the Dutch had played a role. With uncertain conditions prevailing, Chesapeake planters had availed themselves of Dutch shipping entering the capes. Following the Restoration, the passage of the Navigation Act of 1660, and the decline of prices, Sir William Berkeley on behalf of the Virginians publicly charged in England that the plight of the tobacco planters was the direct result of the collusion of forty English merchants, traders given an artificial monopoly by the late parliamentary statute. Later in the century another Virginian sarcastically sounded the same note in referring to "our poverty (our predominant Vertue)," one "prescribed us by our learned Physician[,] the merchants of London." These complaints did not reflect the real situation. In Bristol alone there were at least twenty-five men engaged in importing tobacco and between two hundred to three hundred in London, where the number of traders engaged in Chesapeake commerce had tripled between 1634 and 1677.[26] There was no evidence of collusion among them to fix prices.

Spokesmen for the Virginia planters probably never admitted the consequences of increasing output of tobacco upon prices.[27] Initially they sought to allow the Dutch into the carrying trade; failing that, to restrict production or to diversify the economy by adding more exotic crops. The colonists might produce silk, flax, hemp, and potash, with the initial capital investment to be borne by taxes on tobacco. Actually expanding production of more prosaic crops would have been more practical. The failure at this early date to diversify by turning to ordinary cereal grains, along with pork and beef, for the West Indian and Atlantic islands may have been a failure in entrepreneurship. In devoting themselves primarily to tobacco, the planters were following their short-range interests.

A greater emphasis on foodstuffs and less on tobacco would have enabled the Chesapeake planters to take advantage of the market opening up in the Caribbean and the increasing commitment in the islands to sugar cultivation, a market the New Englanders had already entered and one Englishmen on the Delaware and Hudson would exploit to establish the base for a prosperous agricultural economy. What was required of the planters on the Chesapeake was a shift in emphasis in crops already established, a change not requiring much capital. But not until the end of the century would the larger planters depart from what had become the traditional and, apparently for the short run, the safer system.[28]

During Berkeley's second administration attempts to resolve the chronic problem of overproduction of tobacco on the Chesapeake depended on agreement between the governments of Virginia and Maryland—difficult to achieve, much less to implement—and a consensus between the larger and the smaller tobacco importers as well as rival merchants in London and the western outports. Moreover, any proposal to decrease the volume of colonial tobacco shipped threatened to reduce the revenue of the proprietor and the English crown. To protect this source of royal income, by statute the planting of tobacco was prohibited in England and Ireland, a prohibition fully supported by both colonial planters and English importers.[29]

There was little agreement on the various proposals to limit the amount of tobacco produced and the conditions for carrying the crop to England. While in London, Berkeley in association with several planters and shipmasters proposed to the Privy Council late in August 1661 that no ships leave the Chesapeake for England with tobacco before 1 May. Presumably the arrival in colonial waters of all buyers and merchantmen for the season at roughly the same time would result in more uniform prices. Under such an arrangement, the merchantmen of the outports, having a shorter outgoing and return passage than the Londoners, would lose the advantage of returning with their cargo to the market sooner. The ministry took no action that year.[30] Spokesmen for the planters and local merchants in Virginia again petitioned in the spring of 1662 that no ships be allowed to leave the Chesapeake with tobacco before 1 May and no tobacco be planted after 1 June 1663. This "stint" would reduce the available supply of tobacco and allow the planters to begin producing other staples: silk, flax, hemp, pitch, and potash.

Charles II's council set aside a day, 20 June 1662, for all interested parties, planters, merchants, shippers, and the proprietor of Maryland to testify on the question. Evidently no agreement was possible.[31]

Later that summer Berkeley approached the Privy Council on the benefits of promoting silk, hemp, flax, and naval timber. It would free the mother country of the need to import from foreign sources. But the Virginians needed skilled workers to instruct them in the mysteries of such staples and a stock, that is, capital funds. Royal revenues from tobacco duties might provide the five hundred pounds needed.

The governor also joined with Sir Henry Chicheley, Edward Digges, and Richard Lee in pressing for the enforcement of the ban on tobacco production in England and on early sailings of the tobacco ships from the Chesapeake. Various shipmasters now entered their objections, particularly against the duty imposed by Berkeley's government on tobacco exported from the colony. They had been compelled to give heavy bond, a total of twelve thousand pounds, to pay the duty of two shillings on every hogshead, yet there was no fort erected in Virginia or other defenses for their vessels. Among the merchants in England there was no agreement on banning ships from leaving the Chesapeake before 1 May. About forty traders, including John Jeffreys, supported the proposal, but another forty-two objected, complaining that their ships would be tied up in colonial waters. Restricting the date of departure would result in cargoes arriving in England at about the same time, thus glutting the market.[32]

After conferring with the lord treasurer and the chancellor of the Exchequer, Berkeley departed for the Chesapeake, leaving Richard Lee to continue the struggle at Whitehall. Had it been the best of all possible worlds, the governor might have been able to carry out the instructions so cavalierly given him by the ministers of Charles II. Berkeley must encourage the planters to build towns on every river in the Old Dominion. In this the Virginians could have no better example than that of their neighbors to the north in Massachusetts, who in just a few years had created a wealthy and powerful province. The governor must also promote the production of silk, flax, hemp, pitch, and potash and appoint commissioners to treat with counterparts from Maryland on a program to restrain the planting of tobacco. They must also consider what rules might be appropriate on the schedule for ships to arrive and depart from the Chesapeake, the merchants and shipmasters in London having reached no decision on this question. Despite the complaints registered by the shipmasters, the crown confirmed the Virginia statute imposing a duty on tobacco carried from the colony and any other reasonable impost the assemblymen would think fit to levy for the support of the government. Finally, Berkeley must strictly enforce the Act of Navigation and encourage the growth of staples. The gain in customs accruing to the crown by strict enforcement of the Act to Encourage Shipping presumably would offset any loss from the diversification of the economy of the colony.

Berkeley found it impossible to implement these instructions. The poorer sort in the colony saw little need for towns, while the richer, whose financial support was essential if these shipping centers were to be established, held little attachment to the colony, he felt. They still looked back to England, hoping after making their fortunes on the Chesapeake to retire there. They expended no more in the colony than what was needed to permit them eventually to return to the mother country.

The governor was no less critical of the traders of England and their factors, who offered little assistance. Money from England, either from private sources or the royal revenue, was necessary to provide a capital stock to diversify the economy, yet the merchants of the metropolis had sent over "not one peck" of seed for planting hemp and flax. But Berkeley was not optimistic over the chances to diversify and to reduce the reliance on tobacco, because the merchants through their correspondents were actually working against any possible stint by offering higher prices than usual and by dispatching sufficient shipping to carry off the crop. Through their factors they were spreading the tale that they had opened a new vent, another market in the dominion of the czar of Muscovy.[33]

The governor met with success in one area. In the spring of 1663 commissioners from Maryland and Virginia reached an agreement to limit the growth of tobacco. But the pact was subject to ratification by the provincial legislatures, and the Maryland assembly, with the concurrence of governor Calvert, repudiated the arrangement on the grounds that no program would succeed unless it included the tobacco-producing regions of Albemarle, the Delaware, and the West Indies.

The agent for Virginia in London, Sir Henry Chicheley, and Alderman John Jeffreys protested the action of the Maryland legislature. They argued in Whitehall that it was essential to limit production, since the market was already so glutted and prices were so low as to render it impractical to pay customs. The solution, already approved in Virginia, was to regulate planting and the shipping schedules and promote the production of other commodities. Disagreeing sharply, the proprietor of Maryland questioned the contention of Jeffreys that the warehouses of the merchants were overstocked. Little was to be gained by regulating the schedule of shipping. The planters on the Chesapeake, he argued, must maintain their production to meet the cost of goods they imported from England. What the proprietor did not mention was that he himself derived an income from a duty on every hogshead of tobacco exported from Maryland.

Officials in England, particularly those on the Customs Board, were concerned with the adverse consequences to the royal revenue by any reduction in tobacco. While the Committee for Foreign Plantations agreed to a proposal designed to foster the production of pitch, hemp, and tar, the concession it recommended was slight: a waiver for a period of five years of the duties on naval stores imported from the Chesapeake. The committee agreed with Baltimore that it was unwise to place a stint on tobacco and to regulate the departures of the merchantmen from the colonies.[34]

War and disease intervened. Dutch marauders and plague kept the annual tobacco fleet in England in the fall of 1665. Stocks of tobacco in the colonies grew. Berkeley continued to press on Arlington and Clarendon the need for a crown subsidy to hire skilled workmen to promote the planting of hemp and silk and to encourage the planters to accept these alternatives. In 1666 commissioners from Maryland and Virginia reached an agreement to prohibit the planting of tobacco for a year, provided the governor and assembly of Albemarle concurred. There was already so much tobacco on hand on the Chesapeake it would require three years' shipping to take it off. The agreement depended on acceptance by the rank and file of the planters, or lacking that, the power of the provincial governments to enforce it. Both were doubtful. But they were not put to the test. In England, Lord Baltimore vetoed the program. Berkeley and the Virginians protested, but in vain.[35] Baltimore continued adamant against a political solution to the economic problems on the Chesapeake. A prohibition against planting would be effective only if the quantity of tobacco was appreciably reduced, but this would lessen the king's revenue. Moreover, restraining the crop of the poorer, smaller planters, men who were solely dependent on tobacco, would lead to unrest. Baltimore won his point. The crown dismissed the complaints of the government of Virginia.[36]

In 1667 nature and the Dutch again combined to accomplish what government had been unable to do. In the spring a hailstorm destroyed many of the tobacco seedlings, and excessive rains, high winds, and floods further reduced the crop. When Dutch raiders sailed up the James River, they burned the king's frigate and destroyed or captured twenty-nine merchantmen.

In the spring of 1668 rains again washed out many of the tobacco plants. That summer Berkeley wrote a correspondent: "This year we have little tobacco to spare from this place." But when the next crop was in, he promised to ship at least two hundred hogsheads, "if you send me word what you think it will yield me and if I find it will be above the market here." In conjunction with the council and the burgesses the governor continued to press Charles II for artisans to develop other staples. Could not the king's consuls at Naples and in Sicily recruit men skilled in the making of silk?[37] To the market for grain, beef, and pork, one the farmers in the other English colonies were finding so rewarding, the Virginians paid little attention.

War and natural calamity continued to plague the Chesapeake. Sickness struck the colonists in the winter of 1670. Many persons died of the gripes. Rainstorms again reduced the tobacco crop. The next year provisions were reported very "scarsy" in Virginia. The tobacco crop was also poor. The following year war again broke out with the United Provinces of the Netherlands. In July 1673 a Dutch fleet under Cornelis Evertsen sailed up the James River destroying and capturing merchantmen and carrying off more than nine thousand hogsheads of tobacco. The winter of 1675 was a hard one on the Chesapeake. Harvests had been poor the previous autumn, and squirrels had devoured much grain. Many of the cattle did not survive. Although New Englanders brought in provisions, they "exacted very much" for them. At the end of April 1675, the *Black Cock* of London returned from the Chesapeake with news that there had been a poor crop. Tobacco would be "very bad and scarce." Masters of merchantmen from England had not been able to find enough tobacco to make up return cargoes.[38]

Better than any other man in America, and for a longer time, Sir William Berkeley had served the crown of England. With a governor appointed by the king, Virginia had depended directly on the monarch at Whitehall, an arrangement officials in England regarded as most proper for the American colonies. Yet on the Chesapeake there existed an obvious conflict between the financial needs of the crown and the desire of the planters for higher prices for their tobacco. Ironically, it had been a proprietor, Lord Baltimore, who had prevailed over Berkeley at Whitehall to block any attempts to mandate a reduction in the volume of tobacco grown in the Chesapeake colonies. For proprietary Maryland and royal Virginia, their political and economic problems unresolved, upheaval and civil strife threatened.

The inroads of war, natural disasters, a depressed economy, and rising indebtedness as well as sustained high taxes all contributed to the mounting unrest in Virginia. The situation was ripe for ambitious men, frustrated by their inability to rise, and for demagogues. They had their counterparts in Westminster and Whitehall.

CHAPTER 9

Whitehall and Westminster, 1673–83
Years of Discord and Instability

Fʀᴏᴍ ᴀʟᴍᴏsᴛ ᴛʜᴇ ᴏɴsᴇᴛ of the rule of Charles II, men in America, especially the more zealous Puritans in New England, had expected the restored monarchy to collapse. As one year succeeded the next, Charles remained on the throne, although the king and his ministers seemed unable to exert their will on the plantations across the Atlantic. But during the second decade of the reign, a dramatic political crisis, a violent controversy directly touching religious fears and prejudices, threatened to topple the Stuarts and to bring about the victory of militant Protestantism.

Charles II proved to be a much more adept politician and a more tough-minded ruler than his father. He survived the hysteria raised by the Popish Plot and broke the attempt by the parliamentary opposition to control the throne by excluding his brother from the succession. During this extended crisis at home, king and ministers could devote little attention to affairs across the Atlantic. By the close of 1682, however, the monarchy seemed in a stronger position as a result of the reaction to the extremist tactics employed by the political opposition in and out of Parliament. In the interval New Jersey, New Hampshire, New York, Maryland, Albemarle, and Virginia all experienced either social upheaval or open rebellion. And in Boston, the commonwealthmen of Massachusetts remained as uncompromising as ever. To the north, the French of Canada, allied with Indians hostile to the English, were poised, ready to invade. Only then did Charles and his ministers attempt to impose some order. But time had almost run out; Charles had but a short time left to his life.

The frequent alterations in ministries during these years were somewhat disconcerting to the ubiquitous William Penn: "A Man may miss ye door ye Knocks by proxy; for Courts, too often like loose grounds, are perpetually to be watcht & markt."[1] Political life at Whitehall and Westminster continued to be marred by opportunism, cynicism, and fierce competition for power by men with few scruples, eager for the fruits of office.[2]

To explain, to exculpate, to justify their behavior, politicians fell back on religion, the defense of local and traditional rights, and above all on the threat from some enemy, external or domestic, the Sun King at Versailles or the pervasive, sinister Papists. In the early years of the reign resistance to religious toleration, at least for Dissenting Protestants, centered in the House of Commons, dominated by the Anglican gentry. On two occasions members had rejected attempts by Charles II to grant indulgences. In 1673 the House of Commons had imposed the Test Act. The holder of any office, civil or military, had to take the sacrament of the Lord's Supper according to the rite of the Church of England as well as to swear an oath against the Catholic doctrine of transubstantiation. Three years before, by the secret provisions of the Treaty of Dover concluded with Louis XIV, articles known only to the two Roman Catholic members of the cabal, Charles in exchange for French gold had given an empty promise, one he could not, and probably had not intended to, fulfill: to restore Roman Catholicism in England. Charles, as well as the men who later in the decade were to lead the opposition in Parliament in the name of resistance to Popery and tyranny, was not above using the French Catholic monarch for his own purposes. Leaders of the Parliamentary country party themselves accepted money from Louis XIV to enable them to bribe members to join the persecution of the Catholics and the anti-French minister, the earl of Danby, the man chosen by Charles to lead after the king broke with Shaftesbury. In return for French gold the leaders of the nascent Whig party forwarded the foreign policy of Louis XIV. The cynicism of these proceedings can "never have been surpassed, and seldom equalled."[3]

The Test Act forced Thomas Clifford from the Treasury and the duke of York from the Admiralty. Charles broke with Shaftesbury, Arlington, and the others of the cabal and turned to Sir Thomas Osborne, created earl of Danby in June 1674, to head the Treasury and to build a court party in Parliament. By exploiting every authorized source of royal revenue and economizing on every expenditure, Danby hoped to make the king independent of Parliament and France. But the parsimony he practiced crippled the crown's ability to carry out a program, military or political, in the American colonies. Although improved and more efficient administration as well as the increase in customs receipts resulting from a boom in trade enabled Charles to carry on his government in the latter years of his reign, any attempt to wage war would have made him again dependent on supplies voted by Parliament. The treaty with Louis XIV notwithstanding, the English court was increasingly concerned over the growing commercial and colonial threat of the Bourbon monarchy. The French were thought to have instigated the Indians of New England in their attacks against the

English; their activities in Newfoundland and in the West Indies raised anxieties.[4]

In 1678 Shaftesbury and the opposition leaders in Parliament put to good use one of the most sensational incidents of the reign, the so-called Popish Plot, in their effort to exclude the duke of York from the succession to the throne and to control the monarchy. The notorious John Scott of Long Island, now a self-promoted "colonel," was one agent they used to strike at James. An early victim of the plan to weaken the king and the duke of York was Samuel Pepys, a known associate of the royal duke and secretary to the Admiralty. During the hysteria of the Popish Plot, Scott, under the protection of Shaftesbury and the duke of Buckingham, testified before the House of Commons, accusing Pepys of betraying secrets to the French. Ultimately Pepys was able to clear his name, but the "revalations" against him served to implicate an associate of the duke and to promote a bill to exclude James from the succession.[5]

For months after the body of Sir Edmundbury Godfrey, the magistrate to whom Titus Oates had revealed the details of the purported Popish Plot, had been discovered, the opposition leaders whipped up sentiment against Catholics and the Stuarts. Rumors were circulated that the duke of York and even the king and his Portuguese queen were all privy to the murder of Godfrey in an attempt to suppress any revelation of the Catholic conspiracy and to subvert the government. The king himself was accused of consenting to the plot by his brother and the Papists to ruin "all good Protestant subjects and their religion." Men openly called the duke "the greatest traitor that ever was hatched" in England, a "Papist dog" and "cowardly rogue." Only the return of Shaftesbury and the Whig leaders to power would save the nation. To serve this end the Whigs formed a Green Ribbon Club, whose members met at the King's Head tavern—the symbolism could not have been lost—at the corner of Chancery Lane. Their "brisk boys" were not above using their swords to intimidate men. Shaftesbury's allies on the council of the City of London were busy organizing support for petitions,[6] tactics similar to those John Pym had used in 1641 to create and to focus public pressure on the monarch and his supporters.

With the opposition in the House of Commons threatening to impeach Danby, the king dismissed the lord treasurer and exiled his brother James to Scotland. On 21 April 1679 he commissioned a new Privy Council of thirty-three members, including the leaders of the opposition and Shaftesbury as lord president. Ostensibly the king's service would be carried on with the advice of the entire council rather than by a select committee or what one clerk of the council called "the private committee."[7] But the opposition leaders, having forced themselves upon the king, would not have the monarch's confidence or real power. To prevent passage of a bill excluding his brother from the succession, that summer Charles first prorogued and then dissolved Parliament. From Edinburgh the royal duke expressed the hope that all men both in and without Whitehall would now behave, especially when they saw that the king was resolved to support his friends and go without the assembly at Westminster for a while. [8]

Charles appointed young courtiers to office, among them Sidney Godolphin and Laurence Hyde, younger son of the late lord chancellor, Clarendon. Utilizing the skills of Charles Spencer, earl of Sunderland, the king was able to detach some of the leaders from the parliamentary opposition and to exploit differences among the others.

The struggle between Charles and Shaftesbury then shifted to the courts of justice. Would Shaftesbury and his followers control the judicial process as they had attempted to manipulate the legislative? Whoever controlled the sheriffs and the corporations of the municipalities would control juries and elections.

In London riotous and prolonged campaigning had secured the return of two republican sheriffs. The Whigs could now pack juries in the capital. Such a jury refused to indict Shaftesbury when, on orders of the crown, he had been sent to the Tower on 4 November 1681, accused of high treason. A few days later on the last day of the term at the Old Bailey, a jury packed by the Whig sheriffs refused to indict the Protestant earl. The verdict was greeted with noisy shouting by the common people. Bonfires were lighted in the streets. Passersby were forced to give money to sustain the fires and to slake the thirst of the crowd; they were compelled also to drink to the earl's health. The news was most welcome as well in Massachusetts.

Outside of London the attempts by the Whig leaders to reduce the legal process to an adjunct of party politics was not as successful. The tide began to turn in favor of the court when the king published the evidence against Shaftesbury. A reaction against the violent excesses of the Whigs had already set in among the more sedate citizens, and when James returned to London from his Scottish exile in May 1682, the fickle mob sang his praises. The discovery some months later of the Rye House Plot, a republican conspiracy to assassinate the king and his brother, further aided the Stuart cause. While Nonconformists denied their complicity, there was no doubt some of the conspirators had at one time moved in Cromwellian and Anabaptist circles. [9]

To the king the electoral process, disrupted by violence and fraud, and the magistracy, an essential bulwark against disorderly elections, must be secured for the crown. If London could be brought into line by vacating its charter, then action against other boroughs would follow. Inasmuch as nearly five-sixths of the members of the House of Commons sat for chartered boroughs, much more was at stake: a safe Parliament, one loyal to Charles and his government.

At the time, whether corporate charters could be forfeited was doubtful; the question might have been decided either way if left to an unhindered decision. But Charles obtained a favorable verdict against London by manipulating the appointment of judges to the Court of King's Bench and by considerable pressure behind the scenes. With the traditional tactics of patronage and influence now considered inadequate or uncertain, the king resorted to calling in and remodeling the charters of the municipal corporations to control the electoral process in the boroughs. This had been done before, shortly after the Restoration, on a much smaller scale to maintain men sympathetic to the government in control. The attack aroused surprisingly little opposition in 1682-83.[10]

Was there a deliberate, conscious effort on the part of Charles—one later followed by his brother—to subvert Parliament, to alter drastically the administration of government, and to employ the armed forces on a model then presumably employed by the French monarchy to rule England and the plantations across the Atlantic?[11] Or were such charges the fanciful rhetoric of opposition politics?

Sheer inefficiency and the conflict of various interest groups made a mockery of attempts by royal officials to govern. Nothing better illustrated the inability of the central government to cope with resistance on the local level than the repeated efforts over three decades to stamp out the cultivation of tobacco in the western and northern counties of England, planting outlawed by Parliament and deemed by royal officials prejudicial to the navigation of the nation, the revenue of the crown, and the economy of the foreign plantations. Local interests were too entrenched in Gloucester, Hereford, Warwick, York, and Lincoln.

The bureaucracy remained too small and administration too haphazard and lax to allow for a rapid development of an efficient government. In reply to an order to submit periodic, systematic accounts of English overseas trade, the Commissioners of Customs protested that the accounts for London for one year filled some thirteen hundred leaves of parchment; those for the outports and the colonies came to nearly as many more. Entries were made for each commodity imported in the order of the arrival of ships carrying them, so that the different classes of merchandise and their origin could not be readily ascertained. To analyze the trade for London would require the time and labor of half a dozen clerks working the year round and as many more for the outports. Even this might not be sufficient.[12]

Information needed for adequate administration was often lacking. Since some of the colonies originally had been private ventures, copies of their records never reached governmental files. When ministers left office, they did not draw a sharp distinction between state and private papers. They took important documents with them. The files were so broken that Sir Robert Southwell, the clerk of the Privy Council charged with drafting a report on New England, was forced to write to Clarendon's son to search his father's papers for documents relating to the royal commission sent to America fourteen years before. Not until the end of 1679 were the bundles of papers and books relating to the colonies lodged in the office of the Committee for Trade and Plantations and a list of them was left with a clerk of the council as a guide to the work of the councilors. Not all of the relevant or needed documents were available. In 1676 the last letter available to the Committee for Trade and Plantations from the governor of Virginia had been received five years before! Sir William Berkeley and Thomas Ludwell had been corresponding with the secretary of state; he kept their letters among his private papers.[13]

An effort was made during the later years of the reign of Charles II to make imperial administration more efficient. The bureaucracy was expanded, and lesser officials were given the task of collecting and maintaining records and assisting the privy councilors on the Committee for Trade and Plantations. But the most telling comment was that made by William Blathwayt, more than anyone else the man most familiar with what had occurred in the administration of the overseas possessions. After a quarter century he complained in 1700, "Ye Security of our Colonies & rend[e]ring them more usefull to England etc. are common places that have entertain'd us these many years but the means which are very plain have always been opposed or not prosecuted."[14]

Sheer inertia, ministers operating at cross purposes, and the varied interests of those seeking to influence governmental decisions made a mockery of any design to centralize the authority in the empire and to subject Englishmen in America to the wishes of men at Whitehall and Westminster.

Administration of overseas colonies and trade during the first half of the reign had been handicapped by the rapid succession of bloated boards, committees, and councils staffed by courtiers and merchants, one superimposed upon another. The fall of Shaftesbury from favor, the breakup of the cabal, the victory of Danby over Arlington, and the desire of the new treasurer to institute economy, as well as the weakness of a purely advisory body, all led in 1675 to the dissolution of the Council for Trade and Plantations and the creation of a standing committee of the Privy Council.[15]

Evidently the Lords for Plantation Affairs were not assiduous in attending to their duties. In May 1676 the number necessary for a quorum to transact matters was reduced to three. The requirement of five councilors impeded business![16] This was not an auspicious beginning for the Plantation Office.

Poor attendance and the death and retirement of men familiar with colonial affairs allowed the principal secretaries of state or the clerks of the council to play a greater role than previously. But neither Sir Joseph Williamson (1674–79), a knowledgeable man who had begun as a clerk in Arlington's office, nor Sir Henry Coventry (1672–80), had much standing. Moreover, their area of responsibility included not only colonial but also domestic and, especially, foreign questions. Williamson retired in February 1679 and Coventry in April 1680, to be succeeded by the very able earl of Sunderland, William Penn's "ancient and Noble" friend, and Sir Leoline Jenkins, a former judge in the High Court of Admiralty. Sunderland was the stronger of the two, and the affairs of the colonies went to him as they had to Coventry. Sunderland's vote on the Exclusion Bill in the House of Lords temporarily lost him the favor of the king. For a time he was replaced by an inept third-rater, Edward, Viscount Conway. Conway's term as a secretary of state was brief, but while he held office, he had as his undersecretary William Blathwayt.

Early in 1683 Sunderland was back in Whitehall as a principal secretary, a post he held for some years until James II dismissed him in October 1688 on the eve of the revolution. Sunderland concentrated on developing an efficient administration. With little aptitude himself for routine work, he left the day-to-day details to his undersecretary, William Bridgeman, and to Jenkins. It was during Sunderland's initial tenure in office that an order in council was issued requiring all governors overseas and their councils to maintain a journal of important occurrences, to be transmitted quarterly with their observations and opinions for the information of the Plantation Office, and it was under Blathwayt that this agency was first established as an organized department.[17]

William Blathwayt was one of a small group of lesser-ranking men, subordinates fairly low in the pecking order at Whitehall, who initially served as clerk or private secretary to some political figure and then followed their patrons as undersecretaries in the still largely undifferentiated apparatus of Stuart administration. The day-to-day work of government, if not decisions on policy and patronage, lay with them. They might influence the course of events by their suggestions, however. Engaged in similar tasks, they had common interests and outlooks. Thomas Povey, the merchant who had served the Protectorate as an advisor on overseas commerce and colonies and had survived the Restoration, had among his circle of friends Pepys; John Evelyn; Sir Robert Southwell, a senior clerk attending the Privy Council; and Joseph Williamson, Arlington's secretary. When the Lords of Trade replaced

Shaftesbury's advisory board, Southwell, a clerk on the regular establishment, was assigned specifically to attend the new committee on a permanent basis to maintain its correpondence and deal with day-to-day affairs. In need of an assistant, Southwell took on William Blathwayt, Povey's nephew. The young Blathwayt—he was under thirty at the time—was well grounded in modern languages and had some legal training and diplomatic experience.

Within a year the lords of the committee recognized Blathwayt's abilities by allowing him an annual salary of £150. When Southwell was out of town attending to private affairs in Ireland or Bristol, it was Blathwayt who kept him informed of what was happening at Whitehall. By the summer of 1678 Blathwayt had arrived: he had come to the attention of the king as one who had been suddenly cured of ague by a Doctor Taber, a physician Charles II held in esteem for his certain remedy for this fever. Charles sent over Taber, accompanied by Blathwayt, to Paris to minister to his niece, who had lain ill for some months. To the amazement of the French court Taber effected an immediate cure. Blathwayt, who was already noted for the pains he had taken in plantation business, now stood even higher with Charles II. Through the efforts of Southwell and his patron, James, first duke of Ormonde, he was now admitted to be sworn a clerk of the council extraordinary, that is, on a supplemental appropriation.[18]

Southwell and his assistant were instrumental in compiling, drafting, and perhaps formulating reports for the committee of the Privy Council. In 1677 Southwell sent Ormonde a sample of his work, laws for Jamaica, a model for the governor, Lord Carlisle, to establish, inasmuch as the assemblymen of the island "flew high and were in fair way of treading, in time, the footsteps of New England." Southwell was assigned to draft a representation censuring the Puritan government of Massachusetts. In the summer of 1678 he complained to his patron that he had been plunged into "a long and difficult task of unravelling all the business of New England from the beginning, in order to bring that unruly place into some better tune and a more apparent dependence on the Crown."[19]

Despite shifts in personnel Blathwayt remained a constant figure in plantation affairs. Appointed Charles II's envoy to Brandenburg in 1679, Southwell sold his clerkship to his son-in-law, Francis Gwyn, although he continued to advise his associates at the Plantation Office on colonial matters. As a clerk of the council in ordinary (that is, on the regular establishment), Gwyn nominally attended meetings of the Committee on Trade and Plantations, but after December 1679 Blathwayt, as secretary to the earl of Conway at the northern department, played the greater role. When Sunderland returned to office, he brought with him William Bridgeman, one of the most efficient bureaucrats of the age. Between them and Blathwayt there was little difference of opinion on colonial affairs, and only rarely did they interfere with the details of plantation business.[20]

With the counsel of Southwell, Blathwayt began systematically organizing the Plantation Office. His old chief had suggested he bring in as an assistant John Ellis. The agency was not held in high esteem by all. Ellis, "kept up in the air" by the duke of Ormonde's promise of a secretary's post in Ireland "as by the Loadstone of Mahomet[']s tomb," chose rather "to feed upon expectations" across the Irish channel "than to look like a clerk in the Plantation office." Then as later, junior boards were not highly esteemed. Blathwayt finally brought in his cousin, John Povey, to assist him. He particularly needed a "fit man for Abstract Work" and to bring the plantation laws into some order. By the spring of 1682 he was able to boast to Southwell that "we are grown bigger of late by many Volumes" bound methodically together; Povey "like St. Xtopher wades through the deep of that never failing stream."[21]

Blathwayt acquired other posts—auditor general of the plantation revenue and secretary at war, an office he purchased from Mathew Locke, a distant relative of Southwell. (The latter position was of special significance after William of Orange came to the throne of England in 1689. Deeply involved in leading a wartime coalition against Louis XIV, William III when on the Continent employed Blathwayt, because of his linguistic ability, as a third secretary of state.) Whatever other positions Blathwayt held in the decade after 1679, he continued as a clerk of the Committee for Trade and Plantations, constantly in attendance and at the center of business, but he was a subordinate seeking to influence higher-ranking ministers who made decisions on patronage and policy.

The work of Southwell and Blathwayt to render more efficient the administration of the Plantation Office reflected initially the decision made by the Lords of Trade to obtain more information from the colonies and to exercise more control over and through the governors appointed by the crown. The provincial executives were required before departing for their posts to take oaths and once there to communicate on a regular schedule. No governor appointed by the king was to leave his charge to return to England on any pretense whatsoever without first obtaining permission. Their power to appoint and to dismiss officials in the provinces was also circumscribed.[22] By such procedures, Whitehall hoped to render its control more certain.

The government of Charles II made a critical mistake, one prejudicing effective administration of the overseas colonies, by insisting on economy and financial stringency and passing on to the colonial regimes as much of the expense of government as possible. Given the

king's domestic political problems during the years of the Popish Plot
and the Exclusion Crisis with a House of Commons dominated by opposition leaders, the decision was understandable, but its long-range
consequences damaging. In 1679 the Privy Council ordered the lords of
trade and plantations to investigate how far the monetary allowances for
maintaining government in the colonies might be reduced without
prejudicing the king's service. Revenue was a tender subject.

The earl of Danby at the Treasury made every effort to cut down
expenditures and to exploit sources of income, including funds from the
plantations. From Thomas, Lord Culpeper, the treasurer received a
scheme for increasing the king's income from colonial produce. It was
potentially explosive in its political and constitutional implications, as it
aimed at lessening the king's financial dependence on Parliament.
Culpeper declared himself convinced that the monarch was seized "Jure
Coronae of an absolute right of property" in all the plantations in the
same manner as he held Dunkirk and Tangier and as former kings held
territories beyond the seas, without any dependence on the Lords and
Commons of England. While the monarch could not raise taxes in the
colonies without the consent of the assemblies there, with the consent of
the elected representatives of the planters he might, if the Parliament of
England continued reluctant to support his government, impose duties
on sugar, tobacco, and other commodities exported from the plantations. The planters would have liberty to seek the best immediate
market without the restriction to employ English vessels and to pay
customs in England. Parliamentary acts of trade and navigation would
be ignored. Charles should in no way allow or permit the legislature of
England "to intermeddle" with the governance of the colonies.[23]

Under the provisions of a law enacted in Virginia, a duty of two
shillings per hogshead of tobacco exported from the colony was imposed
for the support of the provincial government. The statute carried a
provision that the money raised was not to be used without the approval
of the assembly. When Culpeper arrived at Jamestown to take up his
duties as governor, he had with him the draft of a bill prepared at the
Plantation Office at Whitehall for continuing this duty under the king's
name and without the restraining clause.[24]

At the same time, the king's ministers sought to reduce the expenses
in America and the West Indies chargeable to the crown. In June 1679
shortly before Charles dissolved Parliament, the Privy Council approved
a civil and military establishment for Barbados, Jamaica, the Leeward
Islands, New York, and Virginia. Given the magnitude of the task, the
sums agreed upon were trifling. The royal treasury would nominally
expend £800 annually for the governor but no other official in Barbados;
£1,000, £600, and £100 each for the governor, his deputy, and the major

general of the forces on Jamaica. Just under £4,000 went for the upkeep of the forts on the island and two companies of soldiers. For the Leeward Islands £700 was allowed the governor, and £2,778 was allowed two companies of troops. Another £1,000 went to maintain the fort and garrison in New York. For Virginia, which had recently experienced a large-scale rebellion and a civil war £1,000 was allocated for the governor, £600 for the lieutenant governor, and £300 for the major general, in addition to £600 for fortifications, £3,327 for two companies of troops, and £371 for an engineer to supervise the construction of military fortifications and for a gunsmith and two mates. Evidently it cost more to save men's souls than to heal their bodies; £121 was allocated for a chaplain, only £91 for a military surgeon. The grand total came to £17,517 annually! The first British empire was being run on the cheap. It was with good reason Blathwayt later complained, "You cannot but known under how many keys our Excheq[ue]r here is kept."[25]

To ensure maximum returns, the Treasury appointed Blathwayt auditor general of the king's revenue in the plantations, and the committee of the council imposed procedures for collecting and accounting. The Commissioners of the Customs must report periodically on all commodities imported and exported as well as on the ships carrying them and their destinations, information supplied by naval officers in the colonies appointed under the Great Seal of England.

Ironically, there was resistance in England to these procedures. The Commissioners of Customs complained that, with the limited staff available to them, they could not easily comply. To compile the desired information for one year entailed going through roughly twenty-five hundred leaves of records for London and the outports by a dozen or so clerks. After submitting an initial account, the Customs Board expressed the hope that the Lords of Trade would not expect them to continue with such troublesome and expensive reports. The last account took the clerks three months to prepare and put all other business in arrears. More assistance must be allowed if such compilations were to be regularly required. The Customs Board received little sympathy. The Privy Council ordered the commissioners without any further excuse or delay to furnish the returns in the future as required.[26]

The drive to reduce expenses and to squeeze every last penny from the sanctioned sources of revenue led to renewed efforts to enforce the acts of trade and navigation. Farmers in the western and northern counties of England in violation of parliamentary statute had continued to plant tobacco, thus reducing the market in England for imported colonial leaf, which paid customs duties to the crown. Repeatedly, the king in council issued warrants to the surveyor general of the Customs and to the lords lieutenant in the western and northern counties of

England to put down illicit tobacco planting.[27] Evidently local officials were not complying. Enforcement of the navigation code even in the royal colonies in America seemed haphazard, subject to various interpretations. Jurisdiction in the plantations had been entrusted to the governors, but under the provisions of the Act of 1673 for Better Securing the Plantation Trade, the collection of duties paid in America fell to officials of the Customs Board.

Administrative and enforcement procedures were haphazard, if not chaotic. In the fall of 1675 the customs commissioners had to admit that they could not tell who in America had authority to administer the requisite oaths to the governors to enforce the acts of navigation. Few of the officials in the plantations had returned the bonds required of ships arriving in the colonial ports. To complicate further the situation, the meaning of the laws was not certain even to officials in England. A particular problem had arisen relating to New England vessels engaged in the carrying trade. If a shipmaster arrived in a colony to take on tobacco but had not given bond to return enumerated tobacco to England yet paid the one penny per pound, was he exempted from posting bond and free to carry tobacco to any port? In the opinion of Sir William Jones, the attorney general, he was not. Colonial vessels taking off tobacco from the colonies must pay the duty of one penny and also give bond to carry their cargo to an English port. They could not avoid the remaining duty in England by sailing directly for Europe.[28]

Ships bound for the colonies from England, as the customs commissioners appreciated, usually carried foreign items imported from Europe. Half of the customs they paid on entry remained to the crown when they were reexported. The Act for the Encouragement of Trade passed in 1663 prohibited carrying commodities from Europe to the colonies except when shipped via England. Given the limited resources of the New England merchants and the size of their ships, the volume of their direct trade with European ports could not have been very great. Nonetheless, certain groups protested against this traffic. As viewed by the ministers of the crown, this law, often called the Staple Act, did not create a monopoly for the merchants and manufacturers of England in supplying the colonies with goods, but required routing commodities from Europe to the colonies through England.[29]

For the king's officers what mattered was revenue and the employment of national shipping; for certain English merchants and artisans it was a question of rivals undermining their business.

Among these protesting the illicit direct trade between America and Europe were the mercers and silkweavers of London. At one time silks and "stuffs" made in England, when out of fashion, had been sent to Ireland, evidently a less discriminating market, but this trade had been disrupted after the Restoration by the ban on importing Irish cattle to England. More recently, the mercers complained in the spring of 1676, New Englanders contrary to law had been carrying silks and other textiles as well as brandy, oil, and refined sugar directly from France and Italy to the colonies.

Twenty-eight other London business men—middlemen in the import and export trades—added their protests. Of late the New Englanders were trafficking directly with Europe and encouraging "strangers," that is, foreigners, to come to the colonies. By avoiding the payment of customs duties the New Englanders undersold the English merchants and deprived the crown of revenue. Some merchants in London with correspondents in Boston—John Wyborne and William Hawes at Tower Hill, John Harwood at Mile End Green, Philip French of Canning Street, and others who could be found at the Exchange—should be called in, they suggested, and questioned at the Plantation Office. They could testify whether or not New England vessels had gone directly to France, Holland, Spain, Scotland, and Hamburg with sugar, logwood, and tobacco and returned to America with French and Spanish brandy, silks, ironware, and other manufactures. On 24 April 1676 traders dealing with New England were summoned, one by one; some were "shy" to "unfold the mystery," others pretended ignorance, but there were those who declared plainly that the charges were true. The New Englanders were carrying staples to European ports to be exchanged for manufactures sold in America at some 20 percent less than English merchants observing the law could sell their wares.[30]

At this point the lords of the Committee for Trade and Plantations concluded there was nothing to be gained in punishing past transgressions, but resolved for the future to recommend that royal officials be settled in New England to collect customs and oversee the enforcement of the acts of trade. They did not suggest the use of military forces in America. Should the Bay Colony refuse to admit royal customs officials, the king's ships could interdict her trade.[31]

The attempt to install officers of the royal customs service in Massachusetts initiated a long, drawn-out contest with the commonwealthmen of the Bay Colony. The treatment meted out to the king's collector, Edward Randolph, left little doubt that the heirs to the founders of the Puritan commonwealth would brook no interference. By 1682 it was clear also that the enforcement of the acts of trade and navigation was weakest in the chartered colonies, including the proprietary ventures, those provinces not directly under the crown (that is, where the governors were not appointed by the king). Indeed, the last proprietary charter was issued in 1681 to William Penn, but the Quaker was a personal friend of the king and his brother and Sunderland. The next year in response to a petition from the earl of Doncaster and Dalkeith for a proprietary grant for colonies in Florida and Guiana and a request from Robert Barclay for confirmation of East New Jersey to its proprietors, the Lords of Trade concluded that it was unwise to constitute any new proprietary in America. The king ought not to grant any further powers which might render the plantations less dependent on the crown.[32]

After more than a decade during which the commonwealthmen of Massachusetts had refused to recognize the claims of the crown or to accept any supervision, Charles and his ministers in 1683 finally decided to institute legal proceedings to vacate the charter of the Bay Colony. Did they plan, as some men accused the king and his brother, James, of a plot to alter fundamentally the political structure of the overseas plantations? Was a trial against the charter of the Bermuda Company in 1681 a test case, a preamble to an attack on Massachusetts Bay and the other corporate colonies? Was an attempt to impose on Jamaica a constitutional arrangement comparable to Ireland under Poynings Law merely the first manifestation of a concerted drive to do away with representative government for Englishmen in the colonies?[33] A detailed examination of the legal contest over the Bermuda patent, a farcical episode, showed that the trial at times was close to collapse, in part due to lack of interest by the court, and that Charles II finally acquired the island as a royal colony "in a fit of absence of mind."[34]

From a constitutional viewpoint, an element of considerable weight with the ministers of state, Jamaica, like Ireland, might not fall into the same category as other plantations. It was conquered territory, taken from Spain, and not an "uninhabited" land initially settled by English subjects. In November 1677 the lords of the Committee for Trade and Plantations had recommended that, as was the case in Ireland, no laws be passed in Jamaica but those proposed to the Privy Council in England. But at the next meeting of the legislature in Jamaica the assembly declared itself opposed to the "new Constitution"; Charles Howard, earl of Carlisle, the governor, consequently advised the Privy Council to give up the new frame of government as distasteful to the planters and impractical to implement because of the great distance separating the island and Whitehall. In June 1680 the privy councilors put the question to the crown law officers and the royal judges: were the Jamaicans entitled to the laws of England, or could they be ruled only by royal proclamation, Jamaica being a conquered country and all laws formerly settled by legislative authority now being expired? The legal authorities declined to give an answer. In October several merchants and planters in London presented a petition praying for the restoration of legislative authority. The royal government pursued the matter no further. On 3 November 1680 the Privy Council passed a commission enabling Carlisle to call an assembly to enact laws as before. The project to govern Jamaica directly from Whitehall was dead by the end of 1680.[35]

This inconstancy, this timidity, was not untypical. Early in the reign royal commissioners had traveled to America in an attempt to resolve outstanding disputes. After two years they had achieved little in New England. At that time the monarchy had been too weak to impose its will by force. Indeed, it had thought it necessary to call on the Dissenter governments in New England to aid New York against the French of Canada. Little had changed since 1667. War with the Dutch, hysteria over the Popish Plot, a crisis with Parliament over the proposal to exclude James from the succession to the throne, the king's need for money, inadequate information over the state of affairs in America, a bureaucracy too small for the task assigned it in the administration of plantation affairs, and above all, lack of will had combined to allow matters to drift.

Finally, after twenty years the court would move against the commonwealthmen of the Bay Colony. The decision to proceed against Massachusetts grew out of the determined insistence of the Puritan faction not to recognize any royal authority over the Bay Colony. By coincidence, during 1684 several disparate incidents in the southern proprietary colonies threatened the royal customs revenue. Although events in Carolina and Maryland as early as 1677 and 1681 had given the ministers of the crown an opportunity to act against the charters, they had taken no action at these early dates. The government of Charles II had no overall plan; it reacted to disparate events as they occurred in the individual American colonies.

CHAPTER 10

Virginia, 1674–84
"The troubled waters of popular Discontents"

VIEWED FROM America, the confused scene in London offered little prospect for political stability. The New Englanders were well content with the situation, according to the Royalist governor of Virginia; they were openly predicting that civil war would once more rack the mother country.[1] Ironically, Virginia herself was to be torn by internecine strife and open rebellion, both seeming to call for direct English intervention. The colony suffered from certain chronic dilemmas, difficulties aggravated by new problems in the last quarter of the seventeenth century. All contributed to heightened tension and discontent, thus creating an explosive situation.

Class animosities were evident. In 1670 the right to vote had been limited to freeholders and house keepers who were rateable. Men without land were considered to have little permanent interest in the country and were thought to have been responsible for previous tumults at local elections. One magnate, reflecting the resentment held against the mass of servants—mostly young unmarried men—coming into the colony, referred to them as "the Rabble of which sort this country chiefly consists, wee serving but as a sinke to drayn Engl[an]d of her filth and venom."[2]

Competition among the local gentry at the upper level of society had intensified in recent years, as the provincial regime had created only three new counties. The most prominent, the most successful among them found their gratification on the governor's council. But these desirable posts had not been awarded without discrimination. Half of the forty-four men appointed to the council between 1660 and 1676 came from just three counties, Charles City, James City, and York, clustered about the provincial capital. Four of the men for whom Berkeley secured appointments were his relatives, another eight his close friends. Among these were Thomas Ludwell, secretary, and Nathaniel Bacon, "a most worthy person" of a "very good family in England," appointed provincial auditor.[3]

As Sir William grew older, he seemed to have relied on his close friends, a tendency which might have deepened divisions in the provincial capital. Among those hostile to Berkeley were Richard Lawrence, William Drummond, and Giles Bland. A graduate of Oxford, Lawrence was said to have had no visible means of support, but lived in Jamestown with a black female slave. Drummond, a Scot and former governor of Albemarle, was well off. Bland was the son of Sarah Green, daughter of a former English member of Parliament, and John Bland, a London merchant with commercial connections in Spain and Tangier and property in Virginia. Giles, newly commissioned a royal collector of customs, had come to America to manage the family holdings. Soon after, a squabble broke out over the Bland lands.

This legal quarrel may have been the cause of a bitter dispute between Giles and Thomas Ludwell, the provincial secretary. Both men had been drinking heavily when an altercation occurred. After an exchange of verbal insults, Bland reportedly called Ludwell "pittifull fellow, Puppy, and Son of a whore." The two exchanged gloves, a challenge to duel. The next day the hotheaded Bland hastened to the spot appointed for the encounter, but not finding Ludwell, he nailed the secretary's glove on the door of the statehouse along with an insulting message: the owner of the glove was a "son of a whore, Mechanic fellow, puppy, and a coward." Berkeley and the other councilors ordered the young man to apologize, but Bland took the offensive, alleging he was being prevented from executing his office of collector of the king's customs by the threats of the governor. He held himself accountable to the Customs Board in London, and to no others.

In the spring of 1676 Bland took his charges to his father-in-law, Thomas Povey, and to Joseph Williamson, the secretary of state: he found matters so confused in Virginia that if corrective actions were not taken immediately, the annual revenue of one hundred thousand pounds Virginia afforded the king would be jeopardized. Berkeley and his clique were oppressing the colonists and neglecting to take adequate measures for their defense, so much so that a number of them had volunteered to band together. They were led by "persons of quality," including one Nathaniel Bacon, a recent immigrant related to the councilor of the same name. According to the collector, Virginians were complaining of heavy and unequal taxes, with the poorer sort paying as much by the poll tax as planters with twenty thousand acres of land. Moreover, the charges for representative government, the cost of sending two burgesses to Jamestown, came to five hundred pounds of tobacco daily for each county, although many of the counties were so sparsely settled as to have not even four hundred tithables.[4]

In London before the Lords of Trade, Thomas Ludwell and two other provincial agents, Francis Moryson and Daniel Parks, attempted to refute the "dirt" thrown upon the "whole Government" of the colony. The Blands were forced to retract the "unadvised and offensive expressions" contained in the petition they had submitted.[5] These charges were not new. For some years the supporters of Berkeley on the Virginia council, branding his opponents as merely ill-affected, vexatious persons, had defended the governor: in ruling the colony for nearly three decades with prudence and justice, Berkeley had gained the love and reverence of the inhabitants.[6]

Regardless of the sentiments Virginians held for Berkeley, many of the difficulties confronting them were clearly not of the governor's doing. In addition to chronic, long-standing problems, an infestation of squirrels and bad weather had destroyed crops. Prices received by the planters for tobacco were generally low, while taxes to meet the needs of the provincial government were high, particularly after 1669. Many of the smaller planters were in debt, some barely able to subsist. Most men in the colony probably never appreciated the consequences of over-production of inferior tobacco on prices or the reasons why the regime at Jamestown found it necessary to levy taxes. The shortcomings of the provincial government in fending off threats to the colony were more evident to them. A chronically depressed economy, natural disasters, and mounting debts in conjunction with what seemed to be expensive, yet inept, government at Jamestown provided fertile ground for ambitious men discontented with their role and the more ignorant rank and file barely able to scrape a living from the soil.[7]

For some years the government had levied heavy taxes to defray the cost of constructing fortifications to protect the colony against attack by hostile Indians and to fend off Dutch raiders, and to contest the grant of rents from the soil made by the king to Arlington and Thomas Culpeper. Its efforts had met with little success, so it seemed, by the spring of 1676. Berkeley and his council had argued after the last Dutch raid in 1673 that the Virginians were simply too poor to provide adequately for the defense of the colony. They had not arms enough to outfit even one in ten men raised in the militia.[8] To defray the charges of the agency in London contesting the grants to Arlington and Culpeper, the government of Virginia imposed an additional levy of fifty pounds of tobacco on every poll. In 1675, after Thomas Culpeper was named governor-designate of Virginia to take effect on the death of Sir William Berkeley, Thomas Ludwell and his colleagues petitioned the crown for a patent to allow Virginia to purchase the proprietary rights of Culpeper and Arlington. The Privy Council approved this request but, for some reason not known to the agents or even to Sir Robert Southwell, the senior clerk of the council, took no action despite an order from the king to the attorney general and the solicitor general to prepare a patent. Early in the following spring the Virginia agents again petitioned for an order to the lord chancellor to pass the patent. The king in council agreed on 19 April, but less than two months later the proceedings were brought to a halt.[9]

News had come that Virginia was racked by war with neighboring Indians and civil strife among the white settlers.

A major conflict had broken out the previous year between the New England colonies and the northern tribes. The war had spilled over onto the Chesapeake frontier, the Susequehannocks having murdered some settlers in Maryland on the adjoining frontiers. To meet the threat it was necessary to levy another fifty pounds of tobacco on every poll. The assembly had called out a force of five hundred men to occupy posts on the heads of the rivers and to patrol against incursions by hostile Indians. Ammunition was in short supply, however.

Berkeley's regime was in a precarious position. As the governor confided to Ludwell in London, "secret villains" were fomenting mutiny, telling the planters the high taxes would bring no benefits.

To meet the threat of belligerent natives, Berkeley, the few councilors resident about Jamestown, and the burgesses adopted a policy of static defense, one distinguishing between friendly and hostile Indians and relying on the resident tribesmen as a buffer against raiding warriors. Berkeley entrusted the regularly appointed militia officers—the councilors were colonels of militia in their respective counties—to carry out this program. To prevent potentially hostile tribesmen from obtaining supplies, the government restricted the traffic in guns and ammunition. Some men charged that Berkeley was conspiring to engross the trade.

Among those engaged in the Indian trade were William Byrd and his partner, Nathaniel Bacon, the younger, both cousins of the governor's wife, Frances Culpeper. Bacon had been sent out to Virginia in the summer of 1674 by his father, a well-to-do gentleman of Suffolk, in the hope that in the colony the extravagant and unbridled young man might be able to redeem himself. With his family connections and financing, Bacon secured an appointment to the provincial council and an estate along the upper James River. In the spring of 1676 he and his trading partner Byrd, along with two other planters, James Crews and Henry Isham, paid a visit to the men who had gathered to go out against the Indians. Crews may have primed the volunteers to appeal to the young councilor. Crying out, "A Bacon! A Bacon!" they prevailed on him to assume the lead in pressing an aggressive campaign against all Indians. Supporting this movement, Giles Bland wrote to Whitehall to reinforce the grievances and charges raised by the discontented element, among them that Berkeley's administration was inept and ineffective in defense and had levied heavy and unfair poll taxes. By this levy the poor sort paid as much as the grandees.[10]

Bacon and his followers launched a campaign against the friendly Pamunkeys and Occaneechees whom Berkeley had hoped to use as a buffer against the marauding Susquehannocks. "How shall wee know o[ur] enemys from our friends, are not ye Indians all of a Colour?" the aggressive frontiersmen asked. It was impossible "to distinguish one nation from another." Berkeley's policy, they charged, was a plot by the governor and the grandees to monopolize the Indian trade.[11]

Berkeley moved quickly to quiet the opposition. On 10 May he declared Bacon in rebellion and dismissed him from the council, but offered to pardon all who returned to their homes. Bacon and two others exempted from this general pardon were promised a fair trial. The governor also ordered elections for a new assembly to provide adequate measures against the Indians and to redress any grievances. All freemen, not only freeholders, were qualified to vote and to present their complaints against the governor. Bacon, insisting on warring against all Indians, appeared at the elections held in Henrico County accompanied by a band of armed men. Not surprisingly, he and one of his lieutenants were chosen to represent the county.

The newly elected burgess soon created a furor. According to William Sherwood, an attorney in Jamestown, Bacon was a man of little experience who stirred up indigent and disaffected persons. Berkeley's supporters on the council were more emphatic in their denunciation: Bacon was "young, hair-brained and highly Atheistical," a rebel whose "only aim had always been and is, nothing else but a total Subversion of ye Government, and out of its Ruines to repair ye lost fortunes of him." The governor himself soon was in despair, as he confessed to Secretary Coventry. Exhausted from riding throughout the colony he described himself *"not able to support myself at this age six months longer and therefore on my knees I beg his sacred majesty would send a more vigorous Governor."*[12] This desperate plea written on 3 June by the apparently defeated septuagenarian was the last news the secretary of state at Whitehall received for some months. The tone and content of Berkeley's letter strongly influenced the reaction of the royal government to the situation in Virginia.

On 5 June the newly elected assembly met at Jamestown. The following day Bacon appeared with fifty armed men. He then held a secret meeting, lasting for three hours, with William Drummond and Richard Lawrence. The governor had him apprehended, but then released him on his own parole. Rumor had it that hundreds of men were marching on the capital at the news of Bacon's arrest. In the presence of the assembly Bacon asked for pardon, and on the recommendation of both the burgesses and the councilors, Berkeley relented and restored him to his seat, promising also to issue him a commission to raise volunteers against the Indians. Shortly after, Bacon left Jamestown. He did not return until 23 June.

During Bacon's absence the assembly drafted the so-called June Laws in response to the crisis. Commissioners later empowered by the crown to investigate the rebellion some months afterwards assumed that during the elections held in May, "such was the Prevalency of Bacon[']s Party" that the planters "chose instead of freeholders freemen, yt had butt lately crept out of ye condicōn" of servitude, men who had never been eligible for this office and thus men who sided with Bacon. But an analysis of the known members of the June assembly does not reveal a bias in favor of Bacon against Berkeley. The voters in some counties returned their former burgesses, and when they did not, they probably chose others because of circumstances peculiar to the particular county rather than acting as oppressed yeomen desiring to change the existing order.

The twenty laws drafted by the burgesses in June 1676 were designed not so much to alter the power of the provincial government as to eliminate abuses at the local, county, level and to reduce the cost of government for the debt-ridden planters. The bills included provisions to return the franchise to freemen, to reestablish local elections of vestries by parishioners, to end the practice of closed meetings by the justices when setting the annual rates and framing local ordinances, to prohibit some plural officeholding, and to eliminate the exemption from paying taxes by the provincial councilors and their right to sit on the county benches. The burgesses directed these reforms against the county magistrates and the councilors in their functioning on the local courts. Absent for much of the session, Bacon had little to do with these reforms of local government. They could hardly be called his; in fact, he repudiated them.[13]

Bacon did not return to Jamestown until 23 June, when the reform bills were being completed and two days before the session closed. He arrived with about five hundred armed followers—William Sherwood described them as "the scum of the country." Parading his men with guns leveled and cocked before the statehouse, Bacon demanded that he be commissioned general of the provincial forces for a war against all the tribesmen. Threatened by the guns of Bacon's men, the assembly complied. At the urging of several of the burgesses and Thomas Ballard, the councilor Berkeley would later call his "Mary Magdalene," the governor issued Bacon a commission. Bacon also obtained an act of indemnity and a public letter of approval to the king signed by the governor and assembly—all, Philip Ludwell charged, were coerced at the point of guns—to be sent to England and presented at Whitehall by Bacon's father. To offset these accounts, William Sherwood and Philip Ludwell wrote to Secretary Williamson of the rebellious activities of Bacon and his "rabble."[14]

In addition to the coerced address from the government of the colony, the dissidents sent to England another document, "The Virginians' Plea for Opposing the Indians . . . ," an account designed to exonerate the rebels. In another relation, allegedly by Bacon himself, they accused the "great men" of the colony of supplying the savages with munitions and portrayed the governor as perfidious, a man filled with hate against the planters.

Bacon saw little merit in the reforms of the June assembly. The poverty of the colonists was such that all power lay in the hands of the rich, who, having the common folk in their debt, had always oppressed them. It was pointless to appeal to the very men against whom the complaints were charged. An emissary of the people, Giles Bland, would take ship for England to counter the misrepresentations sent by Berkeley and his supporters.[15]

To some men loyal to the governor it seemed that "the Rabble, of which sort this country chiefly consistes," were rallying to Bacon. Nicholas Spencer in describing the insurgent leaders revealed the prejudices of the hitherto ruling magnates: Bacon was a "known and declared Atheist," Ingram, a debauched young man, who, rumor had it, less than a year before had been "a paddlar" in England, while one Brinnington, a carpenter, some years before had fled Maryland with another man's wife. Spencer regarded Giles Brent, whose mother was an Indian, as "himself wholly of their brutish nature and principles."[16]

With support for the governor apparently declining, Berkeley fled across the Chesapeake Bay to Accomack on the eastern shore. Bacon sent out a call to the planters there remonstrating that they were "deluded and gulled by that abominable juggler" under whose oppression they had long suffered. What Bacon was undertaking, he professed, was in defense of the royal interest by a power derived from the king: a commission signed by the royal governor at the request of the assembly and ratified by an act of the legislature. No reasonable man then could claim the commission had been given under compulsion. In repudiating Bacon, Berkeley himself was committing treason! Such had been Berkeley's folly that Charles II must consider him unfit to govern. By such logic Bacon arrogated for himself the power of government. As one observer later commented, he was "a witty wicked Rogue!"[17]

Styling himself "general" by the consent of the people, Bacon issued a declaration of the populace against the governor. He condemned Berkeley for having on "specious pretences" constructed public works and raised unjust taxes to enrich his friends and for other "sinister ends," but to no visible or adequate effect. During his long tenure Berkeley had not in any way aided the colony by building fortifications or towns or furthering trade. He had abused and rendered contemptible the king's justices by appointing scandalous and ignorant favorites to the county benches; he had wronged the king's prerogative and interest by assuming a monopoly of the beaver trade; he had betrayed and sold the king's colony and the liberties of his loyal subjects to the barbarous heathen for unjust gains. Having emboldened the Indians against the settlers, he had not appointed anyone to compel them to give satisfaction for their robberies and murders, but had, rather, frustrated volunteers campaigning against the tribesmen.

For these offenses Berkeley was judged guilty of treason, as were those who had aided and abetted him, his wicked and pernicious councilors and confederates. Bacon condemned nineteen men by name, among them Henry Chicheley, Philip Ludwell, Robert Beverley, Richard Lee, Thomas Ballard, and William Sherwood. All persons aiding or sheltering them were to be considered as confederate traitors to the people and were to have their estates confiscated.

On 3 August at the rendezvous at Captain Otho Thorpe's house at Middle Plantation, a meeting controlled by Bacon, sixty-nine men, including Councilor Thomas Swann, calling themselves sober and discreet gentlemen, affirmed Bacon's allegations and pledged to support the general against the common enemy. Inasmuch as it was thought Berkeley had informed the authorities in England that Bacon and his followers were in rebellion, Bacon required those signing the declaration—whether through force or conviction was not clear—to oppose any troops sent from England until Bacon's emissary could fully inform the king of what had occurred.[18]

Early the next month Bacon was reported to have met with John Coode of Maryland, who attempted later to overthrow the proprietary government. This meeting may have had some connection with an outbreak shortly after in Calvert County.[19]

Giles Bland and his lieutenant, William Carver, crossed the Chesapeake to capture Berkeley, while Bacon set out against the Pamunkey Indians. The local tribesmen had not betrayed or injured the English settlers, but as was later noted, "among ye Vulgar itt Matters not whither they be foes soe they be Indians." In a manifesto issued in September Bacon asserted that all of the neighboring Indians as well as other tribes were outside the protection of the law.[20] Fortune now turned away from the insurgents. Bland allowed himself to be captured by Berkeley's ally, Philip Ludwell. Returning to Jamestown, the governor offered to pardon all rebels but the leaders, Bacon, Drummond, and Richard Lawrence. Bacon reacted quickly. He proclaimed freedom for all servants and slaves belonging to planters who adhered to the governor, and then moved on the capital. Berkeley once more took sanctuary across the bay in Accomack, and Bacon on 19 September occupied Jamestown. After burning the capital, Bacon then retreated to Gloucester County. En route his men plundered loyalist planters.

Bacon's movement was already faltering. Giles Brent went over to the loyalists, and when Bacon died suddenly on 26 October of the "bloody flux" (dysentery), the rebel movement disintegrated. With the aid of loyalist ship captains Berkeley took the initiative. Controlling the rivers and the bay, his forces attacked and destroyed the rebel parties piecemeal; Robert Beverley was especially active against the harried insurgents. On 2 January 1677 Thomas Grantham, master of the thirty-gun *Concord,* forced the surrender of Joseph Ingram and other rebel leaders at West Point. By 16 January the whole colony had submitted to Berkeley's authority.[21]

By 22 January Berkeley was back at Green Spring, his plundered plantation, where he issued a summons for a free assembly to convene at his home, the statehouse being burned with the rest of Jamestown. A week later the *Bristol* dropped anchor in the James River. Aboard were two commissioners from London with instructions from the crown.

Little of the dramatic turnabout in events of the last few months was known in Whitehall. Communication across the Atlantic was disrupted during the struggle for control of the Chesapeake. Henry Coventry, the secretary of state, had received Berkeley's pessimistic letter of 3 June, but as late as 15 November he had received no further direct word from the governor. After conferring with Thomas Ludwell, the ministers of state decided to send over three companies of troops with the arms and munitions Berkeley had desired. More men could have been dispatched, but the provincial agents thought three hundred soldiers would be sufficient. Within a matter of days, however, Ludwell and his colleagues prevailed on the ministry not to take action until further word from the governor and assembly arrived.[22]

There was little agreement on what exact course to follow. Some men begrudged the cost to the crown of restoring order. Colonel Francis Moryson hesitated to send over redcoats; the imposition of martial law would heighten discontent. It might be preferable to send a few discreet commissioners to inquire into the grievances of the planters and to promise redress and pardon for those who laid down their arms, the chief rebels excepted. Thomas Ludwell and Robert Smith were not as hopeful: the troubles in Virginia stemmed, not from the discontent of the better sort, but from the poverty of the meanest men, whose discontent made them susceptible to the blandishments of the insurgent leaders. Many who followed Bacon did so in the belief that they served the king and the colony by fighting Indians. Once they understood Bacon was in rebellion, they would reject him. It was essential to send over a large English force to bolster the loyalists and to establish Berkeley's authority under the crown before Sir William left Virginia.[23]

The paucity of reliable information compounded the problem. Moryson and Sir John Berry, a naval officer, were designated with Colonel Herbert Jeffreys as royal commissioners to investigate the situation. Jeffreys, a relative of the tobacco merchant and alderman of London, was given command of the troops to be dispatched to the colony and a commission as lieutenant governor of the province in the place of Sir Henry Chicheley, reported to have been taken prisoner by the rebels. The commissioners were to inquire into all grievances submitted to them by the colonists, including their views on the causes of the rebellion, information to be obtained from witnesses under oath. The acts of the June assembly, since they were extracted under duress, were to be disallowed, but the governor and the burgesses pardoned for approving them. The grievances of the populace must be remedied, however, and to reduce the expense of government, a known complaint, the assembly must meet, not annually, but once in every two years unless upon some emergency. The burgesses, elected by the freeholders as was the practice in England, were to sit for a limited period, fourteen days, and their salaries to be reduced so as not to burden the country.

By the terms of a royal proclamation issued on 27 October the rebels would be allowed twenty days from the time the proclamation was published in the colony to return to their allegiance and take an oath of obedience in order to win pardon.[24]

The division of authority between Berkeley and Jeffreys and the other commissioners was not made clear, and this later led to considerable confusion and continued factional strife in Virginia. Berkeley, because of his advanced age and at his own request, was ordered to return to England with *all possible speed*. Jeffreys as lieutenant governor *in the absence of Berkeley* would assume authority, but until Berkeley left, the commissioners were to *assist* with their *advice* whenever he might request it. Berkeley, the commissioners, and the brothers Ludwell, as well as the loyal councilors, were empowered by a commission of Oyer and Terminer to try cases in Virginia.[25]

Sir John Berry along with Francis Moryson left Portsmouth on the *Bristol* on 19 November. Two other ships of war, the *Rose* and *Dartmouth,* along with eight merchantmen carrying Jeffreys and the bulk of the English soldiers, held up for some days by headwinds, did not leave Deal until 3 December.

The instructions issued by the crown caused confusion, a situation compounded by rivalry and jealousy in America, where the governor and the men loyal to him were already in control. Their passions aroused by the suffering of their families and the damage to their estates, they were in no mood meekly to give up power and to forgive their enemies.

After a voyage of ten weeks, H.M.S. *Bristol* dropped anchor in the James River on the afternoon of 29 January 1677. Berry sent off a note to Sir William Berkeley informing the governor of the mission to investigate and settle grievances and of the expected arrival of Jeffreys with the bulk of the troops to carry on the war and to suppress the rebellion. The governor came on board almost immediately to give them the good news: Bacon was dead, about twenty of the ringleaders already executed, and the loyalists in control. A good foundation had been laid for peace with the Indians, and the call had already gone out for the assembly to meet on 20 February. The redcoats were not needed; indeed, given the condition of the country, there were no quarters for them. The populace could hardly support the king's soldiers. The governor did express some concern over the distribution of forfeited rebel estates and the propriety of publishing the king's proclamation of pardon. He intended to issue his own. At this point Berry and Moryson could see no need for a prolonged stay in Virginia.

Matters did not go that smoothly. Any indulgence shown the rebels would deprive the loyalists of any hope of recovering their property plundered by Bacon's men. The king ought not to deprive his loyal subjects of the means to redress their grievances, for it was because of their support of the crown that they had lost all they possessed. With other men enjoying their plundered property, some councilors had no bread or beds for their children but what they received from the charity of others.[26] The treatment of accused rebels and those charged with aiding them brought Berkeley and his supporters into open conflict with the royal commissioners. To Berry and Moryson it was essential that regular legal procedures be followed; to Berkeley ordinary legal process did not extend in cases of treason and rebellion, and he cited the precedent of the recent civil war in England.[27] The aged governor saw the issue as a threat to his power and authority.

On the arrival of Jeffreys and the bulk of the troops, the breach with Berkeley and the loyalists widened. Supported by the councilors, Berkeley refused to return immediately to England or to give up his authority. By the terms of the royal commission of Oyer and Terminer, he was continued in the government of the colony. In the last days of February the assembly called by Berkeley the previous month convened. In an effort at conciliation the commissioners suggested measures to alleviate the distressed condition of the planters and to restore peace so that the soldiers might return to England. The assembly ought to reduce the expenses of government—the salaries of the burgesses and fees of the clerks and other officers—to lighten the burden on the populace. The reform measures adopted the previous June, although annulled because of the element of coercion when initially passed, were now reenacted with some modifications.

Loyalists seizing the property of men accused—but not yet convicted—of rebellion or simply reclaiming plundered possessions continued to set the commissioners against Berkeley's adherents. When the governor refused to give them an account of the seizures, the break was complete. The rupture over Berkeley's conduct after the rebellion colored the judgment of the royal commissioners. Ironically, his behavior before and during the rebellion did not become an issue. To the commissioners the responses from the various counties to the call for a statement of public grievances seemed for the most part limited to complaints about salaries and expenses of the assembly, money expended on the forts, and other public accounts. All that now obstructed the quiet of the colony were Berkeley's remaining in Virginia and the rapacious insolence of those calling themselves the loyal party.[28] The commissioners and Berkeley's "loyalists" were laying the basis for a new factional division in Virginia public life.

The public responses on grievances submitted from the counties were varied and wide-ranging. In some instances two conflicting sets were returned. One set from Nansemond charged that the uprising resulted from excessive taxes and other burdens. While the June assembly had satisfied most grievances, a war to destroy all Indians still had not been launched. Yet forty-eight other men signed a counter remonstrance claiming that those responsible for the first return had never consulted many of the inhabitants. Having actively engaged in rebellion, they were now trying to justify their behavior. For Berkeley, who had served Virginia so well, to be so cruelly dealt with was the only grievance. Inhabitants of Isle of Wight also sent in conflicting returns. In a paper said to have been written by a servant, six men declared that they had long lived under great oppression and mounting, unnecessary taxes. They included a detailed list of complaints and cited particularly the behavior of Joseph Bridger, a member of the council. In rebuttal Bridger and over seventy other men from the upper parish charged that those accusing the councilor were merely seeking to justify their own treason and had consulted few of the inhabitants of the county. Envy, malice, and ignorance had caused the rebellion.

As might have been expected, the returns from two counties, Accomack, where Berkeley had found refuge, and Henrico, Bacon's home, strongly differed. The Accomack men, stressing their contributions to Berkeley, asked that the governor remain and that if the war against the Indians be continued, they not be charged for its prosecution, as they were not in any way responsible for the conflict. Berkeley's promise to exempt them from paying all provincial taxes for twenty years ought now to be honored. The planters of Henrico, critical of the provincial regime, attacked the presumed monopoly of the beaver trade and burdensome taxes. They called for a war of revenge against Indians in general. One of their specific complaints centered on the alleged domination of the local county court by men bound together by consanguinity and marriage.

Opinion in the other counties differed widely on the causes of the rebellion and other disparate matters. James City stressed the inadequate prosecution of the war against the Indians and heavy taxes, while Rappahannock pointed to the lack of able, pious, and orthodox ministers as the main cause of the miseries of the previous year. Rappahannock wanted planters to pay quitrents for all the land they held with excess, "concealed land," to go to the informer who brought it to the attention of the government. Voting and officeholding were also of concern in Rappahannock. Freemen as well as freeholders should vote, but no man who had voluntarily assisted Bacon should sit as judge in any court. Offices of public trust ought to be conferred only on discreet and knowledgeable gentlemen; men of slight education ought not sit as justices. The granting of positions of profit and honor to "strangers" also found disfavor. In this connection Bacon and Giles Bland were specifically cited in the return from lower Norfolk.

Several complaints were common to almost all of the returns, especially laments that taxes were too high, not an unexpected grievance in a simple agricultural society suffering from sustained depression and mounting debt. The impositions particularly mentioned were the two shillings per hogshead of tobacco exported, the fort duties, and the sixty pounds of tobacco on every poll to pay the expenses in England of combating the grants to Arlington and Culpeper. Some planters appeared ignorant of the purpose of the last imposition; they implied that it was fraudulent. The administration at Jamestown might have taken more pains to inform the less knowledgeable farmers.

Some returns complained of the manner of levying taxes and advocated a land rather than a poll tax, thus shifting more of the burden to the larger landholders, a measure Berkeley and his council had previously proposed but one the burgesses had opposed. Nor had

Berkeley been responsible for another complaint, making the vestries of the churches self-perpetuating. It was under Moryson as acting governor, when Berkeley had been in England, that a statute had been passed enabling the minister and incumbent vestrymen to fill vacancies in the vestry.

Allegedly excessive fees charged by the sheriffs and the clerks of the counties were another common complaint. But the elected burgesses had voted all impositions and had already provided a remedy for excessive fees. Men dissatisfied with the tax burden, the royal commissioners concluded, ought to have looked to their elected representatives for satisfaction.[29]

What emerged from these complaints was not so much the cupidity or tyranny of Berkeley and his supporters on the provincial council or an attempt by Bacon and his followers to bring about democratic reform of the provincial government as a breakdown over a dozen or so years in the counties, malfunctioning at the basic level, frustration, and failure to communicate. Most men were barely eking out a living. Many, illiterate and uninformed, were but recently emerged from indentured status and were in debt because of a chronically depressed economy brought about by the low prices received for tobacco. Their plight was worsened by the heavy cost of government, unfairly distributed and suddenly increased taxes, and a disruptive Indian war, none very well understood by the rank and file.

Personal animosities had also played a role, and a few men in high places, Colonel Edward Hill among them, had earned the resentment of the planters by abusing their positions.

There had also been a crisis in leadership, as Berkeley and his supporters, whatever their judgment as to the best manner of dealing with hostile and dependent Indian tribes, had wavered. This indecision allowed the more gullible to accept the arguments of opportunists from the upper ranks, ambitious or newly arrived men such as the younger Bacon, Bland, Lawrence, and Drummond, men who under normal circumstances might have enjoyed the power their social rank conferred upon them. Contentious, psychologically disposed to challenge authority, they seized the opportunity the crisis in 1676 gave them. But the resultant conflict also brought to the surface strong overtones of class animosity, resentment of the "grandees" by the lower orders, and contempt by men like Nicholas Spencer for the "rabble" and the "scum."[30]

After analyzing the returns from the counties, the royal commissioners drew a sharp distinction between the difficulties plaguing the colony before and the grievances registered after the rebellion. In the former category they found fault with the dilatory defense made for the colony and the refusal of Berkeley to grant commissions for the newly raised volunteers. The imposition of taxes by the assembly to build forts and to procure a patent from the crown extinguishing the grants to Culpeper and Arlington, the commissioners saw as grievous but necessary measures. The reenactment in February 1677 of the reforms passed by the assembly the previous June had already met several of the complaints made against local government. If Berkeley and his adherents would end their depredations and attend to the instructions from England, they felt there would be little left to do. The commission might terminate its work in a fortnight.

Moryson, Berry, and Jeffreys would have preferred to put a stop to trials and seizures and to restore the goods and property plundered by both sides. They were embarrassed on one point, however, having promised the settlers that Culpeper under pressure from the duke of York would give up his patents. James had assured the commissioners before they left England that the patents so prejudicial to the colony would be vacated without any charge to the Virginians. Culpeper was now reviving his claims. For their part, the commissioners condemned proprietary grants. Carolina and Maryland would in time prove utterly destructive to the interest of the crown and the government of Virginia. Carolina was the refuge of runaway slaves, rogues, and rebels. While some restitution might be allowed the proprietors, their provinces ought to be subject to regulation by the king in council through a governor appointed by the crown.[31]

Berkeley remained adamant that those who had disrupted the peace of the colony and terrorized their neighbors be punished. He refused to vacate his governorship, contesting fiercely with Jeffreys, who was forced to declare publicly that the governor himself had cited his great age and physical weakness: he had been recalled at his own request. Sir William finally left Virginia on 5 May 1677, proclaiming that he would return as governor. From the correspondence of the king and the secretaries of state it was clear that he had lost favor as a result of the reports of the commissioners and his failure to take ship immediately for England.[32]

Determined to hold power, the members of the Green Spring faction in the council—Thomas Ballard, Edward Hill and Philip Ludwell—mounted a campaign to vindicate Berkeley and to undermine his successor, Jeffreys. Robert Beverley carried on the faction's work in the assembly. As clerk of the House of Burgesses he refused to surrender its records to the royal commissioners, standing on the rights of the house, a position the majority of the burgesses supported.[33] His enemies accused him of plundering his victims when suppressing the rebellion.

Berkeley, exhausted and ill, arrived in England in June 1677. He was too weak to testify and died without having an opportunity to give any account. The defense of his administration—Thomas Ludwell having returned to Virginia—fell on Lady Berkeley's brother, Alexander Culpeper. With Berkeley dead, what mattered for the men who had supported him and who now contended with Jeffreys was the reputation of his administration and their continuation in power.

The seizures and confiscations effected by Berkeley and his adherents, as well as the executions of rebels, laid the loyalists open to attack by their relatives both in Virginia and England and by merchants in London whose factors had suffered. By the late summer of 1677, when the Lords of Trade took up the task of assessing the situation, Moryson had submitted the official findings of the commission. They implicitly indicted Berkeley's administration for its dilatory proceedings in providing for the defense of the colony—in conjunction with heavy but necessary taxes, this caused the revolt—and explicitly criticized him for condemning rebels and seizing property without warrant or trial. They had little faith that the assembly of Virginia would do justice in restoring goods plundered by both sides. The crown ought to draft an act of oblivion to repeal the act of attainder passed by the provincial legislature.

The late governor's relations, his brother and his brother-in-law, that fall came to his defense. The taxes imposed in Virginia—admittedly heavy—were lawfully voted by the assembly and necessary for the public safety. It would have been imprudent to rely on volunteers when the assembly and council had appointed regular militia officers. All persons executed under martial law had been notoriously guilty, and whether there was any need to offer royal pardon for survivors had yet to be determined. There was no proof of seizure of property, other than during the heat of the rebellion to aid Berkeley in retaking the province or by act of assembly and court. Alexander Culpeper and Lord Berkeley accused the commissioners of being "impatient" of the "least irregularity" by the governor and the loyalists, although they knew well the rebels had destroyed Berkeley's estate.

With little delay, Anglesey, Craven, Fauconberg, Coventry, Williamson, and the other Lords of Trade accepted the arguments of the commission: Berkeley and the loyalist assembly of Virginia had acted contrary to the royal proclamation of 20 October 1676 by passing their own statutes of attainder and indemnity, and fines.[34]

What of the future? Who would rule in Virginia? What laws did the colony need? Thomas, Lord Culpeper, already commissioned as governor, remained in London arranging with Danby, the lord treasurer, the details of his salary and perquisites of his office. Moryson and Berry busied themselves at the Plantation Office to determine the composition of the council in Virginia. They recommended retaining almost all of the incumbents. Some had not been in the colony during the troubles, and Moryson and Berry could find nothing reflecting against them; others had demonstrated their loyalty and worth or were sober and discreet persons who had upheld the royal commission. Berry and Moryson singled out two men as objectionable. They branded Major Robert Beverley, then clerk of the assembly, as a man of poor education and mean parts. He had been bred a vulgar seaman. Minimizing his service in putting down the rebellion, the commissioners charged Beverley with indiscriminately plundering planters and with fomenting misunderstanding between Berkeley and Jeffreys. They also proscribed Colonel Edward Hill, the most hated man in Charles County.[35]

The optimism of Moryson and Berry as to loyalties in Virginia was somewhat misplaced. Jeffreys, harassed and in ill health, complained of Beverley's continued impudence in condemning the proceedings of the royal commission as unjust and illegal. With Philip Ludwell he continued as mutinous as before. Even Daniel Parks, following his return to Virginia, was disgusted by the tactics adopted by the old guard on the council: they had concealed the proclamation by the king voiding the commission to Berkeley and granting royal pardon to the rebels and, when forced to acknowledge it, had charged that the document had been procured from Charles II under false pretenses. Philip Ludwell presided over a clique in the council, a "Cabal," in conjunction with Lady Berkeley, who carried on as if her husband were still living. Allied with the younger Ludwell were William Cole, Nicholas Spencer, Nathaniel Bacon, and Augustus Warner. The "Green Spring Interest" corresponded with Lady Berkeley's brother, Alexander Culpeper, their "great solicitor" in political matters at Whitehall. Apparently they placed their hopes on a new governor.[36] To compound matters Jeffreys died on 18 December 1678, and the titular leadership of the divided council fell to the inept Sir Henry Chicheley as president.

Opposition was not confined to the council. Moryson complained of the "arrogance" of the burgesses in protesting the demand of the royal commission that their clerk turn over to them the papers of the house. Charles II could not have sanctioned such power in his commissioners, the burgesses had contended, for they could not find comparable power ever having been exercised by the kings of England in the past.

In October 1678 the king in council formally rebuked the assembly for its great presumption in calling into question the authority of the king's commissioners and ordered the Lords of Trade to recommend measures to vindicate the king's authority and to bring the assemblymen to a due sense of their duty. The council ordered the committee to prepare a "scheme," or set of laws, to be transmitted to Virginia. At this point Charles II and his ministers seemed to be contemplating adopting for Virginia the procedure undertaken the previous year for Jamaica. In November 1677 the Lords of Trade had proposed that no laws be passed in the island but those initiated by the council in England. The West Indian planters strongly resisted this "new Constitution";[37] those on the Chesapeake no less so. In neither case did the crown push the matter.

In December 1678 the Lords of Trade accepted several proposals by Culpeper, governor-designate, for amendments in the statutes of Virginia to be enacted by the provincial legislature. Among the proposed laws was an act of indemnity for all rebels except those convicted by legal trial. Another bill, designed to alleviate problems in marketing, proposed setting up towns as commercial centers on the major rivers where ships would load and unload. The following winter the council confirmed the decision to revoke the grant to Arlington and Culpeper for the rents from the southern portion of Virginia. This revenue would now provide money to fortify the colony and to rebuild Jamestown.

Charles II also struck out against the Green Spring faction. The councilors loyal to Jeffreys he continued under Culpeper; those dissenting, Ballard and Philip Ludwell among them, he dropped, although unlike their counterparts in Jamaica, they were not declared ineligible for election to the assembly. Beverley and Edward Hill were banned from all offices, however. The former's refusal to turn over the journals of the house had led the burgesses to affirm their rights, a declaration the Privy Council branded as disloyal and seditious. Once Culpeper discovered the authors and abettors of the declaration, they would receive the marks of the king's displeasure for their great presumption.[38]

In the spring of 1679 word arrived of fresh problems in Virginia. Chicheley, who had succeeded on the death of Jeffreys, sent over a compendious narrative of the suffering of the colonists. Short of food and supplies, they were grumbling over the charges in quartering the unpaid redcoats.[39] Chicheley advised a remission of quitrents.

To provide a more certain fund for defense and yet reduce the financial burden the crown proposed various taxes: two shillings a hogshead on tobacco exported, sixpence for every person brought into the colony to be paid by the captains of vessels, and a fort duty, a direct assessment of shot or a monetary equivalent of one shilling and threepence per ton on all vessels entering Virginia waters. Once enacted, these measures would reduce the need for frequent legislative sessions. Any procedure to reduce public expenditures—including fewer and shorter assemblies—would be welcomed by the populace. Several counties had asked that the governor and the council in emergencies levy taxes without calling the burgesses into session. Shortly after the Restoration, the assembly had granted this privilege to Berkeley; Jeffreys and his council, desperate to pay the troops garrisoned in the province, had raised the issue again. Sessions of the assembly cost as much as providing for the redcoats.[40]

Culpeper seemed not to have felt any urgency to leave England. More than two years had passed since he had taken the oath of office following the death of Berkeley. He failed to board the frigate *Oxford* as scheduled on 10 December 1679. It took a direct threat of dismissal by the king to speed the governor on his way. After a tedious voyage he arrived in Virginia in May 1680.

He spent only a few months in the colony and failed to carry out his instructions. He took no action against either Robert Beverley or Edward Hill. Seeking to ingratiate himself with the Green Spring faction, he backed Colonel Christopher Wormley, the stepson of Henry Chicheley, for the council and Nathaniel Bacon as deputy governor and took on Nicholas Spencer as his financial agent. Culpeper did give support to the Virginians for a restriction of planting to remedy chronic overproduction of tobacco. Some men had already taken matters into their own hands by destroying plants in the fields, but Nicholas Spencer, the provincial secretary, thought the intervention of the crown would be necessary. The "miseries" of the planters were due in part to "our wild and rambling mode of living." The governor prevailed on the assembly to enact modified bills for establishing towns and for raising money, but only by granting concessions, exemptions for Virginians in paying fort duties and the export tax on tobacco. The king in council later disallowed these as inequitable.[41]

After only four months Culpeper left Virginia for New England and then set out across the Atlantic for London to negotiate with the crown for the rights to the rents of the soil in Virginia. He had accomplished little. The basic problems remained. Spencer, for one, predicted the act to establish towns would be of little use in view of the numerous locations allowed in the law for landing and receiving merchandise. All was not well between Chicheley, the president, and the other councilors, and the redcoats remained disgruntled over their lack of pay.[42]

Once the patents to Culpeper and Arlington were vacated, the crown might apply the revenue from quitrents in Virginia to defray expenses in the colony.[43] But as to the other fundamental problem, a cessation in tobacco planting would diminish the crown's income.

As might be expected, the Commissioners of Customs in London seized on the fact that the assembly of Virginia had merely asked that some expedient be employed, without specifying a total cessation, a solution unacceptable to the poorer farmers, although acceptable to the wealthier planters and to the merchants in England. These "engrossers," the customs officials called them, had accumulated large stocks and, as before, were exaggerating the extent of overproduction. An ample market did exist, the customs commissioners contended, in most parts of Christian Europe for Chesapeake leaf. To halt planting in the English colonies would merely invite the Dutch, the Spanish, the French, and even growers in England to take up the slack. Of greater consequence, a curtailment of tobacco production on the Chesapeake would reduce the royal revenue, not an inconsiderable point inasmuch as the average annual receipt in customs for the past three years from the importation of tobacco had been about one hundred thousand pounds.

The provincial legislature was skeptical. It sent an address to the king calling for a total cessation of planting in Virginia, Maryland, and Carolina.[44]

From reports reaching London by October 1681, the seriousness of the situation was clear. Not only was there the threat of hostilities with the Indians, but also of renewed internal disorders because of poverty throughout the countryside. Destitute servants might be driven to rob, pillage, and plunder as they had during the late rebellion. While such conditions prevailed, the Lords of Trade concluded, the redcoats should be maintained in the province and paid. But the chaotic state of the records on quitrents, a source of funds for financing the military and civil establishment, compounded the problem.[45] Culpeper, now back in London, went further in his recommendations: all of the crown's subjects in America ought to be united to protect against Indian raids, foreign incursions, and internal disturbances. He found the situation in the southern proprietary colonies particularly disturbing. Albemarle, the resort of the "scum" and the "refuse" of America, had always been a danger to Virginia; and disturbances had already broken out in Maryland. Inasmuch as disorders there affected Virginia, all offices, military and civil, in the proprietary colony ought to be given to Protestants. It was essential to protect the Old Dominion, for this one colony provided the crown with more income than the other plantations combined. Yet the poverty of the planters, a consequence of overproduction of tobacco, was, Culpeper acknowledged, more easily perceived than remedied; possibly, opening a free trade with Muscovy and providing financial support for establishing commercial centers might provide some relief.

The Lords for Plantation Affairs supported their colleagues at the Customs House. They found the provincial law for founding towns impractical and prejudicial to the royal revenue. The Virginia legislature must amend it. They also reprimanded Culpeper for not informing the burgesses of the king's displeasure at their challenge to his prerogative in supporting the refusal of their clerk, Beverly, to turn over their journals. Such unwarranted proceedings ought not to be allowed to become a precedent. Individuals concerned might win pardon, for both Beverley and Edward Hill had done valuable service during the late rebellion.[46] Culpeper was sent off once more to Virginia with more rigorous instructions.

In the new commission completed in January 1682, the principal men of the colony, including Philip Ludwell and William Byrd, were again named councilors and Chicheley deputy governor. Culpeper was to ask the assembly to do away with taxes levied by poll (a grievance registered during the Berkeley administration) and to substitute an impost on imported liquors, to reduce salaries, and to eliminate harsh or inhuman punishments for white servants and black slaves. The governor had also to promote the construction of towns as exclusive sites for loading and unloading ships, encourage the production of silk, hemp, and flax as alternatives to tobacco, and if he thought fit, consult with the legislature on the expediency of restraining the planting of tobacco. That same month Charles II wrote confidently to Chicheley that as Culpeper was to start shortly for his government, the deputy must call no session of the assembly until November except for urgent reasons and then only with the consent of seven of the council.[47] But Caroline administration did not function so smoothly, and Stuart courtiers were not so attentive to their duties. Culpeper's commission did not pass the Great Seal for another ten months, as he and the ministers squabbled over the perquisites and remuneration of his office.

The deficiencies in administration at Whitehall set the stage for near rebellion in Virginia. Culpeper, anticipating that he would arrive in America in the spring of 1682, had sent word across the Atlantic for Chicheley to summon the assembly in April. The deputy did so; some councilors later charged that he acted at the instigation of Beverley. Subsequently, Chicheley received the order of the king, but by this time the burgesses were already on their way to Jamestown expecting to impose a cessation on planting of tobacco. Sentiment was widespread that unless some expedient was found to raise prices, ruin was almost certain. Obeying the order of the king, Chicheley prorogued the assembly until that fall. Four days later violence erupted in Gloucester County; as the deputy governor put it, the prorogation had "blown this Cole wch hath inflamed the People."

On 1 May desperate farmers in Gloucester banded together. To ensure that there would be no tobacco grown that year, they began cutting the plants in their own fields and then proceeded from plantation to plantation. If their neighbors were unwilling to destroy their crops, they would do it for them. Those farmers whose plants were destroyed then informed on others. The frenzy—so it was called—reached a peak a week later. But local officials hesitated to call out the two companies of royal soldiers. The redcoats, dispirited and "grown rusty with want of action," were on the verge of disbanding for lack of pay.

Mounted provincial militia restored order. Since Robert Beverley had been active in opposition, had strongly supported the call for a cessation of planting, and was known to have a large stock of tobacco on hand, some officials assumed he had instigated the riots. By order of the provincial council he was apprehended and confined aboard the *Duke of York* in the Rappahonnock river to prevent his being rescued by his supporters.

Beverley's political ally and business associate, William Fitzhugh, well appreciated the situation. He wrote a London merchant that he was shipping one hundred hogsheads of tobacco to England. What price they would fetch he did not know, but he hoped the "market may rise upon the news of the great destruction . . . by Cutters & Pluckers." Heavy rains later that year finished the task of the desperate planters who had ravaged their neighbors' fields.[48]

Nicholas Spencer saw the plant cutters as "wild Rabble" and the uprising as a consequence of Bacon's rebellion, but the deputy governor was more to the point when he complained bitterly to his brother in England. Nothing had been done for over two years, time enough, one would think, to initiate some remedy for the depressed condition of the colony.[49]

The Lords of Trade reacted swiftly to this most recent outbreak. Dispatches sent from the Chesapeake in May reached London by the middle of June. Culpeper was called in and informed of what was happening in his government. That same day the Lords of Trade recommended to the king that he be ordered out to Virginia with all possible speed, first to discover and punish the persons most responsible for the insurrection, and only then to propose to the assembly some method to reduce the tobacco crop. Beverley was to be dismissed from all offices.

Ordered to embark by 1 August on a frigate assigned to him, Culpeper lingered, quibbling over his salary and perquisites. The king evidently gave him a severe dressing down, but to no avail. August came and went, as did September and October. Culpeper had gotten only as far as Plymouth; he had failed to pay the clerks of the crown law officers the required fees to have his commission passed. Finally, under extreme pressure the errant governor complied and sailed for America.[50]

Culpeper arrived in Virginia on 16 December 1682. He did not stay long. His behavior was nothing short of amazing, a study in insolence and irresponsibility.

Chicheley had been plodding along with little support. Many of the councilors were either ill or lived distant from Jamestown. On his arrival Culpeper was particularly vindictive against his deputy, blaming him for doing little. That "lumpe, that Masse of Dulnesse, that worse than Nothing," he confided privately to Blathwayt, of whom "noe Notice hath been taken all this while butt to ruene him out." He held Chicheley responsible for the outbreak of rioting and accused him of violating instructions by calling the assembly without the advice of the provincial council or, indeed, anyone but Beverley, the "premier ministre." Culpeper resented having to share his salary with the nonentity, but Chicheley obliged the governor by dying on 5 February 1683.

The governor's anger also extended to Nathaniel Bacon, whose accounts of the salary due him were in error, Culpeper charged. By promoting Bacon to the lieutenant governor's post, Culpeper hoped to take over the offices of auditor and receiver himself, although this was contrary to his "maxime of never being the king[']s Accountant." Nicholas Spencer, the governor's cousin and agent for the Culpeper proprietary in the Northern Neck, was himself eager for the post of auditor should Bacon be moved up.[51]

Culpeper displayed a cavalier disregard for his instructions. He deliberately withheld a letter from the secretary of state to Lord Baltimore, the proprietor of Maryland, for the governments of the two provinces to consult on a program for the reduction in tobacco planting. He encouraged the Virginians to continue production! The planters needed no urging, for a recent rise in prices had induced them to renew their efforts. To Culpeper, nothing but the force of the market over at least two years would compel them to turn to new industries. He did proceed against a few of the hapless men apprehended for the recent rioting; three were arrested and tried, two executed as examples, and one, a youth of nineteen, being very penitent and having fully acknowledged the dignity of government, was reprieved. Culpeper met briefly with the assembly. After the burgesses sat for a few days, the governor gave his assent to their bills, for as he rationalized later, although he did not approve of them, he thought it better that the odium for rejecting the assembly's measures should not fall on him but on the men in Whitehall. Culpeper took no action against Beverley; he claimed he could find nothing against him, except a general sauciness in manner.

Culpeper was far from anxious to deal with the problems in his government. By mid-March 1683 he was already planning to abandon his charge and to return home to propose matters of great consequence, business he would not commit to paper. After appointing Spencer, his fiscal agent for the Northern Neck, president of the council—the senior councilor, Bacon, so Culpeper claimed, would not take the post under any terms—the governor departed for England. As he later explained, he knew that the great crop of tobacco expected on the Chesapeake would plunge the country into further difficulties, and he wanted to be home to consult with the ministers on the best measures to be taken. One observer on the Chesapeake noted that his sudden departure had startled many men; it had become the subject of dangerous talk. The planters of Gloucester were again restless and unruly, but in August a severe storm damaged much of the crop.[52]

Culpeper's behavior—leaving his post without permission in direct violation of an order in council and the report he submitted on his return to England—seemed almost calculated to bring about his dismissal, thus relieving him of an unprofitable, tiresome post and allowing him to contract with the crown for a financial settlement. The displeasure of the king was great and the dismissal of the governor immediate. Early in September 1683 the crown law officers received a warrant to draft a commission for Francis, Baron Howard of Effingham as governor of Virginia.[53]

The new governor lost little time in getting to his post. Despite the lateness of the season he left England in November and arrived in his government on February 20. The next day he was sworn into office. Spencer was set aside as president of the council, and Bacon, the senior man on the board, assumed the position.

The instructions issued the new governor aimed at meeting certain grievances of long standing. All grants exempting some planters from paying quitrents were voided. No man was now to take up more land than he could cultivate. Effingham was to secure a revision of the statutes of the colony, with the complete body of laws to be sent home, and was also to solicit an act—one proposed for some time by the provincial council—allowing the governor and the council to impose a general levy not exceeding twenty pounds of tobacco per poll, to be accounted for both by the crown and the assembly. Allowing the governor and his advisors to raise a limited sum to maintain government would relieve the planters of the charge of too frequent meetings of the assembly. The tobacco riots had been precipitated in part by a call for the burgesses to provide emergency funds for the two companies of redcoats. Effingham's instructions also allowed the stay of execution of John Plaisants, a Quaker convicted in Henrico county for not attending church. Liberty of conscience was permitted to those who were content with the peaceable enjoyment of this privilege without giving offense.[54]

Beverley—the first minister, some had called him—the man whose conduct was thought so offensive to the honor and authority of the king, was tried for high crimes and found guilty by a jury, but later pardoned. As William Blathwayt, secretary at the Plantation Office, explained it, matters having been so altered by that time, it could not be easy properly to resolve his status or the position of the clerk of the assembly. This was so intricate a dispute that it evidently was better to let sleeping dogs lie.

Some problems remained intractable. The winter of 1684 was bitterly cold, and the following summer, heavy rains spoiled much of the tobacco in the fields. Northern Indians again menaced the frontiers, yet the colony could not support the burden of war, the burgesses contended, without the aid of the crown. The king had promised that no quitrents would be due for a period of twenty-one years, but now money was demanded of the planters. By whose authority, they knew not. This branch of the royal revenue ought to be applied to the cost of defense and other public needs. Not surprisingly, the governor yielded on the revenue bills providing for the protection of the frontiers and lent his support to a request that the king reclaim the Northern Neck: it was improper to have a proprietor in the midst of his majesty's dominions.[56]

The retention of the Northern Neck by Culpeper siphoned off revenue in rents the crown might have allocated to the government of Virginia. Another proprietor now menaced the royal income. According to officials at Jamestown, Lord Baltimore was now asserting a claim to the Potomac river and demanding that all ships enter with the officers in Maryland. In the spring of 1684 he prosecuted Thomas Smith, master of the *Constant,* forcing him to give bond to pay port duties to Maryland.[57] More shocking news was to come. On 31 October 1684 Colonel George Talbot, president of the council of Maryland and the man empowered by the proprietor to govern the province in his absence, stabbed to death— murdered, some claimed—Christopher Rousby, the royal customs collector, in a scuffle aboard the ketch *Quaker,* riding at anchor on the Patuxent River. Effingham was quick to link this incident with Baltimore's claim to the customs revenue from shipping on the Potomac. From the circumstances of Talbot's crime and the behavior of the proprietor and his officials, he concluded the proprietary authorities were attempting to subvert the crown's customs revenues.[58]

The pretensions of Lord Baltimore finally brought a reaction in Whitehall. As Blathwayt from the Plantation Office reported the reaction of the crown, the king had sent the proprietor a message requesting that he surrender his power of government in return for royal confirmation of his right to the soil of Maryland. Charles II was prepared to proceed against his charter by a writ of quo warranto should Baltimore refuse. Blathwayt urged Effingham to send over information to provide evidence to be used against the proprietor. Two other charters had recently been vacated. Blathwayt expected a grand sweep. The duke of York was ready to surrender the government of New York to his brother. The proprietors of Carolina and all of the other chartered colonies, Blathwayt predicted, would soon fall under the same obligation. The necessary union of all the English colonies in America, a consolidation to make the king great and to extend his dominions, would then follow.

But was it all that certain? It was now up to Effingham to furnish Blathwayt with proofs and arguments to make good the boundaries of the royal colony of Virginia against the usurpations of Carolina to the south and Maryland to the north.[59] If the decisions had already been made, what need was there for Effingham's proofs and arguments?

How much of what Blathwayt reported was fact, how much hope on his part?

CHAPTER 11

The Southern Proprietaries, 1674–85

MINISTERS OF THE English crown in addressing themselves to the affairs of the overseas colonies in the twenty or so years after the Restoration were most concerned with the obstreperous commonwealthmen of New England, the riotous planters in Virginia, and the war-ridden West Indies. Only in what turned out to be the very last year of the reign of Charles II did they submit the proprietary provinces to closer scrutiny. Even in the appointment of customs officials in 1673 they employed proprietary officeholders in Carolina and Maryland. They had allowed the proprietary system to continue, even to expand, with, as events in Carolina and Maryland dramatically demonstrated, adverse consequences for governmental stability.

The Carolina proprietary board in London had had little influence over the settlements along the Ashley and Cooper rivers and Albemarle Sound. It had not even been able to support its own officials. Vacillating policies and turnovers in proprietary personnel further complicated the problem of governing. At times the proprietors sent out blank commissions for deputations to be filled in by governors at their discretion, ostensibly to reward men who might support the proprietors' cause or to be held over the heads of incumbents who might flout proprietary wishes.[1]

But seated at Saint James's in Westminster far from the infant settlements, they had little success in imposing their authority on Carolina and, particularly, on the West Indians who dominated the southern settlement.

Although the flow of people from the West Indies to Carolina diminished after 1680,[2] the Barbadians and the other Anglicans settled in Charles Town and along the Cooper and Ashley rivers still dominated political affairs. The most prominent among them was John Yeamans. In 1672 he had returned to the colony and claimed the governorship on the grounds that he was the only landgrave resident in the settlements. He quickly became embroiled with the board in London in a dispute over the cost of provisions, clothing, and tools supplied the settlers by the proprietors. Craven, Shaftesbury, and Carteret resented Yeamans's insinuations that they had dealt unjustly with the pioneers by not continuing to feed and clothe them. It must be poor soil not to maintain an industrious people, they had observed sarcastically; they would not be so silly as to contract "desperate" debts to maintain the idle. Although they publicly professed a great regard for Yeamans, the proprietors concluded that the colony had been better managed under Joseph West. They now sent him a patent as landgrave and a commission as governor. Unknown to the proprietors, Yeamans had left the colony for Barbados, where he died in August 1674, and the provincial parliament had already chosen West governor.³ For eight years West attempted to moderate between the proprietors and the Barbadians. He had little success.

A number of problems—relations with Indians, the distribution of land, and the debts of the settlers—continued to plague relations between the colonists and their overlords in London.

West, expected to carry out the orders of the proprietors, almost from the outset was himself dissatisfied, having received but little remuneration for several years of service despite a promise from Shaftesbury and Sir Peter Colleton of a salary of sixty pounds annually to be paid in England. Shaftesbury contended that the governor should be paid in Charles Town from the money owed the proprietors by the settlers and in local produce. West, who knew the inhabitants better, predicted they would not pay even a penny if they could avoid it. The proprietors then agreed to remit all debts owed them for supplies by the colonists, provided they paid West what was due him as governor from the board. The expenses of government ought, they insisted, to be borne equally by all of the inhabitants. The most suitable way to raise money would be a tax on property. But, they assured the Carolinians, they did not intend to raise money "without your own consent in parliament." Nonetheless, West continued to draw bills on the palatine (the earl of Craven) and his colleagues in London.

To the proprietors it was clear that the safety of the infant community required that the powerful and warlike tribes, the Westoes and Custatoes, not be antagonized. In response to complaints over English encroachments and the traffic in Indian slaves, the proprietors recommended that the governor and council adjust the boundaries of the English plantations. They themselves prohibited for seven years colonists trading with these tribes except under license from the proprietors. Traders wishing a license had to pay a fee of £100.⁴

When it became evident that commissioners appointed by the proprietors to settle disputes between the tribesmen and the English had failed in their task, the proprietors intervened; they prohibited the Christians from enslaving or transporting any Indian, and banned whites from settling on the same side of a river within two miles of a native village.

The proprietary board also sought to clarify rules for granting land. Although they had initially issued instructions to establish compact communities, the pattern of settlement in Carolina had resulted in plantations being widely dispersed because, it was alleged, of the great tracts of land taken up by men who did not have families settled on their holdings. To check this evil the proprietors ordered a reduction of the acreage awarded in the head rights for every new arrival. These new allotments were more than an individual and his family could work, but not enough for speculation or for land to be passed on to subsequent generations in a family. For the future, wealthier settlers could not take up land by multiple warrants and thus increase their holdings along the rivers. West and the council were warned to take more care in husbanding the proprietary land. If they did not, the board in London threatened to appoint men who would.[5] The threat proved abortive. Seth Sothell, a member of the board sent out to govern, was captured by Algerine privateers on the high seas.

For more than a decade the influential Barbadians—Maurice Matthews, James Moore, Arthur Middleton, and John Boone—easily frustrated proprietary policy promulgated in London. While holding appointed offices they also controlled the grand council and the provincial parliament by the judicious use of the punch bowl at election time. The Barbadians finessed the proprietors out of the trade with the Indians, supplying certain tribes with weapons for raids against other Indians in order to obtain slaves. And all the while Governor West and other officials had held their tongues.[6]

By the spring of 1682 the proprietors decided to establish a counterweight to offset the Barbadians. The failure of Shaftesbury and the Whigs to secure legislation to exclude the Catholic duke of York from the succession to the throne induced many Dissenters, including Presbyterians in Scotland, to contemplate removing to America. Huguenots in France were already feeling pressure from the Sun King, Louis XIV, to accept Catholicism. On 21 March 1682, Shaftesbury, Craven, Sir Peter Colleton, and the Quaker John Archdale (he now owned a Berkeley share) met with the earl of Bath at the Carolina Coffee House in Birching Lane to answer inquiries from Dissenting Protestants considering a move to Carolina. Once they had agreed on conditions, a number of influential men, among them Joseph Morton, Benjamin Blake, and Daniel Axtell, later that year led a migration of several hundred Dissenters from England across the Atlantic. Blake, the brother of the famous admiral of the Commonwealth, was probably related to

Archdale. His son, Joseph Blake, later served as Archdale's deputy and acquired his proprietary share. In Carolina the Dissenters took up lands along the Edisto River.

The proprietors sought to endow the newcomers with some political power. They dismissed West on the ostensible grounds that he had tolerated the Carolinians trafficking with pirates—then a sore point with the crown. Craven, the palatine, commissioned Morton governor, and Archdale named Axtell as his deputy, while Shaftesbury sent over a blank commission to be filled out with the name of a man amenable to the proprietary cause. Later that year the proprietors concluded an agreement with Sir John Cockram and Sir George Campbell wherein they authorized a group of Scottish Presbyterians under Lord Cardross to settle in Carolina outside the jurisdiction of Berkeley County, the center of Barbadian influence. Charles II supported the move of his northern subjects.[7]

The Scots as well as the other Dissenters were unhappy with existing governmental arrangement in Carolina. The constitution promulgated by the proprietors was insufficient to guard against oppression: members of the grand council were appointed for life; judges, sheriffs, and other magistrates were chosen by the proprietors, while juries were named by proprietary officials. To meet these objections the board in London decided to allow the Carolina parliament to punish members of the grand council or any other official for misbehaving, presumably by removing them from office, and to have juries chosen by lot.

The proprietors were contemplating further changes to secure the settlers in their rights, when reports reached London of irregularities and abuses in voting for vacancies in the council. In 1683 Craven, Bath, and Colleton rescinded their concession allowing their deputies and the representatives to ratify alterations in the government voted by the parliament. For the future the parliament would consist of twenty men, ten from Berkeley and ten from Colleton County, to be elected by freeholders holding five hundred acres of land. Craven County was thought to have too few inhabitants. There would be no further alteration in the constitution except by the consent of all the proprietors, the councilors, and the members of two successive parliaments.[8]

To strengthen support for the proprietary regime the board exercised its patronage. It named John Moore provincial secretary and receiver general. Along with John Godfrey and Robert Quary, a recent arrival, Moore also became a proprietary deputy. Inasmuch as Maurice Matthews and James Moore, two of the Barbadians, had contemptuously disobeyed proprietary orders concerning the trade in Indian slaves, Craven, Bath, and Colleton dismissed them and warned their proprietary colleagues, Seth Sothell and John Archdale, against employing them. No deputy put out by a majority of the proprietors could be reinstated by another without their consent.[9]

The attempt to build a proprietary party through patronage and the emigration of Dissenters from the British Isles met with little success. Joseph Morton proved to be a weak governor, an executive unable to control the Barbadians in parliament or to regulate elections in the manner required by the proprietary board. In April 1684, as another contingent of Scots was leaving Glasgow for Port Royal, the proprietors appointed as governor Sir Richard Kyrle, an army officer who had served in Ireland. He had orders to put the province in a state of defense against an expected Spanish assault from Florida. Many of the Scots under Henry Erskine, earl of Cardross, and William Dunlop did not long survive at their exposed settlement (Stuart Town). They bore the brunt of the Spanish attack. Kyrle too succumbed early. He died at Charles Town before the year was out.

Kyrle in his brief tenure of office had not pleased his masters in London. He violated his instructions on several points and signed a bill into law suspending the prosecution of debts owed individuals outside the colony. In nullifying the statute, the proprietors lashed out at the justices and sheriffs in the counties involved in procuring the measure, one repugnant to the laws of England. They were to be dismissed and replaced by men of better principles. For the future all laws enacted by the provincial parliament, unless confirmed by the proprietary board, were to be in force for only two years. By the time this rebuke reached Charles Town, Kyrle had died, and the council had elected Joseph West, the man the proprietors had dismissed three years before, as acting governor.

West was reluctant to take the post, given the opposition of the Indian traders to the election procedures mandated by the proprietary board. The proprietors now allowed West to fill vacancies among their deputations on the provincial council, but Maurice Matthews, James Moore, and Arthur Middleton were proscribed until they and their cohort showed promise of more acceptable behavior.

The displeasure of the proprietors extended to the populace, a "factious" people. Was West to govern the people, the proprietors asked, or were the people to govern him? The Barbadians dominant in Berkeley County had refused to allow equal representation in parliament to the planters in Colleton. Was it just that the Scots at Port Royal should have no representation in the provincial legislature? Was it fair that all of the inhabitants of Carolina be subjected to laws made by an assembly elected only by the inhabitants of Charles Town and the immediate vicinity, where the dealers in Indian slaves boasted that for a bowl of punch they could get whom they wanted chosen for the assembly?[10]

Proprietary patronage did not curb the local leaders, nor did the effort to weaken the power of the Barbadians by introducing other ethnic and religious elements responsive to the interests of the proprietors prove successful. But the program of encouraging diverse national groups into Carolina had great consequences.

By 1685 strong ethnic, national, and religious animosities flawed the social and political structure of southern Carolina. With few exceptions where "a man came from, when he came, and how he worshipped" became the basis of factional politics. The Anglicans from Barbados who settled in and around Charles Town along the Ashley and Cooper rivers had early dominated the colony. These "Goose Creek" men formed the first party opposed to the proprietors. Their leaders were more Barbadian than Anglican. Settlers from England also adhering to the Anglican faith were divided in their political sympathies. Stephen Bull, who had come early to the colony, resenting the dominance of the Goose Creek men, tended to support the proprietors; Ralph Izard, Job How, and George Muschamp, Anglicans arriving later from England, aligned themselves with the Barbadians; Scots, English Dissenters, and French Calvinists made up the bulk of the Protestant Nonconformists and generally supported the proprietary board. There was also a tendency for the earlier arrivals to unite in opposition to newcomers.[11]

Bickering, petty jealousies, and instability characterized political life in Carolina. Frustrated and disillusioned, Joseph West threw up his post and moved to New York. The proprietors did not know for certain who was governor. First Robert Quary and then Joseph Morton served as executive. At Stuart Town the Scots under Lord Cardross resisted the authority of the council at Charles Town. At one point, Quary issued a warrant for the commitment of Ralph Izard for appropriating a box of public papers. At the palatine court in Charles Town he publicly railed against the appointment as high sheriff of Berkeley County of Bernard Schenkingh, a man notoriously unfit, one who had once been fined by the sheriff's court and ejected from the grand council for drunkenness and scandalous behavior. The crowning insult to proprietary authority came in 1685 with the election to the council of Maurice Matthews and James Moore despite the explicit ban decreed against them from London.[12]

A decade of overlordship had done little for proprietary authority in the northern reaches of Carolina among the nearly four thousand settlers about Albemarle Sound. The Virginians across the border regarded these settlements with contempt, as little more than a refuge for thieves, pirates, debtors, criminals, and runaways. The great bulk of the inhabitants eked out an existence from subsistence agriculture and raising tobacco. The shallow waters of the sound prevented large vessels from entering and thus limited the freighting of tobacco to market for the most part to small sloops and ketches employed by coastal traders from New England who sailed across the sandbars blocking the inlets and brought in supplies from the outside world. Since Virginia had imposed a tax on Carolina tobacco, a few New England coastal merchants and captains, Benjamin and Zachariah Gillam, Joseph Winslow, and Mordecai Brown, among them controlled the economy of the Albemarle region.

There were other problems: troubles with the Indians and the policy followed by the proprietors in granting lands. Terms were not as liberal as those in Virginia, under whose authority the earliest planters had once lived. Moreover, land titles from the proprietors seemed uncertain, since the territory, initially part of Virginia, had been added to the Carolina proprietary by the charter of 1665.

To resolve some of the confusion Governor Peter Carteret had returned to England, leaving a council under John Jenkins in charge. Predominating on this board—some of whose members were unable to sign their names—were the older leaders from Virginia. Valentine Bird had once presided over the Albemarle assembly, and Richard Foster, John Jenkins, and John Willoughby were proprietary deputies. By the fall of 1674, however, the commissions issued by Carteret in the name of the proprietors had expired. Was there any authorized government? Jenkins continued to act as governor and in 1675 sanctioned an election for members of the assembly. Thomas Eastchurch, a kinsman of the former lord treasurer of England and the provincial surveyor general, won the speaker's post.

Factional animosities were soon manifest as Jenkins, George Durant, and John Culpeper moved against Eastchurch and his supporters. Durant was one of the more prominent planters. Culpeper had come from Barbados to Charles Town with a commission as surveyor general, but had fled north, according to Sir Peter Colleton, in order to avoid hanging for endeavoring to set the poor against the rich (such as they were). In Albemarle he joined with Jenkins and Durant to undermine Eastchurch by bringing charges against Thomas Miller, an adherent of the speaker, for allegedly referring disrespectfully to the king and his father as well as the proprietors and for blaspheming the Lord's Supper. When Culpeper brought these charges against Miller to John Nixon, a magistrate, the justice dismissed them on the ground that the word of one witness, Culpeper, was insufficient. Nonetheless, Durant, the attorney general, formally indicted Miller, and Jenkins attempted to dissolve the assembly. Although Jenkins was to base his claim to authority on election, there was at this point no division between a popular, or antiproprietary, party and a proprietary faction.[13] As speaker, Eastchurch had had the backing of the assembly elected in 1675, while Jenkins and his followers on the council had accepted deputations from the proprietors.

Adding to the difficulties in Albemarle was the economic impact of the Act for Better Securing the Plantation Trade passed by the English Parliament in 1673. Commonly called the Plantation Duty Act, it required captains who loaded enumerated tobacco without having previously given bond to land their cargo in England, to pay a duty of one penny per pound before clearing the province. In 1675 a box of documents from the Customs House in London arrived in Albemarle, containing commissions and instructions for a collector and a surveyor of this plantation revenue. Timothy Biggs, a Quaker lately arrived from the Ashley River settlements, secured the post of surveyor, and Valentine Bird, a follower of Jenkins, obtained the collectorship. Apparently neither Bird nor Jenkins intended to collect the export duty on tobacco. William Crafford (or Crawford), a New England shipper then in Albemarle, sought to persuade the planters that if the shippers paid the duty, they would then be forced to pass on the cost by increasing—doubling, it was said—the prices they charged for commodities they sold to the settlers in Albemarle. At this, people were said to have become "mutinous," reviling and threatening those councilors who had favored appointing the customs officers. The issue was used in the political struggle that followed.

During the spring of 1676 both factions in Albemarle vied for control. On behalf of the Jenkins group John Culpeper sought to arraign Thomas Miller before Governor William Berkeley of Virginia (one of the proprietors) and his council at Jamestown for using seditious and treasonable language. The Virginia authorities then occupied with the Indian disturbances and Bacon's challenge took no action, and in July Miller took passage on the *Constant* of London to join Eastchurch and to present his case to the proprietors in England. George Durant crossed the Atlantic in behalf of the Jenkins regime.

For some time the proprietors had been unhappy with the administration in Albemarle for having encouraged the traders of New England and for failing to promote the settling of the region south along the Pamlico and Newse rivers. They suspected that the leading planters, who had captured control of the trade with the Indians, feared competition by settlers located close to the Indian villages. To correct various ills the proprietors in 1676 decided to appoint Eastchurch—he was a

gentleman of "good fame" and related to the former treasurer, Clifford—governor. They also secured an appointment for Thomas Miller as
crown collector with John Radcliffe and Timothy Biggs as deputies and
commissioned these three to sit as their representatives on the provincial
council.

Eastchurch and Miller then set out for America. Durant, who had
not been able to win his case before the proprietary board, was known to
have declared that Eastchurch would not be governor. He had even
threatened a revolt. The disgruntled Durant took passage with Zachariah
Gillam, a shipmaster who was returning to Albemarle with, among other
cargo, a load of arms.

Some proprietors suspected that Culpeper, Durant, and the New
Englanders planned to capture the trade to northern Carolina, not only
to avoid the customs due on tobacco but also to dictate prices to the
planters. They were charged with offering the Albemarle planters but
half the price the Virginians received for their tobacco. Shaftesbury,
Craven, and their colleagues sought to reassure the settlers: they had no
intention of selling any portion of the colony and were resolved to
maintain and preserve the inhabitants in their English rights and
liberties. Although they approved the action of Jenkins and the council
in assuming control of the government once Carteret had left, they
decided the tactics of trying persons without a jury or sending Miller or
any man to be judged in Virginia as a derogation of their authority, one
derived from the grant by the king. They now required the assembly to
fill any vacancies on the grand council. This body along with the
assembly was to answer any complaints of oppression.[14]

Since no vessel was then sailing directly to Virginia, Eastchurch and
Miller took passage on a ship bound for Nevis, where Eastchurch,
"lighting upon a woman yᵗ was a considerable fortune," took advantage
of the opportunity thus presented and married her. He sent Miller on to
Albemarle to take charge until he would arrive. Miller sailed on the
shallop *Success,* arriving in Albemarle in July 1677. He carried with him
a commission as president of the council from Eastchurch. But did the
appointment of a presiding officer rest with the governor, or with the
other councilors by cooption?

In an attempt to minimize the events that followed, the proprietors
later repudiated Miller, charging him with "many extravagant things,"
among them imposing strange conditions for "ye choyce of ye
Parliamᵗ," imposing fines, and issuing warrants for the apprehension
(dead or alive) of the most influential men of the colony. By such
behavior he had allegedly "startled and disaffected the people towards
him."

Others testified differently: the faction headed by Jenkins had sought to make matters as difficult as possible for Miller; they had "poisoned the ears of the people," had "unsettled their minds," and had spread false and dangerous rumors that the proprietors intended to increase the quitrents threefold. One adherent of the Jenkins faction, Richard Foster, violently assaulted Miller. Threatening to run him through with a knife, he declared that Miller would never settle the royal customs in the colony as long as Foster lived.[15]

Miller persisted. Appointing Henry Hudson and Timothy Biggs as deputy collectors, he held Valentine Bird to account for any shortages in customs due for the past two years.

On 1 December 1677 Zachariah Gillam's ship, *Carolina,* arrived from London. On board was George Durant and a cargo of arms— weapons, Gillam later testified, he intended to sell to the colonists to enable them to defend themselves against the Indians. Miller sought to fine Gillam for failing to pay required duties on tobacco he had previously carried away from the colony.

Acting swiftly, Gillam and his son Benjamin, George Durant, Richard Foster, William Crafford, and John Culpeper overthrew Miller. They armed their followers with weapons from the *Carolina* and seized the collector and his papers. They then issued a manifesto to the outlying districts charging Miller with denying free elections and cheating the planters of 130,000 pounds of tobacco. Officials appointed by Miller— Biggs, Hudson, and John Nixon—were seized. Some supporters of Miller fled north into Virginia. The Quakers, who refused to support the uprising, were harassed. The junto then dispatched Richard Foster to summon the planters of Currituck to select burgesses for a new parliament. On assembling, the farmers "by a shout of one and all cryed out wee will have noe Lo^{ds} [proprietors] noe Landgraves noe Cassiques we renounce them all and fly to the King's protection." This went on for about half an hour until Foster bluntly informed the farmers what they proposed would not do, whereupon the fickle, or perhaps merely con- fused, planters cried out, "Up ye Lo^{ds} againe," and proceeded to choose representatives to the parliament.

The eighteen men elected to this revolutionary assembly met at the home of George Durant. They included James Blount, Patrick White, John Jenkins, and even William Sears, drummer of the insurgent forces. Once convened, the assemblymen insisted on a free trade and liberty for Albemarle tobacco to be carried anywhere without duties being paid.

Miller was to be tried for several "odious crymes," especially for "cheating the County" of 130,000 pounds of tobacco he had demanded as payment for past due royal customs. Jenkins, Crafford, Blount, Bird,

White, and Foster constituted a court to try Miller and his allies and empaneled a grand jury out of their own followers. The foreman was a New England trader, Mordecai Bowden. Accompanied by the beating of a drum and the shouting of their armed supporters, Culpeper, Bird, and Durant made their accusations, raking up in addition the old charges against Miller of blasphemy and treason. Timothy Biggs, Miller's assistant and the earl of Craven's deputy, they accused of murder; John Nixon, Sir Peter Colleton's deputy and the magistrate who three years before had thrown out Culpeper's charge against Miller on insufficient evidence, of treason.

The grand jurymen were hardly equipped to perform their duty; only four of them could read or write. However, Zachariah Gillam made certain they had enough liquor to drink. When Culpeper informed the foreman he must return an endorsement of *billa vera* (a true bill), Bowden wrote instead "bill of error," on the indictment. Snatching up the paper, Culpeper hastily informed the court that the verdict was a mistake. The hapless foreman replied he had merely done what Culpeper had told him to do. The court altered the return and ordered the sheriff to empanel a petty jury. The foreman turned out to be Joseph Winslow, another New England trader.[16] The arrival of a proclamation from Thomas Eastchurch halted the farce.

By this time the governor had managed to interrupt his honeymoon and arrive in Virginia. While in Nansemond County he had probably been informed from refugees fleeing Albemarle what had happened. He laid the blame for the uprising on the disaffected merchants of New England. Foster, Crafford, Bird, and Blount sought to prevent Eastchurch from taking control. They sent armed men north to the Virginia border and presented their case to the authorities at Jamestown: they had seized Miller, a man illegally commissioned by Eastchurch as president of the council, and had charged him with blasphemy against God, treason against the king, and infidelity to the lords proprietors of Carolina.[17] Fortunately for the insurgents Eastchurch died within a few days, and with Miller closely confined in a small log house and the proprietary deputies in prison, they apparently faced little opposition.

In the spring of 1678 Timothy Biggs, the deputy of the earl of Craven, broke jail and managed to reach London. The proprietors must quickly suppress the uprising even though it might cost them dearly, he pleaded. Initially the proprietors seemed to accept Biggs's views, but before he and the duke of Albemarle could appear before the lord treasurer to swear out his charges, the proprietors ordered him to desist and to return to America. They had decided to send Seth Sothell out as a proprietary governor. Evidently they did not know quite what to believe or whom to trust. It was "a very difficult matter to gitt a man of worth and trust to go thither." As a "sober discreet gentleman," Sothell, they hoped, would win the submission of the planters along the Albemarle. But unfortunately, Sothell was captured on the high seas by Algerine privateers and held for ransom.

As a conciliatory gesture the proprietors sent off commissions and deputations for some of the more moderate planters, who, they expected, would manage the government more circumspectly. They named John Harvey, a man who had apparently taken little part in the uprising, as president of the council with authority to issue out writs for the election of freeholders to serve in the assembly and authority to select the men who would sit with the proprietary deputies on the president's council. But all persons, Quakers excepted, were to swear allegiance to the king and the proprietary government.[18] Possibly Shaftesbury, Craven, Carteret, Albemarle, and Colleton wanted to keep matters as quiet as possible in view of the charges made shortly before against Carolina and Maryland by the royal commissioners sent out to investigate the rebellion in Virginia.

The discord in Albemarle could not be so easily muted. Biggs and his deputy, John Taylor, arrived at Albemarle from London early in 1679. The junto meeting at Durant's home, "ye usuall place" of their "Randezvouse," issued a warrant summoning Biggs to appear and to turn over all papers. Instead Biggs, who was the deputy of the earl of Craven and comptroller and surveyor of the king's customs, published his commission and posted an announcement on the court door: as the only officer for the king in the province, he would officiate in the king's affairs. Culpeper tore down this offensive paper and posted his own notice as collector appointed by the insurgent government, charging all men to ignore Biggs. He would seize the goods of any person attempting to enter or clear a vessel with Biggs. Nor would he give Biggs any account of the customs he should have collected for the past year or so. The "Country" having impowered him to collect tobacco paid in lieu of duties, Culpeper would dispose of it as he saw fit.[19]

John Harvey died shortly after receiving the proprietary commission as president. To consolidate power and eliminate any opposition, the councilors again brought up Miller on the old charges of blasphemous and treasonous speech. But with the aid of Biggs, John Taylor, and Henry Hudson, Miller escaped and made for Virginia, where he could take ship for England. To answer any charges he would make in London, John Culpeper took passage with Benjamin Gillam to Boston and then continued on to London with Zachariah Gillam. Evidently Culpeper arrived in London first. After quieting the fears of the proprietors and giving bond to deliver the tobacco due for payment of customs duties, Culpeper boarded Gillam's ship in the Downs to wait for favorable winds to carry him back to America.

In December 1679 Miller arrived, armed with depositions from Taylor, Biggs, and Hudson as to what had occurred in Albemarle. Crown officials acting on Miller's complaints promptly arrested Culpeper. After a hearing before the Commissioners of Customs Culpeper was committed to Newgate, charged with treason in having abetted a rebellion, imprisoned the king's collector, and appropriated the royal customs. Culpeper confessed his guilt and prayed for pardon. The attorney general in his report to the Lords of Trade recommended that no mercy be shown Culpeper unless he made good the three thousand pounds in tobacco allegedly due from the customs revenue.[20] Apparently in 1680 the king's ministers were concerned with the monetary loss, not in striking at proprietary or chartered governments.

The proprietors themselves preferred to minimize the affair. In a narrative submitted by Sir Peter Colleton, the board pledged that thereafter the king's revenue would be protected under a proprietor sent from England. Robert Holden, the receiver of the proprietary rents, had sent word from Carolina that "all is now quyett & Peaceable."

Gillam submitted a written statement that he had not been concerned in the upheaval on the Albemarle, but had merely sold his goods for tobacco and skins and had returned to England, where he had paid customs. He had refused Miller's demand for a penny per pound on tobacco before lading, for he intended to pay customs in England. Gillam did not address himself to the requirement that, having loaded in the colony without having given bond to return enumerated produce to England, under the Plantation Duty Act he had to make payment as Miller had demanded. The New England captain admitted having been present at the court when the junto had indicted Miller for treasonable words, but he claimed to have taken no part in the affair. Yet, he had "given drinke to ye peopell," but it was "as they was customers to him (noe otherwayes) & Mr Miller had his sheare of itt."

The Lords of Trade read Gillam's denial on 19 February and decided there was no direct evidence against him. They dismissed the case. At best the committee of the council and the commissioners at the Custom House were determined that the proprietors submit some proposal for settling the government and for collecting the customs revenue.[21]

Despite protests by Miller against Shaftesbury's intervention in behalf of John Culpeper and the petition of twenty-nine men from Albemarle pleading for help against the provincial council, the ministers allowed Shaftesbury and Sir Peter Colleton ample time to answer for the behavior of the officials in Albemarle. Finally, at the end of August 1680 the proprietors submitted a report—it was an abbreviated version of one submitted earlier in February—to the Lords of Trade. They repudiated Miller and the men who had aided him. Ignoring the commission issued by Thomas Eastchurch, their governor, they charged that Miller had acted without legal authority and had been imprisoned by the people for his arbitrary behavior and drunkenness. They further disregarded the sworn affidavits presented in behalf of Miller and the armed resistance offered Eastchurch after he landed in Virginia and neared the borders of Albemarle. The proprietors now announced that they were sending out a new governor, a Captain Henry Wilkinson, who, being unknown to the inhabitants, would be able to moderate matters.

At the trial for treason at the Court of King's Bench, John Culpeper was acquitted. As Blathwayt at the Plantation Office cryptically put it, Shaftesbury had represented on the basis of information allegedly received from Albemarle, but evidence he did not present to the Privy Council, that matters had been otherwise than Miller and his supporters had reported.[22]

That Miller remained in the royal service in England, assigned to a customs post in Poole, indicated that the ministers gave no credence to the proprietors' charges against him; nor were they inclined to use the sensational events in the colony as the basis of an attack against the proprietary charter. The proprietors themselves had sought to discredit Eastchurch and Miller simply to relieve Culpeper of any guilt after he had been charged with treason. At this point they were content to overlook the past. For the king's ministers it was enough that the royal officials would supervise the collection of customs in the colony and that the proprietors would send out a governor to quiet the factious planters.

Although Craven, Shaftesbury, Colleton, and John Archdale met to confer on instructions, neither these proprietors nor their governor seemed in any great hurry. Almost a year after the proprietors had pledged to send out a representative, Wilkinson had not left. By July 1681 he still had not departed for his post, and was then thrown in prison for debt. There was still Seth Sothell, held captive in Algiers. He was ransomed and sent to America with blank commissions to hold over the heads of the proprietary deputies in Albemarle should they be found unresponsive to the wishes of their lords.

Given the turmoil of the past few years, it was impossible to find men with sufficient stature who had not been involved in the factional struggles. Sothell was soon involved in a dispute with Timothy Biggs, who charged in the winter of 1683–84 that in violation of instructions Sothell had commissioned partisan deputies, men hostile to the royal interest. Evidently the proprietors had not even known the names of those their governor had deputized to act for them. They now ordered that Sothell send home depositions so that they might be able to answer the complaints made at court.[23]

Four years before, the ministers of the crown had been willing to overlook the turmoil at Albemarle and to accept the bland assurances of Shaftesbury, but in 1684 in light of recent developments in northern Carolina, Massachusetts, and especially Maryland, Craven, Colleton, and the other proprietors might have cause for concern.

The Calverts, barons Baltimore in Ireland and lord proprietors in Maryland, had faced a problem comparable to that the overlords of Carolina had encountered, an open challenge to their authority as manifested at least twice by a resort to violence.

The Calverts themselves had contributed greatly to this situation; they may have been their own greatest source of difficulty. Cecilius, the second Lord Baltimore, had never been in the province but had commissioned his son to govern in America. Following a visit with his father in England, Charles Calvert had returned to Maryland in 1670 and imposed new restrictions for the colony. He disenfranchised all freemen with less than fifty acres of land or a personal estate of less than fifty pounds; in this the Calverts may have been following the example set by authorities in neighboring Virginia. Six years later, when Charles became proprietor, he arbitrarily reduced the number of deputies from the counties called to attend the meetings of the assembly from four to two. Ostensibly this would reduce the financial burden on the rate payers. He later substituted direct purchase for headrights in granting land. It would now be more difficult for freed servants to obtain land and to participate in local government.

For the more ambitious planters status and influence would not come as easily, and among the immigrants entering Maryland during the middle decades of the seventeenth century scores had pretensions to the claim of gentry. While marriage, blood connection, and wealth were factors in determining social status, the main avenue for advancement was appointment to public office.[24]

The formation of new counties in response to the increase and spread of population had provided more openings as justices and sheriffs for the ambitious gentry, but the higher posts were reserved, and advancement was closed, except for a favored few. Real power through control of the provincial land office, the governor's council, and the judicial machinery lay with a small group closely linked with the proprietary family by marriage and religion. To these men went the lucrative and more prestigious posts. Ambitious men eager to rise above the level of county office resented the concentration of superior positions in the hands of a small group of Catholic gentry, relations, and friends of the proprietor. Some Protestants received high office, but they too were either friends or relatives of the Calverts.[25]

Several problems common to the Chesapeake area—overproduction of tobacco, Indian raids, adverse weather, depressed prices—further contributed to the general discontent. For most men in Maryland life was hard. Charles Calvert described his proprietary as "very mean and little," with the homes of the planters generally resembling the meanest farmhouses in England. Except for Saint Mary's, where the assembly and the provincial court met—and it contained not more than thirty houses— there was no place to be called a town. Yet the proprietor could boast that, had it not been for the enactment of a law for tolerating all professing Christians, one granting them liberty to worship according to their own consciences without being subject to any penalties, the province might not have been settled.[26]

Pluralism in religion itself created animosities. John Yeo, an Anglican, had been so bold as to complain to the archbishop of Canterbury that Maryland was becoming a den of iniquity with but three priests adhering to the doctrine and discipline of the Church of England among the estimated twenty thousand inhabitants. Men unordained and unconfirmed dispensed the gospel and administered the sacrament of baptism. The Catholics and Quakers provided for their own, and with no law to suppress dissent, the people were falling into Popery and fanaticism.

Baltimore sought to refute these charges. There was no need to support priests or ministers other than by voluntary contributions. It would be impossible for the provincial legislature to maintain the Anglican church, inasmuch as Presbyterians, Anabaptists, Independents, and Quakers made up three-fourths of the populace. The provincial act of toleration granted freedom of worship—the same toleration granted in Carolina, New Jersey, and Rhode Island—and prohibited exactions for religious support. Although the Lords of Trade professed to see a connection between "wicked" living and the uncertain allowance for ministers of the gospel, especially Anglican priests, they limited themselves to calling for further information.[27]

In Maryland religious animosities thus continued to be a vexing problem, particularly as they involved higher political office, resentment over Catholics receiving favors, and discontent over the burden of taxation. The planters on the northern Chesapeake frontier were uneasy over depredations by Seneca Indians. In Virginia, Bacon and his followers had already set an example in challenging constituted authority. Two successive heavy levies of tobacco further antagonized the farmers.

To air grievances some sixty men led by William Davyes, Giles Hasleham, and John Pate met in September 1676. They remonstrated against excessive taxation, too frequent meetings of the assembly, and having to take an oath to the proprietor as if they had no higher duty to the crown of England. They objected further to Baltimore's restricting the franchise and his taxing the poor equally with the rich by poll taxes.

The proprietary council proved unresponsive, branding these sentiments as seditious and the authors as mutinous. Davyes and Pate were apprehended and executed; some of their followers submitted and were pardoned; others, more obstinate, were fined. Thomas Notely, the deputy governor, who defended the poll tax—the rich paid the tax for their servants—was convinced that the heavy levies of tobacco for the past two years had given occasion to the "Malignant" spirits. The "common people," he thought, would never be brought to understand the need for the public charges, the money spent for the common welfare.[28] This was not the first uprising against proprietary authority in Maryland, nor was it the last.

During this crisis Baltimore had been in England establishing connections with Sir Robert Southwell and William Blathwayt at the Plantation Office, with Leoline Jenkins, a principal secretary of state, and with Anglesey, Rochester, and Craven on the Committee for Trade and Plantations. When he left for America, the proprietor probably felt secure. Southwell would inform Baltimore's counsel, Thomas Gilbert, of any matter relating to Maryland coming before the Committee for Plantations.[29]

The proprietor arrived back on the Chesapeake to face several problems: an open challenge to his authority by insurgents charging favoritism and monopoly of office by Catholics, encroachment on territory he claimed by a proposed grant to William Penn along the Delaware River, and a dispute with royal customs officials in Maryland.

In the spring of 1681 four vessels arrived in the Patuxent from London, Liverpool, and Poole with certificates that they were bound for England and Ireland. Although the parliamentary statute disqualifying Irish ports from receiving tobacco directly from the colonies had expired, Nicholas Badcock, the collector, held that by the Plantation Duty Act of 1673 a tax of one penny in the pound on tobacco shipped to Ireland was still due. Nonetheless, Baltimore—ironically, he had recommended Badcock for his post—granted permission to the master of the *Dolphin* to sail out his vessel without paying duty and allegedly promised to defend him against any action by the royal customs official. Badcock was warned not to meddle with ship captains or to interfere with the collections of plantation duties. In reporting this incident to London, Badcock estimated that the tobacco carried by the four vessels was worth at least twenty-five hundred pounds in customs and that the three sons-in-law of the proprietor and the provincial secretary were materially involved in the cargoes. Baltimore and the councilors thought of themselves almost outside the king's authority, he charged, allowing the collector to examine only a few ships' documents and neglecting to return to England lists of ships entering and clearing Maryland.[30] Badcock died that year, but his successor, Christopher Rousby, continued the campaign.

Baltimore attempted to discredit these opponents. He sent several letters to the lord privy seal, the earl of Anglesey, along with a sworn deposition by Vincent Lowe, a member of the council, relating an alleged conversation with Rousby concerning the king's efforts to foil the attempts of the Whigs to exclude the duke of York from the succession. Supposedly, Rousby had declared that Charles II at heart was of the same persuasion as James, that is, a Papist, and that the great men of the kingdom were all knaves and turncoats. Such talk, Baltimore claimed, proved Rousby to be a wicked and seditious fellow, as great a traitor as any man living. Badcock had been little better; he had sought only to cheat the merchants of as much money as he could under the guise of collecting the plantation duty. The ministers at court could see what hungry, indigent fellows were appointed to serve the crown in Maryland, men who dishonored the king, cheated his subjects, and drove all trade out of the province.

What must have been embarrassing for the proprietor was that he himself had nominated Rousby for his post. Rousby himself had friends in London, and through them he ably defended himself, charging Vincent Lowe with falsely testifying. The Lords of Trade and the Commissioners of Customs did not take Baltimore's charges of sedition and treason seriously, and they upheld Rousby's interpretation of the Act for Securing the Plantation Trade. The proprietor had submitted no particulars to the charges and had offered no proof. George Downing and his colleagues at the Customs House concluded that it would prejudice the royal service if the crown's officers were removed. Rousby would return to his charge. In the future, if Baltimore had complaints to make, he should do so in a formal charge supported by evidence.

These recommendations were incorporated into a sharply worded letter approved by the Privy Council on 8 February 1682. There was a further warning. Baltimore's proceedings in obstructing the customs officers and in exhibiting contempt for the laws of England justified the crown seeking a writ of quo warranto against the charter. For the present the king and council were inclined to be lenient, thinking fit only that he be charged with the payment of the twenty-five hundred pounds due in customs.[31] As was the case with Carolina, the crown seemed concerned primarily with customs rather than an opportunity to strike at the chartered governments.

While campaigning in London against the proprietor, Christopher Rousby had sent back to Maryland vivid accounts of the struggle to exclude the Papist duke of York from the throne. The reports of this battle for power, a political contest posed in a religious metaphor, may well have contributed to another attempt in Maryland to overthrow the proprietor and his Catholic favorites.

The events of the previous years on the Chesapeake seemed to be repeating themselves. There were incursions from marauding Indians from the north. With the "heathen rogues" raiding into Maryland and Virginia, some ill-disposed spirits, so Baltimore charged, sought to stir up the planters.

Two men figured prominently in these disturbances. The more dynamic John Coode, a rebellious soul, had been born in Wales, the son of an attorney. After attending Exeter College, Oxford, he had been ordained a deacon in the Church of England and had then served briefly as a priest before moving to Maryland. Although he was later to boast that he could perform a popish mass acceptable either in France or Ireland, his later views were perhaps more those of an atheist than a practicing Christian, let alone a Catholic priest. Shortly after arriving in Maryland, Coode married Susannah Slye, the forty-one year old widow of a well-to-do merchant and landowner. Robert Slye had incurred the displeasure of the proprietor by supporting the abortive rebellion of Josias Fendall. Susannah's father, Thomas Gerard, a Catholic who had served on the provincial council, had also broken with the Calverts and supported Fendall. As a consequence Gerard had lost much of his estate. His children and their spouses continued his feud with the proprietary family.

The wealth of Susannah Slye had attracted the ambitious John Coode despite her age and occasional fits of madness, episodes brought on, it was said, by the death of one of her sons. Coode himself, club-footed and deformed, with a monkeylike face, was not an attractive catch. His physical appearance and addiction to alcohol may have reinforced his rebellious, contentious disposition. Endowed with certain social credentials from England and his marriage to the widow Slye, John Coode rose quickly at the local level. In 1676 he sat on the Saint Mary's county commission and in the assembly. Through his wife's family he was now a member of an extensive network. It included his stepson, Gerard Slye, and his brothers-in-law, Keneln Cheseldyne and Thomas and Justinian Gerard.

Chances for further advancement depended on the proprietor, but Lord Baltimore in appointing men to office at the provincial level awarded posts to Catholics or relatives of the Calverts. And Saint Mary's had perhaps the highest concentration of Catholics of any county in the colony. In such a situation Coode, Slye, and the Gerards could rise no further. Coode's peculiar personality—a need perhaps to compensate for his physical deformities—may also have led him into chronic opposition. He found an ally in Josias Fendall, the one-time deputy governor of Maryland who had led an unsuccessful coup in 1660 against the Calverts.[32]

In 1681, when the inhabitants of Maryland were plagued by Indian raids and heavy taxes and agitated by the news from London of a popish plot, a threat to Protestant liberties, the two men moved against the proprietary regime.

Partisanship colored the accounts of what happened in Maryland that year. In a narrative intended to influence the authorities in England, Philip Calvert charged that Fendall tampered with the justices of the peace in Charles and Saint Mary's counties, incited the planters to mutiny and sedition, and harangued the settlers that they were fools to pay taxes. With a "war" being waged in England between king and Parliament, one reminiscent of the conflict forty years before, a man might say anything, for nothing was treason. It would be a simple matter, he had supposedly intimated, for the local justices to overturn the proprietary government in Maryland. Coode was alleged to have told a friend then engaged in litigation against a Catholic planter over land that he need not trouble himself by going to court for within three months no Papist in Maryland would own any land.

Coode and Fendall then crossed over to Virginia, where allegedly they intended to raise a force against Maryland. Nicholas Spencer openly entertained and "cherished" Fendall in his home and encouraged him in his designs, forgetting that a successful rebellion against Maryland might raise another Bacon in Virginia, where the planters were as ripe and ready for revolt as ever before. Spencer denied any involvement. But he was in communication with Philip Ludwell in London, and it was Ludwell who submitted to the Lords of Trade extracts of letters from some official in Virginia charging dissatisfaction by the Protestants that all of the arms as well as the militia commands in Maryland had gone to Catholics.[33]

The proprietor acted swiftly when Coode and Fendall crossed back into Maryland. He had Colonel Henry Darnall with a troop of horsemen apprehend them. After being hectored by Coode's wife—she was known occasionally to fall into fits—the proprietor released first Coode and then Fendall on bail. Despite efforts by Baltimore to exclude Coode, he kept his seat in the assembly which convened in Saint Mary's City on 16 August 1681. The charge of breach of peace, rather than treason, was insufficient to warrant his removal, the majority of the assembly concluded. A special court consisting of Philip Calvert (the provincial chancellor), William Calvert (the secretary), Henry Darnall (a Catholic councilor), and Diggs (a Protestant councilor) found Fendall and George Godfrey guilty of sedition, but released Coode, the evidence against him being circumstantial. The proprietor commuted the death penalty on Godfrey and fined Fendall forty thousand pounds of tobacco and banished him from the colony.[34]

Coode lost his offices; his stepson, Gerard Slye, moved to London where he continued the campaign against the Calverts.

The proprietor of Maryland faced another problem by this time. In 1680 the Quaker William Penn had appealed to Charles II and the duke of York for a proprietary colony and for a grant of the territory between the Delaware and the Chesapeake bays. The charter issued by Charles I to the first proprietor of Maryland granted him lands unoccupied by any Christian people. In 1632 the English court had not appreciated that some Swedes and Dutch had already settled on the west side of the Delaware Bay, a region later taken by the English forces sent out in 1664 to reduce New Netherlands. James's title to this region rested on right of conquest, a title contested by Lord Baltimore when he established the jurisdiction of Maryland by creating two counties for the region south of New Castle. Two questions were at issues: where did the line of 40° north latitude marking the southern boundary of Penn's colony run, and had there been any survivors of the initial Dutch and Swedish settlements at the time Charles I issued the charter to Baltimore for lands uninhabited by Christians? When Baltimore, Penn, and their officials could not resolve their questions in America, both proprietors crossed the Atlantic to defend their claims in London.

The men to whom Baltimore entrusted the government in Maryland jeopardized not only his claim to the disputed lower counties on the Delaware river but also his proprietary charter by presuming a right to the customs revenue of ships entering the Potomac and by killing a royal customs officer. Given the warning issued by the crown two years before, Baltimore's charter was in jeopardy.

When Baltimore departed for London, executive power devolved on a board of deputy governors. But the proprietor had made his cousin, Colonel George Talbot, a Catholic, rather than the senior councilor,

George Taylor, a Protestant, presiding officer. On the night of 31 October 1684, it was Talbot who killed the royal collector Rousby in a drunken brawl aboard the ketch *Quaker* in the Patuxent river. In reporting this incident, the governor of Virginia linked the killing of Rousby with Baltimore's refusal to allow shipmasters to pay customs on the Virginia side of the Potomac. William Digges, Baltimore's collector, ostensibly on orders from the proprietor, threatened to seize any merchantman paying duties in Virginia. Officials at Jamestown also charged that the councilors of Maryland, many of whom were friends and relatives of Talbot, were lax in apprehending the accused murderer.[35]

These events in 1684 seemed decisive. There had been ample opportunity several years before for the ministers at Whitehall to act against the proprietary governments of Maryland and Carolina if they had planned in 1681 to consolidate royal power in the colonies. At that time Charles II and his principal ministers of state had shown concern only that the proprietors of Carolina and Maryland make good the several thousand pounds due in customs and restore order to the governments of their respective colonies. In February 1682 Baltimore had been given an explicit warning, apparently to no avail. The behavior of the proprietor of Maryland and his officials in 1684 again seemed to threaten the royal revenue. But before any action could be taken, Charles II died on 7 February 1685.

With the accession of James II his proprietary colony of New York became a royal province. From the Plantation Office William Blathwayt reported that the new monarch was resolved to reduce all of the chartered colonies to an immediate dependence upon the crown; that is, their governors would be appointed by the king in council. The decision was not as certain or as extensive as Blathwayt hoped, for he was forced to call on the governor of Virginia to provide evidence to be used against the proprietors of Maryland and Carolina. Later that summer he wrote Effingham that Baltimore was "respited" until the situation was more quiet, although he thought James II was still resolved to bring Maryland under the crown.[36]

Within a few days the Commissioners of Customs received a letter from Nehemiah Blakiston, appointed earlier that year by Lord Treasurer Rochester as collector in Maryland, claiming the murder of his predecessor was being "seconded" by Talbot and his adherents on the Maryland governing council. There was little hope the principal magistrates under the proprietor would bring Talbot to justice. Moreover, they were obstructing Blakiston in the performance of his duties: they had disowned his commission, destroyed certificates he had issued to ship captains, and cleared vessels without his knowledge.

Baltimore's councilors had arrogated to themselves the power to deputize others—William Digges, Henry Darnall, and Nicholas Sewall—to collect customs. By these obstructionist tactics the king would lose annually several thousand pounds in revenue.[37]

Immediately on reading Blakiston's charges, the Lords of Trade ordered Baltimore to attend their next meeting and instructed Robert Sawyer, the attorney general, to prosecute a writ of quo warranto against the proprietor's charter. Baltimore handed in his reply a week later. Clearly, from the information supplied by Lord Howard of Effingham, Talbot's escape was due to the "corruption" of the guard and not to officials in Maryland, who now kept the accused man under close detention. Blakiston's complaints of obstruction were groundless. The proprietor had long since ordered that shipmasters should apply to the king's collector as well as to those appointed by the proprietary government. He had appointed Digges and Sewall as crown officers only until some successor to Rousby should arrive from England. The interference with Blakiston—serving him with warrants—may have been at the suit of one of the collector's many creditors.

The proprietor now went over to the attack, charging that it was Blakiston who had defrauded the king by turning several thousand pounds of tobacco taken in payment for customs over to his private creditors. To conceal the shortage in his accounts he had charged the proprietary officials with obstructing him in the performance of his duties.[38] Almost a year lapsed with no further action by the crown.

The following spring the ministers of state were considering action against colonial charters, but as part of a plan to revise the patents in the colonies to provide rights for Roman Catholics. The writ of quo warranto against Baltimore's charter was ordered prosecuted on 30 April 1686. William Blathwayt's expectations notwithstanding, it was never completed. James II and his ministers did not pursue the attack on the charter. Consistency of purpose and steadfastness in execution did not characterize the men at Whitehall in their handling of the southern proprietaries. The same was to be true of their reaction to the English colonies on the Delaware and the Hudson.

CHAPTER 12

The Delaware and Hudson Proprietaries, 1674–85

THE REACTIONS of the ministers at Whitehall to developments in the settlements along the Hudson and Delaware rivers were a charade, a burlesque of rational, purposeful rule. Their reactions render doubtful the notion that during the reign of Charles II they sought to impose authoritarian, absolutist government. Rather, they tended to let matters drift. Only after the death of Charles II did financial exigencies and the threat of a clash with the French in America force them to impose some order, to increase the military capabilities of the English on the exposed northern frontier.

Political instability and ethnic and religious animosities had poisoned relations among the colonists in New Jersey and New York and had rendered impotent the proprietary governments. Claimed by force of arms from the Netherlands in 1664, the area included a diverse ethnic populace with few attachments to the new English rulers, but with many grievances. Dutchmen and Swedes were now under alien rule. The settlers in the English towns, an overflow from Congregationalist New England, never fully accepted the rule of the Catholic duke of York or the proprietors, Sir George Carteret and Lord John Berkeley, to whom James Stuart had given New Jersey. The government the duke established for his own province had not allowed representation for the villagers in a provincial legislature, and so provided a source of dissatisfaction for the New Englanders who preferred the jurisdiction of Connecticut. The townsmen in New Jersey, while they chose representatives to an assembly, had other grievances; unlike their fellows in the New England corporations and contrary to the terms initially extended them by the governor of New York, they had to pay quitrents to the proprietors as a condition for holding their lands. James himself at times was rumored willing to sell his burdensome territory, a colony where only a few "indigent officers" commissioned by him had benefited.[1]

The duke's servants had indeed been eager to retake the lost territories following the easy reconquest by a Dutch fleet in 1673, but

231

force proved unnecessary. By the terms of the Treaty of Westminster, concluded in 1674, the Dutch restored the region between the Connecticut and Delaware rivers to the king of England.

In the summer of 1674 Charles II issued letters patent to James granting him the proprietorship over the lands between the Connecticut and the Delaware and vesting him with authority to govern, a grant made necessary by the interlude of the Dutch conquest. James then issued a commission to Major Edmund Andros as governor of his province. As sovereign, Charles II had bestowed on his brother the government and the soil, but had James any right to deed more than the title to the land to Carteret and Berkeley? If he did not under English law have the authority to divest himself of the power to govern, then the governor of New York commissioned by the duke as proprietor under the royal grant had jurisdiction. Charles and James may have been ambivalent or perhaps simply careless, but they issued contradictory and confusing warrants. On 13 June 1674 the king signed a letter commanding all persons in New Jersey to obey the government set up by Sir George Carteret.

That same summer James ordered his legal officers to prepare a grant of land to Carteret. The power to govern was not specifically mentioned. In writing to Andros some months later, the duke's secretary, Sir John Werden, referred to Carteret's "pretensions" to New Jersey and cautioned Andros to guard all matters relating to the duke's prerogative and income as they had been until further orders. As late as the summer of 1676 Werden confided to Andros that he did not find the duke inclined to part with any of his rights; he was merely humoring his protégé in his claims.[2]

Who governed New Jersey, Andros or Carteret's deputy? Further to confuse matters, even before James or his protégé had been legally seized of New York and New Jersey following the Dutch interlude, Lord Berkeley had disposed of his share to two Quakers.

Thus began an extended attempt by the Society of Friends to establish a sanctuary in America separate from the other colonies.

In 1671 George Fox had undertaken an extensive tour of the English plantations in North America and the West Indies. On his return the Quakers resolved to establish a colony for themselves, or at least to control a province. Among the Friends was William Penn, son of an officer of the Protectorate and Restoration navy and a young man fortunate in enjoying the friendship of important men, including the duke of York and the earl of Sunderland. Among the other converts to Quakerism were Edward Byllynge and John Fenwick. Byllynge, a brewer, although described by his contemporaries as a "cunning fellow," had suffered financial losses. By 1673 he was deeply in debt. To recoup his fortunes Byllynge through Fenwick entered into an agreement with Lord Berkeley for his share—whatever it was worth—of New Jersey. What Berkeley sold for £1,000 was a questionable half interest in the soil of New Jersey.

Relations between the two Quakers further complicated matters. Technically, the share Berkeley sold went to Fenwick, who put up the money, to be held in trust for Byllynge. When Fenwick decided to use his interest independently, the two men quarrelled. Fenwick finally agreed to accept one-tenth of the land and a cash settlement, and Byllynge prevailed upon Penn; Gawen Lawrie, a merchant in London; and Nicholas Lucas, a maltster from Hertfordshire, to act as trustees for his share. By an agreement signed on 3 March 1674/5, Fenwick, Lawrie, Byllynge, Lucas, and Penn divided the Berkeley share of the property into 100 portions, with 10 going to Fenwick. He then departed for America to found a settlement, Salem, on the Delaware River.

A year later Lawrie, Penn, and Lucas finally prevailed on Carteret to recognize Berkeley's sale to Fenwick and Byllynge and to agree on a new boundary to divide East and West New Jersey. The Quinquepartite Deed was signed on 1 July 1676.[3]

Acting in conjunction with other leading Quakers, the trustees began selling shares and portions to West New Jersey. Over the next few years 120 individuals became proprietors of the Quaker colony. What they purchased was uncertain. Was it the right to exercise governmental authority or even ownership to the soil? The Quinquepartite Deed, negotiated only with Carteret, had not been recognized by the duke of York, to whom the king had granted the government of the territory acquired from the Dutch by the Treaty of Westminster. Andros, the duke's governor in New York City, and his deputy on the Delaware River, Edmund Cantwell, refused to acknowledge the claim of Fenwick. After the Quaker proprietor arrived at Salem, he had himself elected governor by the settlers he had brought out with him. Andros would have none of it, yet wisely allowed members of Fenwick's board at Salem to remain in control of the town, but as overseers and under Andros's jurisdiction.

The Quakers who had purchased shares from the trustees went ahead with plans to settle their own colony in West New Jersey. In London on 3 March 1676/7, they adopted a document entitled "Concessions and Agreements." A substantial migration of Quakers from England to West New Jersey now began. Until an assembly could be convened in the colony, under the terms of the Concessions and Agreements commissioners appointed by the proprietors in England managed the province.

The first ship with settlers and nine of the commissioners arrived in August 1677. All but two of the commissioners themselves were proprietors. Thomas Ollive and Daniel Wills led the group. Before reaching their destination they stopped off at New York City, where Andros contested their claim to exercise any authority. To avert a clash Ollive, Wills, and their colleagues agreed to accept commissions as justices of the peace from Andros until the issue was resolved in England. Following an election at Burlington, the capital of the new settlement, Andros issued a new commission, appointing five of the eight men chosen by the residents. Unhappy with the powers claimed by the duke's governor, the Quaker leaders in New Jersey pressed for confirmation of their right to govern. They were particularly concerned with demands by Andros that the residents pay a duty on goods carried up the Delaware River.

The duke of York was in a difficult position. Anti-Catholic hysteria was high as a result of the charges levied by Titus Oates and the pressure exerted by the Whig opposition in Parliament for an investigation of the Popish Plot. Except for a few months during 1682, he spent the crisis in exile in Scotland. William Penn was pressing James to recognize the rights of the Quaker proprietors, as was Robert Barclay, a Quaker in Edinburgh, who enlisted the aid of a kinsman, the earl of Perth, an intimate of the duke.

The issue as seen by the royal duke's secretary, Sir John Werden, was whether the grants to New Jersey empowered the proprietors to erect distinct governments or whether they were subject to the laws of New York. James referred the matter to Sir William Jones. The entire procedure, including the ensuing decision, may have been arranged. In a piece of legal sophistry, Jones avoided the central question and treated import duties as profits, as a form of property, not as an element of general governing authority. Inasmuch as James in his grants to Berkeley and Carteret had not specifically reserved to himself any profits, the duke could not legally demand taxes from the settlers.

Later that summer in 1680 James released all his rights in both East and West New Jersey, the former to Sir George Carteret, the latter to Edward Byllynge. In his haste to gratify the Quakers, the duke had made one, perhaps two, errors, laying the ground for future difficulties. He may not have had any legal right to convey the power of government. In investing only Byllynge, James excluded the Quaker proprietors who controlled 90 of the 100 shares and who had founded the West New Jersey settlements under the assumption that they had purchased title to both the soil and the government.[4]

On the advice of William Penn, Byllynge designated as his deputy Samuel Jennings, a respected Quaker, but a man he had never met. In America Jennings hesitated to make public his commission from the unpopular Byllynge, but the resident proprietors and settlers, demonstrating their faith in Penn, still a trustee, decided to accept Jennings on a conditional basis.

At a general convention, or assembly, held in November 1680 they adopted a series of resolutions, designated as fundamental propositions, vesting the government of West New Jersey in a governor, elected council, and assembly. The governor merely executed laws passed by legislature. Jennings subscribed to these fundamentals, and not surprisingly the following spring the assembly elected him governor. His status was now that of an elected governor rather than the appointed deputy of Byllynge. Having now "usurped" the right of government—so Byllynge claimed—the assembly in Burlington unanimously resolved that the land and government of the colony together had been purchased from Byllynge. The Concessions and Agreements subscribed to by the proprietors and settlers alike in 1677 constituted the basis of government in West New Jersey.

Only about a fourth of the proprietors had come to America. How over a hundred men, most of them living three thousand miles away across the ocean, were to conduct a government remained to be seen.

The more immediate threat to the Quaker community on the Delaware came from the claims of Edward Byllynge. He had the support of the crown. In November 1683 the king signed a letter addressed to the inhabitants; the royal duke having granted to Byllynge the powers of government and Byllynge having declared his intention of executing this authority himself, Charles II required all persons in West New Jersey to recognize Byllynge and his deputies.[5]

The controversy was not so easily resolved. Early the following spring the assembly in special session authorized Jennings and Thomas Budd to deal directly with Byllynge in England. They found him adamant. When they threatened to take their case to officials in Whitehall, however, some of the prominent Friends in London suggested the dispute be settled by arbitration. Both parties then chose a panel of fourteen (including George Fox) and agreed to accept a decision rendered by any eight of the arbitrators.

After a number of hearings extending from 31 July to 11 October 1684, eight of the panel issued a judgment favoring Byllynge: the frame of government set forth in the concessions of 1677 by the proprietors had no legal status, since the right of government at that time had not been vested either in Byllynge or in the trustees of his property. Only in 1680 had the duke of York granted governmental authority to Byllynge, and he could not be divested of it without his consent. Moreover, it was not possible to divide such authority into one hundred persons; it must rest in a single person or a corporation under a charter.

Jennings and Budd refused to accept the decision. Remaining in London, they took the issue to the crown's officers. In a long letter, one filled with complaints against Byllynge, they asked the king—James II had succeeded on the death of his brother early in February 1685—to allow the proprietors in America to nominate a governor.[6]

By this time larger issues were at stake. The fate of West New Jersey became enmeshed in colonial matters of wider concern.

Even before the controversey among the Quakers had flared into the open in 1684, the personal antagonisms and legal battles experienced in the settling of West New Jersey had demonstrated to William Penn, not the most patient man among the Friends, the need for a single proprietorship as a prerequisite to planting a settlement.

The ubiquitous William Penn was himself in a favorable position, given his numerous personal contacts and connections varying from the most high—the king, his brother, and the earl of Sunderland—to strategically placed bureaucrats. Two other factors worked in Penn's favor: the desire of the king to offer some refuge for the Quakers and the debt the crown owed the estate of Admiral Penn. With interest, it came to sixteen thousand pounds.[7] The Lords of Trade decided in the fall of 1680 to make no recommendation on Penn's petition for a grant of territory west of the Delaware until they had first consulted Sir John Werden as to any possible conflict with the territory held by the duke of York. Agents for Lord Baltimore, Barnaby Dunch and Richard Burke, were also active to prevent any proposed grant to Penn from encroaching on Maryland.

The duke was willing that Penn have a grant for the land north of Newcastle "colony" beginning at about 40° north latitude under such regulations as the Lords of Trade might deem fit. In November 1680 Sir Francis North, the attorney general, Sir Creswell Levinz, and others, possibly including Henry Compton, bishop of London, scrutinized the draft proposals Penn had submitted, among them the arrangement incorporated in the patent to Lord Baltimore that the proprietor with the consent of the freemen could make such laws as he thought fit, provided they were consonant to reason and as conformable as possible with those of England. North thought it wise to include some mechanism to ensure that the crown would determine whether provincial bills were proper; he proposed a clause to enable the king within a number of years to repeal legislation. Another clause was added, one possibly reflecting the difficulty experienced in forcing Massachusetts to answer in London for transgressions, requiring the proprietor to maintain an agent resident in London and answerable for offenses against the navigation code.[8]

After "many waitings, watchings, solicitings, and disputes in Council," so it seemed to Penn, the patent for the new colony passed the Great Seal of England on 5 March 1680/1.[9] Despite some restrictions— limitations not found in previous proprietary grants—Penn's charter was a liberal one. The constraints resulted from the difficulties arising in the past years with Massachusetts Bay, Maryland, and the Albemarle settlements. The provision specifically subjecting Pennsylvanians to customs duties voted by Parliament was probably a reaction to New England and Albemarle shippers avoiding the Plantation Duty Act of 1673. Penn himself saw little difficulty in the requirement that laws enacted in the province be sent to England within five years, whereupon the king in council had six months to either allow or disallow them. It would be a simple matter to avoid this limitation by reenacting laws shortly before the expiration of the five-year period.[10]

Within weeks following the granting of the charter, Penn sent over a cousin, William Markham, to America. By Penn's orders, his deputy was to strive to satisfy the planters on the Delaware and with "meekness & sweetness, mixt wth Authority" to carry on the government for his own and the proprietor's honor. It would take more than a Friend or even a saint to brew such a potion! Penn himself remained in England to negotiate the transfer of the lower counties on the Delaware from the royal duke and to draw up a frame of government for the colony, one conforming to the requirements imposed in the charter. The day the patent passed he wrote to Robert Turner, a wealthy Quaker linen draper in Dublin and a proprietor of New Jersey, "I shall have a tender care to the government, that it will be well laid at first."[11]

After some weeks of consultation with several eminent Friends in London, Penn produced a draft. While he proposed to limit his own power and that of his heirs to do mischief, to prevent the will of one man from hindering the good of the entire community,[12] Penn was well aware of the confusion in New Jersey. In planning for the government and development of his colony he sought to win over the more prosperous and stable elements of the Society of Friends residing in the British Isles.

Many of the settlers who emigrated from England to Pennsylvania in the months to follow were yeomen and artisans. But Penn also attracted a far smaller number of wealthier men to purchase the land he offered for sale. They would establish a strong commercial base and bring stability to the infant colony. To them he offered inducements, special concessions in the purchase of land and political office. The various drafts of a frame of government Penn produced while in England reflected the role he proposed the wealthier men to play. In the final version the upper house of the legislature consisted of seventy-two of the most eminent men of the colony elected by the freemen. They initiated legislation. The assemblymen of the lower house—also a large unwieldy body, restricted to a nine-day annual session—merely approved or rejected bills proposed by the council. Penn and his advisers proposed to give the franchise to any Christian male twenty-one years of age or more who owned 100 acres of land (50 if he had completed an indenture within the preceding year) or who paid scot and lot, a local rate paid by householders in the English boroughs. But governmental offices were the preserve of the well-do-do, the men who had demonstrated ability by amassing an estate.[13]

Penn actively promoted his colony to potential investors and emigrants. The eight thousand people who settled in Pennsylvania during the first years included Welsh, Irish, and English Quakers and German Pietists. Several groups were organized to promote land sales and migration. Most prominent was the Free Society of Traders, with Nicholas More as president, John Simcock deputy, and James Claypool treasurer.[14]

In the summer of 1682 the proprietor prepared to leave England, a country marked by strife, for America. To his friend Colonel Henry Sydney who had resolved to keep out of harm's way at The Hague, Penn wrote that the voyage "will Secure me from ye revenge of my enimys." Penn was somewhat of an enigmatic man, one little understood in England. That winter, a newsletter circulated in London that in America Penn had professed himself to be a Papist and had died in the communion of the Church of Rome.[15]

Penn received a deed for the lower Delaware lands on 24 August from the duke of York and six days later boarded the *Welcome* at Deal to cross the Atlantic. About eight weeks later she dropped anchor off New Castle. Penn then travelled up river to Upland (Chester), where he held his first court and summoned a convention of delegates from the three Pennsylvania counties (Philadelphia, Chester, and Bucks) and the three Delaware counties (Kent, Sussex, and New Castle) to approve the frame of government and forty laws previously drafted in England.

On 4 December 1682 forty-two representatives met at Chester. Most of Penn's supporters—men he had appointed to office—had secured election. But from the lower counties the Swedish, Dutch, and English settlers had returned deputies little beholden to the proprietor. They attacked the laws Penn and his advisers had drafted as well as the charter for the Society of Traders. A stalemate resulted.

In elections held several months later, Penn's supporters won control of the council, but again few of the men returned to the lower house—Quakers and non-Quakers, Englishmen, Dutchmen and Swedes, old settlers and newcomers—were connected with the proprietor. The men from the older settlements on the lower Delaware, mainly non-Quaker, sought to establish in the assembly a body they would control, an institution to limit Penn and the council dominated by Quakers from the northern counties in Pennsylvania. A protracted contest ensued, with the assemblymen demanding to be allowed to initiate legislation. At best, the councilors condescended to allow them the privilege of conferring with the upper house. This compromise, contained in a document entitled the Frame of 1683, or the Charter of Liberties, satisfied few men.[16]

In the months to come the Quaker experiment in government by brotherly love proved to be little different from government in the other provinces of America, as relations between the council and assembly and between factions in each body became inflamed, as men pursued commercial gain, personal advantage, and political office. Ethnic, national, and religious difference also divided the inhabitants. During these early years Quakers, both English and Welsh, dominated in Pennsylvania, but not in the lower counties. Here the Dutch, Swedes, and English tended toward Lutheranism or Anglicanism, if any formal religion.

Of more immediate concern to Penn was the refusal of the Catholic proprietor of Maryland to accept the deed for the lower counties granted the Quaker by the Catholic duke of York. Both proprietors appealed to ministers at Whitehall, but at the Plantation Office matters were deferred until the spring of 1684 when Baltimore was expected to arrive from America.[17]

Penn decided to return to London himself to fight his case, the "revenge" of his enemies in England holding no terror for him. To protect his interests against the potentially disruptive factions in Philadelphia, he appointed as public and proprietary officials men sympathetic to his cause. Rather than naming a single deputy governor, he vested executive authority in the entire council, an elected body under the presidency of Thomas Lloyd, the keeper of the provincial seal.

In August 1684 Penn left the Delaware. After a passage of almost seven weeks he arrived in England, but found to his chagrin that he had not taken with him the papers and affidavits given before the mayor of New York proving settlement by Christians under the Dutch regime on the lower Delaware prior to the patent being issued to the proprietor of Maryland. Through the intervention of the duke of York he secured a postponement of any action by the Privy Council until the following year, when he was able to present his evidence. In 1685 on the recommendation of the Lords of Trade, the king in council ordered the peninsula between the Delaware and the Chesapeake to be divided, the western portion going to Baltimore, the eastern to Penn.[18]

From England Penn hoped to control the situation in both the lower counties and Pennsylvania, to manipulate the situation in America, relying on Thomas Lloyd to bring around the "wiser" men, the more "discreet and reputable" leaders.[19]

As he later learned, however, his coreligionists in Pennsylvania, as elsewhere, were too "governmentish," too faction-prone, too open in their dissatisfaction. Good intentions and common religious beliefs did not necessarily ensure tranquility.

Penn and the Quakers were also involved in the tangled affairs of East New Jersey, where for some years the proprietary governor, Philip Carteret, had been occupied with both the contentious New Englanders in the East Jersey townships and the aggressive governors of New York. As was the case in West Jersey, it was unclear where governmental authority lay, whether with the proprietor and his deputy or with the duke of York and his governor. Edmund Andros at New York did not acknowledge the authority of the East Jersey regime and demanded that the residents pay the same duty on imports as the residents of New York paid. In 1680 the duke recalled him for consultations on complaints of the Friends in West Jersey and the Carteret family.[20]

Sir George Carteret had died earlier that year, leaving his property in East Jersey in trust for the benefit of his creditors. After some difficulties, Lady Elizabeth Carteret, the executrix of the estate, and the trustees in February 1682 sold the moiety to East Jersey for £3,400 to a syndicate of twelve men, among them William Penn and Edward Byllynge. With the exception of Robert West, a lawyer of the Middle Temple, and possibly Thomas Wilcox, a goldsmith of London who sold out almost immediately, the purchasers were Quakers, merchants and tradesmen in and around London, some of whom were proprietors in West Jersey.

Almost immediately the new proprietors decided to take twelve more partners, by each selling a half share. Interest ran high. By the first week in September all but one of the twenty-four shares had been sold, and proprietors would not let that go for under £350 with another £50 demanded for expenses already incurred.[21] The additional proprietors included six Scots, two of whom were Quakers. Among the Scots were James Drummond, earl of Perth; his brother John Drummond (later Viscount Melfort); Robert Barclay, a cousin of the Drummonds; and their uncle, the merchant Robert Gordon. The English partners included two Londoners, Thomas Rudyard, the lawyer whose home had served as the office for Penn to dispose of his lands in America, and William Dockwra. In influence the Scots were apparently more highly ranked, especially when they added to their number Sir George Mackensie of Tarbet (later Viscount Tarbet), lord register of the northern kingdom.

Although Charles II was willing to encourage the Scots in their American ventures, the king's northern subjects wanted a greater measure of protection. In the summer of 1682 the Scottish and Quaker proprietors petitioned the king to sanction Robert Barclay as governor and confirm their interest in the land and government of East New Jersey. It did not take the Lords of Trade long to decide. On 30 September they gave it as their opinion that it was not "convenient" to constitute a new proprietary in America or to grant any further powers which might render the plantations any less dependent on the crown.[22] But the proprietors had not waited; five days before, Rudyard (Barclay's deputy) and Samuel Groome (the proprietary surveyor) had sailed on the *Globe* for America.

When Rudyard arrived in the fall of 1682, Philip Carteret resigned his office to the new deputy appointed by the British proprietors. Rudyard retained three members of Carteret's council, including the most prominent of the "old settlers," Captain John Berry, and added three new men to his board, among them Benjamin Price of Elizabethtown, one of the few of the New Englanders to have paid quitrents during the Carteret regime, and Lewis Morris, a man influential among the Quakers.[23]

Almost at once Rudyard found himself involved in controversy. The surveyor, Samuel Groome, "grown into an angry pettish humour," he charged, "had goaded" the Quakers and the residents of Navesink district into using the patent issued almost twenty years before by the governor of New York as grounds to claim an exemption from quitrents. The assemblymen were also pressing Rudyard for a bill to enlarge their privileges and to diminish those of the proprietors.[24]

Across the Atlantic the British proprietors repudiated Rudyard. They removed him as deputy governor—he was allowed to remain as secretary and register—and in July 1683 appointed one of their own, Gawen Lawrie, in his place. The new deputy arrived in East New Jersey the following year, bringing with him a fresh code and regulations for the distribution of lands. George Keith as surveyor and Lawrie had orders to safeguard the interests of the proprietors in allocating lands.

The proprietors resident in East Jersey set up their own board, however. Except for Lawrie and Thomas Warne (formerly a Dublin merchant), all of its members were Scots, and they excluded from their board the provincial councilors appointed by the British proprietors. Both sets of proprietors faced another challenge from leaders among the older settlers, John Berry, Samuel Dennis, and Richard Hartshorne.

They insisted on the privileges granted the inhabitants of the towns by Governor Richard Nicolls in 1664 and the right to a separate legislature, courts, and officials for the towns of the Navesink district.

The right of the proprietors to exercise governmental authority in East New Jersey was not certain, for the Scottish and Quaker proprietors in Britain had unsuccessfully sought confirmation from the king in 1682, and one of the proprietors, Sir George Mackensie, the lord register of Scotland, had pursued the matter with the duke of York. In a rather ambiguous vein he wrote to the duke's secretary that the proprietors desired to have "our government holden by Charter of his R[oya]ll H[ighne]ss yn as it is at pr[e]sent by transmission from our authoris [the estate of Sir George Carteret] without any augmentacôn of our priveledges, but only to be und' ye Duke[']s imêiate protection."

Did the proprietors desire to rejoin New Jersey with New York and send representatives to an assembly there, the duke having finally agreed to institute a representative legislature, Werden inquired, or did they want to have their government held in New Jersey by charter from James? Was the phrase "under the duke's immediate protection" to be understood only as the duke's confirmation of their rights and possessions in East Jersey as derived from the grant to Sir George Carteret? Evidently so, for in March 1683 James issued a warrant for his legal officers to prepare a deed confirming to Perth and the other proprietors of East New Jersey the powers granted to Carteret. This was executed on 14 March 1682/3.

What was not clear was whether James, who was not the sovereign, could confer on others the powers of government vested in him by the king. The matter was not definitively resolved that November with the publication of a proclamation approved by the king in council, a document confirming the sale of East Jersey and charging all persons to obey the laws made by the proprietors.[25] At this time James may well have been disillusioned with the entire business in America. He had divested himself of the Jerseys and the Delaware counties. And it was rumored in 1684 that the royal duke was thinking of selling his remaining possession, New York, to the Dissenting merchant of London, Major Robert Thompson.

The proprietors in Britain assumed—or so they informed their deputy in East Jersey—that the new grant from the duke included the full power of government.[26] They were not yet free of pressure from the duke's officers in America, particularly the new governor of New York, Colonel Thomas Dongan, who argued that it would be to the considerable advantage for the duke's affairs and the quiet and satisfaction of the inhabitants that East New Jersey be annexed to the government of New York. In March 1684 the commissioners appointed to manage

James's revenue broached the matter with the earl of Perth, the lord justice of Scotland and a leader of the proprietors of East Jersey: it would be convenient for all parties if East Jersey returned under the government of the duke, with landowners there being confirmed in their possession under the usual quitrent. Would Perth inquire of the other proprietors whether they were willing to surrender the government to James and on what terms? The Drummonds and Mackensie emphatically rejected this proposal. They asked the earl of Sunderland to oppose on their behalf any violation of their rights and William Blathwayt at the Plantation Office to keep them apprised of any matters germane to their colony.[27]

Circumstances far beyond Blathwayt's control—even had he been inclined to protect proprietary governments—intervened. Early in February 1685 Charles II died, and James became king. The proprietary colony of New York became a royal province. From New York City came pleas from local officials that the economic and military well-being of the colony required the annexation of adjoining territory. William Dyer, a customs collector with jurisdiction over New York and East New Jersey, complained of abuses and injuries to the king's service, particularly efforts to foil prosecution of ships violating the navigation code.

The response of the Privy Council under James II was swift. It directed the attorney general to sue out a writ of quo warranto.[28] The officials in New York apparently had prevailed over James's Scottish and Quaker friends.

New York, with its diverse, polyglot population, had proved more burdensome than profitable to its proprietor. The commercial resources of the colony were meager; consequently, the revenue expected to accrue to the duke had fallen far below expectations. By 1675 James still owed Thomas Delavall, the provincial auditor recruited from the English customs service, some two thousand pounds for back salary and expenditures. Delavall had paid out fourteen hundred pounds of his own funds to sustain the soldiers of the garrison in New York. The first English governor, Richard Nicolls, before he left the province in 1668, had been forced to borrow over eight thousand pounds for the government and small garrison.[29] Collection of taxes had been difficult in view of the widespread resentment of the duke's regime by both the English townsmen and the conquered Dutch, many of whom had collaborated when a fleet from the Netherlands had taken the province in 1673.

Following the retrocession to the crown of England, James appointed three officials to restore English and proprietary authority.

Major Edmund Andros, an experienced officer married to the niece of William, earl of Bath, received a commission as the duke's governor and the authority to raise a company of one hundred soldiers from the streets of London to garrison the province. The deputy commander was Lieutenant Anthony Brockholes, a professed Catholic excluded from service in England by the Test Act passed the year before. Appointed to be the duke's collector of customs was William Dyer. His father had been a founder and secretary of Rhode Island, but his mother, a Quaker, the Massachusetts authorities had executed for contumacy. Dyer, Brockholes, and Andros took up their stations in America that fall. Several other Englishmen—lawyers and traders—arrived about the same time, men who saw New York as a temporary station where they might repair or enhance their fortunes.

Sensitive to the situation, James and his advisers had instructed Andros to satisfy both the English and the strangers, that is, the Dutch and the Huguenots in New York. The governor was to maintain discipline among the soldiers and act only according to law against persons who had behaved treacherously. Andros was to remove from office aliens of doubtful loyalty, but allow religious toleration and follow the procedures employed in New England for granting lands as far as possible. As a concession to the Dutch a few vessels under license could sail directly between the Netherlands and New York.

How far the public revenue collected in the colony would support the charges of government was a particular concern. In response to a suggestion given Andros for an elected assembly to facilitate raising money, the duke urged the governor to discourage such a notion as unnecessary. The general assize, probably staffed by the same persons who would be elected as representatives of the towns, could satisfy any grievances. James viewed assemblies as dangerous bodies, apt to assume privileges destructive to the peace of government. However, if Andros found an elected assembly to be necessary, James professed himself willing to consider any proposals to that end.[30]

Critical to the proprietor's policy were the state of finances and the competition for office. Several of the Dutch had served as schout, burgomaster, and schepen during the interlude of Dutch conquest. How were the returning English authorities to treat them? Previous English governors had been financially dependent on the wealthier of the Dutch families, particularly the Van Cortlandts, for loans to support their regimes. How would the newly arrived English lawyers and traders react to any favors granted them?

During the interlude of Dutch occupation, some of the towns on Long Island had again come under the jurisdiction of Connecticut. Although the townsmen petitioned to be allowed to continue this arrangement, Governor John Winthrop, in response to protests from Andros, denied having entered into any permanent engagement with the Long Islanders. The protection extended them by Connecticut had been only temporary until the king made known his will. John Winthrop and his sons continued with Andros the good relations they had established with previous governors of New York. For his part Andros backed down from an armed conflict over the disputed boundaries of the two provinces. The proprietor himself was unwilling to have Andros attempt to force the issue, hoping for a more convenient means of settling the dispute. But the revival of the claim by Andros of all territory east to the Connecticut river, the bounds claimed by the Dutch, might be useful later.[31]

Andros faced another test from eight Hollanders who had enjoyed office under Stuyvesant, Nicolls, and Lovelace, but who had repudiated their former allegiance to the English government and had accepted office under the Dutch conquerors. Indeed, Cornelius Steenwick had actively aided the Netherland forces in 1673. Under orders from the proprietor, Andros excluded them from office. They then refused to take the oath of allegiance unless he would assure them that they would not be required to take up arms against the Netherlands in case of another war. Andros had them jailed. While Johannes DePeyster capitulated within a month, the others persisted and were found guilty by the magistrates— mostly Englishmen from Long Island—of promoting faction and rebellion and of trading illegally. Not having taken the oath of allegiance, technically they were aliens.

After an unsuccessful attempt to have the States General in Europe intercede for them in London, the seven defendants submitted and asked to take the oath. Eagidius Luyck and Anthony DeMilt apparently withdrew from public life, while Cornelius Steenwick, the most prominent among them, did not gain political office again until 1683, when he became mayor of New York. Others were able to gain seats on the board of aldermen, Johannes DePeyster in 1676, Johannes Van Brugh and William Beekman in 1678, and Nicholas Bayard in 1683.[32]

Andros found himself drawn into another controversy in the Dutch community, a religious conflict pitting Nicholas Van Rensselaer against Jacob Leisler and Jacob Milborne. Van Rensselaer had first appeared in London to represent his family interests in England. After ordination in the Church of England he had obtained a license to preach to the Dutch congregation in Westminster. With the close of the Third Anglo-Dutch war he had migrated to America carrying a recommendation from the duke of York. At about the same time, on the death of his brother, he became director of the colony (patroonship) of Rensselaerswyck near Albany. In response to the request of the proprietor Andros had appointed him to assist at the Dutch Reformed Church. The elders protested—having been ordained in England, he was not qualified to administer the sacraments according to the rites of the Dutch Reformed Church—and complained to the classis in Holland, a consistory of senior clergymen.

A few months after Van Rensselaer's forced installation at Albany, Leisler and Milborne accused him of having used some dubious words in a sermon. Both men at times exhibited paranoid behavior. In 1689 they were to go into open revolt against the authorities in New York. Milborne, whose brother was an Anabaptist preacher, had once been an apprentice and was now a bookkeeper for Thomas Delavall. Leisler, born in Frankfort on the Main the son of a Calvinist pastor, had migrated to New Amsterdam as a soldier employed by the Dutch West India Company. Three years later in 1663 he married Elsje Tymens, the widow of a merchant of means, Pieter Van der Veen. The marriage provided him with capital to trade in furs, wine, and tobacco and a possible entry into the prominent families, the Loockermans and Van Cortlandts. His self-serving, contentious personality, however, alienated his relations. When Govert Loockermans, his wife's stepfather, died without leaving a will, Leisler entered into an extended suit for possession of the estate.

Leisler was driven to attack Van Rensselaer and the governor who supported him. He was not representative of an established upper class bypassed by the English regime. He was a latecomer capitalizing on a fortunate marriage and driven by a flawed, compulsive personality into opposition. Once under attack, Van Rensselaer brought charges against Leisler and Milborne, accusing them of false testimony, defamation, and blasphemy.[33] They then charged him with heterodoxy and poor preaching! The affair divided the congregation. Andros removed the pastor for offensive living, but called Milborne before the council at New York City for libelling the governor. Milborne then sought satisfaction in London by swearing out complaints against Andros for false arrest.

While some in the Dutch community may have resented the governor's role in the affair and scorned Van Rensselaer as a man imposed on them by the alien English, the incident actually divided the Dutch: the Van Cortlandts, the Van Rensselaers, and the Schuylers opposed Leisler and supported Andros. They had made their accommodation with the English rulers, had made the best of the situation. Their children would marry among the English, and prestige and position remained with them. Leisler by his marriage was also well off, and three of his daughters married Englishmen, but this did nothing to enhance his career. The failure to master the English language further limited his chances for public office. The bitterness he later showed in open revolt may well have stemmed from his inability to break into the charmed circle.

While Andros had at times been tactless, he had not launched a systematic attack on the Dutch or their culture. He sought to minimize conflict and to avoid interfering in the affairs of their churches. By 1680 his policy of rewarding prominent lay church officials, such as Van Cortlandt, Nicholas Bayard, and even Cornelius Steenwick, with office helped allay ethnic fears.[34]

The major challenge to Andros and the other proprietary officials came not from the Dutch but from discontented Englishmen. The proprietary governor had turned his attention to implementing a program worked out with the duke of York and his household officers for the trade of the province. They planned to stimulate the economy of the colony and thus increase the revenue from foreign commerce. The program aimed, first, to improve the quality, enhance the reputation, and thus widen the market for New York's agricultural produce and, second, to channel exports and imports through New York City. It was not that Andros and his council sought to channel trade away from the Netherlands to England or to disadvantage resident Dutch merchants.[35] The comparatively modest estates of most of the local merchants indicated that their commercial ventures had not been very extensive under the Dutch West India Company.

Some of the newcomers who arrived following the retrocession of New York by the States General proved very aggressive. Robert Livingston lived and worked in a Dutch community and learned the language. In 1679 he married a Dutch woman. That same year James Graham, a merchant based in New York City and engaged in the West Indies trade, wrote to Livingston to inquire about placing his brother as an apprentice in Albany. The youth could more easily learn the Dutch tongue there. An English merchant so trained or a man like Frederick Philipse, with a Dutch father and an English mother, enjoyed an advantage over Samuel Staats or Johannes DePeyster, whose command of the language of the conqueror was poor, or Jacob Leisler, whose use of English made him a laughingstock to his contemporaries.[36]

Before Andros initiated his program, the merchants and shippers of Boston, men who commanded more wealth and better connections with the outside world than the Yorkers, dominated the commerce of New York, controlling the carrying trade in provisions to the West Indies and manufactures from Europe. Andros initiated a concerted effort to improve quality, the reputation, and thus the demand for New York flour and other staples. Expanding trade and channeling it through New York City would both increase and facilitate the collection of import duties for the proprietor.

Despite some brief periods of depression, over the next twenty years this program led to impressive gains in the shipping and overseas commerce of New York, but not without initially evoking hostility within certain elements of the population. New York City was made the entrepôt for the entire province. Here exports would be inspected for quality and weight. Freemen of the city held the exclusive right to mill and pack flour and biscuits for export. Townsmen elsewhere were prohibited from exporting directly, but had to deal through the metropolis. For the settlers on Long Island who had dealt with the middlemen of Boston, the new regulations meant a reorientation of their trade. Hitherto Boston had served as the principal emporium for the distribution of European and English wares.

The collection of import duties essential for financing the proprietary government provided a major challenge to Andros at New York City.

A group of English factors and ship captains involved in the trade of New York and New Jersey—Christopher Billop, William Pinhorne, and Edmund Tudor among them—complained in London that the duke's governor was corrupt, was engaged in illegal trade, and had unduly favored certain Dutch merchants in the colony, Frederick Philipse and Stephanus Van Cortlandt. Some of the charges against the governor bordered on the preposterous: he was accused of allowing a Dutch rather than an English style of whipping post, so that the Englishmen in the colony were "rendered thereby the more ridiculous to ye Netherlanders" and held in great derision by them. That the duke of York and his household, men concerned primarily in protecting the provincial revenue, after reviewing the evidence, dismissed the charges indicated there was little truth behind them. They may have stemmed from the frustration of Englishmen who ordinarily might have enjoyed political prerogatives commensurate with their economic and social position but had been denied by Andros. Undoubtedly Van Cortlandt and Philipse benefited from their relations with the governor and had received high political office from him, since Andros and his predecessors had been so dependent on short-term loans to keep the government going. These established merchants were the only men with enough credit to sustain the proprietary regime.

In response to various complaints James recalled Andros for consultation and sent out one John Lewin to investigate the situation in New York. The evidence Lewin collected was at best suggestive rather than conclusive. It was based on the tales of one merchant, Edward Griffin, that the collector, William Dyer, had allegedly told him: that the revenue collected was actually double the amount entered into the records and that both Andros and Dyer had discriminated in favor of

Philipse and Van Cortlandt by allowing their goods to be undervalued when imported. Two visiting Dutch Labadists, members of a Quietist sect, hardly the best informed of men, were probably responsible for the other charges leveled against the governor, among them that Andros, through secret partners, was engaged in illegal trade with Holland.

In a hearing held the following year in London before the duke of York's solicitor, John Churchill, Lewin could not sustain these charges, accusations so detrimental to the duke's revenue. Andros and Dyer were both cleared and went on to hold offices of greater trust and responsibility.[37]

In New York a crisis developed over the collection of customs duties. On orders from the proprietor these duties had been renewed in 1677 for three years, but Andros before leaving for England had failed expressly to extend them. When a ship from London arrived on 9 May, merchants in the city refused to pay customs and sued William Dyer for detaining the cargo. Samuel Winder brought charges of treason against him. Only one Dutchman, Cornelius Steenwick, sat on the grand jury; the rest were all English merchants or factors residing in the city or townsmen from Long Island. Englishmen also dominated the court of assizes.

The charges against Dyer were that by collecting taxes he had "trayterously, maliciously and advisely used and exercised Regall Power and Authority over the King's Subjects" and had "traiterously, maliciously and advisely plotted . . . Innovacôns in Governm^r and the subversion . . . of the known Ancient and Fundamentall Lawes" of the kingdom of England. He had imposed and collected unlawful customs on the goods of the subjects of the king trading to New York "contrary to the great charter of Libertyes [Magna Charta], Contrary to the Peticon of Right" of 1628, and contrary to other unspecified statutes.[38] Dyer's crime as expressed in this pretentious, redundant language was that he had violated the rights of merchants arrived from England trading in the colony. The men who charged Dyer made up a clique of English merchants operating in New York and New Jersey. They simply employed the familiar political rhetoric of London and Westminster in the colonial arena.

Not to be intimidated, Dyer demanded to know by what law the court presumed to try him. Taken aback, the justices decided to ship him home on the *Hope,* commanded by a merchant, George Heathcote, to be tried in England. Samuel Winder, his accuser, was to post £5,000 before the council to prosecute Dyer in England.

At this same session of the assizes another attack was mounted, this by John Tudor, against the mayor's court and by implication against the Dutch. A tavernkeeper who had arrived in the colony in 1674, Tudor had been tried before the local tribunal for allowing gambling and convicted without benefit of jury. Tudor now charged William Beekman, Johannes Van Brugh, Guillen Verplanke, and the other Dutch alderman who convicted him of treason, on grounds that they maliciously plotted and contrived to practice innovations in the fundamental laws of the realm of England. Much the same evocative rhetoric was employed against Robert Livingston, collector at Albany, for attempting to collect the excise on rum.

The disturbances in New York and the threat to the proprietary revenue were decisive for the duke of York and his servants. The charges against Dyer were dismissed in London. Samuel Winder had failed to appear to prosecute them, despite public notice being given in the *Gazette*. Winder himself was accused in Southampton of infamous conduct to a maid of good repute, but not having the five pounds he had promised her by way of satisfaction, he chose to flee.[39] Lewin's charges against Andros fell through, and Jacob Milborne was able to prosecute the governor only for having him falsely arrested some years before in New York. The damages awarded were insignificant, forty-five pounds.[40] Milborne then returned to New York, purchased land, and made a good marriage. He had done well for himself.

Many of the leaders of the protest against the duke's officials in 1681 came out well from the affair, as the proprietor in England and the new governor he appointed sought to placate the dissidents and to widen the basis of political participation in the colony. There had been little evidence of widespread popular participation in the protests. English merchants and factors who operated in New York and East Jersey made up the movement. They ranked somewhat lower on the political ladder than the men who enjoyed power under Andros, and they forced the duke's hand in the matter of the legislative assembly. To them it offered an alternative for advancement.[41]

By March 1682 the duke of York condescended to allow a representative assembly on the condition that the colonists agree to raise money to discharge the public debt and settle a fund sufficient to maintain the garrison and the government. Benjamin Apsley, John Werden, and the other members of the duke's household then worked out the instructions for a new governor, the Roman Catholic Colonel Thomas Dongan, and the new collector, Lucas Santeen. An invitation was extended the Scottish proprietors of East New Jersey to join New York, send representatives to the assembly there, and share the expenses of government.[42]

Thomas Dongan arrived at his post late in the summer of 1683. On 13 September he issued writs for the residents of the towns and settlements to elect representatives to a legislative assembly. During the course of a three-week session they passed fifteen bills, including a Charter of Liberties and Privileges, probably the work of Mathias Nicolls, a lawyer by training and profession.

From the outset Dongan attempted to placate those who had challenged the duke's government. Jacob Milborne became a justice of the peace and a captain of militia; William Pinhorne, who had taken part in the attack on Dyer, became an alderman, and John Tudor, who had charged the mayor and alderman with treason, became sheriff. While Dongan in making these appointments hoped to end factionalism, disgruntled men in New York could well conclude that opposition, a challenge to authority, could be made to pay.

Dongan faced other problems. To establish a buffer against the French in Canada he committed himself to support the Iroquois Indian confederation. Without the tribesmen the defense of the colony would be more difficult and more expensive. When ordinary means to raise funds proved inadequate, he too borrowed from private individuals, in return granting his creditors special considerations. Seeking other sources to finance the government, he recommended to the duke's servants at Saint James's that the jurisdiction of the colony be enlarged and thus the base for revenue expanded by acquiring East Jersey, the region disputed with Connecticut, and even the corporation of Rhode Island.

In March 1684 the commissioners for the duke's household met several times in London to consider Dongan's proposal. Andros, who attended these sessions, agreed it would certainly be advisable to regain East Jersey if it could be done. The commissioners for their part were hopeful that the earl of Perth and the other Scottish proprietors would see the convenience of coming under James's government if their lands were confirmed to them under a small quitrent. In this they were to be rudely surprised. Perth, John Drummond, and George Mackensie informed them in no uncertain terms that they insisted on their full rights both in respect to the government of the colony and in the right to trade in the ports and harbors of East Jersey. As to Rhode Island, the commissioners could not perceive what grounds Dongan had in calling for a writ against the charter.

By March 1684, Sir John Werden, the earl of Rochester, and their colleagues in the duke of York's household had accepted the major provisions of the bill for the Charter of Liberties and Privileges passed the previous fall by the New York assembly. They then took up a proposal submitted by the mayor and aldermen to have the city incorporated. Later that year, on 4 October 1684, James signed and sealed the bill for the provincial charter. That same evening it was sent to be registered and then delivered to Captain Mark Talbot, who would carry it to New York.[43] It never crossed the Atlantic. Why is not clear.

Charles II died on 6 February 1684/5, and James, duke of York and proprietor of New York, became king of England. Eleven days later the lords of the Committee for Trade and Plantations ordered Werden to deliver the records of the colony to the Plantation Office. At a full meeting of the committee at the council chamber at Whitehall on 3 March, with the more influential ministers—Sunderland, the brothers Rochester and Clarendon, and George Savile, marquis of Halifax—in attendance, the charter of New York was considered. Some noted the proposed bill contained privileges they thought inconvenient and arrangements they viewed as at variance with those in other colonies. At this point James II was pleased to direct that the government of what was now the royal colony of New York be assimilated into the constitution to be established later for Massachusetts.[44] Yet no immediate action was taken, and the legislature at New York continued to meet.

The events of 1684 in Maryland, the Jerseys, and New England had brought matters to a head. A concerted plan was needed. Other developments seemed to reinforce this decision. Dongan argued that if vessels were allowed to enter in East New Jersey without paying duties at New York, it would be impossible to prevent smuggling. The loss of the Jerseys, western Connecticut, and the region west of the Delaware to William Penn, in addition to the diminished base for revenue, led Dongan to recommend the recovery of the lost territories. Adding their pleas were the mayor and council of New York City: the safety of the New Yorkers and the interests of the crown required the Delaware lands and New Jersey to be reunited to New York and the province to be extended eastward into New England.

The issue at this point for the Stuart monarchy was consolidation of the diverse provinces, not the abrogation of representative government. Charles II had recently authorized a popular assembly to be convened in New Hampshire, and although the charter for the Somers Island company had been vacated, the freeholders of Bermuda were also permitted an assembly. And despite the adverse action taken by the king in council in March 1685, the assembly in New York under Dongan continued to meet. Its fate rested upon a decision to be made for Massachusetts and the other New England corporations. Most of the ministers of the crown in 1685 assumed that the settlers in New England would continue to elect representatives to an assembly.

CHAPTER 13

New England Divided, 1673–84

THE UNITY OF Puritan society in New England, often precarious, was severely tested during the latter years of the reign of Charles II as the inhabitants of the several colonies there competed for control of strategic lands. In these squabbles speculators in Massachusetts played a leading role in the attempts to dismember Rhode Island, the outcast among the New England provinces, and to resist the claims of Robert Mason to New Hampshire. The more orthodox Puritan regimes of the United Colonies had never recognized Rhode Island, had never admitted her into the Confederation of New England. The protagonists in these conflicts did not restrict themselves to competing in the local arena; when it suited their purposes, they appealed to a more distant authority, officialdom in London.

Among the more worldly men, whose horizons were not confined to the New England Zion, were the descendants of the Puritan patriarch, John Winthrop, first governor of the Bay Colony. His son, a governor of Connecticut, had proved himself most adept at lobbying in the warrens of Whitehall. The younger Winthrop had several children; one daughter, Martha, married Richard Wharton, a major entrepreneur engaged in land speculation and overseas trade, a man well connected in English commerical circles. Two of Winthrop's sons, Fitzjohn and Waitstill (Wait) had spent some time in England. Subsequently, Fitz had settled in New London, a town Connecticut officials hoped to develop as a major port, while Wait took up residence in Boston. Despite the unresolved dispute over the boundary between Connecticut and New York, the Winthrops, father and sons, remained on good terms with the proprietary governor at Manhattan, Sir Edmund Andros. He was in a position to further the family interests and had confirmed to the Winthrops a gift from local Indians, Fishers Island, located just off the Connecticut shore opposite New London.

There were larger stakes to be won. Following a visit to New London by the royal duke's deputy, Fitzjohn Winthrop wrote Andros at the behest of the proprietors of the Narragansett country—they included

Richard Wharton and the Winthrop brothers—that he use his influence at the English court in their behalf. If Charles II did not think it proper to place the disputed King's Province under the jurisdiction of either Connecticut or New Plymouth, he ought to grant letters of incorporation to the proprietors rather than allow them to suffer under the authority of the Rhode Islanders. Andros, who was then about to return to London, seemed receptive. The Atherton Associates could write him at the home of his father-in-law, the earl of Craven, or through William Blathwayt at the Plantation Office in Whitehall.[1]

The squabbles dividing the government at Providence and the disruptive relations among the towns invited Connecticut, New Plymouth, and Massachusetts men to attempt to encroach upon and even to dismember Rhode Island. The devastation incurred during the conflict with the Wampanoaug and Narragansett Indians further weakened Rhode Island and whetted the appetites of neighbors for her lands. New Plymouth coveted the Mount Hope peninsula in the north-east corner of the colony, the home grounds of King Philip, the vanquished Wampanoaug sachem, while the Atherton Associates and speculators from New Plymouth, Massachusetts, and Connecticut, claimed the mainland west of the Narragansett Bay. Strife between towns, among the Rhode Islanders themselves, aided the interlopers. William Harris and his supporters had long contested both with Roger Williams, George Baxter, and Arthur Fenner of Providence and with the followers of Samuel Gorton, Randall Holden, and John Greene of Warwick over ownership of Pawtuxet lands. Harris later threw in with Richard Smith and Francis Brinley, agents for the Atherton Associates, in the contest over the Narragansett country.

Outmaneuvered in the local provincial arena, the contentious Rhode Islanders did not hesitate to take their case to London. As William Harris put it when he complained against the Providence men, the colonists enjoyed the same privileges as the free and natural-born subjects of the king in the realm of England. Only the intervention of the crown could allow him due process of law in Rhode Island. The char-tered governments in New England no more than any corporation in England could refuse to answer the king's writs.[2] In 1678 Harris's op-ponents for the disputed Warwick lands travelled to England to present their case. Harris followed suit. Agents for the Bay Colony then in London, William Stoughton and Peter Bulkeley, entered into the controversy, belittling Samuel Gorton and Randall Holden as seditious malcontents, men full of the most absurd opinions and notorious heterodoxies, some bordering on blasphemy. Both sides accused local judges and magistrates of being biased.

These dissensions seemed to confirm for the Lords of Trade and

Plantations the need for the crown to appoint some general governor or overall authority for New England.[3] It was too difficult for officials in London to resolve the matter, given the absence of some parties to the controversy over the Pawtuxet lands and the great distance involved. They suggested the magistrates of neighboring New Plymouth gather evidence and then report to the king.[4]

Harris was now involved in a larger dispute over the jurisdiction and soil of the Narragansett country, a small region, but one reputed rich in minerals and claimed by land speculators on the basis of a forfeited mortgage from the local Indians.

By 1679 the Atherton Associates had expanded their membership to include more than twenty partners, most of them merchants of Massachusetts. In addition to the Winthrops, they included Simon Bradstreet, Elisha and Edward Hutchinson, Daniel Denison, Amos Richardson, William Hudson, and Richard Wharton of Massachusetts; the two Richard Smiths (father and son) and Francis Brinley of Rhode Island; and Josiah Winslow, Thomas Willet, and Richard Lord of New Plymouth.[5]

The Atherton partners ignored the claims of the regime at Providence by arguing that the Rhode Island authorities had forfeited suzerainty by abandoning the defense of the region during the conflict with the Indians. John Saffin as agent for the proprietors entered their claim to the lands with the General Court at Hartford and asked for the benefit of Connecticut law to protect their rights. Saffin, Elisha Hutchinson, and Simon Bradstreet (deputy governor of Massachusetts), as a committee for the proprietors, published a printed sheet in Boston placing the lands "purchased" from the Narragansett and Niantic Indians for sale. Legal right had been allowed by the commissioners of the United Colonies and recorded in the records of Connecticut, under whose jurisdiction the lands were, so the advertisement read.[6]

About Christmas time, 1679, the agent for the Atherton Associates, William Harris, left Boston—secretly, so Governor John Cranston of Rhode Island complained—for London. But a Barbary corsair captured the vessel on which he sailed, the *Unity,* and carried the seventy-year old Harris away, a slave, to Algiers.[7]

From Hartford, Governor William Leete and Secretary John Allen appealed to the earl of Sunderland, a principal secretary of state, and the Winthrops and their brother-in-law sought to enlist the ubiquitous William Blathwayt, governor Andros of New York, and the peripatetic governor of Virginia. Lord Culpeper was then spending the hot summer months in New England. The protagonists of Rhode Island had been encouraged to approach Blathwayt on learning of the industry he had shown in promoting the affairs of New Plymouth.[8]

From captivity in North Africa, Harris, the agent for Connecticut to whom had been entrusted the papers containing the colony's pretensions to the disputed region, had written Blathwayt asking that nothing be concluded to the prejudice of his employers until he had an opportunity to present his evidence. Blathwayt so moved before the Lords of Trade and Plantations, and in the interval he volunteered to place into the hands of a good solicitor any evidence Richard Wharton might submit. Because of the conflicting charter claims of the two colonies the crown legal officials had recommended that no action be taken until the parties involved were heard. Harris was not ransomed until late in the spring of 1681, after the Connecticut officials and Atherton Associates had raised two thousand dollars in London to redeem him. A broken man when he finally arrived in England, he died within a few days.[9]

In the fall of 1681 Lord Culpeper brought the dispute in New England before the Committee for Plantation Affairs. He was probably the official who recommended empowering commissioners in America to examine and report on the conflicting claims of the litigants. He also suggested the names of men in New England—men favorable to the Atherton Associates and to Connecticut—to serve on the commission. Edward Cranfield, newly designated royal governor of New Hampshire, and Edward Randolph, surveyor of customs in America, were added.[10] An impecunious and avaricious man, Cranfield later sought to exploit the situation in southern New England. In all probability he had been misled by the exaggerated reports of Robert Mason, the putative proprietor of New Hampshire, as to the financial gains to be realized into believing that a fortune was to be made by squeezing the townsmen of New England for rents and fees. The would-be proprietors of Narrangansett had no knowledge of Cranfield's plans.

Richard Wharton, after purchasing a large tract of land at Pejepscot in Maine from local Indians, on his return to Boston stopped off at Portsmouth to confer with Cranfield on the hearing to be held in Rhode Island. A month later, in August 1683, Cranfield and the other commissioners, Edward Randolph, William Stoughton, Joseph Dudley, Samuel Shrimpton, John Pynchon, and Nathaniel Saltonstall of Massachusetts and Fitzjohn Winthrop and his brother-in-law, Edward Palmes, both of Connecticut, assembled in the Narragansett country. Here they issued a call to all interested persons to meet at the home of Richard Smith to give evidence. Governor William Coddington and other officials of Rhode Island met beforehand at Warwick, having provided themselves with what they considered all the records necessary to prove their claim to the territory. But Cranfield and his associates conducted the investigation without them. Coddington now wrote to

London requesting the Lords of Trade to take no action until all sides were heard. The Rhode Islanders professed themselves ready to render full obedience; they deemed it their duty to uphold the king's authority in New England, an obvious reference to the behavior of the commonwealthmen in nearby Massachusetts.[11]

Cranfield's account of what occurred in the Narragansett country was entirely different. He accused the Rhode Islanders of rude and obstreperous behavior; they were in no way fit to govern so important an area. Not surprisingly, Cranfield found that Wharton and the other gentlemen from Boston were the fair purchasers and Connecticut, with its more ancient (by one year) patent the governing authority of the lands in question. Yet he could not resist the opportunity to condemn all of the chartered governments in New England. There was sufficient evidence, he claimed, to furnish grounds for vacating their patents. If the king were to bring them directly under his government, it would effect a general reformation.

Cranfield was not a disinterested observer. He wrote privately to Blathwayt for the benefit of the secretary at the Plantation Board and others in his circle to suspend passing on any documents the Rhode Islanders sent to the Lords of Trade until Cranfield and the other commissioners submitted their report. The Narragansett proprietors in Boston intended complimenting Blathwayt with a parcel of land in the territory. There was something also for Lord Clarendon: an order for a thousand acres of land to the late lord chancellor passed some years before. If the earl would send Cranfield a power of attorney, he would get him a good sum of money for the land.[12]

On 11 October 1683 Richard Wharton and several other associates met at the home of George Monk in Boston and decided to finance the presentation in England of the report of the Cranfield commission. Cranfield and the other commissioners did not meet to sign their report until a few days later, but before they could send it off to London, Edward Randolph arrived with a claim of the duke of Hamilton to the Narragansett country. Cranfield and the others then rounded up as many of the Atherton Associates as they could to marshal a rebuttal to the pretensions of the latest interloper.[13]

In London Richard Wharton's son, joined by Thomas Deane and Lord Culpeper, pressed for acceptance of the commission's report. In February 1683/4 they petitioned that the Narragansett country (since 1665 called the King's Province) now be recognized as falling within the jurisdiction of Connecticut and that Rhode Island be dismembered. Despite the report by Cranfield and the further recommendation by Governor Thomas Dongan of New York that the charter of Rhode

Island be vacated, the ministers took no action. With the death of
Charles II early the following year, the Whartons, Deane, and Culpeper
then petitioned James II for confirmation of the Narragansett lands.[14]

The fate of the corporation of Rhode Island and the royal colony of
New York would await a decision on the other New England provinces.

During the protracted contest for the Narragansett country both
sides in New England employed the services of the ubiquitous William
Blathwayt. Indeed, when Richard Wharton had sought out Blathwayt,
he had been sensible of the favor and industry the secretary to the Lords
for Trade and Plantations had shown in promoting the affairs of New
Plymouth.[15] Officials of the first English province established in New
England were in a vulnerable position, since the colony had no charter
from the crown. The existence of the province as a legal entity rested on a
dubious patent from the defunct English corporation, the Council for
Plymouth (or Council of New England). Not only was the authority of
the government in question, but its boundary with Rhode Island was also
in dispute. Immediately in contention between the two colonies were the
lands of the vanquished Wampanoaug Indians.

The commissioners of the confederation of New England had sided
against Rhode Island and had awarded the Mount Hope Peninsula north
of Aquidneck Island to New Plymouth, for, as Nathaniel Morton,
secretary of Plymouth had informed the king, the government at
Providence being in the hands of Quakers during the recent Indian war,
the Islanders had not shown the proper "English spirit" in assisting their
distressed neighbors or their own outlying plantations. A third party
entered the dispute when John Crown petitioned the court, asking that
the Indian lands be granted to him as compensation for valuable
property his father lost when the French took Nova Scotia.[16]

Confronted by conflicting claims and unable to come to any conclusion, the Lords of Trade and Plantations in England requested that
the New England colonies submit further information.

Meeting at Boston in August 1679, representatives of the more
orthodox New England regimes undertook concerted action to reinforce
the claims against Rhode Island. Winslow signed a certificate that the
colony of New Plymouth by its "patent" of 1629 was bounded on the
west by the Narragansett River (Bay), and the commissioners for the
other colonies (Thomas Danforth, Joseph Dudley, and John Richards of
Massachusetts, John Allyn for Connecticut, and Winslow and Thomas
Hinckley for New Plymouth) sent off a remonstrance to Whitehall
supporting the awarding of lands conquered from the Indians, Mount

Hope and the Narragansett country, to New Plymouth and Connecticut.[17]

The scales seemed weighted in favor of the men of Plymouth, as the Lords of Trade and Plantations recommended awarding them the Wampanoaug lands. As a reward for their efforts in enlarging the king's dominions and their allegiance during the war, the king should, when the colonists made due application, confer on them a charter; a royal patent would bring them to a nearer dependence on the crown and would confer on them such rights and privileges as would be thought reasonable and fit.[18]

Officials in New Plymouth took the hint. Apparently encouraged, Governor Winslow initiated a correspondence with the secretary of the Plantation Board in order that Blathwayt might advise the Plymouth agents in their quest for a patent comparable to that granted Connecticut in 1662. Henry Ashurst, the treasurer of the Corporation for Propagating the Gospel in New England, was to provide the funds. Blathwayt would have preferred that Winslow himself come to England, but the governor, the last of the Plymouth executives to contest the policies and the authority of Massachusetts, died in December 1680. Thomas Hinckley, of Barnstable, succeeded him. Parliamentary business and political matters at court prevented Blathwayt from pressing for a patent for the colony for some time.[19]

It was Lord Culpeper, the much travelled governor of Virginia who had visited New England in 1680 and had assured the authorities of New Plymouth that there would be no doubt of their securing a charter, who took up the case. In the spring of 1681 he testified before the earl of Craven, the bishop of London, the secretaries of state and the other lords of trade, that the men of New Plymouth were well inclined to the king's government and deserved to be encouraged. The members of the Committee for Plantation Affairs agreed, but thought the general affairs of New England took precedence.

The authorities at Plymouth persisted. To speed matters along, Deputy Governor James Cudworth of Scituate crossed the Atlantic to assist Blathwayt, but he died shortly after arriving in London. In the spring of 1682 Hinckley wrote Blathwayt stressing the desire of the colonists for a charter comparable to those charters given Connecticut and Rhode Island. The crown ought also to include the King's Province in such an award.[20] Evidently communications between the government at New Plymouth and London broke down. By the fall of 1683, as the royal court was taking legal steps against the charter of Massachusetts Bay, Blathwayt complained to Hinckley that he still had not received an authentic copy of the patent issued to New Plymouth or a map of the

Narragansett country. Yet, as the secretary to the Committee for Plantation Affairs appreciated, it was not probable that anything would be determined at court until the ministers of the king resolved matters relating to Massachusetts. They would then model a charter for New Plymouth.[21]

Hinckley and his colleagues persisted. In an excessively fulsome, fawning petition to Charles II sent late in 1683 they recapitulated their efforts to obtain a royal charter bestowing on them the power of government. Among the privileges they desired was liberty of conscience in religious worship. But they had no wish, they emphasized, to infringe on the liberty of those persons who thought otherwise than they. Among them one rule prevailed: when a majority in any town agreed to have an orthodox minister, he would, notwithstanding small differences as to church order and discipline, be supported by the taxes paid by all in the community. This petition Randolph delivered to the Committee on Plantation Affairs in February 1684. As late as November of that year the Lords of Trade were still considering the request from New Plymouth for a chartered government.[22]

As Blathwayt had indicated, however, any decision on New Plymouth had to await the resolution of the dispute between the crown and the Bay Colony, but it was clear by late 1684 that there had been no decision to consolidate the provinces of New England.

Royal government suffered grievous damage to its reputation in northern New England. The limitations of the man Charles II had sent out to act in his name in New Hampshire, a petty, unscrupulous courtier, intent merely to make his fortune, compromised the cause of royal authority in the minds of the settlers residing in the four small, exposed towns between the Merrimack and the Piscataqua and inclined the majority among them to support the Puritan regime at Boston. Whatever else, the government of the Bay Colony had granted lands freely and had extended its protection to the exposed frontier settlements, as the presumptive proprietary Mason family in England had not done. By supporting the claims of Robert Mason, Charles II also damaged his cause in New Hampshire.

The decision to uphold Mason's claims to the proprietary rights of New Hampshire and Naumkeag, the region about Salem, Massachusetts, may have resulted from a desire to weaken the jurisdiction and authority of the Bay Colony. It would have been much less expensive ultimately and much more rewarding politically to have bought out Mason, thus removing the source of friction with the inhabitants of New Hampshire. But in these years crown officials were endeavoring to hold down the cost to the crown of governing the colonies while seeking more closely to control them.

While some among the old planters and Anglicans in the New Hampshire towns had expressed their opposition to the Bay Colony when royal commissioners from London had toured the colony, the failure to offer them direct support had left them with no alternative but to continue under the jurisdiction of Massachusetts. The few small, scattered communities were too dependent on the resources of the regime at Boston, particularly during the devastating Indian war of 1675–76.

The tie to Massachusetts was further strengthened in Portsmouth and Dover with the emergence of a small group of men, closely related by marriage, common religious convictions, and economic connections with Puritans in the Bay Colony. It included the brothers Cutt (or Cutts), Richard and John, William Vaughn, Richard Waldron, Richard Martin, and Elias Stileman. These merchants along with Joshua Moody, perhaps the most influential man among those supporting the Bay Colony, had formed the first Congregational church in Portsmouth. Richard Waldron, for many years representing Dover at Boston, had served as speaker in the General Court. Richard Martin was married to a daughter of Samuel Symonds of Ipswich, while Moody had taken as wife the daughter of Edward Collins, a merchant of considerable means and a deacon of the church at Cambridge. Moody, influential in the Piscataqua Association, led the clerics of the northern towns and enjoyed considerable prestige with the magistrates and ministers of the Bay Colony.[23] For such men these communities were a northern extension of the Puritan commonwealth. Family, trade, and religion united the leading residents of the New Hampshire towns with Massachusetts against any threat mounted by outsiders.

The principal challenge came from Ferdinando Gorges and Robert Mason, claimants to portions of northern New England under grants made the Council for Plymouth. At one point the putative proprietors seemed prepared to surrender to the crown their patents in exchange for new grants, with a third of the revenue going to the king. This would have allowed Charles II to name a governor general and check the encroachments of the regime at Boston. According to a Dissenter merchant of London, John Collins, some courtiers at Whitehall suggested the king purchase Maine and New Hampshire for his bastard son, the duke of Monmouth. The authorities of the Bay Colony would do well, Collins advised them, to make good their title, the papers verifying their claim formerly sent to the "Puritan" lords on the Privy Council having been lost in the Great Fire of London. The earl of Anglesey had sent for Collins to discuss the situation but was taking it ill that of late the commonwealthmen of Boston had ignored him.[24]

In 1675 Mason had the field to himself in testifying before the newly formed committee of the Council for Trade and Plantations. Vindicating the grants claimed by the Mason and Gorges families, he argued, would be the first step in bringing all the colonies in New England under closer "inspection" and "management." Despite the judgment of the attorney general, Sir William Jones, and the solicitor general, Sir Francis Winnington, that both Mason and Gorges did have good title to the lands of New Hampshire and Maine and the conclusion of the Commissioners of Customs that the merchants of the Bay Colony were violating the acts of trade and navigation, the Lords of Trade were not inclined to send out a commission to investigate as Mason had asked. It would be too expensive. There was also the potential damage to the prestige of the crown if it met with an affront such as Nicolls and his colleagues had met a decade before. Moreover, such a procedure might indicate to the colonists of the Bay that the crown had decided the issue without giving them an opportunity to be heard.

Over the protests of Mason and Gorges, the ministers decided to inform the authorities of Massachusetts of the complaints against them and to require the Bostonians to send over agents to answer for the provincial government.[25]

The man selected to carry the message to New England—a relative of Mason—would hardly inspire confidence in the rulers of the Bay Colony. Edward Randolph, a petty functionary, was a man of poor judgment. Although Josiah Winslow of New Plymouth and other New Englanders were willing to work with him in later years, the Puritan authorities of the Bay Colony came to regard him as an anathema, an agent bent on the destruction of their commonwealth.

Governor John Leverett and the dominant commonwealth element in Boston based the claim of Massachusetts to the four New Hampshire towns, as well as to Kittery, York, and Wells, north and east beyond the Piscataqua, on the voluntary submission by the settlers to the Bay government and on the boundaries of the colony specified in the royal charter granted by Charles I in 1629. The northern boundary of Massachusetts ran east and west three miles north of the "most northerly" portion of the Merrimack river.[26] When Peter Bulkeley and William Stoughton, agents for the Bay Colony, arrived in London to present this claim, they further stressed the great expense Massachusetts had incurred in protecting the towns against the Indians, a service Mason and Gorges could not have offered the exposed settlements.

The Lords of Trade concluded, however, that the issue was simply a legal one and deferred to the views of Sir Richard Raynsford and Sir Francis North, chief justices of the courts of King's Bench and Common Pleas.

Raynsford and North in their report of 17 July 1677 based their decision purely on the sequence of patents and grants issued earlier in the century and the probable state of knowledge as to the source of the Merrimack River in 1629 when Charles I granted the charter for the Massachusetts Bay Company. They would not examine claims as to ownership of lands or titles held by the colonists, for it would be improper to decide any title to the soil without hearing the terre-tenants or their attorneys. On such points the parties concerned ought to have recourse to the courts in Maine and New Hampshire.

The justices then proceeded to determine who was entitled to exercise governmental authority. The Council for Plymouth, a trading corporation in England, had received a patent encompassing title to the soil and the legal jurisdiction. Under English law this patent did not entitle the company to give up to others the power to govern. Consequently the Council for Plymouth could only issue grants of land to Mason and Gorges. By 1629 it had itself presumably forfeited the government of New England through negligence. It had been necessary for Charles I that year to issue a charter to another corporation, the Governor and Company of the Massachusetts Bay. But by this grant the authority of the Bay Colony extended only to three miles north of the course of the Merrimack River as then known. Authority to govern the territory north of the Piscataqua, the king had granted by patent in 1640 to Sir Ferdinando Gorges. Henceforth the title to both the soil and government of Maine rested with the heirs of Gorges, but the government of New Hampshire remained with the crown. It was for the local courts to decide the ownership of the soil of New Hampshire as between Robert Mason, the heir of John Mason, and the terre-tenants, the settlers in the towns.[27] Stoughton and Bulkeley could add nothing material in rebuttal.

In a bold move, the authorities of the Bay Colony offered to purchase from Mason and Gorges their rights. Through an intermediary, John Usher, a Boston merchant then in London, Gorges accepted and turned over Maine to Massachusetts for the sum of £1,200. Mason declined, however, and petitioned the crown to buy out his rights to New Hampshire. He may have been seeking to play off one potential buyer against another, but in any case the Committee for Plantation affairs rejected his request. Stoughton and Bulkeley now found it advantageous to stand by the legal decision issued the previous July. Title to the soil as between Mason and others who had as good a claim, the inhabitants who had been in possession for half a century, had yet to be determined. The contest was simply a matter of rights between private subjects. For the crown to declare in favor of Mason would prejudice the claims of the residents of Salem, Newbury, and the New Hampshire towns.[28]

With the agents of Massachusetts pressing to be allowed to return home, the ministers of state in 1679 forced through a compromise, but one generally favorable to Mason. Massachusetts must give up Maine on being reimbursed the purchase price, but the northern province would not be joined to New Hampshire as Mason requested. Mason must agree to waive all rents and demands due from the inhabitants of Dover, Exeter, Portsmouth, and Hampton as of 24 June 1679 and to make them a clear title for improved lands on condition that they become his tenants and for the future pay him an annual quitrent on all improved land. The woodlands, or unimproved waste lands, remained with Mason.

In accepting the validity of the grant by the defunct Council for Plymouth—the same corporation had provided the "patents" for the New Plymouth and Connecticut towns—Charles II and the Lords of Trade committed a blunder of major proportions. They jeopardized the welfare of the settlers and placed them at the mercy of an unscrupulous, undeserving profiteer whose subsequent actions eroded whatever favorable sentiment for the crown the townsmen in New Hampshire held. It would have better served the interests of the government at Whitehall to have bought out Mason and confirmed the titles of the settlers.

For the present the crown placed the government of the new royal colony of New Hampshire in the hands of a council at Portsmouth to administer justice according to the laws of England, circumstances permitting, with freedom of conscience for all Protestants. Appeals in criminal and civil cases could be carried to England, and a general assembly called to enact laws and vote taxes.

In nominating members of the New Hampshire council, the Lords of Trade relied on men familiar with the situation on the Piscataqua, the timber merchant Sir William Warren and the Massachusetts agents Stoughton and Bulkeley. The commission to govern New Hampshire, dated 18 September 1679, named John Cutt president and Richard Martin, William Vaughan, and Daniel Thomas of Portsmouth, John Gillman of Exeter and Christopher Hussey of Hampton, and Richard Waldron of Dover. It empowered them to nominate and choose three others to fill out the board.[29] In following the suggestions of Warren and the agents for Massachusetts the Lords of Trade had nominated wealthier landowners and merchants engaged in the timber trade, men most likely to contest the claims of Mason and bound by religious sentiment and commercial interest to Puritan Massachusetts.

Edward Randolph carried the royal commission across the Atlantic late in 1679. He delivered it to John Cutt, the aged and infirm president-designate, in December. Despite pressure from members of the Puritan community Cutt took the oath of office. The other councilors, led by Richard Martin and Richard Waldron and encouraged by the authorities at Boston, refused. When Cutt remained adamant, Waldron, Martin, and the others reluctantly accepted office, fearing that if they did not accept, others would. Cutt and the council did send an address to the king protesting their separation from Massachusetts, but also explained to the officials at Boston that the division was not of their doing.[30]

The transition from government under Puritan Massachusetts to royal council made little difference. In March 1680 the council voted to continue the laws promulgated by the General Court at Boston imposing the death penalty for idolatry and for blasphemy as prescribed in Exod. 22:20; Deut. 13:6, 10; and Lev. 24:15, 16.[31] The subsequent reaction in England was harsh and emphatic. Randolph as surveyor of the royal customs was to get nowhere. In an effort to bring the provincial trade into conformity with the English navigation code, he appointed Thomas Thurton, Walter Barefoote, and William Beckham as deputies. Over the ensuing months and years they met with verbal and physical abuse as well as legal impediments. Thurton and Barefoote were called before the board, charged with accusing the councilors of violating the king's authority. Waldron and Martin declared that the customs officials were all rogues and that neither they nor the king had anything to do with New Hampshire.

Complaining of the plight of revenue officers under the civil authorities in New Hampshire and Massachusetts, Edward Randolph asked the board in London to grant him a new commission with stronger authority. Sir George Downing and the other commissioners at the London customs house hesitated, fearing for their own authority, until Blathwayt appealed to the Treasury and had the business expedited. From Whitehall Blathwayt chided Randolph, "You may now be sensible of the great difficulties that have arisen from grasping too great a power without due advice; matters of Power & Governm[en]t by new ways & forms being not rashly to be propos[e]d nor easily brought to pass."[32] Blathwayt himself, the other ministers at Whitehall, and Charles II might well have taken this advice in dealing with the New Englanders.

When John Cutt died, Waldron, Martin, and their allies dominated the government of New Hampshire, successfully blocking Randolph in his efforts to regulate the shipping of the colony and Mason in his suits in the provincial courts. They sought to justify their administration: the statutes enacted for the colony were not repugnant to the laws of England, but were, as far as they could make them, consonant with those of the mother country. The New Hampshire code provided the death penalty for, among other offenses, sodomy, bearing false witness against a man's life, murder, bestiality, blasphemy against the Trinity, arson, and worshipping any but the true God. Taking the offensive, the councilors charged Mason with intimidating the poorer folk, using unfair means to collect names in support of his litigation on land, and usurping the authority of the king in summoning the councilors to testify.[33]

Mason was not without allies in New England. Walter Barefoote joined the old Gorges faction from Maine in attacking the Puritan councilors, charging them with antimonarchical sentiments and seeking to subvert royal government. Richard Chamberlain, an attorney sent out from London to be provincial secretary, gave added weight to those charges against the Puritan element and "their archbishop," Joshua Moody. The quarrel with Mason, he contended, was the fault of the councilors; Mason had no differences with the populace. Chamberlain also condemned the entire legal code adopted by the legislature. It came from the statute book of Massachusetts. Certain laws were repugnant to the laws of England; they punished manslaughter by death, disallowed marriage ceremonies performed by ministers (that is, denied the sacramental basis of marriage), and imposed arbitrary sentences for fornication.[34]

The adoption of the statutes of Puritan Massachusetts, with its Mosaic code, as well as the behavior of the councilors toward Randolph's deputies told most heavily against the regime at Portsmouth. In unusually harsh language, Craven, Clarendon, Secretary Jenkins, and the other committeemen for plantation affairs condemned the public acts adopted in New Hampshire as unequal, incongruous, and absurd and the proceedings of the government there as inconsistent with the service of the crown and the settlement of the province. The methods employed by the assembly and the council were so clearly repugnant to the terms of the commission from the crown that there appeared to be no alternative but for the king to appoint a "faithful and capable" governor to prevent further irregularities and render the country useful to the crown and capable of defending itself from invasion. Unfortunately, the choice for this delicate position fell on Edward Cranfield, an unscrupulous adventurer whom William Blathwayt persuaded to accept the post in northern New England.[35]

Robert Mason may have had something to do with Cranfield's decision. Evidently he fed Cranfield tales of wealth in New Hampshire, of the revenues there and money to be made. To ease the cost to the crown of governing the colony, Mason in January 1682 offered to contribute one-fifth of all the rents, profits, and revenues not only from New Hampshire but also the lands he claimed in Massachusetts around Salem. Both Cranfield and the king would have a strong financial incentive to support the proprietor's claims. These were recited in the commission to the new governor as well as the provisions of the agreement made in June 1679 whereby Mason undertook to forego arrears in rents, to confirm all possessions, and to receive only sixpence in the pound annual rent on improved lands. The crown named Mason and his allies, Walter Barefoote and Richard Chamberlain (the provincial secretary), to the provincial council, but ordered Waldron and Martin suspended pending an investigation by Cranfield. It further prohibited the new governor from holding sessions of the council in taverns or other places of public entertainment.

Cranfield delayed his departure for months until August 1682. He was so strapped for money that to enable him to set out for his government the king had to allow him three hundred pounds from the secret service funds.[36] Thus provided with the king's commission and his bounty, Cranfield departed from Plymouth harbor aboard H.M.S. *Lark*, a sixth-rate frigate. His behavior in New England was to be inconsistent and his tenure of office stormy.

After a passage of almost seven weeks the *Lark* dropped anchor off the coast some fifteen leagues south of the Piscataqua. The wind being foul, Cranfield traveled overland to Portsmouth, arriving on the evening of 3 October. Waldron sent his son to invite the new governor to his own home, where the councilors were assembled. There Cranfield read his commission and officially inaugurated his government. As required by his instructions, he issued writs for the election of deputies to the General Assembly and suspended Waldron and Martin, charged with denying the king's commission to John Cutt and obstructing royal customs officers.

Within a few weeks the governor restored them to the council. Witnesses had failed to sustain the accusations of Randolph and Mason. Cranfield now professed to appreciate that Mason had deceived him and the ministers of state with greatly exaggerated accounts of the wealth and profits to be had from New Hampshire. The governor waxed sarcastic over the gross deception. So poor were the people in the four mean towns that they were able to pay no more than one hundred pounds in taxes. As for the revenue to the royal government from the fifth portion of the rents and fines, Cranfield informed Blathwayt, "(If you will give me leave to be merry with you) it's a fantasticall fiction & immateriall substance," existing but in Mason's imagination. The tale the proprietor had told in London of the readiness of the settlers to admit the Anglican Book of Common Prayer was a "meer dream" as evidenced by the fact that the entire populace was then preparing an address to return thanks to the king for not imposing the Church of England upon them. As Cranfield saw it, the only means to make his administration financially viable lay in joining Maine to New Hampshire, a proposition supported in a petition on behalf of the eastern towns presented by Francis Champernoun. The condition of New Hampshire was too mean. If Mason dispossessed the towns of their woodlands, it would be impossible for more than a few families to subsist. Cranfield sent a further indictment of Mason to the Lords of Trade: by intimidating Waldron, Martin, and Joshua Moody, the proprietor had hoped to frighten the populace into complying with his demands.

Within two months Cranfield had had enough of New England. He would rather be in a "warmer Country where I can Account more than ye Game of ye Whole Governm[en]t of New England is able to produce. We are up to ye knees in Snow, ye weather is Cold & comfortless."[37] Not unmindful of what was going on, Mason complained that Cranfield was wholly swayed by the proprietor's opponents.

Until a more lucrative post opened up in a warmer climate, Cranfield had to make the most of New Hampshire. Consistency and virtuousness were not strong suits with him; he could turn a complete about-face if it served his purpose.

Within a matter of a few weeks Cranfield was writing the Lords of Trade that the council and chief inhabitants of New Hampshire were part of a grand combination of church members and Congregational assemblies in New England. The ostensible cause of this revelation was the failure of a jury to return a verdict against the *George,* a vessel owned by a Scot, George Jaffrey, and the negligence of Elias Stileman in allowing the ship to escape. The actual cause may well have been the realization that he would not be able to prevail on the assembly to make ample enough provision for his salary.[38]

The crisis came during a session of the assembly beginning on 9 January 1683. The representatives from the towns insisted on the right to nominate judges and appoint courts of justice and rejected the bill Cranfield proposed for raising a revenue for the support of government. Cranfield charged Moody and the other ministers—men who would suffer no laws but such as would establish Congregationalism—with the responsibility for the intransigency of the assemblymen. He dissolved the assembly on 20 January, resolving to continue the taxes previously voted.

What followed was pure opéra bouffe.

Edward Gove, an assemblyman from Hampton, raising a dozen or so apprentices, artisans, and youths against Cranfield, protested that his commission as vice admiral of the colony, a patent from the duke of York, the lord high admiral of England, was illegal. The royal duke being a Papist, this indicated a design to introduce Popery in New Hampshire. Cranfield was but a pretended governor, for his commission had been signed in Edinburgh. Local authorities quickly apprehended and jailed Gove and his followers. Mason and Randolph sought to make the most of the incident, charging that the Puritan leaders in New Hampshire were in league with their colleagues in Boston in the attempt to overthrow the government but that when Gove rose prematurely, Richard Martin and the others had to turn on him to conceal their own complicity.

Others were more charitable. Hannah Gove thought that her husband suffered from some "distemper" and "lunacy," while Gove
himself later explained that he had been so distressed at Cranfield's arbitrary behavior that he had been unable to sleep. He might have
declared Cranfield to be a traitor, but at the time he scarcely knew what
he was doing.

Gove and his luckless followers stood trial before a special commission in New Hampshire. Some confessed their guilt; others claimed
to have been compelled to join Gove. The governor respited all but Gove
and sent him off in chains to England in the charge of Edward Randolph.[40]

Cranfield than launched an indiscriminate attack. He urged the government at Whitehall to grant him wide latitude: unless he had power to
appoint and displace ministers of the churches, he would never be able to
govern in New Hampshire, for Moody and the others were too turbulent
and enjoyed too much influence. He now confessed he had judged
Waldron and Moody too charitably. They, not the would-be proprietor,
had been responsible for the failure of Mason and the inhabitants of the
towns to come to terms. He wanted an order to allow trials under his
aegis to resolve matters between the proprietor and the terre-tenants and
sought to create the impression that Gove's attempted coup was one
facet of a larger conspiracy by the Puritans of New Hampshire, Massachusetts *and England*. It was held against the governor that he had proposed to the Congregational ministers that baptizing children and administering the sacrament of the Lord's Supper were essential duties of
their office. Such was the involvement of the Independents, encouraged
by the Dissenters of England, in the affairs of government that they were
certain to oppose the duke of York should he come to the throne.

In thus portraying to his superiors in Whitehall the situation in New
England, Cranfield was motivated by something more than serving the
crown of England. To the secretary at the Plantation Office he portrayed
rich pickings for Blathwayt, Francis Gwyn, and himself. Settling the
rents in Maine would yield at least three thousand pounds; the parties involved in the dispute over the Narragansett lands would not be adverse to
paying three or four thousand pounds for a decision favorable to them;
men in Boston would pay another eight or ten thousand pounds for a
pardon from the king for having obstructed the royal government; the
renewal of several grants of town lands would yield another two thousand pounds, while another five thousand pounds had been collected for
the Corporation for Propagating the Gospel in New England.[41] As
auditor general of the plantation revenue, Blathwayt could recognize the
absurdity of this proposal.

In 1683 Cranfield sought to capitalize on the friction between the
merchants of Strawberry Bank, who had dominated the royal council

since its establishment under John Cutt, and their rivals from Great Island. He made the latter community his administrative center. Here Cranfield resided in the home of Walter Barefoote, while Chamberlain, the provincial secretary, took up lodgings at George Walton's inn. Cranfield moved the highest court to Great Island and there established a court of chancery to deal with equity cases. Merchants from Great Island supporting the governor began to play a larger role, as Cranfield dismissed Waldron, Martin, and John Gilman from the council and appointed to high administrative and judicial posts the Anglican Nathaniel Fryer and his sons-in-law, Robert Elliot and John Hinckes.

On the basis of titles derived from Robert Mason, Cranfield's allies George Walton and Walter Barefoote brought suit for lands initially granted by Massachusetts to Robert Wadleigh, Jeremy Walford, and John Amazeen. The jurymen, who themselves held lands by virtue of town grants from the Bay Colony, found against Walton and Barefoote, who then appealed the decision to the crown of England. When the appellants failed to appear, the Privy Council dismissed the case.[42] As Cranfield's deputy, Barefoote supported the governor's dismissal of Waldron, Martin, and Gilman. So unsafe was the Portsmouth area that Cranfield had been forced to retire to Boston. Gove's followers had forcibly and riotously entered the governor's dwelling house. The governor himself was particularly concerned to know what had become of Gove. If the sentence against the rebellious assemblyman was not executed, he warned Blathwayt we shall "all be knock[e]d on ye head."

Cranfield's fears counted for nothing. Confined in the Tower of London, Gove petitioned the king for mercy and applied to Edward Randolph to intercede on his behalf with the Lords of Trade. As Randolph later told it, it was Blathwayt who was responsible for setting Gove at liberty on his good behavior in order to relieve the king of the expense of maintaining him, a fitting enough reason given financial state of the monarchy. Eventually James II pardoned Gove.[43]

In New England Cranfield seemed to have lost all restraint. In the fall of 1683, with the consent of the merchants of Great Island on the council, he issued a proclamation directed against shippers in the Bay Colony who allegedly violated the parliamentary acts of trade and injured the commerce of New Hampshire. No ships from the other New England colonies, unless licensed by the governor of New Hampshire, were to carry away timber from the Piscataqua. Cranfield also moved against Waldron, Vaughan, and the other merchants and landowners in their dispute with Mason. But when the proprietor brought suit against the principal landowners, he and the provost marshal, Thomas Thurton, were met with resistance—gunpowder, scalding water, and hot spits. Many of the inhabitants of Hampton and Exeter signed a paper of

protest against Mason. After circulating a subscription, Nathaniel
Weare, a former assemblyman, left for England early in 1684 to
challenge the proprietor before the royal council. Vaughan provided him
with letters to his former master, the London merchant Sir Joshua Child,
whom Weare prevailed on to aid the campaign against the governor and
Mason.[44]

Desperate over the deteriorating situation in New Hampshire, the
governor sought to implicate his opponents in the pathetic coup launched
by Gove. He singled out Joshua Moody, the leader of the Puritan
community, for special treatment. Cranfield hoped to convince the
Lords of Trade in Whitehall that resistance to the crown by the Puritan
element in Massachusetts was linked with opposition to the governor in
New Hampshire. The cause of royal government would suffer in both
colonies if the adherents to the Congregationalist churches held public
office. Their ministers allegedly professed the doctrine that oaths of
allegiance and supremacy were unlawful. It was essential that no men be
admitted to office except those who conformed to the rites of the Church
of England. In December 1683 Cranfield, with the advice of his council,
issued an order for the ministers to administer the sacrament of the
Lord's Supper to all persons not scandalous in their conduct and to
baptize their children. When Moody refused, Cranfield had his attorney
general file a writ of information on the grounds that under English
statutes clerics must administer the sacraments as prescribed by the
Anglican Book of Common Prayer. Moody's defense—he was not
ordained or maintained under the English law, and the statutes did not
extend to the colonies—was ignored. Cranfield had Moody jailed for a
time, but then relented.[45]

Resistance to the governor spread. The assembly refused to pass any
bill for the support of government, and when Thomas Thurton, the
deputy appointed by Randolph, attempted to collect duties, he was set
upon and beaten by William Vaughan. Cranfield continued to call for
strong measures, but he was begging to get out from under an impossible
situation. Unless his patrons in Whitehall found him some other employment, he professed himself ruined. In securing the governorship of
New Hampshire, he had expended all he had in the world.[46]

Nathaniel Weare had already reached England and had presented to
the king at Hampton Court the grievances of the inhabitants of the
province against the governor: Cranfield had acted in collusion with
Mason. Through a mortgage from the proprietor he had a material
interest in the soil of the colony. The governor had unjustly manipulated
the judicial process and deprived the subjects of legal remedy; he had
arbitrarily fixed the value of money and committed men to prison and
executed laws without the consent of the assembly.[47]

The Lords of the Committee for Plantation Affairs ordered Cranfield to return to England to answer the charges and to allow the inhabitants in New Hampshire to take copies of all public records relating to his administration to be sent to Whitehall. All depositions must be taken in writing by properly authorized persons.

Cranfield defended his actions and his relations with Mason. Since the king had made no allowance for the support of the governor, Mason had generously promised Cranfield £150 a year for seven years out of the proprietor's own estate. Surely it was not a crime for Mason to dispose of his own property or for Cranfield to accept what was offered him. The governor claimed never to have received a penny of this money or any portion of the quitrents reserved to the king. Cranfield ended his defense on a pious note: he called on God to witness that he had done nothing but for the king's service and for the maintenance of justice. If he had gratified the Puritan merchants in their illicit trade and denied Mason his day in court, he would not now be called upon to defend his administration. But it was clear to Cranfield, even as he penned his justification, that his days in New Hampshire were numbered.[48]

In the spring of 1685 the Privy Council returned a verdict against the governor: he had not followed his instructions to return to London a fair and impartial relation of the dispute over land titles. In order to remove the principal cause for conflict in New Hampshire—the differences between Mason and the settlers—the king in council on 8 April 1685 allowed William Vaughan to bring an appeal from all verdicts given in the provincial courts relating to his suit with Mason.[49]

Cranfield had already left New Hampshire. By the end of the year he was in England, where he suffered a further rebuff. He had concluded a contract with Mason and Samuel Allen, a London merchant, by which one-third of the great masts cut in New Hampshire were assigned to him for a period of twenty-one years. He now offered to dispose of his share to the king. The Navy Board rejected the offer. No dependence could be had on naval stores from New England except, as formerly, by dealing with the established merchants in the mast trade. The Navy Board preferred to deal with Sir John Shorter and Sir William Warren, the commercial correspondents of Vaughan and Waldron.[50]

Dismissed from his post and disappointed that he had not been sent to govern at Boston, Cranfield railed at William Blathwayt. He had never wanted to go to Portsmouth; it was only at the urging of the secretary at the Plantation Office that he was made governor there.[51] Cranfield was discredited in London. How far had his behavior in New England compromised the crown in the minds of the commonwealthmen of Massachusetts Bay?

CHAPTER 14

"Lengthening out our tranquility"
Court *versus* Commonwealth, 1674–84

For well over a decade the leaders of the commonwealth in Massachusetts had successfully fended off attempts by the Restoration monarchy to bring into line the Puritan Zion. Yet all was not well in the biblical commonwealth. A devastating Indian war had erupted— evidence of God's wrath, some thought. Over the years proportionally fewer people were able or willing to relate successfully the experience of spiritual regeneration—the visiting of God's grace—and to become full members of the Congregationalist churches. As a result the proportion of adult men qualifying to hold office at the provincial level and to vote for the deputies from the towns declined considerably.[1] The more or-thodox-minded continued to resist the pressures for change both from within and without—the continued insistence of the crown that the Bay Colony accept some supervision and the arguments of moderates in Massachusetts that, rather than lose all by blind resistance, the colony had to come to some accommodation. The commonwealthmen chose to resist, to lengthen out as much as possible their rule under the charter in the hope that Charles would go the way of his father. In the end they forfeited their charter. The moderates were proved correct.

The orthodox-minded leaders in Massachusetts, among them In-crease Mather, who had emerged as one of the more prominent ministers, saw declension in piety, a laxness in religion manifested in the behavior of growing numbers of people. In the fall of 1675 Mather and his allies pushed through the General Court a program for moral reformation. Their complaints illustrated their concern for the deterioration of standards; their determination to maintain control and their persistent refusal to acknowledge any obligation to the government in London may have come from a sense of insecurity, the need to enforce at all costs righteous living in New England.

What concerned the saints? In 1675 the majority among the General Court noted with obvious distress the prideful, immodest behavior of people in wearing long hair and wigs and of women in affecting vain, strange fashions with "naked breasts and armes." Too many people were

273

prone to turn their backs on public worship. Loose and sinful men and women were going about together from town to town on pretense of attending lectures at the meeting houses, but actually to drink and revel in ordinaries and taverns. Such "riotous & unsober" people were subject to fines and imprisonment.

Whereas "idlenes[s] (w[hi]ch is a sin of Sodom) doeth greatly increase," notwithstanding the wholesome laws against it, the General Court ordered local officials to inspect particular families and present a list of names to the selectmen of the town, who would proceed against the unrepentant. Should they remain obstinate, they must be committed to a house of correction. The General Court also found youths and servants remiss; there was a woeful breach of the fifth commandment, a failure to honor parents and heads of families, and a contempt for authority—civil, ecclesiastic, and domestic. Consequently local officials must take strict care to execute the laws against the "evil of inferiours absenting themselues out of families wherevnto they belong in the night, and meeting with corrupt company wthout leaue," a scandalous situation thought to be the root of much social disorder. Unrest and rudeness were also evident among the youth in church, whereby "sin & profaneness" were generally increased. The provincial regime required officials to designate a place in the meeting houses where children and youths must sit in public view under the inspection of some "graue & sober person."

One of the merchants in Boston not in sympathy with the mentality of the men controlling the government was skeptical of the measures adopted to meet the moral crisis. The governor was "crazy" in body, he speculated, and many men were so in their heads.[2]

The authorities continued to be insecure when faced by religious dissent. As late as 1683 Governor Simon Bradstreet refused to allow a Quaker, John Martin, liberty to preach in Boston. Martin, claiming that the Lord had made him a messenger of true tidings, had promised to behave in an orderly fashion and not to create a disturbance. Bradstreet retorted that it would indeed be meet that Martin be heard if he truly had a message from God, but "forasmuch as I believe the contrary and that it is but a delusion or a suggestion of Satan," he could see no reason to grant the request. The governor had read some Quaker books and found them most pernicious and heretical. He would as soon think it "reasonable to let a Jesuit or Popish priest preach" as a Quaker. He ordered Martin out of the province.[3] Anglicans, Friends, and Baptists could not form their own churches.

Moderate men both in old and in New England pointed out the danger of such attitudes as the provincial government continued to flout the orders of the crown to grant religious toleration to peaceable Protestants. Agents who returned from London with a warning that the harsh policy was jeopardizing the reputation of the colony and thus its charter met with ridicule and scorn. Their opponents excoriated them as traitors, seduced by the English court. Any man who temporized or dared to counsel the advisability of reaching an accommodation, the Puritan extremists condemned as an apostate.[4]

On this issue there were three distinct views in the Bay Colony. The defense of the status quo in Massachusetts fell to the commonwealth, Puritan, or so-called popular party. Its leaders were Thomas Danforth, Daniel Godkin, and Samuel Nowell; its strength lay in the House of Deputies and in the rural towns, where less than a majority of the adult men exercised the provincial franchise. Some well-to-do merchants in the Bay Colony, especially in Boston, were excluded from power and consequently could be expected to protest the situation. Others, men who did belong to the Puritan congregations but questioned the wisdom of rigidly resisting any acknowledgement of outside authority, constituted a third, a more moderate element. Too diverse in their interests to make up a party with distinct beliefs and organization comparable to their commonwealth opponents, these moderates became alienated from the dominant group. Some but not all were merchants; some were magistrates; some wanted closer ties with England or desired a form of limited religious toleration. Conscious of a superior social and economic standing, some resented the appeal made by the commonwealthmen to the lower elements. Some were driven to opposition by intemperate charges levelled against them by the more zealous of the "popular" party.

A number of the moderate leaders were linked by a common involvement in land speculation. The support of the government in London might further their interests in the Narragansett country and other tracts in New England. They were also connected by marriage. Joseph Dudley was the son of the second governor of the colony. One of his sisters married Simon Bradstreet; another, Major General Daniel Denison. The younger Dudley himself married a daughter of Edward Tyng. Richard Wharton and the Winthrop brothers were also related to the Tyng family by marriage. Above all, the moderates disagreed with the tactics used to defend the charter. To them it was clear that the rulers of the province must accept a modification of the patent or lose all by blind, obstinate resistance.[5]

The commonwealthmen enjoyed their strongest support among the deputies of the General Court elected to represent the rural towns. In resisting any attempts to reach an accommodation with the English government, they may have thought to outlast Charles II, or they may have been reacting defensively, out of an awareness of the relative decline in the number of men and women committed to the ideals held by many of the first generation of settlers who had crossed the Atlantic during that crucial decade when Charles I and Archbishop William Laud had attempted to impose religious conformity. Charles I had sought by writ of quo warranto to recall the charter issued in 1629. But Providence—so it had seemed—had intervened to save the chosen people. The king had become embroiled first with the Scots and then with the Puritans in the English Parliament and had lost his head in 1649 after suffering defeat in the English Civil War.

Despite the restoration of the monarchy, Charles II had not seemed secure on the throne. Uprisings by various Dissenter groups and challenges from the Whigs under Shaftesbury—all eagerly followed in New England—seemed to indicate that God might again intervene to save the Puritan citadel in New England. By dissembling, by procrastinating, the commonwealthmen might yet survive, might again outlast a Stuart king.

Little had changed over the ten years since the crown had sent a royal commission to England to investigate complaints against the regime in Boston to bring the Bay Colony into compliance with the acts of navigation, to have the regime at Boston accept toleration and political rights for Protestants dissenting from the Congregational establishment, and to resolve conflicting boundaries among the provinces.

By forcing Massachusetts to comply with the navigation code, officials in England were seeking, not to eliminate New England trade to Europe, but to disrupt shipment of enumerated products from the colonies and imports from Scotland and Europe to the plantations without stopping at some English port to pay customs duties. Vessels putting into an English port before proceeding to or returning from the Continent were not molested.[6] There were merchants in Massachusetts who succumbed to the temptation to avoid customs and increase their profits by trading directly with Europe. Several Dissenter merchants in London warned Governor John Leverett that the king and his ministers were disturbed over such practices: it would be in the interest of the colony to be diligent to prevent such violations.[7]

The warning went unheeded.

Early in 1676 twenty-eight English merchants took their complaints to the crown. The New Englanders in bypassing England and avoiding customs were able to carry goods to America cheaper than they could. Certain Londoners connected with the men of the Bay Colony could testify to this illicit trade. That spring the government called in local merchants who corresponded with New England. Some were "shy" in unfolding the "mystery," others pretended ignorance, yet most admitted that illicit trade existed. But the lords of the Committee for Trade and Plantations decided that it was best not to punish transgressors for previous violations but only to prevent mischief in the future by having all governors abroad swear to enforce the acts of trade. Officers ought to be settled in New England to collect duties and to keep track of vessels and bonds as required by the navigation code, and frigates of the Royal Navy empowered to seize vessels violating parliamentary statutes.[8]

Robert Mason, Ferdinando Gorges, and their supporters continued to press their claims against Massachusetts for the recovery of New Hampshire and Maine. Yet the committee of the council, perhaps at the urging of Anglesey, a "Puritan" lord, recommended that the court not decide any issue ex parte; the authorities at Boston ought to be allowed to send over agents to present the case for the Bay Colony.[9] They also rejected Mason's plea that the crown again send over commissioners to Boston. In addition to the expense involved and the uncertainty of such a venture, there was the potential danger of an embarrassing affront should the commonwealthmen repudiate the commission.

The choice of the emissary to carry the king's message was critical. Mason had his own candidate.[10] In accepting Mason's nominee, Charles II weakened the cause of the crown in New England. Edward Randolph was hardly an impartial man. A relative of Mason by marriage, he had held various petty employments and at one time, with creditors hounding him, had been forced to flee his home, wife, and family and to petition the navy commissioners to pay his debts. New England would offer him an opportunity to recoup his fortunes. Obsequious to his superiors and arrogant to those he viewed as his social inferiors, Randolph was a man of poor judgment.

In March 1676 Randolph boarded the *Welcome* bound for Boston, carrying with him orders from the crown that the authorities in Massachusetts send back within six months agents fully empowered to answer complaints so that the king might make a determination on various disputes. But Randolph had also a mandate to conduct a thorough investigation of Massachusetts with respect to its population, government, economy, the number of freemen and church members, ecclesiastical arrangements, the fortifications at Boson, and the disposition of the populace toward the government of England.[11]

Randolph arrived in Boston on 10 June. That same afternoon he delivered the king's letter and the copies of the petitions of Mason and Gorges to the governor and magistrates. He demanded that the authorities give him a full answer. Viewing Randolph as nothing but an agent for Mason, Governor Leverett made little of the matter: Randolph was only a messenger to deliver documents. The authorities of the Bay Colony would answer in their own time. Leverett then wrote Secretary Coventry, branding the complaints against the Bay Colony impertinencies and falsehoods, as the General Court would demonstrate when it met later in the year. An outbreak of smallpox made it now impossible to convene the assembly. Receiving no satisfaction, Randolph spent a few days gathering what information he could from men in Boston discontented with the commonwealth government.

After only a week in the town he sent off a long letter filled with recriminations against Leverett and his supporters. Basking in the glory of having snubbed the royal commissioners more than a decade before, they were now spreading false rumors, tales allegedly sent over from London, that the king was intent on suppressing all Nonconformist meetings, altering the government, and imposing episcopacy in New England. Leverett had purportedly declared that the laws made by the king and Parliament meant nothing in Massachusetts. By the charter the legislative power rested in them; they were free to make laws with no appeal to the king. In this report Randolph denigrated the authorities in Boston. For the most part they were "inconsiderable mechanics," imposed by the prevailing party of factious ministers, since only members of the churches were capable of holding office. Yet seemingly unconcerned about contradictions, Randolph reported many among the magistrates, the officers of the militia, the merchants, and the commoners supported the royal interest. They feared showing their sentiments until convinced the king was fully resolved to reduce the colony to obedience.[12]

Randolph did not tarry long in Boston. Back in London by the end of the summer, he submitted yet another report, further condemning the government of Massachusetts. In New Hampshire many of the inhabitants (not members of the Congregational churches) complained of oppression by the Boston magistrates in not admitting them to the Lord's Supper and in denying them baptism and the liberty of choosing their own officials. In New Plymouth, Governor Josiah Winslow had expressed his disapproval of encroachments by Boston officials. New England could never be secure or serviceable until the king reduced Massachusetts to his immediate government, Randolph concluded. New Plymouth and Connecticut would readily submit, he predicted.

Randolph and his patron placed their hopes in the lord treasurer and Sir Robert Southwell to forward the campaign against Massachusetts. Danby, for his part, seemed to be concerned with what might be done about the New Englanders trading directly to Europe and settling officers from the Customs in Massachusetts.[13] Yet the crown was publicly committed to take no action until agents from the Bay Colony arrived in England and presented a defense for the province. Randolph pressed the issue. On 12 October he submitted a formal reply to the inquiries raised by the Committee on Plantation affairs. Much of what he had to offer was misleading and inaccurate, reflecting his own prejudices and those of the discontented elements in Massachusetts with whom he had spoken during his brief stay. But he also drew heavily and directly from the printed laws of the colony and stressed the usurption of the powers of the sovereign by the Bay authorities, violations of the acts of navigation, and the privileges and prerogatives of members of the Congregational churches (a minority of the population). Randolph's contention that the great majority of the colonists would accept royal intervention was his most serious distortion.[14] It did not follow from the fact that only a minority of the adult men were admitted as members of the churches and freemen of the provincial corporation.

While Randolph pressed his indictment of the commonwealth government, in Boston John Leverett and his deputy, Samuel Symonds, convened a special session of the General Court to deal with the complaints against Massachusetts. With many of the ministers of the province in town, the General Court solicited their advice. They recommended dispatching agents or attorneys to England rather than sending merely a written answer. By mid-September a formal address to the king was drawn and orders and instructions completed for two agents, Peter Bulkeley and William Stoughton. The instructions tightly circumscribed the emissaries. They were to present the claim of Massachusetts to the northern towns by right of the boundary specified in the charter. "To all other clamours and accusations" they were to answer that they had no instructions. If pushed, they were to ask for time to obtain further orders from Boston. Their orders allowed the agents to confer with friends of the Puritan regime in London and to apply particularly to the earl of Anglesey and the other lords of the Privy Council thought to be sympathetic to the Bay Colony.

The two agents departed Boston in the fall of 1676. They did not return until three years later.

By mid-December 1676 Stoughton and Bulkeley had arrived in London and presented an address to the king in council. Mason was reported keeping "a watchfull ey[e] over them" and resolved "not [to] let them rest." He awaited the return to London of Sir Robert Southwell, the clerk of the council assigned to the Committee for Plantation Affairs, "to beginn the Assault."[15] The jurisdiction over the lands beyond the Piscataqua was finally resolved by purchasing Maine from Gorges for £1,200, a negotiation carried through by John Usher, a Boston bookseller then in London. On the basis of a narrow reading of the boundary specified in the charter granted to the Massachusetts Bay Company in 1629 and the priority of the grant made from the old Council of Plymouth to John Mason, the crown law officers and the chief justices of the Court of King's Bench and Court of Common Pleas concluded New Hampshire did not fall within the confines of Massachusetts.[16]

Only after the legal officers had decided the jurisdiction over the northern reaches of New England did the Committee for Plantation Affairs take up the other charges contained in Randolph's report. But when called before the Lords of Trade on 19 July 1677 to answer these allegations, Stoughton and Bulkeley merely repeated the formula required by their instructions from the General Court in Boston: they had no authority to answer. As private persons they might shed some light.

At best the two agents could evade, rationalize, equivocate. Were Whalley and Goffe, the regicides, protected in New England? Yes, but they had escaped, notwithstanding warrants issued by the authorities in Boston. Had the people of the Bay tried to form themselves into a commonwealth? Had they refused to take the oath of allegiance to the king? They had acknowledged his majesty to be their sovereign, submitted to his authority, and had always conformed to the requirements of the royal charter. While they had once of necessity coined money, they had discontinued this act of sovereignty. As to putting any persons to death for matters of religion, the agents denied the charge. There was a law that no Quakers, being strangers, should come into the colony; some, notwithstanding, did transgress the statute and were therefore executed. At present, however, many Quakers resided in the colony. As to the parliamentary navigation code, some private persons, perhaps, traded directly, not understanding the laws, but the governor would submit to the king's orders and swear out bonds as provided by law.

It was, and is, not quite believable.

After reviewing several briefs relating to the laws of the Bay Colony, the Lords of Trade on 27 July 1677 once more called in the agents. They would be wise to remain in England to aid in revising the provincial code. The laws of Massachusetts contained grave faults, and many were repugnant to the laws of England. The king would not destroy the charter but would rather by a "supplemental" patent "set all things right that are now amiss." As a preliminary, the attorney general and solicitor general would review the patent to determine whether the authority of the king was sufficiently preserved and the colonists rendered as dependent on the crown as was deemed necessary. Mason's request that the charter be vacated was rejected.[17]

When the law officers conferred with the agents, Bulkeley and Stoughton were, as they later admitted, "in a manner, ashamed" of the laws of the colony. The attorney general and the solicitor general, Sir

William Jones and Sir Francis Winnington, themselves entered several objections: the statutes of Massachusetts made offenses capital by word of God, called the General Court the chief civil power in the commonwealth, fined people for observing Christmas, and penalized men and women for walking in the streets or fields and children for playing on the Sabbath. The laws failed to require the taking of oaths of allegiance and supremacy to the king, imposed the disproportionate punishment of banishment or death for heresy, and restricted freemanship. On this last point the king in 1662 had required that anyone who adhered to the Church of England might be free in matters of government and equally qualified with others for any office. Although the General Court had modified the law in 1664, few persons were wealthy enough to benefit, and the practice of restricting political office to full church members had continued.

Some on the Committee for Plantation Affairs noted that Governor John Leverett had shown little inclination to obey the crown. They concluded he ought not to be eligible to continue in office unless approved by the king; others thought this unreasonable. Stoughton and Bulkeley tried to make the best case they could in defending the political practices in the Bay Colony, but they failed to mention that the law enacted in Boston in 1664 by which men who were not full members of a Congregational church were made eligible for freemanship imposed such a high tax-paying requirement that few men could qualify. It was not religious commitment that mattered in the selection of civil officers, they argued, but the number of votes. What they omitted was that it was exactly a religious standard which allowed full church members to become freemen and to vote.

The Lords of Trade held to the conviction that the statutes of the colony were repugnant to the laws of England; they must be amended to meet the objections of the crown law officers by an additional or supplemental charter.[18] Bulkeley and Stoughton apparently admitted the past offenses of the government at Boston, begged pardon, and promised it would make amends. But the Lords for Plantation Affairs remained skeptical, particularly since the crown had acted so "fairly," with such "softness" in 1662 and since Bradstreet as agent had promised that the New Englanders would be more obedient. To some on the committee it was now clear that officials in Boston could not be relied on to obey the king's orders. A government supported by the crown was what the majority of the people in Massachusetts wanted.

The attorney general and the solicitor general had to examine several propositions. In view of the prior grant of New England to the Council of Plymouth, had the charter of 1629 been properly issued? Was the charter still valid despite the prosecution by the crown of a writ of quo warranto in 1635? Had the corporation—the governor and company—by maladministration forfeited the patent?

As Sir William Jones and Sir Francis Winnington viewed the evidence, the original charter to the Massachusetts Bay Company had been valid. It had not been abrogated in 1635, for the prosecution of the writ had not been completed under Charles I, and the Act of Oblivion now rendered further prosecution under that writ illegal. However, the violations charged by Randolph, *if proven,* were sufficient now to void the charter. This would require another writ of quo warranto. [19]

Stoughton and Bulkeley seized on the doubt raised by the law officers and sought to undermine Randolph's charge of maladministration by the government of Massachusetts. Randolph's stay in New England had been so short, his acquaintances there so partial, and his prejudices so great that he could not be thought to have accurately assessed the situation. His statements were mere scandals, calumnies, and misrepresentations. The freemen of the colony were free to choose or to leave out whom they pleased as magistrates, and others besides church members could be admitted to the corporation. What the agents omitted in their defense was that property requirement was so high that few men could so qualify. These tax-paying qualifications did not apply to members of the Congregational churches in full communion. Protestants dissenting from the Congregational establishment—Presbyterians, Anabaptists, and Quakers—were not considerable in number, the agents insisted. The General Court required each town by law to maintain a minister. This was done by voluntary contribution, at times by a common tax. The agents insisted that in matters of religion there was full agreement with the articles of the Church of England, although the practice in the colony was Congregational. [20]

Having thus answered the charges by Randolph, or at least having clouded the issue, Bulkeley and Stoughton asked to be allowed to return home to America.

On 30 July 1678 lords Anglesey, Craven, and Berkeley and secretaries Coventry and Williamson reviewed the principal issues. Some were convinced that establishing a general governor and a proper judicature to determine differences was essential for the stability of New England. To the senior clerk of the council, Sir Robert Southwell, they delegated the duty of drafting a solution. It was a long and difficult task, as Southwell complained later that summer, to unravel the entire business of New England from the beginning in order to bring that unruly place into some better order and a more apparent dependence on the crown. Many of the relevant records were not available. [21]

Peter Bulkeley and William Stoughton kept Governor John Leverett informed of the proceedings in Whitehall. When the General Court convened that fall, the commonwealthmen were prepared to answer the objections to the legal code of Massachusetts.

The tactics they adopted consisted of outright denial that the laws of the province conflicted with those of England, special pleading, rationalizations, and promises of reform. In response to the charge that merchants were not adhering to the acts of navigation, the General Court contended that, according to men learned in the law, the statutes of England did not extend beyond the narrow seas, did not reach America. As subjects not represented in Parliament, the colonists did not look upon themselves as limited in their trade by the legislature at Westminster. Yet the king had demanded that his subjects in Massachusetts observe the English navigation code. This could not be done without invading the liberties and injuring the property of the colonists. Nonetheless, the provincial legislature promised to pass a bill incorporating the provisions of the English statutes, although this code discouraged trade and damaged the commerce of the colony. The commonwealthmen were not without hope the king would grant them full liberty to trade directly with Europe. What they did not officially admit was that Boston merchants were then trading directly with French, Scottish, and Dutch ports.

On the question of liberty of conscience for those dissenting from the established Congregational churches in the Bay Colony, the commonwealthmen gave little satisfaction. They remained adamant in their opposition to the Quakers, a people who had carried themselves "insolently and contemptuously against authority, rayling and reuilling" the governor, magistrates, and ministers, denouncing the authorities with "fearful curses in the name of the Lord," and publicly disseminating their "damnable opinions & haethrodoxies." By such behavior they had endangered the true Christian religion and divided the citizenry. Despite repeated warnings and banishment, a few of the Quakers had returned and had suffered the extreme penalty. It could not be argued that the authorities had put them to death for reasons of religion any more than it could be affirmed that the Jesuits and Catholic seminarians had been executed in England in the time of Elizabeth and James I for religious causes. Massachusetts had punished them for breach and contempt of the laws.[22]

That the Puritans of Massachusetts should have drawn a parallel between the threat from Quakers and the menace of Catholics at this time was not without irony. In London, Doctor Israel Tonge and Titus Oates, the latter one of the greatest pathological liars known in recorded history, had already made public their charges of a vast underground conspiracy, a Popish Plot, and Sir Edmund Berry Godfrey, the London magistrate to whom Oates had revealed his tale, had already been found dead under mysterious circumstances. For some time the Privy Council was fully occupied with the purported Catholic conspiracy. Late in October 1678 Oates appeared before the bar of the House of Commons to accuse the queen of treason. Encouraged by Shaftesbury and the Whig opposition, Yonge and Oates recited a series of lurid tales, told of a conspiracy to kill or get rid of Charles II, to install his Catholic brother as king, to impose arbitrary rule, and to massacre the leading Protestants of the realm. In the ensuing hysteria several innocent men were tried, convicted, and executed largely on evidence supplied by Oates.

The administration was shaken. Danby, the lord treasurer, who had built up a faction for the king in the House of Commons, was a political victim. Although he had not approved of securing a subsidy for the king from Louis XIV, under orders from Charles II he had undertaken negotiations with the French court. Throughout 1679 and 1680 and into 1681, the struggle raged to see who would govern England, the king or Shaftesbury and the Whig leaders, many of whom were themselves in the pay of the French king. The conflict was closely followed in Massachusetts. Shaftesbury was charged with high treason late in November 1681, but when a grand jury in London packed by Whig sheriffs threw out the indictment, he was released. Charles II, encouraged by the reaction in the countryside against the excesses of the Whigs, proceeded to move against the charter first of London and then other municipalities.

Occupied with the ongoing domestic political crisis, the king and the ministers of state could devote little attention to the affairs of the Puritan commonwealth across the Atlantic. Robert Mason and Edward Randolph on the one hand and William Stoughton and Peter Bulkeley on the other had been pressing for a resolution of outstanding issues, but Sir Robert Southwell, the clerk of the Committee for Plantation Affairs, had not yet completed the "great Report" on New England when the political crisis broke in London.

Randolph, armed with a commission as surveyor general and collector of the customs for New England, was eager for authority to effect changes in Massachusetts—to widen the franchise, review local statutes, and appoint a governor general to secure New England from the threat of French or Indian incursions. For the time being, Governor Josiah Winslow of New Plymouth, assisted by loyal gentlemen, should command the provincial militia. Southwell was skeptical. More than a dozen years before, royal commissioners had suggested the commonwealthmen accept a much less ambitious program and had failed. Matters must now be maturely weighed, lest the crown be foiled for want of authority to support them. The Lords for Plantation Affairs agreed with Southwell. No good could be expected from the endeavors of any single official.

Except for the decision to remove the communities on the Piscataqua from the jurisdiction of Massachusetts, no further steps were forthcoming. Indeed, in the spring of 1680 the king and his ministers of state resolved to reduce the expenditures of the crown in America, and that summer Southwell seems to have retired as clerk for the Committee for Plantation Affairs, although William Blathwayt sought to persuade him to spend some thought on regulations to "bring the Plantations to a Strict account and correspondency with ye Ministers." According to word received from Governor Cranston of Rhode Island, despite royal orders prohibiting punishment of the king's subjects for matters of religion, the commonwealthmen of Boston had passed newer and stronger laws to prosecute dissenters from the established Congregationalist way.[23]

Occupied with the crisis over the alleged Popish Plot and confronted with the declaration of the agents of Massachusetts that they were not authorized to answer for the provincial government, the lords of the committee agreed to allow Stoughton and Bulkeley to return to America. They would deliver a letter requiring the authorities in Boston to send over fully accredited agents; it would not be possible to resolve outstanding issues unless such agents were present.

Bulkeley and Stoughton, having conducted themselves with discretion, were expected to acquaint the regime in Boston with what was further expected from Whitehall. The authorities in Massachusetts must grant "perfect" freedom of conscience for all except Papists and abolish any religious distinctions in admitting men to the freedom of the corporation. To fine persons dissenting on religious grounds and to deny them the vote was a "severity to be the more wondered at," inasmuch as liberty of conscience was the principal motive for the Puritan settlers first moving to America. Massachusetts must also restore Maine and abolish all laws repugnant to the English statutes on navigation. Many of these conditions Stoughton and Bulkeley had themselves proposed when they asked to be allowed to return to Boston.[24]

If Charles II and his ministers had placed any faith in the willingness of the commonwealthmen to accept an alteration or regulation of their charter, they were quite mistaken. The court required agents authorized to speak for the authorities in Boston to return to London within six months after receipt of the king's letter. Three years passed before John Richards and Joseph Dudley made their appearance at Whitehall.

The reception accorded Edward Randolph when he arrived in Boston in December 1679 further demonstrated unwillingness by the commonwealthmen to moderate their position. Randolph would have his work cut out for him. According to Robert Holden, a customs official in Boston then en route to Carolina, half a dozen traders were engaged in carrying tobacco from Albemarle directly to Ireland, Holland, France, and Spain and illegally returning goods from Europe and the Atlantic islands. Others were illicitly trading in Scottish linen after sailing their ships to Newcastle, Berwick, or Poole to obtain English clearance papers. Some carried on trade with Spain and France under the guise of importing salt.[25] None of this was surprising. Evasion of customs was endemic among merchants both in the colonies and in the mother country.

Within six months after Randolph returned to Boston he was in legal difficulty with the provincial courts for seizing ships he claimed were in violation of the English navigation code. Over the next twenty-four months he brought to trial thirty-six vessels; all but two were released. By parliamentary statute, supervision of the navigation code was left to the governors in the colonies and officials (naval officers) appointed by them. Seemingly complying with this requirement, the General Court after some time passed a law creating naval officers to record the arrival and departure of ships.[26] Randolph conceived this act as contrived to exclude him from participating in the entering and clearing of ships. Puritan officials made Randolph's stay in Boston as uncomfortable as possible. The owner of the house where he boarded, before leaving on a short trip to New York on business, had invited Randolph to be his guest. The local authorities then cited a local law that no woman was allowed to admit a lodger into her home in the absence of her husband. Such harassment, Randolph charged, was part of a plot by Samuel Nowell and Thomas Danforth, now deputy governor, to drive him away.[27]

The commonwealthmen were in a stronger position following the election of May 1680. Expanding the number of magistrates from ten to eighteen as required in the charter had resulted in the election by the freemen in the colony at large—about thirty per cent or less of the adult males—of eight new assistants. At least five were opposed to compromise with the crown. Simon Bradstreet, Jr. complained sarcastically of the choice of a man like Peter Tilton. He might be skillful enough to guide a plowtail, but not the commonwealth. If such rustics were to manage the interest of New England, the younger Bradstreet would not give much for it. The commonwealthmen continued to dominate among the deputies returned by the freemen from the individual towns.[28]

A General Court controlled by the orthodox Puritans would hardly satisfy the demands contained in the royal letter brought back to Boston by Peter Bulkeley and William Stoughton. Although the General Court appointed a committee to review the provincial laws, ostensibly to suggest repeal of any repugnant to the laws of England, as to liberty of conscience it presumed the king did not intend that a multitude of notorious errors and blasphemies should be allowed. After all, there were only eighty to one hundred Anabaptists in the colony, all of the meaner sort, and about half as many Quakers. In Boston, weekly voluntary contributions maintained the ministers; in the other towns, a yearly assessment to which the inhabitants freely assented.

The General Court dismissed as inconsiderable the harm done by irregular trade; the merchants of Massachusetts allegedly paid full customs for what they exported as provided by the Plantation Duty Act of 1673. This ignored the additional duties required under the Act of Tonnage (1660) on enumerated products as well as the customs levied there on merchandise carried from Europe to America. Other complaints the General Court summarily dismissed: the Lords of Trade and Plantations and the king had been misinformed as to conditions in the Bay Colony.

Randolph gave a different story to his correspondents in London. One of the lords of trade, John Egerton, the earl of Bridgewater, concluded it was now clear that the Bostonians were an "unruly & yet dissembling people who when any of them are here pretend great duty" toward the king, but when in Massachusetts would do nothing to acknowledge his authority.[29] To the ministers at Whitehall it was evident by the fall of 1680 that the authorities in Massachusetts had taken little notice of the objections raised against the Puritan regime. The king now gave the provincial government just three additional months to appoint agents competent to answer the charges made against the colony. Should the commonwealthmen fail to respond, the crown would take the "most effectual means" to remedy matters.[30]

Would the Puritans in Massachusetts appreciate the seriousness of the situation?

During 1681 the two contending parties in Boston were at loggerheads over the issues of the agents and the parliamentary navigation code. Frustrated, Randolph pressed his case against the colony for obstructing the acts of trade. He singled out one of the leaders of the Puritan faction, Danforth, the deputy governor of Massachusetts. In open court Danforth allegedly had proclaimed that the parliamentary laws on trade and the king's commission to customs officers were of no validity in Massachusetts. Randolph argued that the officials of the corporation, by removing themselves to America, had violated the requirements of their charter.

Randolph now pressed for a writ of quo warranto. To make this action more palatable he recommended that the king by printed declaration confirm liberty of conscience as well as legal and property rights. Should the commonwealthmen persist, sanctions against their ships trading with the other colonies would bring them to reason. Without trade they could not subsist. Once the charter had been vacated, the king could rely on trustworthy, local gentlemen to support his government: Stoughton, Simon Bradstreet, Bulkeley, the younger Nathaniel Saltonstall, and the other moderate magistrates as well as Samuel Shrimpton, Richard Wharton, Thomas Kellond, Samuel Sheafe, and Wait Winthrop.

Although Randolph had previously described New England as "cantonized" into small corporations, unable to defend themselves or to aid one another, he did not now think it advisable to appoint a general governor. Yet if a united New England under a royal executive was considered necessary, Randolph thought no one better qualified than Thomas, Lord Culpeper who, he claimed, by his administration in Virginia and his conduct in New England had gained the respect of all good men.[31]

The object of Randolph's esteem was then in London backing the claim of the Atherton Associates, Connecticut, and New Plymouth to the Narragansett country. Twice in April 1681 Culpeper appeared before the Committee for Plantation Affairs. The generality of the people in Massachusetts were "very wary" of the authorities in power, officials averse to the government of England, he testified. In contrast, the colony of New Plymouth (then soliciting for a royal charter) was well inclined toward the king's government and deserved to be encouraged. While the members of the committee agreed to report Culpeper's sentiments to the full council, they remained convinced that the situation in New England could not be resolved unless the king sent over a general governor maintained at the expense of the crown.[32]

In a report submitted a few weeks later, the attorney general undermined the case made against Massachusetts by Edward Randolph. The various acts passed to regulate the plantation trade being public laws, the colonists were bound by them without the king having to give specific notice to the authorities in the provinces. Sovereignty remained with the king, and the monarch with his council could receive appeals from the plantations as they did from the Channel Islands of Jersey and Guernsey. But Randolph's contention that the officers and company of Massachusetts Bay, by removing the charter issued in 1629 to America, had violated the terms of their patent was invalid. By this charter Charles I had made the officers and freemen of the company a body corporate. The government of the company rested in them; they might reside in America.

Undaunted, Randolph submitted another list of propositions to the attorney general, designed to show that the authorities of the Bay Colony were interfering with enforcement of the navigation code. On this issue the law officers seemed to support the zealous collector of customs, as did the officers of the Customs House in London.[33]

The administration seemed divided, uncertain as to how to proceed. Some ministers accused Southwell, the committee's advisor, of supporting "fanaticks" in New England. On 18 October 1681, the lord privy seal, Clarendon, Bath, Craven, Halifax, the earl of Conway, Viscount Hyde, Jenkins, and Sidney Godolphin met as a committee for plantations affairs but recommended only dispatching to Boston still another letter, one Blathwayt described as "exceedingly soft and gentle and meddles with nothing but the sending of Agents." In this document, approved by the full council three days later, the king did not enumerate specific objectionable acts, but merely noted the obstructions placed in the way of Randolph and continued religious persecution. Charles II was unwilling to conclude that the failure of agents from Boston to appear in London indicated deliberate intent to procrastinate, but he ordered Bradstreet and his assistants to send fit persons fully authorized without delay and to give all countenance to Randolph in the execution of his duty. Failure to comply would result in legal action against the charter. Despite "ys mild way of Proceeding," Blathwayt yet hoped that "things will goe . . . well."[34]

For months the officials in the Bay Colony had been at loggerheads over the course to be adopted with the crown. Requested by the deputies and assistants to advise on the best way to proceed, the elders of the colony assembled at Boston. They recommended the General Court send over agents to answer any complaint; they would thereby show their obedience to the king as in duty bound. Holy Scripture—the book of Ezra, chapters 4 and 6—was not without instances of those who successfully asserted their innocence against their adversaries. Moreover, experience had demonstrated that dispatching agents to London had been a means of "lengthening out our tranquility." But the agents must not be allowed to do anything that might in the least weaken the government as by patent established. It was the undoubted duty of the saints to abide by what rights and privileges God had bestowed on them, and whatever might come, the Lord forbid that they should in any way part with these.[35]

Early in 1682 Randolph arrived with the royal letter demanding the dispatch of authorized agents to England. For weeks the two factions in the Massachusetts General Court argued over the choice of agents. William Stoughton refused to serve. The vilification he had endured from Danforth made him reluctant to subject himself to further abuse. The futility of such a mission, given the refusal of the commonwealthmen to make any concessions, might also have influenced his decision. The choice then fell on John Richards and Joseph Dudley. English-born but brought over to Massachusetts during the initial settlement by his father, Richards had served as a deputy, speaker, and magistrate. Joseph Dudley was also of impeccable Puritan lineage. Born in Massachusetts, the son of the second governor of the colony, he attended Harvard College and served in the House of Deputies and on the board of assistants. His sisters had married into the Bradstreet and Denison families, and he himself had taken as his wife a daughter of Edward Tyng, another assistant. Of similar backgrounds, Dudley and Richards reacted quite differently to their mission. Dudley's vision was not confined to the backwater of Puritan Massachusetts.

Thomas Danforth and Samuel Nowell controlled the committee charged with drafting the instructions to the agents. Dudley and Richards had little freedom of action. In answering particular charges made against the government, they must represent that Anglicans in the colony had the same liberty as all other subjects, that the laws against Dissenters were suspended, that all Protestants were admitted to the government, and that all acts of trade duly observed. But the charter was the critical issue. The agents must not consent to anything that might infringe upon the liberties conferred by the patent.[36]

Dudley and Richards sailed for England at the end of May 1682. Randolph had already begun his campaign to undermine them in letters to the Treasury, the secretary of state, and the bishop of London. He derided the bill passed by the General Court to enforce the navigation code. The failure of the crown to act the previous year and the expectation of renewed difficulties for the crown in London led the commonwealthmen, encouraged by the Dissenters in England, to hold the king's government in contempt. Nothing would serve but to bring a quo warranto against the charter.

Randolph now submitted another set of articles of high misdemeanor. He categorically denied the claims of the commonwealth faction as stated in the instructions to the agents. No person in Massachusetts could be a magistrate unless first a church member and chosen by the freemen; no man could be admitted a freeman without the approval of one of the Congregational ministers. The government must be placed in the hands of honest, prudent gentlemen who would dutifully receive the king's commands.[37] Randolph saw Joseph Dudley, whom he described as a great opponent of the faction, as such a man.

Randolph's assessment of Dudley seemed to be borne out when the agents reached London. Blathwayt found Dudley to be a discreet and ingenious individual: he got along well with him.

In the last week of August 1682 Dudley and Richards handed in the replies of the General Court of Massachusetts, statements denying any discrimination against Anglicans and claiming full compliance with the king's orders relating to the acts of trade. It was not enough. As the attorney general had remonstrated, there was a great discrepancy between the provincial statutes and the laws of England. Moreover, on 20 September, the king in council held that Richards and Dudley did not, as required, possess sufficient powers to agree to the necessary regulation of the government of the Bay Colony. They must now secure such authority. Should they fail to do so, the crown would seek a writ of quo warranto against the charter on 13 January, the first day of Hilary Term.

Dudley and his colleague then conferred with Secretary Jenkins and several attorneys, but in December, a month before the deadline for the agents to present their authority to agree to modifications of the government, Richards wrote Increase Mather in Boston that it might be well for the minister to suggest to the General Court that a letter be sent through the Dissenting merchant Major Robert Thompson dismissing the agents. Thus the commonwealthmen might postpone action by claiming that the colony was not properly represented. By 24 January 1683, when the agents had received no word from Boston, they could only petition the king for an extension of time.[38]

The news from London did not dishearten Samuel Nowell, for, as he wrote Richards, "Solomon tel[l]s us it shall go well with the righteous, with those that feare before God." The Lord called them out "to honour him by a life of faith," and they must act accordingly. If the government of the Bay Colony granted the agents authority to answer the demands of the crown "we do then pull downe the house ourseues." By the charter "we have full & absolute power to rule & governe, pardon & punish, etc." Consequently the General Court had judged themselves free from appeals to the crown of England. "Either we may finally judge of & determine all things, or else appeals ly, in all cases, wch will make the Goverm^r here . . . a meer cypher, more contemptible than any other Governm^r in all the Plantations." Nowell offered Richards some solace: the "Lord fit you and us for his holy will & pleasure in such trialls as seeme coming."

The behavior of Governor Lionel Cranfield in New Hampshire may have reinforced the determination of Nowell and the other Puritans to resist, but the position they adopted in 1683 was no less rigid than that they held before Cranfield came to New England. Over the pleas of the moderates that some concessions consistent with the purpose in founding the colony, freedom to practice the Congregational religion, be made, Danforth, Nowell, and the other commonwealthmen argued that any regulation of the government would mean attacks on property and religion. By instructions adopted at the end of March 1683 the agents were prohibited from agreeing to any regulation altering the government, curtailing religious liberty, or allowing appeals from decisions of the provincial courts.

To support the Puritans' position the General Court sent the agents a petition signed by the inhabitants of the towns to be presented at Whitehall if any advantage might be made of it. This would prove that "the generality doe not desire a chainge."[39] According to documents presented by Randolph to the Committee for Plantation Affairs later that spring, this address was composed in the General Court. Inhabitants in the towns sixteen years of age and older were directed to sign a blank paper which was then sent to the speaker of the House of Deputies and attached to the address.[40]

Late in the spring of 1683 Randolph presented to the Committee for Plantations a résumé of affairs relating to Massachusetts and articles designed to show the government of the colony was in violation of English law. At a meeting held on 12 June the Lords of Trade, with the lord president (John Robartes, earl of Radnor) and George Savile, marquis of Halifax, present, took quick action. Contrary to the requirements laid down by the king, the General Court of Massachusetts had not given the agents powers sufficient for them to consent to matters necessary for the due regulation of the provincial government. They recommended the attorney general sue out a quo warranto.

The writ was issued at Westminster on 26 June, and on 9 July Richard Normansell, secondary of the sheriffs of London, signed a notice to that effect to the governor and officials of Massachusetts.[41] Randolph suggested to the lord keeper and the Committee for Plantation Affairs that to dispel any false and seditious "insinuation" relating to the future government of the colony and to induce the people more easily to surrender the charter, the king send over some proper person—he had himself in mind—with a declaration promising to preserve their liberties and property. Charles II signed such a declaration on 9 August 1683. He promised to respect all private interests and property in Massachusetts. If the governor and company submitted without further delay, there would be no alterations in the charter other than those necessary for the better support of government.[42]

Under orders to deliver notification of the writ (returnable the next Michaelmas term) to Boston within three months, Randolph was eager to depart. He did not want to give the "disaffected" party any excuse to plead that they had not been given time to answer the summons. While waiting for a ship, he conferred with Dudley.

Realizing perhaps the futility of continued resistance, the agent conferred with Randolph on a possible frame of government for New England. To provide for the security and defense of the region the king would appoint a governor general over the petty provinces with a council selected from the magistrates of the several colonies to assist him. Massachusetts would have a president and a council elected every three years by the freemen, those Protestants taking the oath of allegiance to the king and holding £100 in real or personal property. All laws in Massachusetts repugnant to the statutes of England were to be declared void and the parliamentary acts relating to trade enforced. Subjects would have the right to appeal from the provincial courts to England and to hold their lands under the crown, paying a yearly quitrent not to exceed two shillings and sixpence per hundred acres.

After turning these proposals over to Sir Robert Southwell, Randolph boarded H.M.S. *Golden* early in September 1683 and left for New England. With him he took the summons to answer the writ against the provincial charter, the royal declaration on liberty of conscience and property, and a dozen or so blank passes for New England merchant ships granting them immunity from seizure by the North African corsairs. These passes, he expected, would make him welcome "to the trading party" in Boston.

Whatever the views of the merchants of the Bay Colony, the commonwealthmen would not receive Randolph kindly. According to Cranfield, the ministers there were inciting the populace, arguing that "it is God[']s cause and that they may lawfully draw their Swords in the defence of their Charter and liberties therein granted unto them."[43]

Randolph arrived in Boston at the end of October shortly after Dudley and Richards. The General Court was not then in session. Since he did not plan to stay more than five weeks—he left on 14 December—he wrote immediately to Governor Thomas Hinckley of New Plymouth for attested copies of the grants to further the application made by the Plymouth men for a settlement of their government under the crown.

On 7 November the magistrates and deputies of the Bay Colony assembled at Boston. After they had spent a day in private fasting, Randolph delivered the declaration from the king. It made little difference. Nowell, Danforth, and Increase Mather held up the behavior of Cranfield in Portsmouth as an example of what lay in store if the crown remodeled the government. To encourage opposition someone circulated a letter purportedly from London among the members of the General Court describing the miserable condition of the East Anglican town of Norwich following the surrender of its charter. At least nine deputies and an equal number of ministers were sufficiently unimpressed by this danger to Congregationalism and supported an accommodation with the crown. But they were hardly enough. Another paper, allegedly written by a hotheaded young minister, Samuel Cheevers, was also circulated, a document condemning those ministers, deputies, and magistrates favoring compromise as backsliders and betrayers of the liberty of their country.

Danforth and Nowell prevailed. In a letter signed, not by the governor, Simon Bradstreet, but by the provincial secretary, Edward Rawson, the General Court empowered a London solicitor, Robert Humphreys, to contest the action of the crown. They even suggested the legal arguments he use. A charter exercised in America could not be tried in a court in England, nor could sheriffs in London serve a writ on persons who had never lived there. Randolph had not presented the writ in America until the time for the appearance of the defendants had passed, and the sheriffs had not served the legal process on the agents of the Bay Colony in London. This last point was not without irony, for it had been a cardinal rule of the commonwealthmen not to allow the agents to act in any legal capacity. In a more cogent vein, they referred Humphreys to the reports of the great legal authority, Edward Coke, lord chief justice under James I, concerning the status of the isles of Man, Guernsey, and Jersey, lands determined to be "extra regnum," not liable to judgment at the Court of King's Bench. The royal courts could not hear cases from territory outside the realm of England.

By this argument the majority of the General Court hoped to deny the authority of the judges in England over the Bay Colony. To sweeten the pill, in the spring of 1684 they also sent Humphreys a petition addressed to the king: "We hereby ayming to express our vnfeigned desires to submitt ourselues to his maj'jes favour to be extended towards us for the continuation of the libertjes and priuildges to us granted by his maj'jes royall charter. . . ."[44]

The behavior of the commonwealthmen disgusted the moderates on the board of assistants, particularly Bulkeley and Dudley, who maintained a correspondence with Blathwayt, expecting that the management of New England affairs would pass though their hands. Bulkeley condemned the decision of the majority of the deputies from the towns to contest the prosecution at Westminster, many of whom, ignorant of affairs, did not understand the matter. By "such (apelike) overfondness, wee are hugging our priveledges & franchises to death." Efforts by Governor Bradstreet and the moderate magistrates to impress on them the gravity of the situation and to bring the people to a better understanding had met with little success.[45]

In the contest to influence public opinion, at least in Boston, the moderates lost. On 21 January 1684, Nowell and Mather held forth at a tumultuous town meeting. Men who had not been admitted to the corporation were excluded. Mather exhorted the freemen not to accept the king's declaration on rights or give up the charter. If they yielded, their children would surely curse them. What had happened in London and neighboring New Hampshire gave evidence of what royal rule would mean. Any regulation of the charter by the crown would be destructive of religion and of Christ's kingdom in Massachusetts. They could not consent "without sin and great offence to the Majesty of Heaven." Twice before, in 1638 and 1664, the holy commonwealth had been threatened by the crown, but nothing had happened. The implication was clear. The Lord would again intervene in behalf of the saints.[46]

Nowell, Danforth, and Mather carried the attack against the moderates on the board of assistants into the elections. Bradstreet held the governorship, but by a narrow margin over Danforth. Dudley, William Browne, and Bartholomew Gedney lost their places. Although reelected, Bulkeley and Stoughton refused to take their seats. With the addition of Elisha Hutchinson, Elisha Cooke, William Johnson, John Hawthorn, and Samuel Sewall, the commonwealthmen controlled the board of assistants as well as the House of Deputies. They promptly passed a vote confirming the decision to contest the suit against the charter. Although repudiated by the majority of the freemen, men in full communion with the Congregational churches in the towns, Dudley wrote on their behalf to London imploring that the royal government take no severe action against them but, rather, give assurances for property and an indulgence in religion.[47]

Cranfield's prosecution of Joshua Moody in Portsmouth, an attack viewed as a preliminary to a campaign against the Puritan clergy, may have influenced some people, but it would not have been decisive in Massachusetts. Danforth and his supporters were no less intransigent before Cranfield and Mason arrived on the Piscataqua than after. Nor were the commonwealthmen ever in danger of losing control of the House of Deputies, a chamber elected by the freemen of the towns—the full church members, a declining minority among the adult males in the province. They were in a position to block any compromise. Believing themselves to be the elect of God, they viewed compromise as un- thinkable and, indeed, unnecessary, for the Lord would preserve them. Against the more objectionable opponents, they took immediate action.

They had meted out rough treatment to Edward Randolph, threatening him with the town dock. Guns were set off in his wife's face, his two daughters chased "through the streets with the name of Whores[,] Whores." The harassed customs official had taken passage for London, where at the end of March 1684 a letter from Bradstreet and the moderate magistrates arrived announcing that they were still laboring to bring the people to a better understanding of the situation.[48]

That same month Richard Wharton's son, then on a mission for his father and the other Narragansett proprietors, brought over to London a packet of books and papers sent from Boston by Increase Mather and directed to Abraham Kick, a Dissenter merchant living in Amsterdam. Shaftesbury had died in his house. By order of the secretary of state, the packet was opened, and a letter to Peter Gouge, minister of an English congregation at Amsterdam, read. Edward Randolph identified the author as Increase Mather, although the latter claimed later the document was a forgery, possibly done by Bernard Randolph, Edward's brother. The author of the letter attacked Randolph, criticized the moderates in Boston for violating their oaths to God, and strongly condemned the king's ministers of state as perpetrators of evil, corrupt men who had become "abomnible in theire Wickedness" for persecuting "that great ffreind of God[']s Cause," the earl of Shaftesbury, and the other Whigs implicated in the Rye House Plot to assassinate the king and his brother. The Lord was certain to "Avenge the blood of his Saints."[49]

Forgery or no, the letter attributed to Increase Mather was not needed to influence the course of events at Whitehall or Westminster. Due to a slip by a clerk employed in drafting the writ against the charter, it seemed at one point the prosecution might fail. The attorney general, Robert Sawyer, initially concluded a new writ would have to be issued and Randolph would once more have to cross the Atlantic to serve it. But Blathwayt prevailed on Sawyer to employ another legal process, a writ of scire facias. Seeking to block the Court of King's Bench from issuing the new writ, Robert Humphreys, the solicitor employed by the General Court of Massachusetts, appeared with three chancery practitioners before the lord keeper: inasmuch as the officers of the company had not received notice of the writ, they ought to be given time to answer.

On 21 June Lord Guilford ruled that judgment be entered for the king. If the defendants appeared by the first day of the next term, Michaelmas, the judgment would be set aside. If they did not or were in default, it was to stand.[50]

Writing Joseph Dudley of what had happened, Humphreys now suggested the best course of action for the General Court: the authorities must send witnesses, "men of sense," to London, as soon as possible. "Pray see that I be not pincht for money, since rowing against the wind & tide all hands must be employed & you well know what tools work here." His recommendation did not arrive in Boston until early September 1684. By then it was too late even if the commonwealthmen had been willing to act on it. Temporizing as before, they mocked the threat of a writ against the charter as a "poor, toothless creature." Kept out of the deliberations of the majority, Bradstreet, Dudley, and William Stoughton hoped that the crown would honor its promise of a general pardon, an indulgence in religion, liberty of conscience, and protection of property.[51]

Robert Humphreys waited vainly for word from the General Court. Despite the pleas of the chancery practitioners he employed for a decision to be put off for still another term, the order against the charter of Massachusetts was confirmed on 23 October 1684 and the patent vacated.[52]

The closing weeks of 1684 and the ensuing winter of 1685 seemed momentous for the English provinces across the Atlantic. The king and his brother, James, seemed embarked on a plan to consolidate some governments in America. William Blathwayt seemed hopeful, if not certain, of more. There were indications that the small, weak, and scattered towns of New Hampshire and New Plymouth, the latter still without any legal sanction from England, might be joined to Massachusetts, whose government had devolved directly on the crown, but beyond this what Charles II and his advisors had in mind was not clear. Despite warnings to the proprietor of Maryland and the opportunity presented by the inept handling by the Carolina proprietors in the Culpeper affair, in 1681 the crown had taken no action against the southern proprietaries. That same year Charles II had issued a patent for another proprietary colony in America, and while the Lords for Plantation Affairs in 1682 had recommended that no more charter colonies be established, in assuming the governments of Bermuda and New Hampshire the king had authorized as late as 1682 the calling of elected assemblies. In the same month that the royal courts let stand the writ against the charter of Massachusetts Bay, James, as a proprietor, gave his approval to the Charter of Liberties, establishing an elected assembly in New York. Although he later reversed his position, the legislature was allowed to continue until 1687, and its laws were confirmed.

The decision to move against the commonwealthmen of Massachusetts had come only after twenty years. During this long interval Charles II had shown remarkable restraint. The crown did not act peremptorily even in 1681, when the law officers had agreed that actions of the General Court, if proven, constituted grounds to vacate the charter. After three sets of agents, none prepared to acknowledge the sovereignty of the crown of England, had attended the court in London, Charles II and his ministers had finally moved in 1684 against the charter. The House of Deputies elected by the freemen of the towns—members in full communion with the Congregationalist churches, but a declining minority in the colony—had been the stumbling block to any accommodation with the crown. The men dominating the Bay Colony, self-proclaimed saints committed to the idea of churchmen endowed with the Lord's saving grace ruling an independent commonwealth, had procrastinated, convinced that God would save their Zion as apparently he had before.

During the fall of 1684 and the ensuing winter, events elsewhere in America and in Whitehall broadened the scope of the problem of the overseas colonies. The murder of the royal customs official in Maryland and the extraordinary claims of the proprietary government of Lord Baltimore to the customs of the Potomac River, a development bitterly contested by royal officials in Virginia, now came to the attention of the ministers in London. Rivalry for power in Whitehall may also have been a factor. Although James favored the earl of Rochester (his brother-in-law) over Sunderland as chief minister, the royal duke, Sunderland, and Louise, duchess of Portsmouth (an agent of the French king) were united in opposition to the marquis of Halifax. The nature of the government for Massachusetts once the charter had been vacated gave them an opportunity to attack and to weaken Halifax. Hitherto all but one of the governments sanctioned in the colonies by Charles II had enjoyed an elected lower house of assembly, and as late as October of 1684, James had given his approval for a representative body in New York.

By the autumn of that year the worsening military situation in the northern provinces of America became a factor. Previously the Puritan regimes had undertaken defense against local Indians through a loose arrangement, the United Colonies, or Confederation of New England, whose particularistic members, imbued with a sense of localism, had often squabbled among themselves. Even during the war against the Wampanoaugs and Narrangansetts they had wrangled; their efforts at cooperation had collapsed. Thereafter the confederation was in virtual desuetude.[53] By 1684 it was clear that the tribesmen of northern New England, now backed by the French in Canada, were becoming hostile. Intelligence received in London indicated the Bourbon authorities of New France, long engaged in bloody conflict with the Five Nations, hoped to form a general alliance with the northern tribesmen and to put an end to the Iroquois menace. The French were believed to have inspired attacks on the northern frontiers of the Puritan colonies. In attempting to provide for the defense of New England the crown hitherto had merely charged the various governments to come to the aid of their neighbors.[54] To some observers a more firm union was needed for the common defense of the northern provinces.

On 8 November 1684, lords Guilford, Rochester, Halifax, Godolphin, and Clarendon attended a meeting of the Committee for Plantation Affairs in the council chamber at Whitehall. Sunderland acquainted the board that, the charter of the Bay Colony having been vacated, they should consider how the government might be rendered more fit for the king's service in New England. Charles II and his ministers had consistently aimed at bringing the northern provinces into a closer dependence on the crown by a governor appointed, or at least approved, by the crown. The vacating of the charter of Massachusetts now gave the king an opportunity. He seemed resolved to appoint a professional military officer, Colonel Percy Kirke, most recently commander of the royal garrison at Tangier.

At this point, the Lords of Trade, noting that the government of New Hampshire—Cranfield having complained that it was too small to stand alone—was already in the hands of the crown, recommended placing it under Kirke on the revocation of Cranfield's commission. New Plymouth, having no charter or "Constitution," and Maine, devolved upon the crown with the dissolution of the Bay company, might also be added to Kirke's government. Rhode Island and Connecticut enjoyed charters not yet vacated by any judicial proceedings. Apparently some of the committeemen had in mind bringing these two corporations under closer supervision or even joining them to Massachusetts. No legal grounds as yet existed for such a step.

The new government to be established at Boston as posed by the Committee for Plantation Affairs on 8 November would consist of an elected assembly and a governor and council of twelve men appointed by the king.[55] However, just two weeks later the lord keeper informed the Lords of Trade of the king's desire that until further orders, no mention be made of an assembly in the commission and instructions for the proposed governor of Massachusetts. The governor and council appointed by the crown were to have power to make laws and perform all other governmental functions. Kirke's instructions were, however, to include a grant for liberty of conscience. A domestic political wrangle during the two-week interval between the meetings of the Committee for Plantation Affairs might have influenced the decision against an elected assembly. According to Paul Barillon, Louis XIV's ambassador, the duchess of Portsmouth, the duke of York, and Sir George Jeffreys, now chief justice of the King's Bench, had combined to attack Halifax, to discredit and to drive him from office. The "Trimmer" had argued that an absolute government, that is, one without a representative assembly, was neither a happy nor a safe one. Jeffryes had retorted that "who so capitulatheth, rebelleth," that is, any attempt to define, to limit the power of the sovereign was equivalent to rebellion. Yet the decision against a representative assembly was not firm; in fact when the Lords of Trade and the attorney general and solicitor general the following summer were drafting the commission and instructions for the royal governor of Massachusetts, they assumed that he would have authority to issue writs for the election of representatives from the towns to a provincial assembly.[56]

Nor was there any agreement on the choice of the governor to be sent out to Massachusetts. Randolph hoped to persuade the court that there was need of a more prudent man than the "hott, heady passi[on]ate Soudier," Kirke, to reconcile the New Englanders. Randolph himself drafted plans for a government at Boston, with a council to be made up of leading moderates and loyalists from the Bay Colony, Maine, New Hampshire, New Plymouth, and the King's Province (the disputed Narragansett lands). He also listed twenty-one towns in Massachusetts, nine in New Plymouth, five in Maine, and four in New Hampshire as towns "to haue liberty to Chuse Assembly men." No decision had as yet been made to issue out writs against Connecticut and Rhode Island. The crown might resort to such a course should the two corporations refuse to become part of a general government for New England.[57]

Decisions made at Whitehall relating to the American colonies were not at all certain by the end of 1684. In view of the vacating of the charters of Massachusetts and Bermuda and the proposed consolidation of New Plymouth, New Hampshire, Maine, and the Bay under one governor, Blathwayt was optimistic. The king's brother, he thought, was now ready to surrender the government of New York to the crown. Because of the murder of Rousby and Lord Baltimore's "exactions" on the shipping and commerce of the Potomac River, the king, he expected, would proceed against the proprietary charter of Maryland. The proprietors of Carolina and all others would soon fall, he predicted. It was now time for the governor of Virginia to furnish Blathwayt with proofs and arguments to make good the boundaries of the Old Dominion against the usurpations of Carolina and Maryland.

The secretary at the Plantation Office would have done well at this juncture to heed the warning he himself had given Edward Randolph some four years before. Great difficulty might be expected from grasping too great authority without due advice, "matters of Power & Governm[en]t by new ways & forms being not rashly to be propos[e]d nor easily brought to pass."

The lord keeper, Guilford, doubted whether the colonists in Massachusetts would acquiesce in the vacating of their charter and accept a royal governor. Randolph did not presume to give a definitive answer, but he emphasized that the New Englanders were exceedingly jealous of their liberty under the charter to choose their own officers, make their own laws, and dispose of public lands—rights and privileges they conceived the Lord to have bestowed on them. A charter from God could not be forfeited by the king. Men imbued with such beliefs now held the government in Boston, and they had been told that the king was sending over a regiment of soldiers from Tangier to be quartered among them and a great fleet to subjugate them by force. Randolph dreaded to think how the populace would react if these reports were sent them "with the usual additions of ye Schismaticks in Eng[lan]d or Holland & what mischiefs" they would attempt.

To reassure the populace Randolph advised the lord keeper to send his exemplification of the judgment against the charter together with a commission to honest, fit gentlemen temporarily to exercise authority. They should be informed that in proceeding against the charter—the only way to regulate abuses and free the people from oppression— Charles II aimed only at their good. If the majority of the people could be made to understand and to accept, then the populace of Rhode Island and Connecticut would also acquiesce in the king's laws and governor. Then New Englanders would be united, able to defend themselves against Indian and foreign invasion. If not, a poor example would be set for the inhabitants of the other colonies to the south and the king put to great expense each year to defend New England from the French, who already encroached upon her borders.[58]

Randolph, often given to exaggeration and distortion, had touched on a very real point. The commonwealthmen, convinced of their special relation with the Creator, were resolved to deny the authority of the crown of England and committed to continuing their Zion free of outside interference. Under the charter as administered by the saints, the men with any political voice (with very few exceptions) were those granted the franchise because they were full members of the churches. And the proportion of adult men in the Bay Colony who could pass this religious test had been steadily decreasing. The power of the government rested with a decided minority of adult males. As events later demonstrated, many of those disenfranchised, unhappy with the situation, wanted voting to be more widely spread and wanted a tax-paying qualification— one most men would have been able to meet—as the measure for political participation. A representative assembly, a more liberal franchise—one comparable with those franchises then exercised in the English shires and boroughs—and a pledge of religious toleration, or freedom of conscience, might well have made the difference for many men in Massachusetts in deciding how to react to the Restoration monarchy.

". . . union may make us more formidable"

SOME MEN serving Charles II and his brother may have looked with tacit approval across the English Channel at the attempts by Louis XIV and his minister Colbert to impose order on the chaotic, petty local jurisdictions in France, the remnants of hundreds of years of feudalism, as a model for the English court. But the absolutism of the Sun King outside the close environs of his capital was never great. The attempt of monarchy to rationalize, to centralize administration was frustrated even in France, where the power of the crown was so much greater and its resources so much more extensive than in England, by almost all levels of society tenaciously defending obscure, ill-defined local rights, dating from medieval times.[1]

A no less tenacious defense of local interests by Englishmen doomed the efforts of the Stuart monarchs. The particularistic development of the English plantations in America for over half a century, coupled with rudimentary technology and a still haphazard system of communication and transportation, imposed overwhelming burdens for any significant reform of the administration of the overseas colonies. Charles II and his ministers of state needed to commit massive sums of money and several thousands of royal troops over a long period. Financially and politically this was impossible, as they realized.

When the court at Westminster vacated the charter of Massachusetts, Charles II had been on the throne of England for almost a quarter of a century. In the spring of 1660, when he had returned to London after years of exile in Europe, few observers would have given him that long. His reign had witnessed the further expansion of overseas settlements. The English dominions in America had become even more diverse as the number of separate governments had increased with the explicit sanction of the crown. Hard-pressed at home, the king had sought to hold royal expenditures in the foreign plantations to a minimum, often reducing his officers there to dependence on the local populace while seeking to increase the revenue accruing to the crown under the navigation code from burgeoning colonial trade channeled through English ports. The king had two further goals: to bring the individual colonies into a closer dependence on the crown by commissioning governors and to further liberty of religious conscience. As far as he was able, Charles II remained true to the declaration he had issued at Breda. Limited by the political and religious biases of the Anglicans dominating the House of Commons, Charles had strived in the charters, commissions, and instructions granted over twenty years for the overseas provinces to establish and promulgate the principle of religious liberty, at least for peaceable Protestants.

He died on 6 February 1684/5. His Roman Catholic brother succeeded him.

Because of the initial reaction against the excesses of the Whigs during the last few years, James II began his reign with a large measure of support. An uprising in Scotland led by the earl of Argyle and another in the west of England on behalf of Charles II's bastard son, the duke of Monmouth, were brutally suppressed. When James's first Parliament met, it voted generous grants to overhaul the run-down Navy and Ordinance Department and to pay off the dead monarch's debts by additional duties on imports. Higher rates on tobacco and sugar for eight years were voted, threepence on English colonial tobacco, sixpence on foreign. The new taxes voted in this session and the boom in foreign trade brought the total annual revenue from overseas commerce during the reign of the new monarch to almost a million pounds sterling.[2]

Seemingly secure politically and financially, the new Catholic king embarked on a program to emancipate his coreligionists. In the House of Commons a committee reported favorably on a petition to the crown to enforce the laws against all religious dissenters from the established Church of England. By using extreme pressure James II squashed the report. But many members of Parliament signed the petition, thus indicating their dissatisfaction with the monarch's views.

To men then and later, the character of James II and his program were unclear. Was he a designing bigot, a man who calculated by degrees to reestablish the Church of Rome in England, or was he, however tactless and clumsy, a sincere believer in religious toleration, a king who hoped to win for his fellow Catholics and for other Christians the religious and political rights Cromwell and Charles II had failed to secure?[3] In 1685 Louis XIV was giving Europeans an example of militant Catholicism in power by revoking the Edict of Nantes and coercing French Calvinists by military force.

James openly sought repeal of the penal laws against Catholic and Protestant Dissenters as well as repeal of the Test Act, which deprived all but Anglicans of civil and political posts. When the Anglican Tories would not consent to the destruction of their political and ecclesiastical monopoly, the king turned away from them.

The king acted first on the basis of what he conceived to be the prerogative of the monarch. In a declaration in favor of toleration he expressed his aversion to persecution on religious grounds and his belief in the necessity of allowing his subjects liberty of conscience; he nonetheless pledged to protect and maintain the clergy and the communicants of the Church of England, as by law established, in the full enjoyment of their rights. But he also declared that it was his will that the execution of the penal laws in matters of religion be suspended and that the religious oaths and tests imposed by the Cavalier Parliament should no longer be required of persons holding civil and military office. Quakers benefited immediately; some twelve hundred imprisoned for not attending the Church of England were freed. William Penn and his family were the subjects of a special warrant to the ecclesiastical officials signifying that the Quaker leader and his relations were not to be molested.

James extended this policy to the colonies in the West Indies and in America. On 28 May 1687 the king in council approved a letter to the governors of the plantations. They must publish the king's declaration for liberty of conscience and indulgence in religion. All civil officials responsible for enforcing the laws were commanded to obey.[4]

Reactions in England were mixed. William Penn, a personal friend of the king, publicly supported the monarch. In April 1687 he held forth in a Quaker's conventicle in Gracechurch Street and "magnified" the king's mercy in granting toleration, as did some Presbyterian preachers. But other Dissenters and Anglicans, fearing that equality in religion ultimately would lead to the reestablishment of Roman Catholicism, were suspicious. Would other faiths then be tolerated? Halifax warned Dissenters that the Catholics embraced them now all the better to squeeze them later. Penn himself was suspect as a secret Jesuit. Thomas Marriett, an Anglican who had served more than twenty years as a justice on the commission for peace in several counties, warned him that the king's Declaration of Indulgence was not to be taken seriously, for as a Catholic, James was not his own master. In matters of religion the king's word "must signify noe more than ye Edict of Nantes when ye Pope pleaseth."[5]

James pressed his campaign, seeking a repeal of the discriminatory penal and test acts. After a survey revealed that prospective candidates for a new Parliament would not vote for repeal, the king began a systematic attack on the charters of the boroughs to remodel the corporation so as to ensure that men favoring his policy on toleration would be returned from the boroughs to Westminster. From March to September 1688 thirty-five charters—some previously revised under Charles II—were forfeited or surrendered under pressure. By the terms of the newly issued charters the crown nominated officials of the corporations and retained the right of removing them.

Late in April 1688 the king announced his intention to summon a Parliament, reissued his Declaration of Indulgence, and the following month ordered that it be read in all the churches on successive Sundays at the usual time of divine service. Seven bishops, including the primate of England, petitioned the king, protesting that the royal declaration dispensing with the laws had been founded on a power declared illegal by Parliament on three occasions in the past twenty-five years. For their pains they were charged with seditious libel and committed to the Tower. Two days later, the queen, thought by many to be incapable of having children, was delivered of a son, a Catholic heir to the throne. Rumor had it that the infant was actually the son to a tiler and had been introduced into the royal bed in a warming pan.

On June 29 the bishops were tried, but were acquitted twenty-four hours later. That same day seven notables, all Anglicans, sent off an invitation to William of Orange in the United Provinces. Their allegiance to the Church of England was greater than their loyalty to a monarch who threatened that church. James persisted. He dismissed two of the judges, who in their summations to the jury had ruled that the petition of the bishops was no libel, and he ordered that the chancellors of the dioceses and archdeacons report those clergy who had not read the king's Declaration of Indulgence during the Sunday services. Few had done so; the Anglican priests had almost universally ignored the king's order.[6]

From the Netherlands, William, eager to add England to the alliance of Protestant states he was constructing to save the United Provinces and prevent the establishment of a French hegemony over western Europe, had closely followed the actions of his royal uncle and father-in-law. Among his papers was a newsletter, dated 1 June 1686, apparently written by a clerk at Whitehall—many of the clerks in the offices of the principal secretaries of state supplemented their incomes by conducting a private news service—relating the events of the most recent session of the Privy Council. Writs of quo warranto were to be sued out against the charters of the plantations in order that they might be recalled and new patents issued "wherein a latitude shall be allowed" to Catholics. This might cause revolts, the reporter speculated, which might with difficulty be suppressed, the discontented elements in the colonies being populous and rich enough to have already attempted more than once to set up for themselves and to "defy their mother, Old England."[7]

This account of the session of the royal council revealed a fresh motive for legal action against the charters held by the American plantations, in addition to those motives prevailing during the last years of the late monarch. The desire to bring the chartered colonies to a more immediate dependence on the crown by having the king appoint the governors, the need to coordinate military affairs against the French in America, and the necessity to protect the sources of crown customs revenue in the plantations had led the ministers of state serving Charles II to revoke the charter of Massachusetts and to amalgamate several of the diverse plantations. Another factor loomed large in the mind of James II: religion. The new king was a convert to Catholicsm, and as a convert he was the more zealous in his religion.[8]

One of the clerks of the Committee for Plantations Affairs, William Blathwayt, had speculated within a matter of weeks of the accession of James II that the king intended to reduce the proprietary and chartered governments to an immediate dependence on the crown. When James had ascended the throne, his proprietary of New York had become a royal colony. Despite the threat of a quo warranto against the charter held by Lord Baltimore, a Catholic, his charter was respited that summer until "all things be more quiet."[9] But complaints from customs officers on the Potomac of the continued offenses committed against the crown revenue led the council on 10 July to order the attorney general to pursue the writ against Baltimore's charter.

About the same time, consolidation of the American plantations received further impetus from the complaints registered by municipal authorities in New York. The separation of the territories of New Jersey and Delaware and the policies adopted by their proprietors had greatly reduced the commerce of New York and hence the financial base of the colony. New York was now simply too weak. Halifax, Rochester, Clarendon, and the other lords for plantation affairs then recommended on 17 July 1685 that the attorney general consider legal action to regain the Jerseys and Delaware. The complaints of William Dyer of the customs service strengthened the case against the New Jersey proprietors. He claimed to have been abused when attempting to prosecute a vessel for violating the navigation code. The *Dolphin,* manned by foreigners and laden with European goods, had not entered with him or presented the requisite certificates.

By this time Edward Randolph had presented articles to be used against the charters of Rhode Island and Connecticut. By August Randolph was ready to cross the Atlantic to serve five writs in all. He seemed more than eager to make the journey.[10]

But the court at Whitehall took no action that year except to send off Randolph with a commission for establishing a temporary government under a president and council at Boston. Colonel Percy Kirke, once designated as the royal governor of Massachusetts, had been assigned the task of putting down the rebellion under Monmouth. In view of "the great carnage he has made in ye West" of England, Randolph did not think him a proper man for the colonies. New England needed a "quiet" man a "prudent" and experienced governor such as Edmund Andros, who unfortunately had been "unkindly laid aside" after "unlucky mistakes" in New York.

The following spring Andros did receive the post at Boston, but the fact that the "constitution" for that government was without an assembly led John Povey at the Plantation Office to doubt whether he would have any cause for satisfaction. Andros was apparently unhappy over the situation, complaining that a plantation government "without an assembly seems very mysterious." The omission of a representative assembly was the work of Robert, earl of Sunderland. It was not a decision the ministry as a whole favored. The previous summer, in drafting a commission for the temporary government established at Boston, the Lords of Trade had written to the lord president to learn the king's pleasure concerning a clause for calling assemblies to make laws and raise money. Such a provision was agreeable to the attorney general (Sir Robert Sawyer) and the solicitor general (Sir Thomas Powis) who had reported that, notwithstanding the forfeiture of the charter, the inhabitants of Massachusetts retained the right to consent to such laws and taxes. According to information later supplied by a solicitor in London to Increase Mather, Sunderland intervened with the king to strike the provision for calling an assembly from the commission to the governor. Instead, Andros and Thomas Dongan, the governor of New York, were given authority with the majority of the provincial council in each province to make laws and continue the taxes then in effect.

Andros would have a difficult time, Povey predicted; he would have to use his "utmost dexterity" with a people stubborn enough "to desert" the country and their estates rather than put their confidence in a royal appointee.[11] He did not foresee that the commonwealthmen would find another alternative, revolt.

After a hiatus of almost a year, the king in council, following the recommendation of the Lords of Trade on 30 April 1686, ordered the attorney general to prosecute writs against the proprietaries of Maryland, the Jerseys, and Delaware and the corporations of Connecticut and Rhode Island. A month later it issued a similar order for prosecutions against the charters granted to William Penn and the proprietors of Carolina and the Bahama Islands. The newsletter dated from Whitehall two days later reported that the charters were being recalled and new patents issued "wherein a latitude shall be allowed to the Roman Catholics."[12]

Yet within a matter of a few days, Sunderland, then attending the king at Windsor, wrote the attorney general that James II had thought fit "for some particular considerations" to suspend the proceedings against Pennsylvania. But the law officer was to continue with the prosecutions against the charters of the other proprietors and corporations.[13] One of the proprietors, the earl of Shaftesbury, protested that he did not know on what grounds a writ was being brought against the charter of Carolina. He professed himself as unwilling as anyone to dispute the king's pleasure, but that it was not within the power of any particular man to dispose of the property of others. The proprietors had expended considerable sums of money on the colonial venture, and he could see no probability of their being reimbursed if they surrendered the patent. Despite subsequent complaints by George Muschamp, collector of the plantation duty in Carolina,[14] Whitehall did not press the writs against the charters of Carolina and Maryland during the remainder of James's reign.

What "particular considerations" had led James II to exempt the charter of Pennsylvania from prosecution—his friendship for the Quaker proprietor, Penn's aid in furthering the king's religious policies, or the fact that under the government established by the proprietor, Catholics already could enjoy rights? Did the toleration already established cause James not to move against Maryland and Carolina? Penn claimed that it was by his influence that no writ was issued against his charter and, had he not intervened, "some busy bodys" in Philadelphia who were always disputing about laws and points of government "would have had their mouths stopped for good an[d] all." James's friendship with the earl of Melfort and the earl of Perth (John and James Drummond), who were involved in the East Jersey proprietary, evidently had no effect. Melfort converted to Catholicism that year and then served as Scottish secretary, liaison between his brother who headed the government at Edinburgh and the king.[15]

Whatever the reasons, in the more than fifteen months remaining to James as ruler of England, his government did not press the prosecution of the writs against Maryland, Pennsylvania and Carolina. But New Jersey, Connecticut, Rhode Island, and New York were amalgamated into the Dominion of New England under the governorship of Sir Edmund Andros. Two factors may have been critical: the desire to extend the king's policy on religious toleration and the need to meet the seemingly growing threat of the French and Indian menace from Canada.

Despite the conclusion in November 1686 of a treaty of neutrality for America, a mutual pledge not to become involved in hostilities in the colonies, by James II and Louis XIV, the English king in his foreign policy was not subservient to the court at Versailles.[16]

For some years it had been evident that tensions between the English and the northern tribes, now backed by the French, were increasing. The Canadians for their part seemed determined to check or curb the hostile Iroquois, the bulwark for the English in New York. Governor Thomas Dongan in an effort to strengthen the position of his weak province had been making overtures to the authorities of Connecticut and Rhode Island that they accept a merger with the government at Manhattan, a move Randolph at Boston protested. Should this occur, he wrote with his customary exaggeration, we would be "in danger of Starving for we have [a] great part of Our Corn from Them," the farmers of the two corporate colonies. Dongan for his part argued that without outside aid it would be impossible to defend New York, impossible to build and garrison the needed forts. The New Yorkers required money and hundreds of men from the Jerseys and New England. To offset the efforts of New York, the council established at Boston under Joseph Dudley sent emissaries—among them Wait Winthrop—to Hartford to persuade officials of Connecticut to accept a merger with Massachusetts.[17]

The men at Whitehall decided the contest. New York, the Jerseys, Connecticut, and Rhode Island were merged with the Dominion of New England. "The French have occasion[e]d it by their incursions," Blathwayt, the secretary at war, reported to Sir Robert Southwell; ". . . this union may make us more formidable." It would be "terrible to the French and make them proceed with more caution than they have lately done."[18] Although the ministers of state determined to proceed with writs against the charters of Connecticut and Rhode Island, they later decided by a dubious interpretation of letters from Hartford and Providence that officials there had agreed to accept annexation to the Dominion of New England. Their charters, unlike the patent to Massachusetts, were later deemed to be still in force. But in 1688 in the commission issued to Sir Edmund Andros (Dongan being recalled), the Dominion of New England included all of the English settlements east and north of the Delaware River.[19]

The need to bring the American plantations under the more immediate control of the crown through governors appointed from Whitehall and to consolidate English efforts against the French transcended the politics of the Glorious Revolution. To the Lords for Plantation Affairs later appointed by the Protestant William III, without provincial union and government immediately under the crown of England, the French would easily possess themselves of the dominion and trade of northern America.[20]

For a generation following the restoration of the monarchy, New England, and particularly Massachusetts, had been critical to the measures adopted by the Stuart kings for the American plantations. Would the descendants of the Puritan founders accept the demise of their Zion in the wilderness, the end of rule by saints of an independent commonwealth of God's chosen people?

In the early months of 1685 there was evidence that Massachusetts society was in disarray. Some local officials entrusted with enforcing the orders of the charter government at Boston evidently were neglecting their duties. In March the General Court was forced to order the selectmen, grand jurymen, constables, and tithingmen of all the towns faithfully to discharge their duties so as to prevent Sabbath-breaking, tippling, and carousing in public houses. It was essential to exorcise these evils and to renew "our couenant with God, which hath been neglected too much in the most cheurches." The ministers ought "to use all possible wajes & means for the vpholding of church discipljne."

Now that there was no hope of defending the charter by a suit at law and the choice was either submission or open rebellion, some of the merchants hesitated to support the Puritan faction. The ministers of the colony were divided as to the course to follow. On Tuesday, 31 July 1685, thirty-one of the ministers met in Boston and dined together at the Blue Anchor. That afternoon, following what was called an "uncomfortable" meeting, the Reverend William Hubbard of Ipswich delivered their views to the General Court. The government ought not to give way to another until it had evaluated the commission from the crown. At this several ministers dissented, claiming Hubbard had abused them, that he was not authorized to speak for them.[21]

Later that summer it seemed that the Lord had once more saved his people. Word came from England that put some men in "a hurly burly," "very ful[l] of Joy and Satisfaction at yᵉ Whigg News": the earl of Argyle had defeated the royal forces in Scotland, while the duke of Monmouth, the Protestant candidate for the throne, had routed the Catholic James in battle and with the approval of the entire English nation had been proclaimed king. At this intelligence the General Court in Boston voted a day of thanksgiving, but rescinded the order when accurate reports arrived.[22]

Some were now ready to accept an accommodation. That fall men were publicly drinking the health of the new governor and openly challenging the old regime. In the spring of 1686 Samuel Shrimpton appeared before the board of assistants to assert that there was no Governor and Company of Massachusetts Bay. Governor Simon Bradstreet seemed to think that the charter was indeed vacated, but insisted on a proclamation to that effect being sent over from England. Others remonstrated that the patent of Massachusetts was as void as the charter of London, whose officials had dared not even sit as the Common Council. Danforth pleaded that the government must not be "tumbled down" until the king actually called for it.

Events in the third week of May ended the doubts and indecision. On 14 May 1686, the frigate *Rose* arrived at Nantasket. Randolph came ashore and took coach for Roxbury, where Joseph Dudley, named president of the council nominated by the crown, lived. Major John Pynchon and William Stoughton then went to inform the magistrates that, the king's commands having arrived, Danforth with whomever he pleased to accompany him might come to view the exemplification of the writ vacating the charter and the royal commission bearing the broad seal of England for the new government. The following day, Saturday, Dudley sent for Governor Thomas Hinckley, whose colony of New Plymouth was included within the jurisdiction of the commission to Dudley, along with Major John Richards, Samuel Sewall, and James Russell to examine the documents Randolph had brought over from London.

At noon the next Monday Samuel Phillips met with Dudley in Samuel Willard's home. With Increase Mather and William Stoughton present, he engaged Dudley in "very close discourse," seeking to persuade him not to accept the king's commission. It was to no avail.

That afternoon the General Court met in the town house. Members of the "old government" sat on the north side of the room; Dudley with several of the men named with him in the commission—John Pynchon, Bartholomew Gedney, Robert Mason, Randolph and Wait Winthrop—sat on the left. Thomas Hinckley, of New Plymouth, and James West, former governor of Carolina, were among the spectators filling the room.

Dudley addressed the assemblage. He could no longer treat them as the Governor and Company of the Massachusetts Bay. Taking out the exemplification and his commission, he openly exhibited them to the spectators. It was Danforth's turn. He assumed Dudley and his colleagues did not expect the answer of the General Court at this time. Dudley would not acknowledge them as a legal body and would in no way capitulate with them.

When the president and his associates left the room, Daniel Denison, Major John Richards, James Russell, and Samuel Sewall all spoke, evidently in favor of submission. As Sewell asked: the foundations being destroyed, what could the righteous do? Some proposed sending a protest to England and calling upon the elder to pray, but others thought this "inconvenient," or, perhaps, pointless, since Dudley and his colleagues had declared themselves to be the king's council of Massachusetts.

The key to the situation lay in the attitude of the officers commanding the militia. Richards, Wait Winthrop, Nicholas Paige, and Samuel Sewall, among the officers, were ready to continue in office under the new administration; Captain John Higginson, Richard Wharton's brother-in-law, and Captain Bartholomew Gedney announced that they intended to bring down their troops from Salem on Friday, when the General Court was to meet again. For the time being several of the commanders of local militia companies acquiesced in the royal Dominion of New England. Would they continue to do so?

On Friday, 21 May 1686, the General Court—the Governor and Company of Massachusetts Bay as prescribed by the charter of 1629— met again, for the last time. Samuel Nowell prayed that God would pardon the magistrates and deputies for what they were about to do and thanked the Lord for the fifty-six years of mercy he had shown them. A weeping marshal general declared the General Court, not dissolved, but adjourned. But many knew the truth. They left in tears.[23] Government by God's elect was at an end.

The Dominion of New England would fall, but Massachusetts would never be the same.

List of Abbreviations

Add. MSS	Additional Manuscripts, British (Museum) Library, London.
Adm.	Admiralty, Public Record Office, London.
AHR	*American Historical Review.*
BL	British (Museum) Library, London.
Bodl.	Bodleian Library, Oxford University.
CO	Colonial Office, Public Record Office, London.
CSPC	Great Britain, Public Record Office, *Calendar of State Papers, Colonial Series, America and West Indies.*
CSPD	Great Britain, Public Record Office, *Calendar of State Papers, Domestic Series.*
CW	Colonial Williamsburg, Williamsburg, Virginia.
FDRL	Franklin D. Roosevelt Library, Hyde Park, New York.
HL	Henry E. Huntington Library, San Marino, California.
HMC	Royal Historical Manuscripts Commission, London.
HMSO	His (or Her) Majesty's Stationery Office.
HMPEC	*Historical Magazine, Protestant Episcopal Church.*
HSP	Historical Society of Pennsylvania, Philadelphia.
JAH	*Journal of American History.*
JCBL	John Carter Brown Library, Brown University, Providence, Rhode Island.
LPL	Lambeth Palace Library, London.
MHS	Massachusetts Historical Society, Boston.
MHSC	*Collections of the Massachusetts Historical Society,* 79 volumes in 8 series (Boston, 1792–1941).
MVHR	*Mississippi Valley Historical Review.*
NUL	Nottingham University Library, Manuscripts Department, Nottingham.
NYCD	*Documents relative to the Colonial History of the State of New York,* ed. Edmund B. O'Callaghan and Berthold Fernow, 15 vols. (Albany and New York, 1865–87).
PC	Privy Council Register, Public Record Office, London.

PMHB	*Pennsylvania Magazine of History and Biography.*
PRO	Public Record Office, London.
SP	State Papers, Public Record Office, London.
Treas.	Treasury, Public Record Office, London.
VMHB	*Virginia Magazine of History and Biography.*
WMQ	*William and Mary Quarterly.*

Notes

Chapter 1

1. John Evelyn, *Diary,* ed. Esmond S. de Beer, 6 vols. (Oxford: Oxford University Press, Clarendon Press, 1955), 3:246. Ellipses (. . .) have routinely been omitted at the beginning and end of direct quotations and initial capitalization and final punctuation regularized accordingly.

2. See Violet Barbour, review of Charles Wilson's *Profit and Power,* in *American Historical Review* 63 (January 1958): 469-70; and Frank T. Melton, "London and Parliament: An Analysis of a Constituency, 1660-1702," (Ph.D. diss., University of Wisconsin, 1969), pp. 282, 318.

3. Samuel Pepys, *The Diary of Samuel Pepys,* ed. Robert Latham and William Matthews, 9 vols. to date (Berkeley: University of California Press, 1970-), 3:189, 190; 6:257-58. Unless otherwise indicated, all references to the Pepys's diary are to this edition.

4. Pepys to William Coventry, 23 February 1663/4, Samuel Pepys, *Further Correspondence of Samuel Pepys, 1662-1679,* ed. Joseph Robinson Tanner (New York: Harcourt, Brace [1928]), p. 19; William Bodham to the navy commissioners, 11 February 1664/5, Mary Anne Everett et al., eds., *Calendar of State Papers, Domestic Series, Charles II,* 28 vols. (London: HMSO, 1860-1939), *1664-1665,* p. 200; Hebden to the navy commissioners, 11 December 1666, ibid., *1666-1667,* pp. 337-38. The "bribery" may be traced in Pepys, *Diary,* 3:131; 4:61, 246, 302, 303; 5:215-16, 229-30, 270, 271. For the various contracts and proposals see *CSPD, Charles II, 1663-1664,* p. 270.

5. Spencer to Corbin, 7 August 1676, Coventry MSS, vol. 77, f. 171, Longleat House, Wilts.; Nathaniel Blakiston, Nicholas Greenberry, Thomas Tench, John Court, and Thomas Brooke to Paggen, 21 December 1698, Bridgewater Americana, 9572, Huntington Library.

6. Sanford to Pate, 7 December 1666, in Peleg Sanford, *The Letter Book of Peleg Sanford of Newport, Merchant (Later Governor of Rhode Island), 1666-1668* (Providence: Rhode Island Historical Society, 1928), pp. 14-16.

7. For the chartering of the company after the Restoration and the membership, see orders in council, 17 May, 24 July, PC 2/55/pp. 217, 321; order in council, 14 May 1660, PC 2/55/p. 33; order in council 2 July 1662, CO 5/903/pp. 6-9.

8. See the letters of Knowles, Thompson, Collins, and Edward Rawson (secretary of Massachusetts), in *A Collection of Original Papers Relative to the*

315

History of Massachusetts Bay, comp. Thomas Hutchinson (Albany, 1865), pp. 447, 448, 451–52, 462–63, 463–64.

9. For Wilson's activities on behalf of Boston merchants, see his petition to the king, CO 1/30/64. On Hull's activities, see Hermann Frederick Clarke, "John Hull—Colonial Merchant, 1624–1683," American Antiquarian Society, *Proceedings,* n.s. 46 (1937): 206–21.

10. On the formation of the personal relations in New England's commerce, see Bernard Bailyn, *The New England Merchants in the Seventeenth Century* (Cambridge, Mass.: Harvard University Press, 1955), pp. 78–82, 86–91; and Bernard Bailyn, "Communications and Trade: The Atlantic in the Seventeenth Century," *Journal of Economic History* 13 (Fall 1953): 378–82. Although Bailyn's assessment is not directly concerned with the impact of the acts of trade and navigation, it does incidentally illustrate that the connection between the commercial economy of New England and the mother country was based on personal relations and generally predated the enactment and attempted enforcement of the navigation code.

11. For a discussion of the expansion of English trade, see Ralph Davis, "English Foreign Trade, 1660–1700," *Economic History Review,* 2d ser. 7 (December 1954): 150–66; "English Foreign Trade, 1700–1774," ibid., 2d ser. 15 (December 1962): 285–303; *English Overseas Trade, 1500–1700* (London: Macmillan, 1973); *A Commercial Revolution: English Overseas Trade in the Seventeenth and Eighteenth Centuries* (London: the Historical Association, 1967); and "England and the Mediterranean, 1570–1670," in *Essays in the Economic and Social History of Tudor and Stuart England in Honour of R. H. Tawney,* ed. F. J. Fisher (Cambridge: Cambridge University Press, 1961), pp. 117–37. Attempts to assess the volume of English trade overseas are based on contemporary governmental records. These trade figures must be used circumspectly. Patrick McGrath, ed., *Merchants and Merchandise in Seventeenth Century Bristol,* Bristol Records Society, Publications vol. 19 (Bristol, 1955), p. xx, noted that the Port Books cannot be used to give a statistical account of imports and exports, at least for the out ports. Officials maintained records to keep track of revenue, not to provide statistical material for historians. Faulty record keeping as well as widespread smuggling and evasion of duties make these accounts misleading. Nor do they show a complete account of overseas trade. They record ships leaving for certain ports and arriving from others, but do not indicate any trading ventures between first discharging a cargo and taking on another to be carried to the home port. H. J. Fisher, *The Portugal Trade: A Study of Anglo-Portuguese Commerce, 1700–1770* (London: Methuen, 1971), p. 2, has shown that English customs records ignore the part played by English trade in the commerce of the Spanish and Portuguese colonies in America. Another source for trade records is the annual series produced from 1697 by the inspector general of Customs. The accuracy of the data for the previous years is open to question. Charles Davenant, an inspector general, reported in 1704 that the customs officials were attempting to recover the accounts from 1662 but were doubtful of their ability to reconstruct them accurately "by a Retrospection" of a quarter century or more (Davenant to the Customs Board, 3 July 1704, BL, Harleian MSS 6836, f. 63; Customs Board to Treasurer Godolphin, 12 September 1704, BL, Harleian MSS 6836, f. 65). Customs officials arrived at figures

for imports and exports by multiplying the quantity of each commodity by an official price. With few exceptions these remained unchanged over the years; the aggregate statistics reflect volume and fluctuations, not the value of foreign trade or the balance of payments. The official ratings of reexports, including colonial produce, were sometimes unduly high. Smuggled goods did not find their way into the official records. See G. N. Clark, *Guide to English Commercial Statistics, 1696-1782* (London: Royal Historical Society, 1938); and T. S. Ashton, *Economic Fluctuations in England, 1700-1800* (Oxford: Oxford University Press, Clarendon Press, 1959), pp. 53-54.

    12. Downing to the earl of Clarendon, 25 December 1663, Bodl., MS Clarendon 107, f. 52. See also Violet Barbour, "Dutch and English Merchant Shipping in the Seventeenth Century," *Economic History Review* 2 (May 1930): 261-90.

    13. Ralph Davis, *The Rise of the English Shipping Industry in the Seventeenth and Eighteenth Centuries* (New York: St. Martin's Press, 1962), pp. 1-22.

    14. Quoted in H. R. Trevor-Roper, *Men and Events: Historical Essays* (New York: Harper, 1957), pp. 199-200.

    15. See Maurice P. Ashley, *Financial and Commercial Policy under the Cromwellian Protectorate*, rev. ed. (London: F. Cass, 1962), pp. 12-15; Jacob M. Price, *The Tobacco Adventure to Russia: Enterprise, Politics, and Diplomacy in the Quest for a Northern Market for English Colonial Tobacco, 1676-1722,* American Philosophical Society, Transactions 51, pt. 1 (Philadelphia, 1961); and Ray Bert Westerfield, "Middlemen in English Business, Particularly between 1660 and 1760," Connecticut Academy of Arts and Sciences, *Transactions* 19 (New Haven, Conn., 1915): 413-17.

    16. R. Gravil, "Trading to Spain and Portugal, 1670-1700," *Business History* 10 (July 1968): 69-88; Hermann Frederick Clarke, "John Hull—Colonial Merchant, 1624-1683," American Antiquarian Society, *Proceedings,* n.s. 46 (Worcester, 1937): 206, 213; Bailyn, "Communications and Trade," pp. 379-80; Davis, *Rise of English Shipping,* p. 90; Charles M. Wilson, *Anglo-Dutch Commerce and Finance in the Eighteenth Century* (Cambridge: Cambridge University Press, 1941), p. xiii. See also William Byrd to Perry and Lane, 2 February 1684/5, 20 [November] 1686, *The Correspondence of the Three William Byrds of Westover Virginia, 1684-1776,* ed. Marion Tinling, 2 vols. (Charlottesville: University Press of Virginia, 1977), 1:29, 67 (hereafter cited as *Byrd Correspondence*).

    17. D. C. Coleman, *Sir John Banks, Baronet, and Businessman: A Study of Business, Politics, and Society in Later Stuart England* (New York: Oxford University Press, 1963), p. 28; Patrick McGrath, ed., *Merchants and Merchandise in Seventeenth-Century Bristol,* pp. xv-xviii; Jonathan Howes Webster, "The Merchants of Bordeaux in Trade to the French West Indies, 1664-1717" (Ph.D. diss., University of Minnesota, 1972), pp. 7-23, 197-205; and Spencer to Corbin, 7 August 1676, Coventry MSS, vol. 77, f. 171, Longleat House, Wilts.

    18. Bailyn, *New England and Merchants,* pp. 35-38, 91; "Communications and Trade," pp. 378-87; Clarke, "John Hull," pp. 206, 213, 214-15; Sanford, *Letter Book of Peleg Sanford,* pp. iv-v.

19. J. H. Parry, "Transport and Trade Routes," in *The Economy of Expanding Europe in the Sixteenth and Seventeenth Centuries,* ed. E. E. Rich and C. H. Wilson (Cambridge: Cambridge University Press, 1967), pp. 177–80; Charles Francis Carroll, "The Forest Civilization of New England: Timber, Trade, and Society in the Age of Wood, 1600–1688" (Ph.D. diss., Brown University, 1970), pp. 296, 327; E. E. Rich, "Colonial Settlement and Its Labour Problems," in *Economy of Expanding Europe,* ed. Rich and Wilson, pp. 345–58; K. G. Davies, *The Royal African Company* (London: Longmans, Green, 1957); and G. D. Ramsey, *English Overseas Trade during the Centuries of Emergence* (London: Macmillan, 1957), pp. 224–25, 228–29.

20. The relationship between increased production and falling prices was to be demonstrated again during the years 1717–33 when the market for British sugar was again narrowed by the increased production of the French on Santo Domingo. See the discussion in G. B. Masefield, "Crops and Livestock," in Rich and Wilson, *Economy of Expanding Europe,* pp. 289–93.

21. K. G. Davies, "The Origins of the Commission System in the West India Trade," Royal Historical Society, *Transactions,* 5th ser. 2 (1952): 90–99.

22. Berkeley's tract, "A Perfect Description of Virginia," published in London in 1662, is among the Thomas Povey Papers, BL, Egerton MSS 2395, f. 356.

23. The best discussion of the problem of prices and marketing for tobacco is in Price, *The Tobacco Adventure,* pp. 3–16. The best study of the price mechanism in Virginia, James H. Soltow, *The Economic Role of Williamsburg* (Williamsburg: Colonial Williamsburg [1965]), deals with a later colonial period.

24. Henry Savile to the earl of Rochester, Paris [19/] 30 June 1679, *The Rochester-Savile Letters, 1671–1680,* ed. John Harold Wilson (Columbus: Ohio State University Press, 1941), p. 69. The most extended discussion of the problem of marketing American tobacco in France as well as the fiscal policy of governments for the tobacco trade is in Jacob M. Price, *France and the Chesapeake,* 2 vols. (Ann Arbor: University of Michigan Press [1973]).

25. Petitions of John Strother, n.d., PRO, SP 29/393/no. 14 (a second copy, ibid., no. 115 is docketed as dispatched on 4 May 1677); see also the order in council, dated 4 May 1677, ibid., no. 116. Order in council on the petition of John Jeffreys and Jacob Lucie, 7 July 1680, CO 389/11/pp. 190–91 (another copy in the commercial entry book, CO 388/1/n.p.; and Jeffreys to the secretary of state, Sir Leoline Jenkins, 5 October 1680, SP 29/417/no. 257.

26. An illustration of the nature of the services offered and the charges levied by the merchants in the consignment system is provided by the accounts of John Mathen of Bristol and Major Theophilus Hone, a merchant and sometime resident of Virginia. See the accounts in McGrath, ed., *Merchants and Merchandise in Seventeenth-Century Bristol,* pp. 253–54.

27. The fullest and best discussions—and these reflect the scarcity of documentation for the seventeenth century—deal with the marketing system as it developed late in the colonial period. See Soltow, *The Economic Role of Williamsburg,* pp. 33–43; and Samuel Michael Rosenblatt, "The House of John Norton and Sons: A Study of the Consignment Method of Marketing Tobacco

from Virginia to England" (Ph.D. diss., Rutgers University, 1960), pp. 49-51. While the description of consignment and direct purchase given for the later period is probably valid for the earlier years, the conclusion that consignment predominated in the seventeenth century is open to question. The petitions of the merchants and shippers submitted to the crown often give the impression that shipmasters spent a great deal of time in Chesapeake waters searching out and negotiating for cargoes.

28. Davis, *Rise of the English Shipping Industry,* pp. 188-92; Gary M. Walton and James F. Shepherd, *Shipping, Maritime Trade, and the Economic Development of Colonial North America* (Cambridge, Mass.: Harvard University Press, 1972). See also William Byrd to Perry and Lane, 21 July 1690, in Tinling, *Byrd Correspondence,* 1:118-19.

Chapter 2

1. Evelyn, *Diary,* 3:246.

2. See Ivan Roots, *Commonwealth and Protectorate: The English Civil War and Its Aftermath* (New York: Schocken Books, 1966), pp. 179, 204-5.

3. Evelyn, *Diary,* 3:241; Pepys, *Diary,* 1:50.

4. Pepys, *Diary,* 1:122; entries under 12 May, 13 May 1660, notes transcribed from Goffe's papers, Massachusetts Historical Society, Winthrop Family Papers. For a good summary of the events leading to the Restoration, see Roots, *Commonwealth and Protectorate,* pp. 251-55; for a fuller treatment, Godfrey Davies, *The Restoration of Charles II* (San Marino, Calif.: Huntington Library, 1955).

5. Pepys, *Diary,* 1:115; 2:7; Jack H. Adamson and H. F. Follard, *Sir Harry Vane: His Life and Times, 1613-1662* (New York: Gambit, 1973), pp. 432-35.

6. Pepys, *Diary,* 3:189-90. For a discussion of the Dissenter political interest in both houses of Parliament, see Douglas R. Lacey, *Dissent and Parliamentary Politics in England, 1661-1689: A Study in the Perpetuation and Tempering of Parliamentarianism* (New Brunswick, N.J.: Rutgers University Press, 1969).

7. [Coventry] to Henry Bennet, private, 16 November 1664, PRO, *CSPD, Charles II, 1664-1665,* p. 75; Ramsay, *English Overseas Trade during the Centuries of Emergence,* p. 233. On the role of merchants, see R. C. Thompson, "Officers, Merchants and Foreign Policy in the Protectorate of Oliver Cromwell," *Historical Studies: Australia and New Zealand* 12 (April 1966): 149-65; Ashley, *Financial and Commercial Policy under the Cromwellian Protectorate;* and Violet Barbour's review of Charles Wilson, *Profit and Power,* in *American Historical Review* 63 (January 1958): 469-79.

8. In reporting the debate in the House of Commons on 6 November 1667 on the impeachment of Clarendon, John Nicholas listed among the charges against the lord chancellor that "he hath introduced an arbitrary Government into the [foreign] Plantaĉons" John Nicholas to Edward Nicholas, 7 November 1667, Nicholas Papers, BL, Egerton MSS. 2539, f. 133.

9. Maurice Lee, *The Cabal* (Urbana: University of Illinois Press, 1965), p. 211.

10. For observations of behavior at court and the complaints registered, see Pepys, *Diary,* 2:149; 5:73; 8:181, 286, 354, 355, 378, 450, 505–6, 525.

11. On the strength of the localist traditions in England and France, see Roots, *Commonwealth and Protectorate,* pp. 197–98; Clive Holmes, *The Eastern Association in the English Civil War* (London: Cambridge University Press, 1974), p. 11; J. H. Plumb, *The Origins of Political Stability in England, 1675–1725* (Boston: Houghton Mifflin, 1967), pp. 10–13; Pierre Goubert, *Louis XIV and Twenty Million Frenchmen,* trans. Anne Carter (New York: Pantheon Books, 1970), p. 297.

12. Charles Bryant, *Samuel Pepys,* 3 vols. (Cambridge: Cambridge University Press, 1933–39), 2:4–7.

13. Lawrence Kaplan, "English Civil War Politics and the Religious Settlement," *Church History* 41 (September 1972): 307–25; Lacey, *Dissent and Parliamentary Politics,* pp. 314, 30–31; F. G. James, "The Bishops in Politics, 1688–1714," in *Conflict in Stuart England: Essays in Honour of Wallace Notestein,* ed. W. A. Aiken and B. D. Henning (New York: New York University Press, 1960), pp. 230–31; Robert S. Bosher, *The Making of the Restoration Settlement: The Influence of the Laudians, 1649–1662* (New York: Oxford University Press, 1951), pp. 30–40.

14. The strength of anti-Catholic feeling held by Englishmen brought up on the memory of the Gunpowder Plot and Saint Bartholomew's Day Massacre was reflected in the many rumors of Papist conspiracies to burn London. See for example Pepys, *Diary,* 8:364, 360. Following the Great Fire of London a commission of the House of Commons reported in January 1667 that the blaze had been planned by French Catholics, the Jesuits, and the king's brother, James, duke of York.

15. Bosher (*Restoration Settlement,* p. 106) and George R. Abernathy, Jr., (*The English Presbyterians and the Stuart Restoration, 1648–1663,* American Philosophical Society Transactions, n.s. 55, pt. 2 [Philadelphia, 1965]: pp. 6–80) disagreed on the motives of the king and Clarendon on toleration. Bosher doubted whether they were actually in favor of this policy, and argued that they were merely manipulating the Commons and the clergy. I have tended to follow Abernathy, who accepted their sincerity and credited the failure of comprehension and toleration to the political weakness of the Presbyterians, the divisions among the Puritan groups, and the strength of the Anglicans in the House of Commons. As will be evident through the present work, Charles II during his reign insisted on toleration for Protestants in the colonies.

16. Pepys, *Diary,* 4:5, 44; G. F. T. Jones, *Saw-Pit Wharton: The Political Career from 1640 to 1691 of Philip, Fourth Lord Wharton* (Sydney: Sydney University Press, 1967), pp. 190–94; K. H. D. Haley, *The First Earl of Shaftesbury* (New York: Oxford University Press, 1968), p. 163; George R. Abernathy, "Clarendon and the Declaration of Indulgence," *Journal of Ecclesiastical History* 11 (January 1960): 66–70; Richard E. Boyer, *English Declarations of Indulgence, 1687 and 1688* (The Hague: Mouton, 1968), pp. 11–15.

17. William Penn's letter book, 1667–1675, 99, HSP, Philadelphia.

18. See the various reports and items of intelligence received by Secretary of State Bennet in *CSPD, Charles II, 1661–1662,* p. 591; *1663–1664,* pp. 63, 117, 408, 426.

19. Declaration of Indulgence, 15 March 1671/2, in *The Letters, Speeches, and Declarations of King Charles II,* ed. Arthur Bryant (London: Cassell, 1935), pp. 247–49; Pepys, *Diary,* 8:584; John Leslie Miller, *Popery and Politics in England, 1660–1688* (Cambridge: Cambridge University Press, 1973), p. 107; Haley, *Shaftesbury,* p. 297; Boyer, *Declaration of Indulgences,* pp. 22–24; Edward F. Carpenter, *The Protestant Bishop: Being the Life of Henry Compton, 1632–1713, Bishop of London* (London: Longmans, Green, 1956), pp. 27–28; and Norman Sykes, *From Sheldon to Secker: Aspects of English Church History, 1660–1768* (Cambridge: Cambridge University Press, 1959), pp. 76–77.

20. The ecclesiastical jurisdiction of the Anglican bishops over the foreign possessions was uncertain. Under Charles II the practice developed of having the bishop of London attend meetings of the Privy Council and its committees when colonial affairs were discussed, but during the first dozen years of the reign no attempt was made to place this prelate's jurisdiction on a legal bais. In 1672 or 1673 plans were underway to put the Anglican churches in the colonies on a more formal basis. A charter was prepared placing the churches of Virginia and some other colonies under the archepiscopal see of Canterbury. A bishop resident in the diocese of Virginia would have no jurisdiction, however, over English subjects in New England. The Reverend Alexander Moray (or Murray) was initially considered for the Virginia diocese, but the proposal was never implemented, as Charles cryptically noted when recommending Moray for a living in Ireland, "By reason of several accidents [it] cannot be so speedily and well effected as we desire" (Charles II to the lord lieutenant of Ireland, ? November 1673, *CSPD, Charles II, 1673–1675,* p. 2). In 1675 Henry Compton, bishop of London began a campaign to extend the authority of his diocese, but by the end of the century jurisdiction was still uncertain. See Secretary of State James Vernon to Matthew Prior, Whitehall, 20 October 1698, BL, Add. MSS. 40,722, f. 221.

21. Instructions to Berkeley, 12 September 1662, PRO, CO 324/1/pp. 263–72; Charles II to the governor of Massachusetts Bay, 28 June 1662, PRO, CO 1/16/ff. 168–69; Secretary of State Bennet to the lord chief justice, 7 March 1664/5, *CSPD, Charles II, 1664–1665,* p. 244.

22. Josiah Cole to George Fox, [21 February 1660/1], ARB MSS. I, no. 53, Friends House Library, London; order in council, 28 June 1661, PCR, PRO, PC 2/55/p. 281; Charles II to Governor John Endecott, 9 September 1661, PRO, CO 1/15/f.169.

23. Orders in council, 8 March 1664/5, 5 July 1665, PRO, PC 2/58/pp. 73, 200.

Chapter 3

1. Orders in council, 4 July, 17 August 1660, PRO, PC 2/54/pp. 63–64, 131.

2. The lists of names submitted by the mercantile community are in PRO, SP 29/19/nos. 21–25; see also order in council, 10 October 1660, PC 2/55/p. 5 and the commission of 7 November 1660, PRO, CO 389/1/pp. 1–5.

3. Instructions to the Council of Trade, 7 November 1660, SP 29/19/no. 27 (also Thomas Povey Papers, BL, Egerton MSS 2395, ff. 268, 269; and "Some Heads for Groundes for a Counsell [sic] of Trade," SP 29/19/no. 22, ff. 36–37.

4. Order in council, 19 December 1660, PC 2/55/p. 74; proceedings of the Council of Trade, 3, 8 January 1660/61, SP 29/31/no. 62, f. 119, no. 63, f. 123.

5. Warrants for the Council of Foreign Plantations, 25 October 1660, SP 29/19/no. 45, f. 89, no. 46, f. 90; commission for the council, 1 December 1660, CO 1/14/no. 59, f. 142; proceedings of the Council for Foreign Plantations, 7 January 1660/61, CO 1/14/f. 45.

6. For example, in 1667 the standing committee for foreign plantations undertook to decide what areas in America should be returned to the Dutch at the conclusion of the war then current, while another committee dealt with matters relating to the New England colonies. See the orders in council for 30 August and 2 October 1667, PC 2/59/p. 551; and Thomas Povey Papers, BL, Egerton MSS 2395, ff. 448–49.

7. Order in council, 5 September 1662, PC 2/56/p. 128.

8. Order in council, 31 January 1667/8, BL, Egerton MSS 2543, f. 205; order in council, 12 February 1667/8, PC 2/60/p. 176; and especially Edward Southwell's book of Privy Council memoranda, BL, Add. MSS 38,861, ff. 18, 20.

9. The plan was to unite the old commission of trade with the former commission of plantations (order in council, 23 September 1667, PC 2/59/p. 594).

10. For the members and those attending the early meetings see *CSPD, Charles II, 1667–1668,* p. 607; *1668–1669,* p. 224. George Duke, secretary of the first commission of trade, was replaced by Pierre DeMoulin, a nominee of Arlington. He deserted to the Dutch in 1672.

11. John Nicholas to Edward Nicholas, 18 November, 22 December 1668, BL, Egerton MSS 2539, ff. 281, 305; Samuel Pepys, *The Diary of Samuel Pepys,* ed., Henry B. Wheatley, 10 vols. (London: George Bell, 1897–1910), 8:319.

12. See Joseph Williamson's notes endorsed "Plantations 1669," SP 29/277/no. 129; Evelyn, *Diary,* 3:582–83; Worsley to George Duke, 28 November 1672, CO 389/10/p. 16; instructions to the Council of Foreign Plantations, CO 389/4/pp. 3–5. For the membership and functioning of the Plantation Board, see the royal warrant of 20 March 1670/1, CO 1/26/ff. 121–22 (also in SP 29/288/no. 50).

13. Worsley's resignation caused some comment. A clerk of the Privy Council wrote a colleague: "Amongst those that leave their places upon account of the late Act you would, I suppose scarce have thought Dr. Worsley had been yet he is not to bee so much as suspected as a Catholique, for I dare swear he is far from it" (William Bridgeman to Joseph Williamson, 23 June 1673, *Letters Addressed to Sir Joseph Williamson . . . ,* ed. W. D. Christie, Camden Society Publications, n.s. 8 (London, 1874): 59–60.

14. Evelyn, *Diary,* 4:14.

15. Stephen Saunders Webb, " 'Brave Men and Servants to His Royal Highness': The Household of James Stuart in the Evolution of English Imperialism," *Perspectives in American History,* vol. 8, ed. Donald Fleming and Bernard Bailyn (Cambridge Mass.: Harvard University Press, 1974), pp. 55–79, pointed out the close association of the members of the duke of York's household on the committee for naval affairs and Tangier. He argued that James and his followers dominated decisions on policy and that they aimed to establish both in England and in the colonies overseas an absolutist, statist military regime modeled on the administrative apparatus Louis XIV was supposedly instituting in France. Webb further embroidered on this theme in a book, *The Governors-General: The English Army and the Definition of Empire, 1569–1681* (Chapel Hill: University of North Carolina Press, 1980). John Childs, *The Army of Charles II* (Toronto: University of Toronto Press, 1976) contains much material to question this thesis. On the basis of his father's and his own experience during the Civil War, Charles II was convinced that it was impossible for him to enjoy security without an armed force of some kind. Venner's revolt confirmed this. But the Restoration settlement allowed a mobile force of six regiments with barely six thousand guards at most in addition to static garrisons of nonregimented companies raised locally in England and stationed for the most part in decayed Tudor castles of no strategic value except as convenient quarters for housing these local levies. During Charles's reign the army, never a political force, was subordinate to the civil government. Its officers, except in time of war, were amateurs socially and politically connected with the gentry class. Professional career officers found employment in England only during time of war and then lost their posts, as on three occasions the newly levied forces were cut back. The power of the purse exercised by Parliament was decisive. The king could neither raise nor disband troops without the approval of Lords and Commons. Even in the last four years of the reign, when Charles governed without calling a parliament, he was not able to expand the forces. The army in England then was a weak and often poorly run police force, used to apprehend highwaymen, to preserve law and order, and during two wars with the Dutch, to augment the navy in battles at sea.

   On a few occasions during the reign, troops from England served in the colonies. By 1660 a force of only fifteen hundred men remained of the five thousand soldiers who were sent by Cromwell to the West Indies and had captured Jamaica from the Spanish. They were disbanded, and the defense of the island against the Spanish and its internal security against slave insurrection was entrusted to two thousand part-time militia made up of local settlers. In 1678 two companies totalling two hundred men were sent out to Jamaica at an annual cost of three thousand pounds. Because of financial exigencies even this force was abandoned in 1682 and the militia left to provide security for the island. The Lesser Antilles had been the scene of violent strife with the French, who had attacked and burned the English plantations on Saint Kitts. In 1667 a new regiment of eight hundred men had been organized into six companies and sent out to the West Indies. Half of this force was sent to Barbados, the other half assigned to the English portion of Saint Kitts. As was the case with the garrison

324 *Notes (pp. 44–48)*

on Jamaica, financial exigencies in 1671 led to the disbanding of these troops. Some discharged men were allowed to remain to take up land; two-thirds returned to England, while two companies remained as a garrison.

During Charles's reign royal troops on two occasions were sent to North America. Three hundred men went with Colonel Richard Nicolls to take over the Dutch colony of New Netherland; some soldiers were retained at New York in the face of a potentially hostile, subversive Dutch population. But when a Dutch fleet recaptured the colony, fewer than one hundred men in one company remained in the garrison. By 1679 even these were withdrawn. Earlier in the decade, under the impression that the rebels in Virginia had overthrown the king's governor and threatened royal customs from tobacco, the crown sent out five hundred regulars and another five hundred newly raised volunteers under Colonel Herbert Jeffreys. The mortality rate was so high in the Atlantic crossing that half of these men died by the time they reached Virginia. The governor had already broken the rebellion with the aid of loyal militia. Jeffreys returned to England, leaving two companies totalling two hundred troops in the province. The story of the West Indian companies was repeated. When the crown and the provincial governments did not take up the financial burden, the men were disbanded. After the death of Charles II the outbreak of long-sustained conflict involving England, France, and Spain in North America appreciably altered the situation. Many observers in the provincial governments, acutely aware of the inadequate military capabilities of the local leaders, called for governors with military experience.

16. "An Overture for the Better Regulation of the Forreign Plantations," Leeds Papers, XVII, BL, Egerton MSS 3340, ff. 148–49. Another copy is to be found among the papers of Thomas Povey (BL, Egerton MSS 2395, f. 276) which might have led Charles McLean Andrews, *The British Committees, Commissions, and Councils of Trade and Plantations, 1622–1675* (Baltimore, Md.: Johns Hopkins University Press, 1908), p. 112, to ascribe authorship to Povey. For an intimate view of the functioning and succession of the various clerks and undersecretaries associated with the Privy Council in the decades following the Restoration, see Edward Southwell's memoranda of the Privy Council proceedings, BL, Add. MSS 38,861, ff. 7, 9. Both Southwell and his father, Sir Robert, before him served as clerks.

17. John Collins, employed as a clerk under Henry Slingsby, claimed that the Council for Trade and Plantations was abolished to save the charges to the crown (*Report on the Manuscripts of Lord Montagu of Beaulieu* [London: Royal Historical Manuscripts Commission, 1900], p. 178).

18. See, for example, the Lords of Trade to Governor Sir William Berkeley, 14 April 1676, CO 1/36/f. 80.

19. Edward Southwell's Privy Council memoranda book, BL, Add. MSS 38,861, ff. 7, 9.

20. This discussion is based on C. D. Chandaman, *The English Public Revenue, 1660–1688* (Oxford: Oxford University Press, Clarendon Press, 1975), pp. 11–14, 21–28, 33–35, 213, 258; Lee, *The Cabal,* pp. 119–60; Bertram R. Leftwich, "The Late History and Administration of the Customs Revenue in England (1671–1814)," Royal Historical Society, *Transactions,* 13 (1930):

189-94; and Elizabeth E. Hoon, *The Organization of the English Customs System, 1696-1786* (New York: Appleton-Century, 1938), pp. 6-29.

21. Nottingham to Viscount Sydney, 11 September 1691, *Report on the Manuscripts of the Late Allen George Finch . . . ,* 3 vols. (London: Royal Historical Manuscripts Commission, 1965), 3:260; John Nicholas to Edward Nicholas, 10 March 1667/8, BL, Egerton MSS 2539, f. 165.

Chapter 4

1. See Edward Hughes, review of Lawrence Harper, *The English Navigation Laws,* in *English Historical Review* 55 (October 1940): 660; also Ramsay, *English Overseas Trade,* p. 232; and Jacob Viner, *Studies in the Theory of International Trade* (London: George Allen & Unwin [1955]), p. 113. There was no class homogeneity and little sense of community among the businessmen engaged in overseas trade. Merchants were split into warring, highly competitive cliques—gangs, often at odds with each other. On few occasions did men from the same economic class or economic function present a united front. See Charles Wilson, "Economics and Politics in the Seventeenth Century" (review of Christopher Hill, *Century of Revolution*), *Historical Journal* 5, no. 1 (1962): p. 86; and Price, *The Tobacco Adventure to Russia.*

2. For the number of persons involved in the trade at this time, see Paul Clements, "From Tobacco to Grain: Economic Development in Maryland's Eastern Shore, 1660-1750," (Ph.D. diss., University of Wisconsin, 1975), pp. 6-9.

3. For the rivalry between Bristol and London see Patrick McGrath, ed., *Records relating to the Society of Merchant Venturers of . . . Bristol in the Seventeenth Century,* Bristol Records Society Publications, vol. 17 (Bristol, 1952), pp. xxxvi-xxxviii.

4. Richard Chiverton's response to Jacobsen's petition, *CSPD, Charles II, 1663-1664,* p. 33; committee of the Bristol Merchant Venturers to Sir Thomas Day and Major Richard Yate, 16, 21 December 1695, BL, Add. MSS 5540, ff. 84, 87; undated petition of the shipmasters and mariners, circa 1660, PRO, SP 29/440/no. 27; and notes on foreign trade for the year 1662 in the Abraham Hill papers, BL, Sloane MSS 2920, f. 70.

5. On the dispute over the trade to the Canary Islands, see *CSPD, Charles II, 1664-1665,* pp. 98-99, 111-12, 187, 227, 383; *1665-1666,* pp. 49, 75; *1666-1667,* pp. 254, 534-35; *1667,* p. 486. On the Newfoundland dispute, see the petitions in *CSPD, 1663-1664,* p. 353; *1667-1668,* p. 257; PRO, SP 29/224/nos. 55, 56; and order in council of 23 December 1667, SP 29/225/no. 139.

6. Kenneth Gordon Davies, *The Royal African Company* (New York: Longmans, Green, 1957), pp. 39-41, 63-74, 105.

7. The prominent merchants of London trading to the West Indies, thought by some to have been influential in securing the passage of acts to increase and encourage English shipping by which all Englishmen could participate, actually wanted a monopoly charter to exclude all rivals, both English and foreign, not merely Dutch competitors. See Thomas Povey, "Booke of Entrie of Forreigne Letters," BL, Add. MSS 11, 411, ff. 304; Povey's "Reasons Propounded by the

Adventurers for [the West Indies]," BL, Egerton MSS 2395, ff. 103-4; Martin Noell and Thomas Povey, "Overtures for a Council to Be Erected for Foreign Plantations," ibid., ff. 290-91; the draft of an agreement by the principals of the proposed West India Company, ibid., f. 108; and the petition of the West India Company to Cromwell, ibid., ff. 109-10.

8. W. L. Grant and James Munro, eds., *Acts of the Privy Council of England: Colonial Series,* 6 vols. (London: HMSO, 1908-12), 1:49, 129.

9. Ashley, *Cromwellian Commercial and Financial Policy,* pp. 28-29, 133-34; J. S. Kepler, "Fiscal Aspects of the English Carrying Trade during the Thirty Years' War," *Economic History Review,* 2nd. ser. 25 (May 1972): 261-83.

10. Some contemporary writers assumed that this measure was enacted at the behest of English merchants intent on excluding Dutch rivals from the colonial carrying trade. The contention has been debated by later scholars. J. E. Farnell, "The Navigation Act of 1651, the First Dutch War, and the London Merchant Community," *Economic History Review,* 2d. ser. 16 (April 1964): 439-54, argued that a group of London merchants whose trade with the West Indies would have benefited by the exclusion of the Dutch (in what way Farnell did not specify) were the key. While the motivation of national security, the increase of English naval power, weighed heavily with the Council of State, the pressure of these merchants acting with the support of the Hamburg branch of the Merchant Adventurers was decisive. They operated through Benjamin Worsley, a member of the Committee on Trade. Farnell's argument on the connection between Worsley and the West Indian traders is speculative. Moreover, while the act may have aided these merchants in eliminating the Dutch as rivals for the Antilles trade, the Londoners wanted more. They wanted a charter such as that enjoyed by the East India Company excluding any English rivals. The act threw open the trade to all Englishmen. A more general argument in favor of the influence of the trading companies was advanced by Charles McLean Andrews, *The Colonial Period of American History,* 4 vols. (New Haven, Conn.: Yale University Press, 1934-38), 4:35-43, simply on the grounds that these companies stood to benefit from the exclusion of the Dutch as shipping rivals. Lawrence A. Harper, *The English Navigation Laws: A Seventeenth Century Experiment in Social Engineering* (New York: Columbia University Press, 1939), p. 49, was content to conclude that while several factors were involved, the complaints of the trading companies furnished the impetus for governmental action. Harper was concerned not so much with determining motives as in identifying concepts utilized to justify legislation. R. W. K. Hinton, *The Eastland Trade and the Common Weal in the Seventeenth Century* (Cambridge: Cambridge University Press, 1959), pp. 90-91, challenged the thesis that the act was the work of special interest groups. There "is not one scrap of evidence that any company pressed" for a navigation law. The companies wanted an act confirming their privileges by charter rather than an act throwing open trade to rival merchants in England. The remonstrance of the Eastland merchants to the Council of State, in 1659, asking for renewal of the corporation (*CSPD, 1659-1660,* pp. 283-84) illustrates this. While some merchants may have eventually benefited from the law, their interests coincided on this issue with those of the officials of the Commonwealth.

11. Ten years later Worsley wrote, "I was ye first sollicitour for ye Act for ye incouragem' of navigation & putt ye first fyle to it, and after writt ye Advocate in defence of it" (Worsley to [the countess of Clarendon], 8 November 1661, Bodl., MS Clarendon, 75, f. 75). Farnell assumed but did not really demonstrate that Worsley was connected with the London West Indian merchants. However, G. E. Aylmer, *The State's Servants: The Civil Service of the English Republic, 1649–1660* (London: Routledge & Kegan Paul, 1973), pp. 270–72, argued that it cannot be demonstrated whether Worsley was an originator of such major legislation as the act of 1651 or the subsequent navigation laws. Aylmer was more inclined to credit more influential men, such as George Downing. In this Aylmer followed Charles Wilson, *England's Apprenticeship, 1603–1763* (New York: St. Martin's Press, 1965), p. 372, who further denied the influence of the traders. The ministers of state were not mere puppets of the mercantile community, which was itself divided into opposing interests. Whether Worsley actually originated or solicited the act of 1651, when he wrote *The Advocate* he was in a position to know the aims of the Commonwealth officials who promoted the ordinance.

12. John Nicholas to Edward Nicholas, 10 March 1666/7, BL, Egerton MSS 2539, f. 165; and Benjamin Worsley's propositions on trade and plantations submitted to Ashley on 14 August 1668, Shaftesbury Papers, PRO 30/24/49/no. 26.

13. In reviewing the various bills passed during the early years of the reign, Charles Wilson, *England's Apprenticeship*, p. 165, concluded that while the merchants and spokesmen for the commercial interests were consulted, the politicians in administration retained control of policy in their own hands. It might be further noted that at this time the shipping interest had little power in the House of Commons. The Masters of Trinity House, for example, complained in 1664 that there were but two seamen in the house and not more than thirty merchants. It was "no wonder that things of trade go no better nor are better understood" (Pepys, *Diary*, 5:95). The most ambitious claim for the influence of the merchants in promoting the various acts of trade and navigation was made in Arnold Alan Sherman, "Commerce, Colonies, and Competition: Special Interest Groups and English Commercial & Colonial Policy, 1660–1673" (Ph.D. diss., Yale University, 1972). Sherman inferred, but with no positive evidence, that the various laws benefited the East India and Royal African companies. He identified twenty-eight members of Parliament as merchants, most of them connected with the East India Company. But the great majority of the merchants he listed did not enter Parliament until *after* 1663, by which time the basic navigation code was already on the statute rolls.

14. J. R. Tanner, ed., *Samuel Pepys's Naval Minutes*, Naval Records Society Publications, vol. 50 (London, 1926), pp. 22, 31.

15. There is general agreement that the act was intended to encourage English shipping and to increase the earnings of English freighters, thus aiding the balance of payments in foreign trade and establishing an entrepôt in England. Richard B. Sheridan, *Sugar and Slavery: An Economic History of the British West Indies, 1623–1775* (Baltimore, Md.: Johns Hopkins University Press, 1974), p. 42, follows Harper, *The Navigation Laws,* and George Louis Beer, *The Old Colonial System, 1660–1754,* part 1, *The Establishment of the*

System, 1660–1688, 2 vols. (New York: Macmillan, 1912), by adding another motive for enumeration: the channeling of colonial produce through England was intended to swell the profits of English businessmen resident in the various European ports. This does not necessarily follow, for it would have been possible for them to market sugar and tobacco without physically routing these products through English ports. Andrews, *Colonial Period,* 4:86, observed that the enumerated list covered certain valuable raw materials of the colonies for which England would otherwise have been dependent on European rivals. This was not the case for tobacco, which was grown in England. Moreover, the law did not require that enumerated produce remain in England to be processed or consumed there.

16. Order in council, 22 April 1664, PC 2/57/pp. 73–74; order in council, 1 July 1663, PC 2/56/p. 460. In the months following passage of the act to encourage shipping, the council of trade discussed a proposal to make Dover once again a free port for the composition trade, that is, to permit the reexportation of goods imported without the payment of customs duties at the full rate. Due to the pressure of customs officials, however, ships engaged in the plantation trade were not exempted from the provisions of the navigation code when using Dover (Proceedings of the Council of Trade, 3, 8, 31 January 1660/1, SP 29/31/ff. 119, 122, 123; and order in council, 28 June 1661, PC 2/55/pp. 272–73).

17. For evidence of this lawful trade see *CSPD, Charles II, 1670,* p. 173; *1668–1669,* pp. 489, 621; Anthony Thorold to Secretary Williamson, 26 May 1675, SP 29/370/f. 247; Thomas Holden to Williamson, 9 September 1675, 5 March 1676/7, SP 29/373/no. 106, no. 120; Holden to Williamson, 9 November 1676, SP 29/386/no. 224; Holden to Williamson, 21 February 1677/8, SP 29/401/no. 140; Holden to Williamson, 15 August 1678, SP 29/406/no. 9; Francis Bellot to Williamson, 19 August 1678, SP 29/406/no. 25; Bellot to Williamson, 5 March 1676/7, SP 29/391/no. 119.

18. Charles II to the governor of Jersey, 16 May 1666, *CSPD, Charles II, 1670, Addenda,* p. 708. Fiscal considerations continued to rank high. Early in the reign of Anne, when reviewing the treaties between England and the States General of the United Provinces, the English Commissioners of Trade remonstrated against ships from the English plantations conveying goods directly from and to Dutch ports "by which the Queen loses the customs" (Commissioners of Trade to Secretary Charles Hedges, 1 July 1702, SP 34/1/no. 54).

19. The customs commissioners later reported on a cargo of tobacco from French Martinique taken on a prize of war that the difference in the duty upon tobacco of the English plantations and of foreign plantations was intended to encourage the product of the English plantations and to prohibit that of foreign plantations (Customs to the Commissioners of the Treasury, 24 September 1689, PRO, Treas. 1/5/f. 59.

20. Pepys, *Diary,* 6:120. See also the order in council, 28 February 1660/1, PC 2/55/pp. 147, 171–72. Early in the reign of James II, when Parliament raised the duty on imported tobacco to sixpence per pound, the government had more at stake. It issued new orders to destroy plants in the western counties. After the overthrow of James II in 1689, William III empowered the use of troops to assist

in the destruction of the plants (orders in council, 18 December 1685, PC 2/71/pp. 177-78; 27 June 1684, PC 2/73/p. 158.

21. Leo Francis Stock, ed., *Proceedings and Debates of the British Parliaments respecting North America,* 5 vols. (Washington, D.C.: Carnegie Institution of Washington, 1924-41), 1:294-308; and Jacob M. Price, "The Tobacco Trade and the Treasury, 1685-1732," 2 vols. (Ph.D. diss., Harvard University, 1954), 1:197-98, 326-27.

22. Bland's remonstrance, CO 1/36/ff. 141-43; order in council on Downing's reports, 15 August 1662, PC 2/56/p. 101; minutes of the Council for Foreign Plantations, 25 August 1662, CO 1/14/no. 59; and 13th and 14th paragraphs of the instructions to Willoughby approved by the Privy Council, 13 June 1663, PC 2/56/p. 439.

23. Minutes of the Privy Council, 24 June 1663, PC 2/56/pp. 450-51. The letter to the colonial governors was evidently the work of Joseph Williamson. See CO 5/903/11-15.

24. Petition of the shopkeepers, 28 November 1660 and the report of the committee, 14 March 1660/1, *CSPD, Charles II, 1660-1661,* p. 363.

25. Stock, *Debates,* 1:309-20. For details on the Irish and Scottish aspects, see Carolyn A. Edie, *The Irish Cattle Bills: A Study in Restoration Politics,* American Philosophical Society Transactions, n.s. 60, pt. 2 (Philadelphia, 1970), pp. 11-13. The provision excluding Irish ports from receiving enumerated colonial produce directly came partly in retaliation for a vote in the Irish parliament lowering the duties on sugar and tobacco, passed in the hope of drawing trade away from rival English ports. As the crown had promised during debate on the bill, it rescinded a proclamation banning the export of horses to the colonies (order in council 31 July 1663, PC 2/56/pp. 491, 495).

26. Downing to Clarendon, 22 April 1664, in T. H. Lister, *Life and Administration of Edward, First Earl of Clarendon,* 3 vols. (London, 1838), 3:308. Wilson, *Profit and Power,* p. 116 followed Downing's argument, but see Laurence James Bradley, "The London / Bristol Trade Rivalry: Conventional History, and the Colonial Office: Five Records for the Port of New York," (Ph.D. diss., University of Notre Dame, 1971), for the volume of foreign goods legally imported via Bristol and London to New York. Both Harper, *English Navigation Laws,* pp. 59-60 and Andrews, *Colonial Period of American History,* 4:114, concluded that the Staple Act was intended to bind the English colonists to purchase nearly all of their European commodities in England. But a close reading of the law does not support this conclusion. Commercial relations between colonial importers and English middlemen had already been established, and this nexus determined the channels for colonial trade. Commerce to the colonies via English ports from Europe was allowed under the law and was conducted with no interference from the English government. The royal proclamation Andrews quoted objected to direct importation of European goods on the grounds that such commerce was detrimental to fair traders, those who paid customs duties in England, and to the king's revenue. For evidence that colonial ships were stopping at Falmouth, Harwich, Lyme, Rye, and other outports on their voyages between the Netherlands and the colonies, see above, this chapter, note 17.

27. Orders in council, 6, 22 November 1661, PC 2/55/pp. 427-28, 453-55; 24 September 1662 PC 2/56/p. 145; report of the Council of Trade, ? July 1664, *CSPD, Charles II, 1663-1664*, p. 651.

28. John Milward, *The Diary of John Milward, Esq., Member of Parliament for Derbyshire,* ed. Carolina Robbins (Cambridge: Cambridge University Press, 1938), p. 89; Architel Grey, col., *Debates of the House of Commons from the Year 1667 to the Year 1694,* 10 vols. (London, 1769), 1:38-39.

29. English commissioners to the Scots, 16 March 1667/8, PRO, SP 29/236/no. 133; Scottish reply, 25 March 1668, SP 29/237/no. 61; Lee, *The Cabal,* pp. 44-47; and Edward Hughes, "The Negotiations for a Commercial Union between England and Scotland in 1668," *Scottish Historical Review* 24 (October 1926): 30-47. In assessing the interests of various groups in the navigation code, Hughes noted that the Scottish demands for entry into the colonial trade did not call forth a single protest from an English trading or colonizing organization, evidence the code did not result from pressure by those English groups.

30. In order to induce migration to New York, a province recently captured from the Dutch, the proprietor, the duke of York, petitioned the Privy Council that Scots intending to settle there be given liberty to transport themselves in Scottish vessels and to engage in a limited trade. Permission was given for two ships, one of 250 tons and another of 500 tons (order in council, 5 April 1669, PC 2/61/p. 25.

31. T. C. Barker, "Smuggling in the Eighteenth Century: The Evidence of the Scottish Tobacco Trade," *VMHB* 68 (October 1954): 391, noted that during the early French wars there was a considerable increase in sailings from the Clyde River to the American plantations because of the immunity Scottish ports enjoyed from attack by privateers. There were no precise figures for this early illegal traffic by Scottish interlopers, although it may have been fairly heavy during these wars late in the seventeenth and early in the eighteenth century. See also T. C. Smout, "The Anglo-Scottish Union of 1707: Part I, The Economic Background," *Economic History Review,* 2d ser. 16 (April 1964): 455-67; T. C. Smout, "The Glasgow Merchant Community in the Seventeenth Century," *Scottish Historical Review* 47 (April 1968): 56-65; and T. C. Smout, *Scottish Trade on the Eve of Union, 1660-1707* (Edinburgh: Oliver and Boyd, 1963), pp. 26-27, 97, 175-78.

32. Instructions for the Council of Trade, ? September 1668, SP 29/247/no. 14.

35. Stock, *Debates,* 1:353-54; Milward, *Diary,* p. 228; Melton, "London and Parliament: An Analysis of a Constituency, 1661-1702," pp. 251-52.

34. The case of the sugar planters, in CO 1/26/ff. 149-50; Edward Deering, *The Parliamentary Diary of Sir Edward Deering, 1670-73,* ed. Basil D. Henning (New Haven, Conn.: Yale University Press, 1940), p. 92; and Stock, *Debates,* 1:362-76.

35. Stock, *Debates,* 1:376-79; the journal of the earl of Sandwich, in F. R. Harris, *The Life of Edward Montagu, K.G., First Earl of Sandwich (1625-1672),* 2 vols. (London: John Murray, 1912) 2:333-37; and House of Lords MSS, HMC, *Ninth Report,* app., pt. 2, p. 13.

36. Customs to Clifford, 10 February 1672/3, *Essex Papers,* ed. Osmund Airy, Camden Society Publications, n.s. 47 (1890): 55. The act of 1671 for regulating the plantation trade expired in 1680 and by an oversight was not renewed. The crown attempted initially to remedy the situation by an order in council, allowing shippers to take out bonds to return plantation produce only to England (order in council, 16 February 1680/1, PC 2/69/213-14). Parliament provided a statutory remedy in the first year of the reign of James II when it revived the act to regulate the plantation trade and deleted Irish ports from among those eligible to receive enumerated goods directly from the colonies. The respective customs establishments in England and Ireland strongly contested the issue, but the Privy Council finally recommended that the king not dispense with the recently revived law and that the lord lieutenant of Ireland be required to enforce the act (earl of Rochester to the Irish commissioners of revenue, 25 July 1685, SP 63/351/f. 61; Francis Gwyn to John Ellis, 4 July 1686, John Ellis Papers, BL, Add. MSS 28875, f. 433; order in council, 19 June 1686, PC 2/71/p. 290).

37. This opening of trade, the Eastland company protested unsuccessfully through its counsel in the House of Lords, violated its charter rights (House of Lords MSS, HMC, *Ninth Report,* app. pt. 2, p. 31). See also Stock, *Debates,* 1:398-99.

38. See the unsigned proposals offered to the House of Commons, BL, Harleian MSS 1238, f. 1.

39. See the notes made by Secretary Williamson of a conference with the king, the lord keeper, and the attorney general, 12 May 1676, SP 29/366/ff. 82-83; Danby to the Customs Board, 10 March 1674/5, *Caldendar of Treasury Books, 1660-1718,* ed. William Shaw et al., 32 vols. (London: HMSO, 1904-62), *1675,* p. 705; Sir Robert Southwell to William Jones, 28 January 1675/6, CO 1/36/f. 19; Jones's reply, 8 February 1675/6, CO 1/36/f. 20 (both also in CO 324/4/pp. 28, 29-30).

40. See, for example, the opinion expressed by the Commissioners of Customs in 1685, PC 2/71/pp. 105-6. In later years some question arose in Virginia whether the money collected through the payment *in the colony* of the plantation duty on tobacco could be used to establish a college. In reply the Commissioners of Customs noted that the duty was intended not so much to raise a revenue for the crown—they may have meant to raise revenue for the crown in the colonies—as to prevent an unlimited trade current in 1673 of carrying tobacco and other enumerated commodities from one colony to another and then to Europe, a trade diminishing the customs, trade, and navigation of England. In much the same manner commissioners on the board responsible for trade and plantations held that the act was intended to prevent a direct trade in these products from the colonies to Europe without first paying duties in England. See Customs report to the Treasury, 30 June 1692, CO 5/1358/186 (also in PRO, Treas. 64/88/353); the Commissioners of Trade and Plantations to the lords justices, 15 September 1699, CO 389/16/p. 366; and Commissioners of Trade to Secretary Hedges, 1 July 1702, SP 34/1/64.

41. In reviewing the provisions of the act as well as the statements by some officials, Thomas C. Barrow, *Trade and Empire: The British Customs Service in Colonial America, 1660-1775* (Cambridge, Mass.: Harvard University Press,

1967), p. 7, may have read certain statements somewhat out of context. He concluded that the measure was intended, among other things, to restrict the participation of the northern colonies in the export and consumption of materials necessary to English prosperity and to limit the colonial coasting trade generally, with a consequent reduction of shipments of enumerated produce directly to foreign ports. Yet if it were intended to exclude colonial ships from this trade, this could have been done explicitly by statute. During these years England was not suffering from a shortage of tobacco or sugar. Finally, as noted in this work (note 17 above), officials in the English outports did not hinder colonial freighters carrying plantation goods to Europe after they had entered and cleared their cargoes.

42. Within a year English merchants complained that under the guise of supplying the Dutch at New York these ships were engaged in a more extended trade to the other colonies. An order in council rescinded the exemption to Dutch shipping (minutes of the Committee of Foreign Plantations, 17 October 1667, CO 1/21/f. 275; order in council, 23 October 1667, PC 2/60/p. 29; order in council, 18 November 1668, PC 2/61/p. 112.

43. See, for example, Sir Robert Southwell to the secretary of the Customs Board, 23 September 1674, CO 324/4/p. 21; and the report of the Commissioners of Customs to the Committee for Plantation Affairs, 11 October 1675, CO 324/4/pp. 22–25.

44. See the summary of the complaints of the English merchants, SP 29/391/no. 94; Bollan's proposals in the Thomas Povey Papers, BL, Egerton MSS 2395, f. 42; and the complaints transmitted by the lord lieutenant of Ireland in Clarendon to Blathwayt, 30 May 1686, *The Correspondence of . . . Clarendon and . . . Rochester,* ed. Samuel Singer, 2 vols. (London: Camden Society, 1928), 1:418–19.

45. Smuggling on a large scale to avoid customs payments, especially in the outports, was widespread from at least the reign of Elizabeth. See McGrath, *Records of the Bristol Merchant Venturers,* p. 255; and *Merchants and Merchandise in Seventeenth Century Bristol,* pp. 207–8.

46. Bradley, "The London / Bristol Trade Rivalry," pp. 187–99; and Davis, *Rise of English Shipping Industry,* p. 136.

47. See, for example, *CSPD, Charles II, 1668–1669,* pp. 489, 621; *1670,* p. 176; *1675–1676,* p. 181; and SP 29/373/nos. 106, 210; SP 29/386/no. 224; SP 29/401/no. 140; SP 29/406/nos. 9, 25.

48. For example, in consigning a shipment of fish to be sold in Barbados, the Boston merchant Samuel Sewall instructed Nathaniel Green to make up a return cargo in cotton, sugar, and molasses and good bills of credit drawn on a London merchant. They were to be payable to his cousin, Edward Hull, at the Hat in Hand within Aldgate (letter book of Samuel Sewall, 1686–1729, *MHSC,* 6th ser. 1:64–66, 92–93, 112). For the connections of these merchants generally, see Bailyn, *New England Merchants in the Seventeenth Century.*

49. In January 1676, a number of London merchants entered a protest against New England traders who allegedly were importing goods directly from Europe and were thus able to sell them throughout the colonies at rates lower than for those goods shipped legally by the English. Yet as late as the 1680s the

total number of ships engaged in the entire West Indian trade from New England's leading port was not more than 150. The majority of these were small coasting vessels of ten to thirty tons each, carrying, for the most part, fish, timber, grain, and meat. On the other hand, the annual sailings from Barbados to London alone in 1680 numbered no less than 200 large, oceangoing vessels. Whatever the extent of illicit trade by New Englanders in manufactured goods to the West Indies, it did not divert the mainstream of trade from London and the English ports (Vincent T. Harlow, *A History of Barbados, 1625-1685* [Oxford: Oxford University Press, 1926], pp. 224, 288-90; Bailyn, *New England Merchants in the Seventeenth Century,* pp. 126-28; Carroll, "The Forest Civilization of New England: Timber, Trade, and Society in the Age of Wood, 1600-1688," p. 380.

50. On the marketing mechanisms in the West Indies, see K. G. Davies, "Origins of the Commission System in the West Indies Trade," pp. 92-105; and Harlow, *Barbados,* pp. 169-71. The period of the great sustained wars with France, 1689-1713, led to relative stagnation as high wartime freight and insurance rates discouraged sending ships to the Chesapeake. This situation depressed prices and, consequently, production in the colonies, but raised prices and stimulated production in Europe. The removal of the last halfpence per pound of the English duty on reexport in 1723 considerably narrowed the price advantage enjoyed by European-grown tobacco over American leaf. These and other developments in the colonies were to stimulate production there. The opening of the French market to British colonial tobacco led to a golden age for the American producers. See Price, *France and the Chesapeake,* 1:5-9, 15, 509.

51. Bland's remonstrance is in PRO, CO 1/36/ff. 141-43; Berkeley's "A Perfect Description of Virginia," is in LB, Egerton MSS 2395, ff. 354-59. George Louis Beer, *The Commercial Policy of England toward the American Colonies* (New York, 1893), p. 50, points to the additional burden American tobacco labored under in the European market because of the cost of additional freight made necessary by the requirement to first land cargoes at England. Yet, he concluded, for the market north of Cape Finisterre, England was the natural entrepôt. As has been pointed out above, for the market south of Cape Finisterre, the governments of France, Spain, and Portugal adopted protectionist policies.

52. Not until well into the eighteenth century, when the tobacco trade greatly expanded in size, did it fall increasingly into the hands of fewer, but larger, firms. At that time there were definite constrictive, even oligopolistic, influences at work, but they could not be ascribed entirely to government fiscal policy. Other, purely commercial, factors were also then at work (Price, "Tobacco and the Treasury," 2:902-4). For an example of direct purchase, see McGrath, *Merchants and Merchandise,* pp. 198-99.

53. Anderson to Cuthbert Jones, 1 May 1713; Anderson to Richard Lee, 12 October 1713; Anderson to Robert Page, 27 April 1710, University of Virginia, Alderman Library, Robert Anderson letterbook; petition of Thomas Sands, 23 November 1677, CO 1/41/f. 259.

54. Fitzhugh to John Cooper, 18 May 1685, Fitzhugh to Thomas Clayton, 26 April 1686, *William Fitzhugh and His Chesapeake World, 1676-1701: The*

Fitzhugh Letters and Other Documents, ed. Richard Beale Davis (Chapel Hill: University of North Carolina Press, 1963), pp. 166, 180; Anderson to John Mainard, 10 August 1714, and Anderson to Francis Magson and John Gibson, 26 April 1701, Anderson letterbook. See also Fitzhugh's letters to Dains and Gotley, *Fitzhugh Letters,* pp. 355, 86.

55. Fitzhugh to Bligh, 8 April 1696 [1697?], *Fitzhugh Letters,* p. 350.

56. William Berkeley, *A Perfect Description of Virginia,* BL, Egerton MSS 2395, ff. 354-59; Berkeley to Lord ———, 30 March 1663, Egerton MSS 2395, f. 362. Most of the extant data on the marketing of tobacco date from the eighteenth century. Two sources used in the above discussion, the Anderson and Fitzhugh correspondence, in addition to the published letters of William Byrd, contain valuable information on the trade during the latter decades of the seventeenth century. How representative these are for the later period remains a problem.

57. See William Byrd to Eliakim Hutchinson, 2 May 1689, Byrd to Jonathon Walke, 29 May 1689, *Byrd Correspondence,* ed. Tinling 1:103, 104. John C. Rainbolt, *From Prescription to Persuasion: Manipulation of Seventeenth Century Virginia Economy* (Port Washington, N.Y.: Kennikat Press, 1974), p. 86, attributed the failure of the planters of Virginia to take early advantage of the economic opportunity made possible by the expansion of sugar cultivation in the West Indies to the fact that they were indebted to English merchants. This committed them to continued tobacco production in order to make remittances to England. But this argument ignored the possibility that such remittances could easily have been made through bills of credit earned by the sale of provisions to the West Indian planters. The Tidewater planters appreciated this more fully in the eighteenth century. For the immediate future, according to Russell R. Menard, "Economy and Society in Early Colonial Maryland," (Ph.D. diss., University of Iowa, 1975), pp. 314, 321, the planters on the Chesapeake had to lower their expectations and to content themselves with smaller profits. More importantly, a drop in the cost of production, in marketing, and in freighting tobacco later permitted a higher margin of profit. Falling costs allowed the sale of Chesapeake tobacco at lower prices in an expanding market, one not open to the higher priced luxury tobacco produced earlier.

Chapter 5

1. William Blathwayt to James Vernon, 7/17 September 1700, BL, Add. MSS 40,744, f. 305; Council of Plantations to the governor of Virginia, [circa 1660-61], Thomas Povey Papers, BL, Egerton MSS 2395, f. 335.

2. Blathwayt to Thomas, Lord Culpeper, 10 February 1682/3, CW, Blathwayt papers, vol. 17; Governor Francis Lovelace to Secretary Williamson, 3 October 1670, *NYCD,* 3:189.

3. William Blathwayt to Nicholas Spencer, 28 July 1684, CW, Blathwayt Papers, vol. 16.

4. Harlow, *Barbados,* pp. 128-31. A compromise was adopted shortly after the Restoration by which Willoughby ruled as the king's governor for the

remaining seven years of his lease from Carlisle. He received one-half of the profits from a tax on all exports, with the other half allotted to pay off the other creditors of Carlisle. Eventually both portions reverted to the crown to pay the cost of civil government and the military forces sent out to defend against French attacks.

5. James Logan to William Penn, [17 February 1707/8], HSP, James Logan letter books, 1(3):301; Nicholas Spencer to William Blathwayt, 12 August 1682, CW, Blathwayt Papers, vol. 16; and the charges against Bland in the minutes of the Virginia council, 21 November 1674, BL, Egerton MSS 2395, f. 496.

6. Chesterfield to Solomon Dayrolles, 16 November 1753, *The Letters of Philip Dormer, Fourth Earl of Chesterfield*, ed. Bonamy Dobrée, 6 vols. (London: Eyre and Spottiswood, 1932), 5:2059. Bernard Bailyn's analysis, "Politics and Social Structure in Virginia," in *Seventeenth Century America, Essays in Colonial History*, ed. James Morton Smith (Chapel Hill: University of North Carolina Press, [1959]), pp. 90–115, needs some modification. Englishmen of this era held that political office ought to go to men with economic means and social status. Consequently the social was but little distinguished from the political hierarchy. Bailyn perhaps underestimated the degree of social mobility in England and consequently the disparity between social and political leadership. See Paul Seaver, ed., *Seventeenth-Century England: Society in the Age of Revolution* (New York: New Viewpoints, 1976). In America economic opportunity and the arrival of men from England from English mercantile and genteel families provided more individuals with pretensions to political status than the existing governmental structure could provide.

7. James Logan to William Penn [2 April] 1705, HSP, James Logan letter books, 1(2):172; Nicholas Spencer to his brother, 13 June 1672, BL, Sloane MSS 3511, f. 134.

8. Penn to C. Lawton, 21 December 1700, HSP, William Penn letter book, 1699–1703; Penn to his commissioners of state, 12 August 1689, HSP, Dreer Collection, Letters and Papers of William Penn; Samuel Mac. Janney, *The Life of William Penn: With Selections from His Correspondence and Autobiography*, 4th ed. (Philadelphia, 1876), p. 277; and Bonamy Dobrée, *William Penn, Quaker and Pioneer* (Boston: Houghton Mifflin, 1934), p. 203.

9. For the confused and complicated legal claims and grants to New England see Andrews, *Colonial Period*, 1:258–62, 282–83, 292–96, 334–35, 356–59, 417–27; 2:24–25, 32–33, 73–75, 91–92, 120–21, 154, 212, 222, 224–25; Isabel Calder, "The Earl of Stirling and the Colonization of Long Island," in *Essays in Colonial History Presented to Charles McLean Andrews* (New Haven, Conn.: Yale University Press, 1931), pp. 74–88; Robert C. Black III, *The Younger John Winthrop* (New York: Columbia University Press, 1966), pp. 85–86; Mary Jeanne Anderson Jones, *Congregational Commonwealth: Connecticut, 1632–1662* (Middletown, Conn.: Wesleyan University Press, 1968), pp. 23–24, 158–60.

10. Nonetheless, it was accepted in the Bay Colony that an incumbent magistrate should not be voted out of office without cause. See Stephen Foster,

Their Solitary Way: The Puritan Social Ethic in the First Century of Settlement in New England (New Haven, Conn.: Yale University Press, 1971), pp. 180–81.

11. By law in 1647 the General Court permitted freemen in the towns to admit nonfreemen who had reached the age of twenty-four years to elect town officials, provided the freemen remained a majority of the town electorate. Eleven years later householders twenty-four years of age and older, if they owned an estate assessed in a single country rate at twenty pounds, were allowed to vote for town officials, but not for deputies to the General Court.

12. Charles H. Firth, ed., *The Clarke Papers,* Camden Society Publications, 4 vols. (London: Camden Society, 1891–1901), 1:229, 301–2.

13. For the complicated issues of qualifications for voting and the proportions of the adult male population with the franchise, see B. Kathrine Brown, "Puritan Democracy: A Case Study," *MVHR* 50 (December 1963): 377–96; and "Freemanship in Puritan Massachusetts," *AHR* 69 (July 1954): 865–83; Robert Emmet Wall, Jr., "A New Look at Cambridge," *JAH* 52 (December 1965): 599–605; and "The Decline of the Massachusetts Franchise: 1647–1666," *JAH* 59 (September 1972): 303–10; Stephen Foster, "The Massachusetts Franchise in the Seventeenth Century," *WMQ,* 3d ser. 24 (October 1967): 613–23; and *Their Solitary Way,* pp. 173–79; Richard C. Simmons, "Godliness, Property, and the Franchise in Puritan Massachusetts: An Interpretation," *JAH* 55 (December 1968): 495–511; Theodore Burnham Lewis and Linda M. Webb, "Voting for the Massachusetts Council of Assistants, 1674–1686: A Statistical Note," *WMQ* 3d ser. 30 (October 1973): 625–34; Theodore B. Lewis, Jr., "Massachusetts and the Glorious Revolution, 1660–92," (Ph.D. diss., University of Wisconsin, 1967), pp. 41–47; Timothy H. Breen, "Who Governs: The Town Franchise in Seventeenth Century Massachusetts," *WMQ* 3d ser. 27 (July 1970): 460–74.

14. George D. Langdon, Jr., *Pilgrim Colony: A History of New Plymouth, 1620–1691* (New Haven, Conn.: Yale University Press, 1966), pp. 77–78, 81, 87–88, 98; "The Franchise and Political Democracy in Plymouth Colony," *WMQ,* 3d ser. 20 (October 1963): 513–26.

15. David H. Fowler, "Connecticut's Freemen: The First Forty Years," *WMQ,* 3d ser. 15 (July 1958): 312–33; Paul R. Lucas, *Valley of Discord: Church and Society along the Connecticut River, 1636–1725* (Hanover, N.H.: University Press of New England, 1976), pp. 59–71, 74–75.

16. Andrews, *Colonial Period,* 2:55–57; Irving B. Richman, "The Land Controversies of William Harris," Rhode Island Historical Society, *Collections,* 10 (1902): 11–16.

17. For this dispute, see Sydney V. James, *Colonial Rhode Island: A History* (New York: Charles Scribner's Sons, 1975), pp. 82–87; Richard S. Dunn, "John Winthrop, Jr., and the Narragansett Country," *WMQ,* 3d ser. 13 (January 1956): 68–79; the memoranda in *Public Records of the Colony of Connecticut (1636–1776),* ed. J. H. Trumbull and C. J. Hoadley, 15 vols. (Hartford, Conn., 1850–90), 2:541; the deeds and memoranda in *The Records of Proprietors of Narragansett, Otherwise Called the [John] Fones Record,* ed. E. J. Arnold (Providence, R. I., 1894), pp. 1–2; and Amos Richardson to John Winthrop, Jr., 9 July 1659, Trumbull Papers, *MHSC,* 5th ser. 9:7.

18. See "The State of the Colony of Kennebec," BL, Egerton 2395, f. 426.

19. Evidently there were no representatives returned to the Massachusetts General Court from Exeter, the village founded by fugitives from Massachusetts during the so-called antinomian controversy. See the list of deputies from the New Hampshire towns returned from 1641 to 1679 in Nathaniel Bouton et al., eds., *Documents and Records Relating to the Province of New Hampshire,* 40 vols. (Concord: New Hampshire Historical Society, 1867–1943), 1:369–72.

20. David E. Van Deventer, *The Emergence of Provincial New Hampshire, 1623–1741* (Baltimore, Md.: Johns Hopkins University Press, 1976), pp. 5–17; Gary Thomas Lord, "The Politics and Social Structure of Seventeenth-Century Portsmouth, New Hampshire," (Ph.D. diss., University of Virginia, 1976), pp. 53–96; and Peter Ralph Barry, "The New Hampshire Merchant Interest, 1609–1725" (Ph.D. diss., University of Wisconsin, 1971), pp. 34–35, 43. Carroll, "The Forest Civilization of New England: Timber, Trade, and Society in the Age of Wood, 1600–1688," pp. 517–21 is particularly valuable for the economic domination of the merchant group in the life of the towns.

21. Godfrey's letter and information, 14 March 1660/1, PRO, CO 1/15/f. 65 (printed under the date of 14 March 1660 in Maine Historical Society, *Collections,* 2d ser. 4 (1889): 148–51); Godfrey to [Thomas Povey], 7 April 1663, Maine Historical Society, *Collections,* 2d ser. 4 (1889): 251.

22. See the account of the meeting at Wells by the commissioners for Gorges, dated 21 December 1661, CO 1/15/ff. 186–87; their warrant, 11 March 1661/2, CO 1/16/f. 81; and Daniel Gookin to Gorges, 25 June 1663, CO 1/17/ff. 154–55.

23. Foster, *Their Solitary Way,* pp. 182–85 argued that the effort of Bernard Bailyn to establish a distinct outlook by merchants, at variance with that of the orthodox Puritans, is strained. He contended that it is difficult to identify a distinct merchant class separate from the magistrates of the colony and that the Puritan merchants did hold high office within the institutional and electoral system operating until the revocation of the old charter. It might be noted that much of Foster's argument relates to the years after 1673 and that some merchants in the Bay Colony had already left as the result of religious controversies. Supporters of the antinomians, they followed the Hutchinsons and Coddingtons to Portsmouth and Newport.

24. Robert Emmet Wall, Jr., *Massachusetts Bay: The Crucial Decade* (New Haven, Conn.: Yale University Press, 1972), pp. 32, 39, 119–20, 220–29.

25. The Quakers' letter without date is printed in MHS, *Proceedings,* 3d. ser. 2 (Boston, 1909): 359.

26. William Kelloway, *The New England Company, 1649–1776: Missionary Society to the American Indians* (London: Longmans, 1961), pp. 47–48. Richard Baxter, an eminent Puritan divine who had spent some time in New England, had suggested Boyle as head of the missionary society. William G. McLoughlin, *New England Dissent, 1630–1833: The Baptists and the Separation of Church and State,* 2 vols. (Cambridge, Mass.: Harvard University Press, 1971), 1:49, 59, 79, argued that New Englanders did not have to wait for the English act of 1689 or John Locke's famous letters on toleration and that the laws requiring uniformity became dead letters. But at best this meant only that

certain Dissenters were allowed to worship outside the established Congregational church. They still had to support the state church financially. Moreover, McLoughlin's argument ignores the pressure for toleration exerted by the English crown for twenty years. See T. H. Breen, *The Character of a Good Ruler: A Study of Puritan Political Ideas in New England, 1630–1730* (New Haven, Conn.: Yale University Press, 1970), pp. 92–93.

27. Petition of Lionel Copley, John Becx, and others to the Council of Foreign Plantations, n.d., CO 1/15/f. 56; petition of Gifford, CO 1/15/f. 56; petition of Henderson with annexed paper, CO 1/15/ff. 56, 57.

28. Crown's undated deposition, CO 1/15/f. 165; Kellond and Kirke to Endecott, 29 May 1661, CO 1/15/f. 118; Davenport to Thomas Temple, 10 August 1661, CO 1/15/f. 164; and Temple to Secretary of State Edward Morrice, 20 August 1661, CO 1/15/f. 162. Whalley and Goffe had arrived in Boston on 27 July 1660. About two weeks later the authorities of the Bay Colony were in the possession of a printed paper, brought in by a Scottish vessel, an order from the Council of State in London, dated 18 May, requiring that the sixty-six members of the court responsible for the execution of Charles I be apprehended. Daniel Gookin showed this to the two regicides on the night of 9 August 1660. See the entries for 27 July, 9 August 1660, notes transcribed from Goffe's papers, MHS, Winthrop Family Papers.

29. Breedon's narrative and deposition, sworn before the Council for Foreign Plantations, 11 March 1660/1, CO 1/15/ff. 54–55.

30. Maverick to the earl of Clarendon, n.d., *The Clarendon Papers,* vol. 2 of NYHS, *Collections,* Publication Fund Series (New York, 1870): 19–22, 29.

31. Leverett to the Massachusetts General Court, 13 September 1660, in Hutchinson, *Original Papers,* p. 323; the address of the king, *Records of the Governor and Company of the Massachusetts Bay in New England,* ed. Nathaniel B. Shurtleff, 5 vols. in 6 (Boston, 1853–54), 4(1):450–52; petition and address to the houses of Parliament, ibid., pp. 453–54; instructions to the agents, ibid., pp. 455–56. The address to the king delivered in London is in CO 1/15/f. 179. The set of instructions to Leverett which he presented to the Council of Foreign Plantations on 11 February 1660/1 is CO 1/15/f. 181.

32. The king to the governor of Massachusetts, 15 February 1660/1, CO 5/903/pp. 18–19.

33. Report of the Council of Foreign Plantations, 30 April 1661, CO 1/15/ff. 83–84 (draft in CO 1/15/f. 100) (also in the Thomas Povey Papers, BL, Egerton MSS 2395, ff. 299–300; order in council, 17 May 1661, PC 2/55/pp. 216–17.

34. Endecott to Clarendon, 7 August 1661, Bodl., MS Clarendon 75, f. 75; the Massachusetts address to the king, 7 August 1661, CO 1/15/f. 158; Shurtleff, *Records of Massachusetts Bay,* 4(2): 24, 25, 27, 30–31, 32–33.

35. Rawson to Secretary Morrice, 6 December 1661, CO 1/15/f. 181 enclosing the order of the General Court of 27 November 1661, CO 1/15/f. 182.

36. Paul R. Lucas, "Colony or Commonwealth: Massachusetts Bay, 1661–1666," *WMQ,* 3d ser. 24 (January 1967): 93–95.

Chapter 6

1. Charles to Governor John Winthrop, 8 April 1660, MHS, Winthrop Family Papers.

2. Petition of the General Court of New Plymouth, 5 June 1661, Winthrop Family Papers (also in CO 1/15/f. 121); the address of the colony of Connecticut to the king with the instructions to Winthrop, circa 7 June 1661, Winthrop Family Papers; Governor William Prence to Winthrop, 24 September 1661, Winthrop Family Papers, and Prence to Winthrop, 29 September "Winthrop Papers," *MHSC,* 5th ser. 1:392.

3. See Davenport to John Leverett, 24 June 1665, Hutchinson, *Original Papers,* p. 393; Davenport to Winthrop, 23 June 1663, and Leete to Winthrop, 6 August 1661, "Winthrop Papers," *MHSC,* 4th ser. 7:523, 549.

4. See Saye and Sele to Winthrop, 14 December 1661; John Richards to Winthrop, 18 December 1661; and Robert Boyle to Winthrop, 28 December 1661, MHS, Winthrop Family Papers.

5. See the deeds signed in the name of the Narragansett Indians to Atherton, 13 October 1660, CO 1/14/f. 105; Gorton, Green, and Holden to Clarendon, 4 April 1662, JCBL, Clarendon Papers, p. 9; Atherton Associates to Winthrop, 24 September 1661, "Trumbull Papers," *MHSC,* 5th ser. 9:30–31.

6. Clarke's petition is undated, but endorsed as received on 29 January 1661/2; another copy dated 5 February 1661/2 and endorsed as received on the same day, CO 1/15/ff. 7, 11; Winthrop to Clarendon, 7 June 1662, "Winthrop Papers," *MHSC,* 5th ser. 8:75.

7. Minutes by Nicholas, 6 February 1661/2, CO 1/16/f. 29; order in council, 26 February 1661/2, CO 5/905/pp. 5–6; warrant dated 28 February 1661/2, CO 1/16/f. 70.

8. Petition of Clarke, 14 May 1662, *Clarendon Papers,* p. 44; Winthrop to Clarendon, 7 June 1662, "Winthrop Papers," *MHSC,* 5th ser. 8:75; Winthrop to William Thursby, ? August 1662, ibid., pp. 75–76; Winthrop to the Atherton Associates, 2 September 1662, "Trumbull Papers," *MHSC,* 5th ser. 9:33–34; Atherton Associates to Winthrop, 17 September, 18 November 1662, ibid., pp. 37–40, 43; and orders of the Committee for Plantations, 15, 25 September 1662, PC 2/56/pp. 139, 147.

9. [Hooke to Davenport], 2 March 1662/3, *CSPD, Charles II, 1661–1663,* p. 125; Winthrop to John Mason, 4 March 1662/3, "Winthrop Papers," *MHSC,* 5th ser. 8:77–80.

10. This agreement is in CO 1/17/f. 48 (also in "Winthrop Papers," *MHSC,* 5th ser. 8:82–83 and "Trumbull Papers," *MHSC,* 5th ser. 9:51–52.

11. Scott to Edward Hutchinson, 9 April 1663, "Trumbull Papers," *MHSC,* 5th ser. 9:53; petition of Scott and others to the king, n.d. [before 21 June 1663], CO 1/17/f. 145; Charles II to the governors and assistants of Massachusetts, New Plymouth, Connecticut, and New Haven, 21 June 1663, CO 5/903/pp. 222–23 (also in CO 1/17/f. 149) with a draft in Williamson's hand, CO 1/17/f. 148.

12. Edward Hutchinson to the General Assembly of Connecticut, 17 July 1663, *Public Records of the Colony of Connecticut,* ed. J. H. Trumbull and C. J. Hoadley, 15 vols. (Hartford, Conn., 1850–90), 2:542; Connecticut Commissioners to Rhode Island, 9 September 1664, ibid., 2:542; Richard S. Dunn, *Puritans and Yankees: The Winthrop Dynasty of New England, 1630–1717* (Princeton, N.J.: Princeton University Press, 1962), pp. 145–47; Black, *The Younger John Winthrop,* pp. 254–58.

13. The instructions were probably the work of Thomas Danforth, a magistrate. See John Gorman Palfrey, *History of New England,* 5 vols. (Boston, 1858–90), 2:514–26.

14. Report by the Doctors of Laws, 15 February 1661/2, CO 1/16/f. 37.

15. Charles II to the governor of Massachusetts, 28 June 1662, CO 1/16/ff. 168–69; Maverick to Clarendon, n.d., *Clarendon Papers,* p. 37.

16. Orders in council, 15 September 25, 1662, PC 2/56/pp. 139, 147. That Sir William Compton, master of the ordnance, joined the committee for New England affairs later that winter adds futher support (order in council, 6 February 1662/3, PC 2/56/p. 294).

17. Paul R. Lucas, "Colony or Commonwealth: Massachusetts Bay 1661–1666," pp. 96–97; Lewis, "Massachusetts and the Glorious Revolution, pp. 10–11; Shurtleff, *Records of Massachusetts Bay,* 4(2):74.

18. Maverick to Clarendon, 8 March 1662/3 with enclosure dated 20 March 1662/3, *Clarendon Papers,* pp. 48–50; order in council, 10 April 1663, PC 2/56/384; minutes of the Council for Foreign Plantations, 6 July 1663, *NYCD,* 3:46; Scott to Williamson, 14 December 1663, CO 1/17/f. 250.

19. Notes by Williamson, n.d., 1663, CO 1/17/f. 274.

20. Memorandum of points for the settlement of New England, Thomas Povey Papers, BL, Egerton MSS 2395, f. 396; "Considerations for the Establishing of His Majesty's Interests in New England," CO 1/18/ff. 94–96; Clarendon's draft of the private instructions to Nicolls and his colleagues, headed "to be considered & communicated only between themselves," JCBL, Clarendon Papers relating to America, pp. 46–69, especially p. 51.

21. Private instructions, 23 April 1664, CO 1/18/ff. 107–11; public instructions, CO 1/18/ff. 103–6; commission dated 23 April 1664, CO 1/18/ff. 98–99; instructions for the visitation to Connecticut, 23 April 1664, CO 1/18/ff. 120–22; the king to the governor of Connecticut, 23 April 1664, CO 1/18/f. 123; the king to the governor of New Plymouth, 23 April 1664, CO 1/18/f. 124; the king to the governor of Massachusetts, 23 April 1664, CO 1/18/ff. 112–15.

22. Nicolls to [Clarendon], 27 July 1664, JCBL, Clarendon Papers relating to America, pp. 91–95.

23. Lewis, "Massachusetts and the Glorious Revolution," p. 17, estimated from the Boston tax rolls of ten years later that fewer than 1 percent of the inhabitants of the colony's largest town could have qualified under the new provision. In 1665 only seventy-three men presented themselves for freemanship. Foster, "Massachusetts Franchise," pp. 619–20, points out that the provincial secretary, Edward Rawson, did not keep adequate records. Some men may have been made free for whom no record survives.

24. Endecott to Secretary Morrice, 19 October 1664, CO 1/18/f. 286; "The Humble Supplication of the General Court of Massachusetts Colony to the King," 19 October 1664, CO 1/18/f. 287; Shurtleff, *Records of Massachusetts Bay,* 4(2):117-32.

25. Endecott to Clarendon, 8 November 1664, JCBL, Clarendon Papers relating to America, p. 121.

26. Maverick to Nicolls, 20 December 1664, CO 1/18/f. 334; Cartwright to Nicolls, 20 January 1664/5, CO 1/18/f. 16; Cartwright to Nicolls, 19 April 1665, CO 1/19/no. 49; Cartwright to Nicolls, 4 February 1664/5, CO 1/19/no. 20.

27. Secretary Morrice's answer to the Massachusetts petition, 25 February 1664/5, CO 1/19/f. 50 (also in JCBL, Clarendon Papers, pp. 79-80); Clarendon to Nicolls, 11 February 1664/5, JCBL, Clarendon Papers, pp. 87-88; Clarendon to Nicolls, [15 March 1664/5], JCBL, Clarendon Papers, p. 141; Boyle to Endecott, 17 March 1664/5 "Winthrop Papers," *MHSC,* 5th ser. 1:401-2; Clarendon to the governor and assistants of Massachusetts, 15 March 1664/5, JCBL, Clarendon Papers, pp. 135-36.

28. Report of the commission on New Plymouth and Rhode Island, CO 1/19/ff. 335-36, 337; Arnold and Brenton to the commissioners, 3 February 1664/5 with enclosed petition, CO 1/19/ff. 25, 26; Carr and Maverick to the Rhode Island magistrates, 2 August 1665, CO 1/19/f. 213.

29. Report of the commissioners, CO 1/18/f. 131; CO 1/19/f. 334; Lucas, *Valley of Discord,* pp. 65-70.

30. Bailyn, *New England Merchants,* pp. 121-24, saw in the controversy over the royal commission a manifestation of certain latent tensions in the colony. Support for the royal commissioners in Boston centered in the recently arrived merchants, men without church affiliation and without the franchise. Lucas, "Colony or Commonwealth," pp. 88-107, argued that there was another, a more significant group, the moderate faction, no less notable and no less representative of the various elements within the colony than the commonwealthmen with whom they disagreed on the tactics to be employed in the face of the demands from London.

31. Nicolls to John Winthrop, 4 May 1665, MHS, Winthrop Family Papers; Cartwright to Samuel Gorton, 26 May 1665, CO 1/19/f. 124; the Massachusetts declaration, 23 May 1665, and the reply of the commission, 24 May 1665, *NYCD,* 3:95-96, 96; and Bellingham to Secretary Morrice, 31 May 1665, CO 1/19/f. 150.

32. Nicolls to Winthrop, 23 June 1665, 27 February 1665/6, 2 May 1666, MHS, Winthrop Family Papers.

33. Commission for Symonds and Danforth, 2 June 1665, CO 1/19/f. 159; Cartwright to Nicolls, 3 June 1665, CO 1/19/f. 161; Maverick to Nicolls, 18 June 1665, CO 1/19/f. 163.

34. See the correspondence in Bouton, *Documents of New Hampshire,* 1:270-80; Barry, "The New Hampshire Merchant Interest," pp. 60-72; Lord, "Politics and Social Structure of Portsmouth," pp. 136-44; and petition of the New Hampshire towns, CO 1/19/ff. 193-94.

35. The summary report of the commission, CO 1/19/ff. 334–44 (copy in the Thomas Povey Papers, BL, Egerton MSS 2395, ff. 426–35; and Carr, Cartwright, and Maverick to Arlington, 26 July 1665, CO 1/19/f. 191.

36. Bellingham to the king, 1 August 1665, in Bouton, *Documents of New Hampshire,* 1:294–95.

37. Chasey's testimony, 7 April 1681, CO 1/44/f. 251; order of the Massachusetts General Court, 1 August 1665, CO 1/19/f. 206; summons and warrants for the arrest of Corbett, CO 1/19/ff. 245, 251, 260; justices of Maine to Nicolls, 22 November 1665, CO 1/19/f. 316.

38. Charles II to the commission, 5 December 1665, CO 1/19/f. 322; Maverick to Winthrop, 9 August, 29 August 1666, Nicolls to Winthrop, 29 August 1666, MHS, Winthrop Family Papers; royal letter of 10 April 1666, CO 1/20/ff. 88–89; and Clarendon to Nicolls, 13 April 1666, CO 1/20/no. 56.

39. The petition is in CO 1/20/f. 287, also in "Danforth Papers," *MHSC,* 2d ser. 8:103–8, with the names of the men from Boston, Salem, Newbury, and Ipswich.

40. Notes on the debates in the General Court, "Danforth Papers," *MHSC,* 2d ser. 8:98–101, 109–10; the letter of the General Court to the king, ibid., pp. 108–9 (also CO 1/20/f. 291).

41. Nicolls to Secretary Morrice, 24 October 1666, Bodl., MS Rawlinson A, vol. 175, f. 75; Berkeley to [Secretary Arlington], 11 November 1667, CO 1/21/f. 286; and notes by Joseph Williamson in 1667, CO 1/21/ff. 344–46.

42. Resolution of the Massachusetts General Court, ? May 1668, CO 1/22/f. 161; orders of the General Court, 21 May 1668, CO 1/22/f. 167; Nicolls to Arlington, 23 May 1669, CO 1/24/f. 114; Shapleigh to Nicolls, 25 December 1667, CO 1/21/f. 325; Shapleigh to Robert Mason, 20 May 1667, CO 1/21/f. 88.

43. Sandwich's journal, in Harris, *The Life of Edward Montagu, K. G., First Earl of Sandwich,* 2:219, 337–41; Evelyn, *Diary,* 3:584–85; minutes of New England affairs before the Council of Foreign Plantations, CO 1/26/f. 147; representation of the council, 12 August 1671, CO 1/27/f. 27.

44. Minutes of the Council of Foreign Plantations, CO 1/26/f. 147; Gorges's report, 16 February 1671/2, CO 1/28/f. 37; entry for 12 February 1671/2, Evelyn, *Diary,* 3:603.

45. Lewis, "Massachusetts and the Glorious Revolution," pp. 46–56; Lord, "Politics and Social Structure of Portsmouth," pp. 93–96; Lucas, *Valley of Discord,* pp. 65–70, 74–78; and Nicolls to Governor John Winthrop, 27 May 1667, MHS, Winthrop Family Papers.

46. Trumbull and Hoadley, *Records of Connecticut,* 2:543, 545–47, 551.

Chapter 7

1. Minutes of the lord proprietors of Carolina, 23 May 1663, CO 5/286/f. 3; Mattie Erma E. Parker, ed., *North Carolina Charters and Constitutions, 1578–1698* (Raleigh, N.C.: North Carolina State Department of Archives and History), pp. 76–89.

2. Order in council 10 June 1663, PC 2/56/p. 428; order in council, 12 August 1663, Shaftesbury Papers, PRO, 30/24/48 no. 2 (also in PC 2/56/p. 511).

3. Modyford and Colleton to [Albemarle], with the enclosed proposals, 12 August 1663, CO 5/286/ff. 7–8; the proprietary declaration and proposals, 21 August 1663, CO 5/286/ff. 6–8.

4. Proprietors to Modyford and Colleton, 30 August 1663, CO 5/286/ff. 6–7; Albemarle to Willoughby, 31 August 1663, CO 5/286/f. 7; [proprietors] to Modyford and Colleton, 9 September 1663, CO 5/286/f. 9; and the answer of the proprietors to the Barbadian proposals, 9 September 1663, CO 5/286/ff. 8–9.

5. Commission to Berkeley, [8] September 1663; instructions to Berkeley, 8 September 1663; and proprietors to Berkeley, 8 September 1663, CO 5/286/ff. 3–4, 5, 5–6.

6. Concessions and Agreements of January 1665, Shaftesbury Papers, PRO 30/24/48/no. 3; memorandum of agreement of the proprietors, 7 January 1664/5, CO 5/286/f. 11; proprietors to Drummond, 7 January 1664/5, CO 5/286/f. 13; commission to Sir John Yeamans, 11 January 1664/5, CO 5/286/ff. 11, 13; commission to Yeamans, ? January 1664/5, CO 5/286/ff. 9–10.

7. The charter of 1665 is printed in Bartholomew Rivers Carroll, ed., *Historical Collections of South Carolina,* 2 vols. (New York, 1836), 2:42–57.

8. Woodward to Sir John Colleton, 12 June 1665, Shaftesbury Papers, PRO 30/24/48/no. 4; Henry Vassall to [the proprietors], 15 August 1666, PRO 30/24/48/no. 5; and John Vassall to Sir John Colleton, 16 October 1667, PRO 30/24/48/no. 6.

9. Instructions and warrant to Stephens, [18] October 1667, CO 5/286/ff. 14, 15–17.

10. Haley, *Shaftesbury,* p. 241.

11. The memorial of the Surinam planters was received on 24 March 1668/9, CO 1/24/f. 66; agreement of 26 April 1669, PRO 30/24/48/no. 9.

12. At a meeting held at the Cockpit in Whitehall on 21 October 1669 Albemarle was elected the first palatine; Craven, high constable; Lord Berkeley, chancellor; Shaftesbury (Ashley), chief justice; Carteret, admiral; and Peter Colleton, high steward (CO 5/286/f. 25).

13. For a list of the provincial nobles and the proprietary deputies, see the proprietary entry book, CO 5/286/f. 42.

14. Southwell to Ashley, 31 August 1669, Shaftesbury Papers, PRO 30/24/48/no. 14.

15. Instructions for West, CO 5/286/ff. 19–20, 23.

16. It was later called Old Town or Old Charles Town. Ten years later the Carolinians moved Charles Town to Oyster Point, at the junction of the Ashley and Cooper Rivers.

17. Sayle to Ashley, 25 June 1670, PRO 30/24/48/no. 24; West to Ashley, 27 June 1670, ibid., no 25; Sayle and the council to the proprietors, 9 September 1670, ibid., no. 31; Sayle and the council to Ashley, 9 September 1670, ibid., no 29; and Dalton to Ashley, 9 September 1670, ibid., no. 30.

18. Yeamans to the proprietors, 15 November 1670, PRO 30/24/48/no. 46; Brayne to Ashley, 9 November 1670, to [Colleton], 20 November 1670, ibid., nos. 45, 49; Bull to Ashley, 12 September 1670, ibid., no. 35.

19. See Owen's election returns, Shaftesbury Papers, PRO 30/24/48/no. 26; West and the council to the proprietors, n.d., but enclosed in Joseph Dalton to the proprietors, 21 March 1670/1, ibid., nos. 64, 64(iii); and M. Eugene Sirmans, *Colonial South Carolina: A Political History, 1663–1763* (Chapel Hill: University of North Carolina Press, 1966), pp. 26–27.

20. Carolina Instructions, 1 May 1671, CO 5/286/ff. 33–35; temporary laws for Carolina, CO 5/286/ff. 35/36; and additional instructions, CO 5/286/f. 41.

21. Ashley to Yeamans, 18 September, 15 December 1671, PRO 30/24/48/no. 55, pp. 94–97, 100–101; Ashley to West, 16 December 1671, ibid., pp. 105–6; proprietary instructions, 16 December 1671, CO 5/286/f. 42; Ashley to Matthews, 15 December 1671, PRO 30/24/48/no. 55, p. 102; deputation to Matthews, 18 December 1671, CO 5/286/f. 40; and M. Eugene Sirmans, "Masters of Ashley Hall: A Biographical Study of the Bull Family of Colonial South Carolina," (Ph.D. diss., Princeton University, 1959), pp. 40–43.

22. West to Ashley, 1 September 1671, PRO 30/24/48/no. 76; Ashley to Yeamans, 20 June 1672, Ashley to Matthews, 20 June 1672, PRO 30/24/48/nos. 89, 55, pp. 110–11.

23. Ashley to West and the council, 20 June 1672, PRO 30/24/48/no. 55, pp. 112–13; Ashley to Colleton, 27 November 1672, ibid., no. 55, pp. 120–21. As proprietary chief justice, Ashley appointed West provincial register and encouraged him to maintain a constant correspondence with his patron to keep him informed of developments in Carolina (Ashley to West, 20 June, 25 June 1672, ibid., no. 55, pp. 113–14, 115.

24. There is an undated draft of a letter from the Carolina proprietors to Governor Stephens and the council of Albemarle entered in the proprietary entry book (CO 5/286/f. 17) in response to a petition from the assembly requesting that they hold lands on the same terms as those held in Virginia. The proprietors seemed willing to empower the local governor to make alterations, but apparently this did not extend to the tax rate.

25. Berkeley to the council of Albemarle, 7 March 1669/70, in *Ye Countie of Albemarle in Carolina: A Collection of Documents, 1664–1675,* ed. William S. Powell (Raleigh: North Carolina State Department of Archives and History, 1958), p. 38.

26. Even as late as 1686 John Archdale complained from North Carolina, "For present we have not immediate opportunities to send to England by reason there is no settled trade thither" (London, Friends House Library, ARB MSS, 1: no. 68, Archdale to George Fox, 25th of 1st month 1686 [March 25, 1686]).

27. Instructions to Carteret in Powell, *Countie of Albemarle,* p. 45; Carteret and the council to the proprietors, 16 May 1672, ibid., pp. 51–52.

28. Mattie Erma E. Parker, "Legal Aspects of 'Culpeper's Rebellion,' " *North Carolina Historical Review,* 45 (April 1968): 115–17.

29. The authorities of Connecticut put an end to Scott's pretensions as a governor. They carried him off to Hartford and locked him away, despite a plea

in his behalf sent by Governor Richard Bellingham to the governor of Connecticut. Scott was also a lobbyist for the Atherton Associates, whose members were, in the main, prominent Massachusetts residents. See Bellingham to Governor John Winthrop, 2 April 1664, MHS, Winthrop Family Papers.

30. Order in council, 13 April 1664, on the stores of war commanded on 25 February for Richard Nicolls, PC 2/57/p. 18; and warrant for a charter for James, CO 5/1111/p. 78.

31. Wesley Frank Craven, *The Colonies in Transition, 1660–1713* (New York: Harper & Row, 1968), p. 64, subscribed to the latter view.

32. James never did pay Stirling the money, but in lieu of the sum agreed on, in 1674 he granted the earl three hundred pounds a year, to be paid out of the surplus revenue raised in New York. Since there was to be no surplus revenue—indeed there was a chronic deficit—the annuity was constantly in arrears.

33. See the terms of the charter contained in the warrant to the law officers to prepare a bill for the king's signature, CO 5/1111/pp. 7–8.

34. Clinton Alfred Weslager, *The English on the Delaware: 1610–1682* (New Brunswick, N.J.: Rutgers University Press, [1967]), pp. 187–97.

35. Nicolls to Clarendon, 24 October, 26 October, 21 November 1664, JCBL, Clarendon Papers Relating to America, pp. 105, 113–15, 127–31; Nicolls to Governor John Winthrop, 7 February 1664/5, MHS, Winthrop Family Papers; Ludwell to Nicolls, 7 December 1664, HL, William Blathwayt Papers, BL81.

36. Clarendon to Nicolls, 11 February 1664/5, JCBL, Clarendon Papers Relating to America, pp. 87–89.

37. This line was thought not to intersect with the Hudson River when extended northwest. When this proved incorrect, the line was renegotiated in 1683.

38. Black, *Younger Winthrop,* p. 281; and John R. Brodhead, *History of the State of New York,* 2 vols. (New York, 1853–57), 2:53–55. For Nicolls's awareness of his dependence on the New England colonies, particularly Connecticut, for defense against the French and Dutch, see his letters to Governor John Winthrop, 23 June 1665, 27 February 1665/6, 2 May 1666, MHS, Winthrop Family Papers.

39. Laurence James Bradley, "The London / Bristol Trade Rivalry," pp. 131–33; Charles Howard McCormick, "Leisler's Rebellion," (Ph.D. diss., American University, 1971), p. 15; and Albert Rink Oener, "Merchants and Magnates: Dutch New York, 1609–1664," (Ph.D. diss., University of Southern California, 1976). At the time of the capitulation Nicolls had agreed to allow the Dutch for a limited time to engage in direct trade with the United Provinces. At the conclusion of the Second Dutch War, Stuyvesant, with the support of Nicolls, petitioned the crown for a restoration of trade with Holland on the gounds that Dutch goods were essential for the trade with the Indians, whose support was necessary against the French in Canada. Nicolls and his successor seemed to think that as an infant colony inadequately serviced by English shipping, New York needed the connection with Amsterdam. The English Privy Council in October 1667 granted permission—a dispensation from the Act of Navigation—for three vessels in each of the next seven years to sail directly from

the Netherlands to New York. But the following year this was revoked because of objections of the customs officials, the Council of Trade, and merchants in England that Dutch vessels might carry merchandise not only to New York but to other colonies as well. Exceptions to the navigation act were also made for Scottish vessels trading to New York, provided they did not carry colonial produce to any foreign territory. See Nicolls to John Winthrop, 2 March 1667/8 and Francis Lovelace to Winthrop, 24 February 1668/9, MHS, Winthrop Family Papers; minutes of the Committee for Foreign Plantations, 17 October 1667, CO 1/21/f. 275; order in council, 29 September 1668, PC 2/61/p. 49; report of the Council of Trade, ? November 1668, and order in council, 18 November 1668, CO 1/23/ff. 159–61, 163; memorial of the duke of York, 15 April 1669, and order in council, 5 April 1669, CO 1/24/ff. 67, 69. See also Jan Kupp, "Aspects of New York Dutch Trade under the English, 1670–1674," *New-York Historical Society Quarterly* 63 (April 1974): 139–47.

40. Robert Cowan Ritchie, *The Duke's Province: A Study of New York Politics and Society, 1664–1691* (Chapel Hill: University of North Carolina Press, [1977]), pp. 48–53.

41. Robert Cowan Ritchie, "The Duke of York's Commission of Revenue," *New-York Historical Society Quarterly* 58 (July 1974): 177–82; and Lovelace to Williamson, 3 October 1670, CO 1/25/no. 73. Nicolls's arrival in Portsmouth, England in a Dutch vessel was reported in Hugh Salisbury to Williamson, 11 October 1668, *CSPD, Charles II, 1668–1669,* p. 15.

42. See the petition of the eastern towns to the crown, CO 1/28/f. 195, referred to the Council on Foreign Plantations, PC 2/63/p. 275; Ritchie, *Duke's Province,* pp. 64–67; and especially Bradley, "Bristol / London Rivalry," for the backward state of the commerce of New York.

43. Lovelace to John Winthrop, 9 December 1670, MHS, Winthrop Family Papers; Charles Calvert to Lord Baltimore, 26 April 1672, Baltimore, Maryland Historical Society, Calvert Papers, no. 1064.

44. Weslager, *English on the Delaware,* pp. 198–99, and order in council, 19 August 1670, PC 2/62/p. 268.

45. The duke of York's release to Carteret and Berkeley dated 24 June 1664, in Aaron Leaming and Jacob Spicer, comps., *The Grants, Concessions, and Original Constitutions of the Province of New Jersey* (Philadelphia, Pa., [1752]; reprinted Somerville, N.J., 1881), p. 81; and James to Francis Lovelace, [December 1672], BL, Harleian MSS 7001, f. 209. For a discussion of the issue of the powers of government for New Jersey, see Andrews, *Colonial Period,* 3:138 n. 1. Some years later, when opposition to the proprietary claim to quitrents and government broke out in the New Jersey towns, the court sent a royal letter countersigned by Secretary of State Henry Coventry commanding all persons in New Jersey to obey the government established by Carteret and Berkeley, they allegedly having the sole power to settle and dispose of the country as they saw fit. Charles II to John Berry, 9 December 1672, BL Harleian MSS 7001, f. 299 (printed in Leaming and Spicer, *Original Constitutions,* pp. 38–39). This order may have reflected more the king's desire to support what his brother had done than a studied legal conclusion.

46. Leaming and Spicer, *Original Constitutions,* pp. 12–27; Nicolls to Governor John Winthrop, 2 August 1665, MHS, Winthrop Family Papers; Nicolls to the duke of York, [25 November 1665], CO 1/19/no. 138. Four years later Samuel Maverick, writing from New York, reported a garbled tale that Berkeley was under a cloud in England and would lose all of his offices and be forced to surrender the patent for New Jersey. New York would then be restored to its original boundaries. See Maverick to John Winthrop, 29 June, 29 December 1669, MHS, Winthrop Family Papers.

47. Leaming and Spicer, *Original Constitutions,* p. 77; declaration of the governor and council, 28 May 1672; the council to Philip Carteret, 1 July 1672, commission to Samuel Moore as agent in England, *Archives of the State of New Jersey,* ed. Frederick W. Ricord, William Nelson, et al., eds. 36 vols. (Newark: New Jersey Historical Society, 1881–1941): 1st ser. 1:89–91, 91–92, 93–94.

48. James to Lovelace [25 November 1672], Charles II to Berry, 9 December 1672, BL, Harleian MSS 7001, f. 299; explanatory declaration, 6 December 1672, Leaming and Spicer, *Original Constitutions,* pp. 32–34; proprietors to Berry, 10 December 1672, ibid., pp. 39–40; and the proprietors to the deputies of Elizabeth, Newark, and Piscataway, 11 December 1672, ibid., pp. 40–41.

49. See two accounts of the Dutch takeover of New York in CO 1/69/f. 131 and CO 1/30/ff. 117–19.

Chapter 8

1. Affidavit of Cooke, 20 June 1660, of Tilghman, 29 June 1660, CO 1/14/ff. 12, 12(i); Donnell MacClure Owings, *His Lordship's Patronage: Offices of Profit in Colonial Maryland* (Baltimore, Md.: Johns Hopkins University Press, 1953), p. 117; James Welch Vardaman, "The Baltimore Proprietary and the Growth of English Colonial Policy, 1630–1691," Ph.D. diss., Vanderbilt University, 1957), pp. 120–31; Andrews, *Colonial Period,* 2:322–23.

2. A Quaker in the colony reported that there were some men who wanted Fuller's neck but that he was able to withdraw from public life (Josiah Coale to George Fox [21 February 1660/1], London, Friends House Library, ARB MSS I, no. 53).

3. David William Jordan, "The Royal Period of Colonial Maryland, 1689–1715" (Ph.D. diss., Princeton University, 1966), pp. 4–10.

4. In the account of the Calverts (BL, Sloane MSS 3663, f. 26) the population in 1670 was estimated at between fifteen thousand and twenty thousand.

5. William A. Reavis, "The Maryland Gentry and Social Mobility, 1637–1676," *WMQ,* 3d ser. 14 (July 1957): 418–28.

6. Russell R. Menard, "From Servant to Freeholder: Status, Mobility, and Property Accumulation in Seventeenth-Century Maryland," *WMQ,* 3d ser. 30 (January 1973): 37–64.

7. See Secretary Francis Windebank to Charles I, 20 September 1640, in Edward Hyde, earl of Clarendon, *State Papers,* 3 vols. (Oxford, 1768–86),

2:120; and Henry Vane to Windebank, 24 September 1640, in Philip Yorke, 2d earl of Hardwicke, *Miscellaneous State Papers*, 2 vols. (London, 1778), 2:187. According to Archbishop William Laud, Leslie's secretary told two of the gentry of Durham: "We came not unsent for, and that oftener than once or twice, by our own great ones . . . your own lords" (William Laud, *Works*, 7 vols. [London, 1853], 3:293).

8. Berkeley to ———, 4 May 1667, BL, Add. MSS 28,218, f. 16.

9. Warrant dated 17 June 1660, CO 1/14/f. 7.

10. Berkeley's printed treatise of 1662, "A Perfect Description of Virginia," Thomas Povey Papers, BL, Egerton MSS 2395, f. 356.

11. See the analysis in Wesley Frank Craven, *White, Red, and Black: The Seventeenth-Century Virginian* (Charlottesville: University Press of Virginia, 1971).

12. For a contemporary description of the government of Virginia, see the account enclosed in Thomas Ludwell to Arlington, 18 July 1666, CO 1/20/ff. 218–19, 220–21. The best scholarly analysis is Warren Martin Billings, "Virginia's Deploured Condition, 1660–1676: The Coming of Bacon's Rebellion," (Ph.D. diss., Northern Illinois University, 1968), pp. 34–47, 54–77, 99–100, 128–36; and his "The Growth of Political Institutions in Virginia, 1634 to 1676," *WMQ*, 3d ser. 31 (April 1974): 225–42.

13. Spencer to his brother, 13 June 1672, BL, Sloane MSS 3511, f. 134.

14. For the rewards of the posts connected with finance and revenue, see William Fitzhugh to Henry Fitzhugh, 5 April 1687, *Fitzhugh Letters,* ed. Davis, pp. 215–16.

15. See Warren M. Billings, "The Causes of Bacon's Rebellion: Some Suggestions," *VMHB* 88 (October 1970): 409–35 (based on his dissertation), as a corrective to Bailyn, "Politics and Social Structure in Virginia," pp. 90–115.

16. Thomas Ludwell to [Arlington], 9 August 1665, CO 1/19/f. 213; Ludwell to Arlington, 18 July 1666, CO 1/20/ff. 219–20; Berkeley to Clarendon, 20 July 1666, Bodl., MS Clarendon, 84, ff. 230–31; governor and council of Virginia to Arlington, 13 July 1666, CO 1/20/ff. 199–200; Ludwell to Lord John Berkeley, 24 June 1667, CO 1/21/ff. 116–17; order in council, 13 December 1667, PC 2/60/p. 92; and Thomas Ludwell to Arlington, 7 June 1669, CO 1/24/f. 118.

17. See John Berkeley's letter of attorney to his brother, 8 November 1649, BL, Add. MSS 15,857, f. 38.

18. Berkeley and the council to ———, 28 March 1663, BL, Egerton MSS 2395, f. 365; Berkeley to Lord ———, 18 April 1663, ibid., f. 365; and Charles II to the governor and council, 3 August 1663, CO 1/17/ff. 177–78.

19. Thomas Ludwell to Arlington, 7 June 1667, CO 1/21/ff. 116–17; Norwood to Joseph Williamson, 17 July 1667, CO 1/21/f. 156 with enclosure, ibid., f. 158; and Ludwell to Arlington, 7 June 1669, CO 1/24/f. 118.

20. Petition of Saint Albans et al., CO 1/25/ff. 6–7; Charles II to Sir William Berkeley [26 January 1669/70], CO 1/25/f. 8.

21. Memorandum by Alexander Culpeper and annexed agreement signed by Arlington and Thomas Culpeper, CO 1/28/ff. 41, 43; order in council, 23

June 1675, CO 389/3/11. Revenue from the tax of two shillings per hogshead of tobacco exported from the colony and the duties shipmasters paid to raise funds for munitions for the forts were also diverted to finance the activities of the agents, according to Robert Beverley, *The History and Present State of Virginia,* ed. Louis B. Wright (Chapel Hill: University of North Carolina Press, 1947), pp. 75-76.

22. Price, *France and the Chesapeake,* 1:509. Data for prices on a year-to-year basis for the tobacco trade are difficult to come by, and the literature is often contradictory. One scholar's year of prosperity is another's year of depression. There is agreement that the years following the Restoration witnessed a general decline in the price for tobacco on the Chesapeake. For an assessment of prices received by planters in Maryland during these years, see Russell R. Menard, "Farm Prices of Maryland Tobacco, 1659-1710," *Maryland Historical Magazine* 68 (Spring 1973): 80-85.

23. John Bannister to Robert Morison, 6 April 1679, LPL, Fulham Palace Papers, XI, f. 8. For the varieties of tobacco grown and the problems in marketing, see Arthur Pierce Middleton, *Tobacco Coast: A Maritime History of the Chesapeake Bay in the Colonial Era* (Newport News, Va.: Mariners' Museum, 1953), pp. 97-98; Jacob M. Price, "The Economic Growth of the Chesapeake and the European Market, 1697-1775," *Journal of Economic History* 24 (December 1964): 496-500. The European governments quickly discovered they could extract a significant revenue by taxing tobacco at rates exceeding 100 percent of cost. In England and a few other places this revenue was obtained by import or excise duties alone. In Spain, Portugal, most of the German and Italian states, and France (in 1674), it was found that the highest yield could be obtained by a state-sanctioned monopoly. Before 1674 high duties on foreign tobacco protected the leaf produced in the French colonies. Domestic planting was also restricted by the French monarchy (Price, *France and the Chesapeake,* 1:xviii, 5-15, 17.

24. Berkeley to Richard Nicolls, 4 October 1664, HL, Blathwayt Papers, BL 67. For shipping problems and freight rates see Ralph Davis, *Rise of the English Shipping Industry,* pp. 285-89.

25. For information on the various marketing procedures and evidence that the Virginians were not locked into any single method or forced to deal with a particular merchant, see Davis, *Fitzhugh Letters;* and Robert Anderson's letter book, Alderman Library, University of Virginia, Charlottesville, especially Anderson's letter to Micajah Perry and Company, 10 August 1714; to John Page, 27 April 1710; to Francis Magson and John Gibson, 26 April 1701; to Cuthbert Jones, 17 July 1705; 19 September 1709; and to Richard Lee, 11 January 1713.

26. Berkeley's printed paper, BL, Egerton MSS 2395, ff. 354-59; James Ming to ———, 30 June 1692, BL, Portland MSS, Loan 29/285. For a list of Bristol merchants engaged in the trade in 1665, see their petition for a convoy, PRO, SP 29/133/no. 66. For the London merchants, see Paul Gilbert Clements, "From Tobacco to Grain: Economic Development in Maryland's Eastern Shore, 1660-1750," (Ph.D. diss., University of Wisconsin, 1974), pp. 6-9.

27. Billings, "Coming of Bacon's Rebellion," pp. 157–58, 174.

28. See Clements, "From Tobacco to Grain." The present author cannot agree with Clements that diversification, simply putting more emphasis on grains and less on tobacco, would have been very difficult, provided the planters were not concerned with immediate, short-term gains. Rainbolt, *From Prescription to Persuasion,* p. 86, appreciated that the economic revolution in the West Indies offered the Chesapeake planters a market for provisions and livestock. But, he argued, with the commitment to tobacco, the indebtedness of the Virginia and Maryland planters to English merchants (actually these were credits extended by the merchants) had grown to an estimated fifty thousand pounds by 1664. This required the planters to continue producing tobacco in order to make remittances to England. This explanation ignored the possibility of the Chesapeake growers obtaining remittances by bills of exchange, by credits earned through the sale of provisions to the West Indies. Rainbolt thought that officials during Berkeley's later administration were not ignorant of what was happening in the West Indies but gave scant encouragement to trade there, perhaps, as he speculated, because of their adherence to traditional mercantile doctrine, their concern to serve the mother country directly. This explanation seems weak, if only because of the strong opposition of Berkeley and others to the navigation law and their effort to retain Dutch shippers in the tobacco trade. An exception among the Virginians was William Byrd, a merchant and a planter, whose activities illustrated how the economy of the Chesapeake might have been better integrated into the commerce of the Atlantic community. He corresponded with English merchants, New Englanders, and Barbadians and dealt in rum, sugar, Madeira wine, earthenware, and any suitable commodity and, if necessary, made remittances in bills of exchange. See, for example, Byrd to Elisha Hutchinson, 29 May 1689 and Byrd to Jonathan Walke, 29 May 1689, *Byrd Correspondence,* ed. Tinling 1:103, 104.

29. See the orders in council on the statutory prohibition and the petitions of the merchants for proclamations to execute the law, 21 December 1660, 28 February 1660/1, 20 March 1660/1, PC 2/55/pp. 76, 147, 171–72.

30. Orders in council, 28 August, 6 September, 27 September 1661, PC 2/55/pp. 357, 370, 384–85.

31. Petition of the planters and merchants of Virginia, 14 May 1662, CO 1/16/f. 145; minutes of the Privy Council, 26 May 1662, CO 1/16/f. 161; petition of John Bland and others, 13 June 1662, CO 1/16/ff. 165–66; orders in council, 13 June, 29 June, 1662, CO 1/16/f. 167, PC 2/56/p. 33.

32. Petition of Berkeley [July 1662], CO 1/16/ff. 183–84; petition of the shipmasters, 18 August 1662, CO 1/16/f. 207; petition of Berkeley, Chicheley, Digges, and Richard Lee, 26 August 1662, CO 1/16/f. 220; petition of Tilghman and others, 6 September 1662, CO 1/16/ff. 227–28, 229–30; petition of Jeffreys and others, 8 January 1662/3, CO 1/17/f. 1.

33. Royal instructions to Berkeley, 12 September 1662, CO 324/1/pp. 263–72 (also in CO 5/1354/ff. 270–81); order in council, 3 September 1662, PC 2/56/p. 123; Berkeley to Lord ———, 30 March 1663, BL, Egerton MSS 2395, ff. 362–63.

34. Virginia remonstrance, 10 August 1664, CO 1/18/f. 202; order in

council, 10 August 1664, PC 2/57/p. 181; Virginia petition and representation, 16 November 1664, CO 1/18/ff. 311, 312-13; Baltimore's case, 19 November 1664, CO 1/18/ff. 318-19; orders of the Committee for Plantations and orders in council, 5 October 1664, PC 2/57/p. 234; 16 November 1664, PC 2/57/p. 293, 25 November 1664, PC 2/57/pp. 302-3; memorandum by Secretary Bennet, 19 November 1664, CO 1/18/f. 322.

    35. Berkeley to Arlington, 1 August 1665, CO 1/19/ff. 202-3; Berkeley to Clarendon, 20 July 1666, Bodl., MS Clarendon, 84, f. 230; articles of agreement by the Virginia and Maryland commissioners, 12 July, 11 December 1666, CO 1/20/ff. 193-94, 238; Berkeley and the Virginia council to Arlington, 13 July 1666, CO 1/20/ff. 199-200; Thomas Ludwell to Arlington, 12 February 1666/7, CO 1/21/f. 37; Baltimore's disallowance, 24 November 1666, CO 1/20/f. 319; Berkeley and the Virginia council to the king, ? June 1667, CO 1/21/ff. 109-12.

    36. Virginia representation, CO 1/21/ff. 118-21; Baltimore's answer, CO 1/21/ff. 269-70; orders in council, 16, 30 October 1667, PC 2/60/p. 23, 40-41; report of the Committee for Plantations, 30 October 1667, CO 1/21/f. 281.

    37. Berkeley to [Arlington], 11 November 1667, CO 1/21/f. 286; Berkeley to [Richard Nicolls], 7 July 1668, HL, Blathwayt Papers, BL75; governor, council, and burgesses to Charles II, 22 July 1668, CO 1/23/f. 41; Berkeley to the Committee for Plantations, 22 January 1671/2, CO 1/28/f. 9.

    38. Conditions on the Chesapeake were reported in shipping intelligence in the western outports. See *CSPD, Charles II, 1670,* pp. 104, 178, 219; *1667-1668,* pp. 85, 346, 333; *1671,* pp. 2, 133; *1675-1676,* pp. 81, 98, 134, 141, 342.

Chapter 9

    1. William Penn to William Bridgeman, 1 [August] 1683, *PMHB* 6, no. 4 (1882): 473-74.

    2. James Rees Jones, *The Revolution of 1688 in England* (New York: W. W. Norton, 1972), pp. 24-27; Plumb, *The Origins of Political Stability,* pp. 10-11.

    3. Jones, *Saw-Pit Wharton,* pp. 240, 223. See also Francis S. Ronalds, *The Attempted Whig Revolution of 1678-1681* (Urbana: University of Illinois Press, 1937); and J. R. Jones, *The First Whigs: The Politics of the Exclusion Crisis, 1673-1683* (London: Oxford University Press, 1961).

    4. See *CSPD, Charles II, 1675-1676,* pp. 435, 438; notes by Williamson of talks with Sir Peter Colleton about Martinique and Barbados, 20 December 1676, SP 29/366/269; and order in council, 5 May 1675, on a report of the Committee for Plantations, 15 April 1675, PC 2/64/pp. 413-16.

    5. On the role of Scott in the attack on Pepys see Bryant, *Pepys,* 2:203-7; G. W. Keeton, *Lord Chancellor Jeffreys and the Stuart Cause* (London: Macdonald, 1965), pp. 125, 129; Clayton Roberts, *The Growth of Responsible Government in Stuart England* (Cambridge: Cambridge University Press, 1966), p. 228; and Haley, *Shaftesbury,* pp. 520-21.

    6. Haley, *Shaftesbury,* p. 520. For an example of the charges levied against the duke of York, see Michael Browne to Thomas Conyngsby, 27 October 1682, SP 29/421/nos. 36, 37, ff. 68-75.

7. The reference to the "private committee" was made by William Blathwayt in a letter to Sir Robert Southwell, 18 September 1676, NUL, Portland MSS, PwV51. This may simply have been a reference to the committee of foreign affairs.

8. James to the duke of Lauderdale, 16 December 1679, BL, Add. MSS 23245, f. 31.

9. That is the conclusion of Gerald R. Cragg, *Puritanism in the Period of the Great Persecution, 1660-1668* (Cambridge: Cambridge University Press, 1957), p. 25, generally sympathetic to the Nonconformists. Charles Bryant, *King Charles II* (London: Longmans, Green, 1931), pp. 242-43, 257, 262-69 is more certain in his conclusion. See also Maurice Cranston, *John Locke: A Biography,* (London: Longmans, Green, 1957), p. 219.

10. Plumb, *Origins of Political Stability,* pp. 52-56; Arthur G. Smith, "London and the Crown, 1681-1685," (Ph.D. diss., University of Wisconsin, 1967), pp. 278-87; and Jennifer Levin, *The Charter Controversy in the City of London, 1660-1688, and Its Consequences* (London: Athlone Press, 1969), pp. 60-68.

11. Plumb, *Origins of Political Stability,* pp. 62, 113, 123-25, deals with the consequences of the large-scale involvement in international wars between 1689 and 1714, when the English monarchy was engaged in the first of a series of extended continental and colonial conflicts with France. Prolonged war on a scale vastly beyond anything English governments had been called upon previously to wage led to a great expansion of governmental activity and an increase in the number of persons employed and an augmentation of the power of the Treasury. The most extravagant claim is that in Webb, " 'Brave Men and Servants to His Royal Highness,' " one aspect of a much larger study Webb plans to publish. His thesis is that English imperialism was always militaristic and statist and that the instrument for this imperialism was the corps of royalist officers sent out to govern the colonies and to establish garrison regimes. Also important were the men in the royal duke's household in coordinating the administration of imperial government. James presided over an interlocking directorate of officials, extending to every department of colonial administration except Shaftesbury's Council of Plantations, an agency terminated in 1675. In addition, James had drawn about him Royalist military men who during the years of exile after the Civil War had served with James in the campaigns of the French army in Europe. These were the men later sent out after the Restoration to rule in America. While serving in the French army, James had learned, according to Webb, that effective political control depended on force, a lesson confirmed in the bitter political struggles after 1660. Royalism, French militarism, and absolutism shaped the policies of the duke for the empire and in reestablishing what Webb sees as the Cromwellian network of garrison towns in England. Once this had been accomplished in England, the same technique of military government could be applied to the colonies. For a criticism of Webb's thesis on the use of the army see above, Chapter 3, note 15.

As to the view that the men of the duke's household constituted an interlocking directory controlling almost all of the offices of government for the colonies, Stuart bureaucracy was simply not that efficient—neither was

Bourbon—and the opposition to the royal duke or to any other politician was just too strong in the chaotic world of Restoration politics. That James and the men he employed were Royalist goes without question; that they were militarist and statist is not proven. The military forces sent out to the colonies—even the force under Colonel Herbert Jeffreys dispatched to end a civil war in Virginia—were totally inadequate for the purpose of intimidating the English settlers.

There was a more sensible and indeed more obvious reason for the dispatch of experienced officers with relatively small detachments to the colonies to lead the English settlers, a reason made clear by Professor Ian Steele of the University of Western Ontario at the annual meeting of the Organization of American Historians on 10 April 1976, when he commented on a paper delivered by Webb. In the twenty-three years after 1652 the English were at war in the Western Hemisphere with the Dutch and the Spanish during all but one year (1671). During that period the Dutch captured Antigua, Montserrat, Saint Christopher's, and New York. That thirteen years of peace would follow could not have been predicted at the time. Even before the outbreak of prolonged conflict with France in 1689, it was clear that the English in America would be drawn into the hostilities already raging between the French and the Iroquois in North America. And once the conflict with the French broke out, the fires which destroyed Canso, Deerfield, Schenectady, Nevis, and Saint Kitts gave evidence that military leadership was indeed needed. Few colonists had the requisite military ability. The colonels of the English army were sent out to the colonies to provide leadership and military experience for the colonial militia in an age of chronic war. The detachments of redcoats accompanying Edmund Andros, Richard Nicolls, and their colleagues were simply too small to be used to overawe and to coerce the English population in America. And the experience of the officers who served as governors hardly demonstrated an intention, much less an ability, to dominate the English subjects by force.

12. Customs to the Committee for Trade, 3 November 1681, SP 29/417/no. 75; order in council, 3 March 1681/2, CO 324/4/pp. 81–82.

13. Entry for 6 December 1679, journal of the Committee for Plantations, CO 1/43/f. 312; Southwell to Clarendon, 18 September 1678, CO 1/42/no. 127; Lords of Trade to Clarendon, 24 May 1678, CO 1/42/f. 168; Committee for Plantations to Berkeley, 10 April 1676, CO 1/36/f. 80. Many of the letters from Berkeley and Ludwell are among the private papers of Henry Coventry at Longleat, Wilts.

14. Blathwayt to James Vernon [Het] Loo, 7/17 September 1700, BL, Add. MSS 40, 774, f. 305.

15. "An Overture for the Better Regulation of the Foreign Plantations," Thomas Povey Papers, BL, Egerton MSS 2395, f. 276 (also in Danby Papers, BL, Egerton 3340, ff. 148–49); order in council 12 March 1674/5, CO 389/10/pp. 1–2 (also in CO 324/4/pp. 7–8 and PC 2/64/p. 395). During the crisis over the Popish Plot, when the king was forced to reorganize the council in April 1679, this committee was greatly expanded, but it is doubtful under these circumstances whether it was allowed any real power. See William Blathwayt's "Establishment and Accounts of the Committee for Trade and Plantations," vol. 1, BL, Add. MSS 9767, p. 62 and PC 2/68/p. 1. After 1675 other councilors

with particular interests in the colonies were admitted to the committee: Henry, earl of Saint Albans, and Henry Compton, bishop of London, in 1676. Compton, on becoming bishop of London in 1675, almost immediately put forth claims for his see to ecclesiastical jurisdiction over the American colonies and offered specific reforms for the parishes in Virginia. His memorial (17 July 1677) is in CO 1/41/ff. 48-50 (in the colonial entry book, CO 5/723/p. 27 it is misdated 26 July 1677). There was no written record that the Privy Council granted Compton the authority he requested. The crown law officers in 1725 concluded that indeed none had been granted. See the minutes of the Committee for Trade and Plantations, 24 January 1675/6, 19 July 1677, 15 April 1685, Fulham Palace Papers, vol. 36, ff. 11, 13, 15, LPL; and the discussion in J. H. Bennet, "English Bishops and Imperial Jurisdiction, 1660-1725," *HMPEC* 32 (September 1963): 175-88; Carpenter, *Life of Henry Compton,* pp. 252-54; Arthur Lyon Cross, *The Anglican Episcopate and the American Colonies* (New York: Longmans, Green, 1902), pp. 15-29.

16. Order in council, 5 May 1676, CO 389/3/p. 71.

17. Blathwayt to Lord Culpeper, 4 April 1680, CW, Blathwayt Papers, vol. 17; Florence May Grier Evans, *The Principal Secretary of State: A Survey of the Office from 1558 to 1680* (London: Longmans, Green, 1923), pp. 148-49, 318-19; John P. Kenyon, *Robert Spencer, Earl of Sunderland, 1641-1702* (London: Longmans, Green, 1958), pp. 80-81, 91.

18. Report of the Plantation Committee, 24 April 1676, and order in council, 3 May 1676, CO 389/3/pp. 69-71; Southwell to Ormonde, 13 July, 27 August 1678, in HMC, *Ormonde MSS,* 10 vols. in 2 ser. (London, 1895-1916), n.s. 4:444, 449. See also Blathwayt to Southwell, 18 September, 9 December, 16 December 1676, NUL, Portland MSS, PwV51.

19. Southwell to Ormonde, 20 November 1677, 27 August 1678, HMC, *Ormonde,* n.s. 4:386, 447.

20. Gertrude Ann Jacobsen, *William Blathwayt, a Late Seventeenth Century English Administrator* (New Haven, Conn.: Yale University Press, 1932), pp. 106, 187-88.

21. Blathwayt to Southwell, 25 July 1679; 23 April, 21 May, 11 June, 29 July, 22 October, 8 November 1681; 5 April 1682, NUL, Portland MSS, PwV51, 52.

22. Southwell to Bridgeman, 10 January 1675/6, SP 29/378/f. 82, no. 54; orders in council, 28 April, 3 May 1676, CO 389/3/pp. 68, 69; Blathwayt to Lord Culpeper, 5 April 1680, CW, Blathwayt Papers, vol. 17; order in council, 12 December 1679, CO 1/43/f. 317; order in council, 8 November 1680, CO 1/46/f. 76.

23. Order in council, 6 June 1679, CO 1/43/f. 123; PC 2/68/p. 90; CO 389/11/p. 168; customs commissioners to the Treasury, 14 April 1679, CO 1/43/f. 72; and "Some Observations about the Plantations," endorsed as a memorial concerning the plantation trade from Lord Culpeper, n.d., Danby Papers, BL, Add. MSS 28,079, ff. 84-85.

24. Blathwayt's report to the Treasury on the revenue in the plantations, 4 October 1689, PRO, Treas. 64/88/ff. 26-27; Blathwayt to Culpeper, 2 September 1680, CW, Blathwayt Papers, vol. 17.

25. Order in council, 27 June 1679, PC 2/68/150-51; Blathwayt to Nicholas Spencer, 28 July 1684, CW, Blathwayt Papers, vol. 16.

26. Representation of the Committee for Plantations, 28 October 1680, CO 389/11/pp. 208-9 (also in SP 29/414/no. 129); order in council, 6 November 1680, CO 389/11/pp. 210-11; journal of the receiver general of the plantation revenue, Treas. 64/88/ff. 19-20; Customs to the Committee for Plantations, 3 November 1681, SP 29/417/no. 75; Blathwayt to Henry Guy (secretary to the Treasury), 14 February 1681/2, SP 29/418/no. 107; report of the Committee for Plantations, 28 February 1681/2, and order in council, 3 March 1681/2, CO 324/4/pp. 81-82.

27. Orders in council, 17 July 1674, 7 July 1675, 7 July 1680, 30 June 1681, PC 2/64/262, 462, PC 2/69/32, 312.

28. Robert Southwell to Charles Bertie, 23 September 1675, CO 324/4/p. 21; Customs to the Lords of Trade and Plantations, 11 October 1675, CO 324/4/pp. 22-25; Southwell to Sir William Jones, 28 January 1675/6, CO 324/4/p. 28; Jones to the Committee for Plantations, 8 February 1675/6, CO 324/4/pp. 29-30. See also Customs to the lord treasurer, 11 October 1675, CO 1/35/f. 237; and Southwell to William Bridgeman, 10 January 1675/6, SP 29/378/no. 82.

29. Customs Board to the Lords of Trade, 22 April 1678, CO 1/42/f. 120.

30. Petition of the mercers, read at the Committee of Trade, 10 April 1676, CO 1/36/f. 79; petition of the twenty-eight London merchants, CO 1/36/f. 16 (also in CO 5/903/pt. 2, pp. 85-88); minutes of the Lords of Trade, 28 January 1675/6, CO 5/903/pt. 2, pp. 85, 108-10; questions to be asked of the New England (London) traders, 18 April 1676, CO 1/36/ff. 83-84; and Robert Mason to Danby, 5 March 1675/6, Danby Papers, BL, Egerton MSS 3340, f. 155. This trade at times involved stopping at an English port to obtain clearance papers to cover voyages there undertaken and to load goods in Scotland or Europe. See Robert Holden to the Customs Board, Boston, 10 June 1679, CO 1/43/ff. 124-26. This pattern demonstrated that the object of the trade was not to avoid expensive, burdensome "jogs," stops at English ports, but to avoid paying customs.

31. Report of the Lords of Trade, 6 February 1676/7, CO 1/39/f. 57 (also in CO 5/903/pp. 179-81).

32. See the orders of the Committee for Trade and Plantations for letters to the governors of New Jersey, Connecticut, and Rhode Island, CO 389/11/pp. 265-66; and the Lords of Trade to the king, 30 September 1682, CO 324/4/pp. 84-85.

33. Those are the arguments of Stephen Saunders Webb, "William Blathwayt, Imperial Fixer: Muddling through to Empire, 1689-1717," *WMQ*, 3d ser. 26 (July 1969): 379-410; and Philip S. Haffenden, "The Crown and Colonial Charters, 1675-1688," *WMQ*, 3d ser. 15 (July and October 1958): 297-311, 452-66.

34. Richard D. Dunn, "The Downfall of the Bermuda Company: A Restoration Farce," *WMQ*, 3d ser. 20 (October 1963): 501.

35. See the account by the secretary of state, James Vernon, BL, Add. MSS 40,774, f. 341.

Chapter 10

1. Sir William Berkeley to Secretary Arlington, 11 November 1667, CO 1/21/f. 286.

2. Nicholas Spencer to ———, 6 August 1676, Longleat House, Coventry MSS, vol. 77, f. 170.

3. William Berkeley to Lord John Berkeley, 18 March 1674/5, Coventry MSS, vol. 76, f. 337; Berkeley to Henry Coventry, 1 April 1676, ibid., vol. 77, f. 68.

4. Giles Bland to Williamson, 28 April 1676, with enclosed paper, CO 1/36/ff. 109, 111–12; order of the General Court at Jamestown, 17 October 1675, CO 1/35/f. 245; minutes of the Virginia council, 21 November 1674, Povey Papers, BL, Egerton MSS 2395, f. 486; order of the General Court, 21 November 1674, CO 1/31/f. 228, and the relation of John Bland, n.d., CO 1/36/f. 14. For the younger Bland's charges on enforcement of the trade laws, see Giles Bland to Sir William Berkeley, 16 September 1675, Povey Papers, BL, Egerton MSS 2395, ff. 511–13.

5. Papers submitted by John Bland to the lord treasurer, Longleat, Coventry MSS, vol. 77, f. 329; petition of Sarah Bland to the king, n.d., CO 1/36/f. 86; memoranda and report of the Lords of Trade, 15 June, 27 July 1676, CO 1/37/ff. 14, 15.

6. Memorial of the Virginia council, n.d. but endorsed as received 11 October 1673, CO 1/30/f. 179.

7. The best discussion of the situation in Virginia at this time is in the dissertation by Billings, "Coming of Bacon's Rebellion," pp. 155–75. See also his "The Causes of Bacon's Rebellion," pp. 409–35.

8. Sir Henry Chicheley to Sir Thomas Chicheley, 16 July 1673, with enclosed petition from Berkeley and the council, CO 1/30/ff. 113, 114.

9. Southwell to Coventry, 7 March 1675/6, CO 1/36/f. 57; petition of the Virginia agents read in council 19 April 1676, CO 1/36/f. 84; orders in council, 19 April, 31 May 1676, PC 2/65/187, 243 (also in CO 389/3/pp. 66–67, 84).

10. Berkeley to Thomas Ludwell, 1 April 1676, CO 1/36/ff. 67–68; Berkeley to [Williamson], 1 April 1676, CO 1/36/ff. 65–66; Bland to Williamson, 28 April 1676, with enclosed "Considerations upon the Present Troubles in Virginia . . . ," CO 1/36/ff. 109, 111–12.

11. "A Narrative of the Rise, Progress, and Cessation of the Late Rebellion in Virginia," compiled by Samuel Wiseman, secretary to the royal commission sent out to investigate the uprising, Wiseman's entry book, Pepys 2582, Magdalen College Library, Cambridge University. Another copy is CO 5/1371, printed with commentaries, by Charles McLean Andrews, ed., *Narratives of the Insurrections, 1675–1690* (New York: Charles Scribner's Sons, 1915), pp. 107–40.

12. Sherwood to Williamson enclosing Berkeley's declaration, 1 June 1676, CO 1/37/f. 1; Virginia council to the Lords of Trade, 31 May 1676, Coventry MSS, vol. 77, f. 96; Berkeley to Coventry, 3 June 1676, Coventry MSS, vol. 77, f. 103 and Berkeley's call for elections, 10 May 1676, CO 1/36/f. 137.

13. Wilcombe E. Washburn, *The Governor and the Rebel: A History of Bacon's Rebellion in Virginia* (Chapel Hill: University of North Carolina Press, 1957), pp. 58–66; Billings, "Coming of Bacon's Rebellion," pp. 101–4, 111–12; Billings, "Causes of Bacon's Rebellion," pp. 430–33; and Philip Ludwell to [Williamson], 28 June 1676, CO 1/37/ff. 35–38. For a more traditional view of these acts and of Bacon as a reformer, see Richard L. Morton, *Colonial Virginia*, 2 vols. (Chapel Hill: University of North Carolina Press, 1960), 1:256–58.

14. Thomas Bacon to the king, n.d., with address, CO 1/37/ff. 31, 33; Sherwood to Williamson, 28 June 1676, CO 1/37/ff. 39–40; Philip Ludwell to Williamson, 28 June 1676, CO 1/37/ff. 35–38.

15. "The Virginians' Plea," CO 1/37/ff. 29–30; Bacon's account, misdated 18 June 1676, in Thomas Povey Papers, BL, Egerton MSS 2395, f. 551; "Bacon's Letter," n.d., CO 5/1371/pt. i, pp. 241–46; Giles Bland to Povey, 8 July 1676, CO 1/37/f. 84.

16. Berkeley to Secretary Coventry, 1 July 1676; Spencer to [Lord John Berkeley], 6 August 1676, Longleat House, Coventry MSS, vol. 77, ff. 146, 170.

17. Bacon's appeal, CO 5/1371/pt. i, pp. 254–63, and the characterization of Bacon, probably by Samuel Wiseman, ibid., p. 263.

18. Bacon's "Declaration of the People," in Povey Papers, BL, Egerton MSS 2395, ff. 547–48 (also in CO 1/37/f. 128; in Hyde Papers, Add. MSS 17,018, f. 110; and Bodl., MS Rawlinson, A, 180, f. 306); "Declaration of the People of Virginia" [3 August 1676], Povey Papers, BL, Egerton MSS 2395, f. 552 (also in CO 1/37/ff. 130–31); "Declaration of the Chief Persons in Virginia" [4 August 1676], Povey Papers, BL, Egerton MSS 2395, F. 553.

19. Information presented by Berkeley, CO 5/1371/pt. i, pp. 232–40. See also the cryptic document, "Complaint from Heaven with a Hue and Cry and a Petition out of Virginia and Maryland," CO 1/36/ff. 213–18, charging a conspiracy by Baltimore, the Papists (in conjunction with the French in Canada), and Berkeley, turned into a covetous fool by marriage with a young woman.

20. "A Narrative of the Late Rebellion," Pepys 2582, Magdalene College, Cambridge; Bacon's manifesto, CO 1/37/ff. 178–79.

21. For detailed accounts of the rebellion, see Washburn, *The Governor and the Rebel;* Billings, "Coming of Bacon's Rebellion," and the narrative compiled by an investigating commission, Pepys 2582, Magdalene College, printed in Andrews, *Narratives of the Insurrections,* pp. 107–40.

22. Henry Coventry to Sir William Berkeley, 15 November 1676, BL, Add. MSS 25,120, f. 94; Coventry to Berkeley, 10 July 1676 [marked as not sent], Add. MSS 25,120, f. 82; Coventry to Berkeley, 14 July 1676, Add. MSS 25,120, f. 88; minutes of the meeting of the committee endorsed, heads of dispatch, Virginia, 22 August 1676; Longleat, Coventry MSS, vol. 77, ff. 187–92; warrant to the attorney general, 9 September 1676, CO 324/2/p. 99 (also in CO 5/1355/pp. 94–96).

23. Arlington to Williamson, 2 October 1676, SP 29/385/f. 217; Moryson to Sir William Jones, ? October 1676, CO 1371/pt. i, ff. 8–13 and "Proposals," by Ludwell and Smith, n.d., CO 1/38/f. 35.

24. Commission to Jeffreys, Berry, and Moryson, 3 October 1676, CO 5/1355/pp. 83–85; order in council, 10 October 1676, CO 389/6/pp. 137–38; additional instructions to Berkeley, 13 October 1676, CO 5/1355/pp. 111–14; proclamation of 27 October 1676, CO 1/38/ff. 12–14 (also in CO 389/6/pp. 140–44 and CO 5/1355/pp. 129–32).

25. Coventry's particulars to be considered by the Committee for Foreign Affairs, Bodl., MS Rawlinson A. 185, f. 259; Williamson's notes, 3 October 1676, CO 1/37/ff. 209–11, 213–17; Charles II to Berkeley, and to Chicheley, 5 November 1676, CO 5/1355/pp. 127, 128; warrant for a commission for Jeffreys, 7 November 1676, CO 5/1355/pp. 86–90; royal instructions, 11 November 1676, CO 5/1355/p. 120; Coventry to Berkeley, 15 November 1676, BL, Add. MSS 25,120, f. 94. On the commission of Oyer and Terminer, see Coventry to Sir William Jones, with memorandum, 14 November 1676, CO 389/6/pp. 183–84, 184–85; and Williamson to Coventry, 13 October 1676, SP, 44/43/p. 119.

26. Berry and Moryson to Berkeley, 29 January 1676/7, CO 5/1371/pt. i, pp. 17–20; Berry and Moryson to Williamson, 2 February 1676/7, CO 1/39/ff. 52–53; Berry and Moryson to Thomas Watkins, 2 February 1676/7, CO 1/39/f. 56; declaration of Berry and Moryson, 6 February 1676/7, CO 5/1371/pt. i, pp. 39–40; Berkeley to Coventry, with note by Thomas Ballard and Philip Ludwell, 9 February 1676/7, Longleat, Coventry MSS, vol. 77, f. 382.

27. Berry and Moryson to Watkins, 10 February 1676/7, CO 1/39/ff. 66–67; Berkeley to Moryson, 11 February 1676/7, CO 5/1371/pt. i, pp. 68–70; Washburn, *Governor and Rebel,* pp. 110–13.

28. Commissioners to Coventry, to Williamson, and to Thomas Watkins, 27 March 1677, CO 5/1371/pt. i, pp. 132–47, 152–59, 168–75.

29. The royal commissioners drew up commentaries and replies for each of the county returns. The latter are to be found as follows: Nansemond, CO 1/39/nos. 96–97, 99; Isle of Wight, CO 1/39/nos. 82, 84; Accomack, CO 1/39/no. 76; Henrico, CO 1/39/no. 90; Elizabeth City, CO 1/39/no. 94; James City, CO 1/39/no. 58; Lancaster, CO 1/39/no. 77; New Kent, CO 1/39/no. 86; Northampton, CO 1/39/no. 74; Stafford, CO 1/39/no. 64; Surrey, CO 1/39/nos. 68, 69; Warwick, CO 1/39/no. 80; Westmoreland, CO 1/39/no. 72 and York, CO 1/39/no. 92. These returns in a more legible hand with commentaries by Moryson and Berry are in the commission's entry book, CO 5/1371/pt. ii.

30. Washburn argued that the rebellion cut across class lines, that leaders on both sides held large amounts of land, while followers of each group possessed but modest estates, and that the leaders of the movement against Berkeley were men with large tracts of land on the frontier and with a record of aggression against neighboring tribesmen. On occasion the governor had punished them for their actions against the Indians (*The Governor and the Rebel,* pp. 160–237). While there were a few gentlemen—or those who had some claim to be so called—among the rebels, some of these men took the oath to Bacon under compulsion. Colonel Thomas Swann was compelled to sign but was able to keep his son from so doing (Craven, *Colonies in Transition,* p. 143).

One gets the distinct impression that, overwhelmingly, the upper orders supported the governor and were plundered by the rebel forces. See, for example, the names and characters of the men executed (entry book of the royal commission, Pepys 2582, Magdalene College, Cambridge University); the analysis of the commissioners of the behavior of the leading men in the province (CO 1/41/ff. 278-80); and John Berry's description of the men who suffered by the rebellion (CO 5/1371/pt. ii, pp. 179-81).

31. See Moryson's and Berry's account, CO 5/1371/pt. ii, pp. 423-27; the review and conclusion by the three commissioners, CO 5/1371/pt. ii, pp. 411-19; Moryson to Culpeper, 14 April 1677, the commissioners to Thomas Watkins, 14 April 1677, CO 5/1371/pt. ii, pp. 201-4, 205-7; Moryson to Berkeley, 21 April 1677; commissioners to Coventry, 31 April 1677, CO 5/1371/pt. ii, pp. 208-11, 193-98.

32. See the letters of the king and Coventry, 15, 16 May 1677, CO 389/6/pp. 188-98, 201-5.

33. Jeffreys to Williamson, 11 June 1677, CO 1/40/f. 225; Ludwell to Coventry, with duplicate to Williamson, 14 April 1677, CO 1/40/ff. 54-55, 56-57.

34. See the commission's account, breviary, and conclusion in Samuel Wiseman's entry book, Pepys 2582, Magdalene College, Cambridge University; Alexander Culpeper's answer, CO 1/41/ff. 275-76; minutes of the Lords of Trade, 4 December 1677, CO 1/41/ff. 273-74; memorandum of the Lords of Trade, 6 December 1677; order in council, 7 December 1677, CO 1/41/no. 122; order in council, PC 2/66/pp. 236-37 (also in CO 5/1355/pp. 222-29).

35. Minutes of the Committee for Foreign Affairs, 9 December 1677, Longleat, Coventry MSS, vol. 77, f. 144; Charles II to Jeffreys, 27 December 1677, CO 389/6/pp. 235-36; order of the Lords of Trade, 6 December 1677 with annotated list of the council presented by Berry and Moryson, CO 1/41/ff. 277, 278-80.

36. Jeffreys to [Moryson], 1 April 1678, to Coventry, 4 July 1678, Longleat, Coventry MSS, vol. 78, ff. 206, 214, 215, 268; Thomas Ludwell to Coventry, 17 April 1678, ibid., f. 226; Moryson to Coventry's secretary (Cook), 28 May 1678, ibid., f. 273; Thomas Ludwell to Williamson, 17 April 1678, CO 1/42/f. 111; Daniel Parks to Williamson, 30 January 1677/8, CO 1/41/f. 304; William Sherwood to Williamson, 8 August 1678, CO 1/42/f. 304; and Sherwood to Williamson, 1 July 1678, CO 1/42/no. 103.

37. Moryson to Blathwayt, 25 October 1678, representation of the burgesses to Jeffreys, and order in council, 30 October 1678, CO 1/42/ff. 346, 352, 353. See also Secretary James Vernon's notes on Jamaica, BL, Add. MSS 40,774, f. 341; John C. Rainbolt, "A New Look at Stuart 'Tyrany'; The Crown's attack on the Virginia Assembly, 1676-1689," *VMHB* 75 (October 1967): 398-99, concluded that it was doubtful Poyning's Law (a constitutional provision for Ireland by which the English Privy Council initiated all legislation) was actually intended for Virginia.

38. Journal of the Lords of Trade, with proposals from Culpeper, CO 1/42/f. 372; order in council, 14 March 1678/9 on the report of the Lords of Trade of 18 February PC 2/67/pp. 132-33.

39. Chicheley to Coventry, 20 May 1679, Chicheley to Charles II, ? May 1679, CO 5/1355/pp. 360-61, 362.

40. Charles II to Culpeper, 5 December 1679, CO 389/8/p. 16; warrant to

Culpeper, 8 December 1679, CO 1/43/f. 315: Culpeper's instructions, 6
December 1679, additional instructions, 7 December 1679, CO 5/1355/pp.
326-56, 404; Rainbolt, "New Look," pp. 398-401.

41. Proclamation by Culpeper, 8 July 1680, CO 1/45/f. 187; Culpeper to
[Coventry], 8 July 1680, CO 1/45/f. 8; Spencer to Coventry, 9 July 1680, CO
1/45/f. 188; Culpeper's heads of requests to the king, 12 August 1680, CO
1/45/f. 268; Blathwayt's report on the state of the plantation revenue, 4 October
1680, PRO, Treas. 64/88/ff. 26-27; Lords of Trade to Culpeper, 14 October
1680, CO 5/1355/pp. 388-92; order in council, 14 October 1680, PC 2/69/p.
121.

42. Spencer to Coventry, 20 August 1680, CO 5/1355/pp. 396-98.

43. Entries for 15, 30 June 1680, receiver general's books, Treas. 64/88/ff.
8, 19-20; Blathwayt to Culpeper, 2 September 1680, CW, Blathwayt Paper, vol.
17.

44. Customs Board to the Lords of Trade, 10 January 1680/1, CO 1/46/f.
165; Spencer to Leoline Jenkins, 13 May 1681, CO 1/46/f. 324; and the council
and burgesses to the king, n.d., CO 1/47/f. 80.

45. Lords of Trade to the king, 31 October 1681, CO 5/1356/pp. 1-2;
Blathwayt's reports. PRO, Treas. 64/88/ff. 47, 50-51; and Charles II to
Culpeper, 1 October 1681, CO 389/8/pp. 83-84.

46. Lords of Trade to the king, 13 December 1681, CO 1/1356/pp. 3-6;
Commissioners of Customs to the Lords of Trade, 13 December 1681, CO
1/47/ff. 252-53; Culpeper's projects, 18 October 1681, CO 1/47/f. 180;
Culpeper to the Lords of Trade, 25 October, 12, 15 December 1681, CO 1/47/ff.
193-94, 258-60, 276.

47. Commission and instructions to Culpeper, 27 January 1681/2, CO
389/8/pp. 97-106, 107-22; Charles II to Chicheley, 20 January 1681/2, CO
389/8/p. 92.

48. Chicheley to Leoline Jenkins, 8 May 1682, CO 1/48/f. 28; Lord
Baltimore to Blathwayt, 26 March 1682, CO 1/48/f. 185; Chicheley to Charles
II, 8 May 1682, HL, Blathwayt Papers BL86; Spencer to Jenkins, 8 May 1682,
CO 1/48/ff. 230-31; Chicheley to Jenkins, 8 May 1682, CO 1/48/f. 28; Spencer
to Jenkins, 28 May 1682, CO 1/48/f. 26; Baltimore to Jenkins, 31 May 1682,
CO 1/48/f. 277; Fitzhugh to John Cooper, 5 June 1682, *Fitzhugh Letters,* ed.
Davis, pp. 125-26; Spencer to Blathwayt, 10 June 1682, CW, Blathwayt Papers,
vol. 16.

49. Spencer to Blathwayt, 12 August 1682, CW, Blathwayt Papers, vol. 16;
Spencer to Leoline Jenkins, 12 August 1682, CO 1/49/f. 106; Sir Henry
Chicheley to Sir Thomas Chicheley, 12 June 1682, CO 1/48/f. 321.

50. Lords of Trade to the king, 14 June 1682, CO 5/1356/pp. 74-77; orders
in council, 17 June 1682, CO 5/1356/pp. 77-81; Culpeper's petition to the king,
14 July 1682, SP 29/419/no. 154; Culpeper to Jenkins, 16 October 1682, CO
1/49/f. 246; and Blathwayt to Jenkins, 1 November 1682, CO 1/50/f. 49.

51. Culpeper to Blathwayt, 20 March 1682/3; Blathwayt to Spencer, 2 May
1683; and Spencer to Blathwayt, 14 August 1683, CW, Blathwayt Papers, vol.
17.

52. Culpeper to George Legge, Lord Dartmouth, 18 March 1682/3, HMC,

Eleventh Report, App., pt. V (London, 1887), p. 80; [Lord Baltimore] to [William Penn], n.d., HSP, Penn MSS, Official Correspondence, 1:1; Culpeper to the Lords of Trade, 20 September 1683, CO 1/48/no. 11; Culpeper to [Jenkins], 20 March 1682/3, CO 1/51/f. 171; Spencer to Jenkins, 15 February 1682/3, 25 March 1683, CO 1/51/ff. 73, 213; Spencer to the Lords of Trade, 29 May 1683, CO 1/51/f. 340; council of Virginia to the Lords of Trade, 4 May 1683, CO 1/51/ff. 316-18; Spencer to Blathwayt, 15 February, 9 May, 12 August, 14 August 1683, CW, Blathwayt Papers, vol. 16.

53. In the winter of 1684 Culpeper successfully negotiated with the Commissioners of the Treasury for the arrears of his salary and for his patents to rent in Virginia. He did not surrender the Northern Neck, however; Charles II preferred to compromise rather than take the issue to law. Culpeper's proposals, 18 November 1683, CO 1/53/ff. 163-64; Blathwayt to the attorney general, 16 October 1683, CO 5/1356/p. 244; Blathwayt to Effingham, 24 February, 8 March, 6 September 1684, CW, Blathwayt Papers, vol. 14; warrant to the solicitor general, 24 June 1684, CO 5/1356/pp. 276-80.

54. Commissioners of Customs to the Commissioners of the Treasury, 26 October 1683, CO 1/53/f. 104; instructions to Effingham, 24 October 1683, CO 5/1356/pp. 205-7; additional instructions, 3 December 1683, CO 5/1356/pp. 265-72; Blathwayt to Spencer, 1 October 1683, 12 March 1683/4, CW, Blathwayt Papers, vol. 16; and Rainbolt, "New Look," p. 401.

55. Blathwayt to Spencer, 28 July 1684, CW, Blathwayt Papers, vol. 16; William Byrd to [Thomas Grendon], 20 May 1684, *Byrd Correspondence,* ed. Tinling 1:20.

56. Spencer to Sunderland, 21 July 1684, CO 1/55/f. 30; Spencer to Jenkins, 4 April, 26 May 1684, CO 1/54/ff. 157, 312; address of the burgesses, 22 May 1684, CO 1/54/ff. 292-97; Effingham to the Customs Board, 20 February 1684/5, and to Blathwayt, 21 June 1685, PRO, Treas. 64/88/pp. 185, 178.

57. Effingham to Leoline Jenkins, n.d., but endorsed as received 17 June 1684, CO 1/54/f. 358; Spencer to the Lords of Trade, 23 June 1684, CO 1/54/f. 374; Spencer to Blathwayt, 23 June, 9 July 1684, CW, Blathwayt Papers, vol. 16; and the council of Virginia to the king, 17 June 1684, CO 5/1356/pp. 303-5.

58. Effingham to Sunderland, 26 November 1684, with enclosures, information of various witnesses, CO 1/56/ff. 96, 98-99, 100, 102, 103, 108. Captain Thomas Allen of the *Quaker* thought that Talbot intended his freshly sharpened dagger for him when he rejected Talbot's homosexual advances.

59. Blathwayt to Effingham, 9 December 1684, draft and fair copies, CW, Blathwayt Papers, vol. 14.

Chapter 11

1. For some examples of patronage, see the proprietary entry books, CO 5/286/ff. 53, 54, 76, 84, 108-9; CO 5/287/f. 23; CO 5/288/f. 15. For a list of the deputies and provincial nobility and the proprietors nominating them, see CO 5/286/f. 42.

2. Richard S. Dunn, "The English Sugar Islands and the Founding of

South Carolina," *South Carolina Historical Magazine* 72 (April 1971): 81–93; and Richard Waterhouse, "South Carolina's Colonial Elite: A Study in the Social Structure and Political Culture of a Southern Colony," (Ph.D. diss., the Johns Hopkins University, 1973), pp. 17–49.

3. Proprietors to ———, 18 May 1674, CO 5/286/ff. 49–50; Shaftesbury's instructions to Andrew Percivall, 23 May 1674, PRO 30/24/48, no. 55, pp. 127–33, 141; Colleton to John Locke, 22 July 1674, Bodl., Locke MS c.6, 217; Locke minute book, Locke MS c.30, p. 13; proprietary commission for Joseph West, 25 April 1674, CO 5/286/ff. 48–49.

4. Joseph West to John Locke, 30 April 1676, Bodl., MS Locke c.23, f. 69; proprietors to the governor and council at Ashley River, 10 April 1677, CO 5/286/ff. 65–67; proprietors to the governor, council and inhabitants, 10 April 1677, CO 5/286/f. 63; proprietors' articles of agreement, 10 April 1677, CO 5/286/f. 63; Haley, *Shaftesbury,* p. 433; proprietary commission and instructions, 17 May 1680, CO 5/286/ff. 77–78; instructions to Percivall, 21 February 1680/1, CO 5/286/ff. 80–81; instructions to Percivall and Matthews, 9 March 1680/1, CO 5/286/ff. 85–86; proprietors to the governor and council, 7 March 1680/1, CO 5/286/ff. 86–87.

5. Instructions to Joseph Morton, 10 May 1682, CO 5/286/f. 95; proprietors to [the governor and council], 5 June 1682, CO 5/286/f. 101; idem, 17 December, 19 December 1679, CO 5/286/ff. 73–74, 74–75; Converse D. Clowse, *Economic Beginnings in Colonial South Carolina: 1670–1730* (Columbia: University of South Carolina Press, 1970), pp. 76–77; and the rules for granting lands, embodied in the directions given the provincial surveyor, 20 November 1682, CO 5/287/ff. 33–34.

6. Sirmans, "The Bull Family of Colonial South Carolina," pp. 60–61.

7. Proprietary commissions, 18 May 1682, CO 5/286/f. 106; articles of agreement with Cochran and Campbell, 31 July 1682, CO 5/287/ff. 8–10; proprietors to Governor Joseph Morton, 21 November 1682, CO 5/288/f. 45; proprietors to Governor Sir Richard Kyrle, 4 March 1683/4, CO 5/287/f. 65; and Charles II to Sir George Haddo and the Privy Council of Scotland, 15 August 1682, *CSPD, Charles II, 1682,* p. 340.

8. Proprietors to the governor and council at Charles Town, 10 May 1682, CO 5/288/ff. 91–92; proprietors to Morton, 21 November 1682, CO 5/288/ff. 4–5; proprietors to the governor and Parliament, 22 June, 30 September 1683, CO 5/287/ff. 22, 39; Sir Peter Colleton to Sir Richard Kyrle, 28 June 1684, CO 5/287/f. 65; proprietors to the governor and deputies, 30 September 1683, CO 5/287/f. 8; third set of the Fundamental Constitutions, 17 August 1683, CO 5/287/ff. 24–32.

9. Commissions dated 21 June, 30 September 1683, CO 5/287/f. 23, 3 June 1684, CO 5/288/ff. 15, 18; Craven, Bath, and Colleton to Sothell, 6 November 1683, CO 5/288/f. 10.

10. Proprietors to Kyrle, 9 June 1684, CO 5/288/ff. 17, 18–19; proprietors to West, 13 March 1684/5, CO 5/287/ff. 54–55, 57–58.

11. Sirmans, *Colonial South Carolina,* pp. 40–47.

12. Cardross and others to the governor and council, 25 March 1685, CO 5/287/f. 67; minutes of the palatine court, 6 October 1685, CO 5/287/f. 74;

warrant for the commitment of Izard, 17 November 1685, CO 5/287/f. 75; Cardross to Quary, 17 July 1685, CO 5/287/f. 68; proprietors to Morton, 9, 10 September 1685, CO 5/288/ff. 32-33, 34.

13. This distinction was seen by Mattie Erma E. Parker, "Legal Aspects of 'Culpeper's Rebellion,' " pp. 118-19; Mattie Erma E. Parker, ed., *North Carolina Higher-Court Records, 1670-1696* (Raleigh: North Carolina State Department of Archives and History, 1968), p. xlii; and Hugh Rankin, *Upheaval in Albemarle: The Story of Culpeper's Rebellion* (Raleigh: North Carolina Charter Tercentenary Commission, 1962), pp. 27-30. For the plot against Miller by Culpeper and Jenkins, see the affidavit by Henry Hudson, CO 1/55/f. 50, doc. no. 25(v).

14. [Sir Peter Colleton's] case between Miller, Culpeper, and others, CO 1/44/ff. 41-42; Henry Hudson's affidavit, CO 1/55/f. 50, no. 25(v); proprietors to the assembly, 21 November 1676, CO 5/286/ff. 58-59; commission to Eastchurch, 21 November 1676, CO 5/286/f. 60; appointments for proprietary deputies, 21 November 1676, CO 5/286/ff. 61-62.

15. Anonymous representation to the proprietors, CO 1/43/ff. 359-64; affidavit of Solomon Summers, CO 1/44/f. 49.

16. Depositions by Henry Hudson, CO 1/44/f. 34; by Thomas Miller, CO 1/44/ff. 36-37; by Timothy Biggs, CO 1/44/f. 55 and CO 1/45/f. 230; affidavit of Solomon Summers, CO 1/44/f. 49; unsigned representation of the proprietors, CO 1/43/ff. 359-64; affidavit of Peter Brockwell, CO 1/44/f. 51. A copy of the charges against Miller signed by Crafford, Bird, and others is in CO 1/44/f. 32.

17. Eastchurch to Herbert Jeffreys, 25 December 1677; Foster, Crafford, Bird, and Blount to ———, 27 December 1677, Longleat House, Coventry MSS, vol. 78, ff. 152, 154.

18. Affidavit of John Taylor, CO 1/44/f. 35; proposals and affidavit of Biggs, CO 1/45/f. 57; affidavit of Thomas Miller, CO 1/44/f. 46; case of the proprietors, CO 1/44/f. 42; proprietary instructions to Harvey, 5 February 1678/9, CO 5/286/ff. 270-72; proprietors' warrant to Robert Holden, 19 February 1678/9; proprietors to the council at Albemarle, 8 February 1678/9, CO 5/286/f. 73.

19. Affidavit of John Taylor, CO 1/44/f. 35; declaration of Culpeper to the inhabitants of Albemarle, 25 February 1678/9, CO 1/44/f. 33.

20. Miller's petition, n.d., CO 1/44/f. 15; Culpeper's petition, n.d., CO 1/44/f. 10; Commissioners of Customs to the Commissioners of the Treasury, 22 January 1679/80, CO 1/44/ff. 30-31; William Blathwayt to Lord Culpeper, 11 January 1679/80, 5 April 1680, CW, Blathwayt Papers, vol. 17.

21. The proprietors' case, CO 1/44/f. 42; Gillam's statement, CO 1/44/f. 58; [Blathwayt] to Henry Guy, 19 February 1679/80; orders in council, 19 December 1679, 4 February 1679/80, 7 April 1680; PC 2/68/pp. 330, 378, 379, 387; Commissioners of Customs to the proprietors, 15 April 1680, CO 1/44/f. 385.

22. Miller's petition, 29 June 1680, CO 1/45/f. 159; petition from Albemarle, n.d., read in council 30 June 1680, CO 1/45/f. 166; petition of Miller, n.d., but read in council 19 July 1680, CO 1/45/f. 185; Colleton to

Blathwayt, 9 August 1680, CO 1/45/no. 73; proprietors to the Lords of Trade, n.d., CO 1/45/ff. 282–83; Blathwayt to Lord Culpeper, 26 August 1680, CW, Blathwayt Papers, vol. 17.

23. Minutes of the proprietary board, 14 December 1683, CO 5/286/ff. 108–9; proprietors to the governor of Albemarle, 14 February 1683/4, CO 5/288/ff. 13–14.

24. Reavis, "The Maryland Gentry and Social Mobility," p. 426; and Menard, "From Servant to Freeholder," p. 61.

25. Jordan, "The Royal Period of Colonial Maryland," pp. 7–9.

26. Baltimore's statement, 26 March 1678, CO 1/42/ff. 86–87.

27. John Yeo to the archbishop of Canterbury, 25 May 1676, Bodl., MS Tanner 114, f. 79; Canterbury to the bishop of London, 2 August 1676, CO 5/723/pp. 27–30; minutes of the Lords of Trade (with paper by Baltimore), 19 July 1677, CO 1/41/f. 61; Lords of Trade to Baltimore, 19 July 1677, CO 1/41/ff. 63–64. Baltimore's paper was in response to memorial from Henry Compton, bishop of London, on abuses of the churches in the colonies (CO 5/723/p. 27).

28. Thomas Notely to ———, 22 January 1676/7, CO 1/39/ff. 20–21.

29. Baltimore to Elizabeth Calvert, 10 July 1679, to Thomas Gilbert, 13 July 1679, Baltimore, Maryland Historical Society, Calvert Papers, MS 174; Baltimore to Blathwayt, 21 April 1680/1, CW, Blathwayt Papers, vol. 18.

30. Badcock to the Commissioners of Customs, 26 May 1681, CO 1/46/ff. 351–52; Badcock to the Commissioners of Customs, 10 July 1681, CO 5/723/pp. 61–65.

31. Baltimore to Anglesey, 28 April 1681, 7 June 1681, with deposition by Lowe, CO 1/47/ff. 43–44, 6, 4; Commissioners of Customs to the Lords of Trade, with enclosures from Rousby, 15 December 1681, CO 1/47/ff. 282–83, 284, 285, 293–94; order in council, 8 February 1681/2, PC 2/69/p. 456; and Charles II to Baltimore, 8 February 1681/2, CO 1/48/ff. 127–28.

32. The best discussion of Coode and the Gerard circle is David W. Jordan, "John Coode, Perennial Rebel," *Maryland Historical Magazine* 70 (Spring 1975): 1–28.

33. Philip Calvert to Colonel Henry Meese, 29 December 1681, CO 1/47/f. 321 (a folio printed in London by A. Banks in 1682); Baltimore to the lord privy seal, 19 July 1681, CO 1/47/f. 75; Nicholas Spencer to Blathwayt, 29 May 1682, CW, Blathwayt Papers, vol. 16; extracts of letters received by the Lords of Trade from Philip Ludwell, CO 1/47/ff. 79, 80, 92.

34. Trials of Fendall, Coode, and Godfrey, 8, 14, 15 November 1681, CO 1/48/ff. 87–102; Baltimore to Blathwayt, 26 March 1682, CO 1/48/f. 185; Cadwallader Jones to Baltimore, 6 February 1681/2, CO 1/48/f. 115.

35. Nicholas Spencer to William Blathwayt, 23 June 1684, CO 1/54/f. 374; Effingham to Leoline Jenkins, 17 June 1684, CO 1/54/f. 358; Spencer to Blathwayt, 9 July 1684, CW, Blathwayt papers, vol. 16; Effingham to the earl of Sunderland, 26 November 1684, CO 1/56/f. 96; Spencer to Sunderland, 27 April 1685, CO 1/57/f. 251; Spencer to Blathwayt, 1 April 1685, CW, Blathwayt Papers, vol. 16.

36. Blathwayt to Effingham (draft), 25 March 1685, CW, Blathwayt

Papers, vol. 14. The date of this draft is uncertain. It is endorsed as 12 February but also marked as sent on 23 February.

37. Blathwayt to Effingham, 2 July 1685, CW, Blathwayt Papers, vol. 14; Blakiston to the Commissioners of Customs, 20 April 1685, CO 1/57/ff. 226–29 and presented by the Customs Board to the Committee of Trade and read on 10 July 1685.

38. Baltimore's answer, [16?] July 1685, CO 1/58/ff. 24–26.

Chapter 12

1. Charles Calvert to Lord Baltimore, 26 April 1672, Maryland Historical Society, the Calvert Papers, no. 1064; John Collins to Governor John Leverett of Massachusetts, 10 April 1674, *Original Papers,* comp. Hutchinson, p. 443.

2. Royal letter countersigned by Arlington, 13 June 1674, in Leaming and Spicer, *Original Constitutions,* p. 49; patent from Charles II, 29 June 1674, ibid., pp. 41–45; royal warrant to the attorney general, 3 July 1674, CO 324/2/pp. 56–57; Charles II to Andros, 12 August 1674, CO 324/2/p. 58; warrant from James to Sir Francis Winnington and John Churchill, 23 July 1674, CO 5/1112/p. 13; Werden to Andros, 13 February 1674/5, 31 August 1676, CO 5/1112/pp. 17, 22–23.

3. Penn to Fenwick [20 January 1674/5]; Fenwick's answer [30 January 1674/5]; Penn to Fenwick, 13 February 1674/5; BL, Harleian MSS 7001, f. 300; memorandum of 31 May 1675, New York entry book, CO 5/1112/f. 18; Quinquepartite Deed, in Leaming and Spicer, *Original Constitutions,* pp. 61–72.

4. See the account of the pretensions of the proprietors of New Jersey to pay no customs at New York, 19 September 1679, CO 1/43/ff. 219–20; memorandum in the New York entry book, 6 August 1680, CO 5/1112/f. 32; warrant from the duke, 6 September 1680, CO 5/1112/f. 33; Werden to Andros, 6 November 1680, CO 5/1112/f. 34; the duke's confirmation of the soil and grant to the government of West New Jersey to Byllynge, 6 August 1680, CO 5/1261/ff. 140–49. The best treatment of the question is in John E. Pomfret, *The Province of West New Jersey, 1609–1702: A History of the Origins of an American Colony* (Princeton, N.J.: Princeton University Press, 1956), pp. 110–12.

5. Royal letter, 15 November 1683, CO 389/9/ff. 245–46.

6. Letter of Jennings and Budd for themselves and the proprietors in West New Jersey, 28 February 1684/5, CW, Blathwayt Papers, vol. 7; Pomfret, *West New Jersey,* pp. 141–45.

7. Joseph E. Illick, *William Penn, the Politician: His Relations with the English Government* (Ithaca, N.Y.: Cornell University Press, 1965), pp. 24–25, argues against the thesis that the proprietary grant to Penn served to allow Charles II to rid himself of Quakers and other Whig Dissenters who would, if they remained in England, oppose the king in Parliament. There is no evidence to support this proposition, and few Dissenters at the time had the franchise.

8. Werden to Blathwayt, 23 June 1680, CO 1/45/f. 154; Werden to Blathwayt, 16 October 1680, CO 1/46/f. 58; draft report undated, with corrections in the hand of Blathwayt to the Committee of Trade, ? October 1680,

CO 1/46/f. 73; the attorney general's observations, n.d., CO 1/46/f. 90; North's observations, CO 1/46/ff. 101, 103; Lords of Trade to the king, 24 February 1680/1; draft charter, 28 February 1680/1; CO 1/46/ff. 210, 211-28; order in council, 28 February 1680/1, PC 2/69/p. 224.

9. Penn to Robert Turner, [5 March 1680/1], *Memoirs of the Historical Society of Pennsylvania,* 14 vols. (Philadelphia, Pa., 1826-95), 1:208.

10. Penn to Thomas Lloyd, 21 July 1686, *PMHB* 80 (April 1956): 239-45.

11. Charles II to the inhabitants of Pennsylvania, 2 April 1681, CO 389/4/pp. 164-65; Penn to Markham, 18 October 1681, HSP, Dreer Collection, Letters and Papers of William Penn; Penn to Turner, [5 March 1680/1], *Memoirs of the Historical Society of Pennsylvania,* 1:208.

12. Penn to Turner and others, [12 April 1681], ibid., p. 210.

13. The best discussion is in Gary B. Nash, *Quakers and Politics: Pennsylvania, 1681-1726* (Princeton, N.J.: Princeton University Press, 1968), pp. 6, 12-27, 34-44; and "The Framing of Government in Pennsylvania: Ideas in Contact with Reality," *WMQ* 3d ser. 23 (April 1966): 186-201.

14. Gary B. Nash, "The Free Society of Traders and the Early Politics of Pennsylvania," *PMHB* 89 (April 1965): 152-62; John E. Pomfret, "The First Purchasers of Pennsylvania, 1681-1700," *PMHB* 80 (April 1956): 137-63.

15. Penn to Henry Sydney, n.d., BL, Add. MSS 32681, f. 209; newsletter, 13 January 1682/3, *The Manuscripts of the Earl of Egmont,* 2 vols. (London: HMC, 1905-1909), 2:126.

16. See Nash, "The Framing of Government in Pennsylvania," pp. 205-9.

17. Penn to Blathwayt, 30 July 1683, CW, Blathwayt Papers, vol. 7; Penn to John Bridgeman, [1 August 1683], CO 1/52/f. 92; Penn to Laurence Hyde, [5 February 1682/3], London, Friends' House Library, Penn MSS, I, no. 15; memorandum read at the Plantation Board, 13 February 1683/4, CO 1/54/f. 66; Baltimore to Leoline Jenkins, 6 April 1684, CO 1/54/f. 159.

18. Penn to Thomas Lloyd, 7 October 1684, HL, HM 22031; John Povey to Sir Robert Southwell, 17 October 1685, NUL, Portland MSS, PwV60.

19. Penn to Thomas Lloyd, 21 July 1686, *PMHB* 80 (April 1956): 236-47.

20. Blathwayt to Lord Culpeper, 26 August 1680, CW, Blathwayt Papers, vol. 17. On the confused jurisdictional question, see also Charles II to Andros and Major Anthony Brockholes, 12 August 1674, CO 324/4/p. 58; Werden to Andros, 13 February 1674/5, 31 July 1676, CO 5/1112/ff. 17, 22-23; account of the pretensions of the proprietors of New Jersey, 19 September 1679, CO 1/43/ff. 219-20.

21. James Claypool to Thomas Cooke, [5, 26 September 1682], *James Claypool's Letter Book, 1681-1684: London and Philadelphia,* ed. Marian Balderston (San Marino, Calif.: Huntington Library, 1967), pp. 146, 158.

22. Charles II to the Privy Council of Scotland, 15 August 1682, *CSPD, Charles II, 1682,* p. 340; order in council, 8 September 1682, *CSPD, Charles II, 1682,* p. 377; report of the Lords of Trade, 30 September 1682, CO 324/4/pp. 84-85.

23. John Robert Strassburger, "The Origin and Establishment of the Morris Family in the Society and Politics of New York and New Jersey, 1630-1746," (Ph.D. diss., Princeton University, 1976), pp. 76-82.

24. Rudyard to Penn [13 January, 13 March 1682/3], London, Friends' House Library, Penn MSS, I, nos. 7, 10.

25. Sir George Mackensie to Werden, 21 December 1682, CO 5/1112/f. 40; warrant to George Jeffreys and John Churchill, 2 March 1682/3, CO 5/1112/ff. 46–47; order in council and proclamation, 23 November 1683, CO 389/4/pp. 171–72.

26. Wait Winthrop to Fitzjohn Winthrop, "Winthrop Papers," *MHSC,* 5th ser. 7: 445–47; Thomas Rudyard to Penn, 30 July 1683, Friends' House Library, Penn MSS, I, no. 12.

27. The duke's commissioners to Perth, 8 March 1683/4, BL, Add. MSS 24928, f. 24; Perth, Mackensie, and John Drummond to Sunderland, 22 August 1684, PRO, SP 29/438/no. 33; Perth and Drummond to Blathwayt, 22 August 1684, CW, Blathwayt Papers, vol. 7.

28. Order in council, 16 October 1685, PC 2/71/p. 143.

29. Petition of Delavall, [24 June 1675], CO 5/1112/ff. 18–19.

30. Instructions to Andros with notations by Werden, 1 July 1674, CO 5/1112/pp. 4–9; James to Andros, 6 April 1675, 28 January 1675/6, CO 5/1112/ff. 17–18, 20; Werden to Andros, 13 February 1674/5, 28 January 1675/6, 7 May 1677, CO 5/1112/ff. 17, 21c–21d.

31. Andros to Governor John Winthrop, 3 November 1674; John Winthrop to Fitzjohn Winthrop, 25 November 1674; Andros to Governor Winthrop, 4 December 1674; Winthrop to Andros, 16 December 1674; MHS, Winthrop Family Papers; James to Andros, 28 January 1675/6, CO 5/1112/f. 20b; Sir John Werden to Andros, 28 January 1675/6, CO 5/1112/ff. 21c–21d.

32. Ritchie, *The Duke's Province,* p. 141; and Jeanne Gould Bloom, "Sir Edmund Andros: A Study in Seventeenth Century Colonial Administration" (Ph.D. diss., Yale University, 1962), pp. 11–13.

33. See the account of the special court at Albany, 25 August 1676, signed by Robert Livingston, FDRL, Livingston Family Papers, Robert Livingston General Correspondence.

34. S. J. Stern, "Knickerbockers Who Asserted and Insisted: The Dutch Interest in New York Politics, 1664-1691," *New-York Historical Society Quarterly* 58 (April 1974): 125–30; Ritchie, *The Duke's Province,* pp. 145–48.

35. Thomas John Archdeacon, "The Age of Leisler: New York City, 1690-1710: A Social and Demographic Interpretation," (Ph.D. diss., Columbia University, 1971), pp. 70–71, speculated that by the terms of the English navigation code all but a few Dutch merchants had the requisite connections to transfer their trade from Amsterdam to London and other English ports. Most of the Dutch and Huguenot traders lost out. The thesis is tenuous, for under the Dutch West India Company, the trade of New Netherlands had been restricted, dominated by merchants from Amsterdam. The Dutch in New Netherlands were, in the main, artisans, laborers, and farmers. Moreover, after the English conquest, trade between New York and Holland continued, as evidenced by the notarial records in Amsterdam, Leyden, and Haarlem. This trade was not illegal if the vessels involved were owned, manned, and captained by Englishmen or denizens of an English colony. The Dutch in New York—and not merely the Van Cortlandts, Philipses, and Van Dams—who married into English families were

able to establish connections with merchants in England. In 1670 a group of traders in the Netherlands hired *The Duke of York,* skippered by Johannes Luyck of New York, for a voyage to America. Eagidius Luyck was designated the agent to dispose of the cargo in New York. Three London merchants, John Iberson, John Burkin, and John Buss, were involved in the cargo. Provided the ship and others so engaged stopped at some English port on the voyage across the Atlantic, there was nothing in this arrangement contrary to the English navigation code. See Jan Kupp, "Aspects of New York-Dutch Trade under the English, 1670-1674," *New-York Historical Society Quarterly* 58 (April 1974): 139-47. Trade from the colonies to Europe in enumerated goods was perfectly legal, provided the vessels, properly owned and manned, entered at some English port. In 1676 English officials noted with no objection that the *Rebecca* of New York carrying tobacco and furs entered at Falmouth and then proceeded for Amsterdam. Two years later the *Margaret* of New York, similarly laden, entered at Falmouth and then left for Amsterdam (Thomas Holden to Secretary Williamson, 9 November 1676, SP 29/386/f. 354; Holden to Williamson, 15 August 1678, SP 29/406/f. 9; Francis Bellot to Williamson, 19 August 1678, SP 29/406/f. 46.

36. Graham to Livingston, 7 April 1679, FDRL, Livingston Family Papers, Robert Livingston General Correspondence; McCormick, "Leisler's Rebellion," p. 23.

37. McCormick, "Leisler's Rebellion," pp. 110-16; Ritchie, *Duke's Province,* pp. 155-63.

38. The proceedings of the court are printed in *NYCD* 3: 288-89; see also the account in John West to Robert Livingston, 6 June 1681, FDRL, Robert Livingston General Correspondence.

39. Adam Cardonnel to Dyer, 14 September 1682, CO 1/49/no. 55 enclosing the certificate of the deputy mayor of Southampton; *Gazette* (London) for 10 August 1682, CO 1/49/no. 24; petition of Dyer, n.d., CO 1/48/f. 355; order in council, 3 August 1682 on the report of the Lords of Trade, 21 July 1682, CO 5/1112/pp. 54-55.

40. The brief for the defense in the action for assault and unlawful imprisonment, a broadsheet, CO 1/50/ff. 259-60; John Churchill's report, n.d., CO 1/53/ff. 163-64.

41. See Lawrence H. Leder, "The Glorious Revolution and the Pattern of Imperial Relationships," *New York History* 46 (July 1965): 203-11 for a more realistic assessment than is to be found in the Whiggish David S. Lovejoy, "Equality and Empire: The New York Charter of Libertys, 1683," *WMQ* 3d ser. 21 (October 1964): 493-515.

42. Sir John Werden to Anthony Brockholes, 11 February 1681/2, CO 5/1112/f. 38; James to Brockholes, 28 March 1682, CO 5/1112/ff. 38-39; minutes of the duke's commissioners, 2 March 1682/3, BL, Add. MSS 24927, ff. 19, 21, 23; instructions to Dongan, 27 January 1682/3; CO 5/1112/ff. 41-44; Werden to the lord register of Scotland, 4 January 1682/3, CO 5/1112/f. 40.

43. Sir John Werden to Dongan, 10 March, 26 August, 1 November, 4 December 1684, CO 5/1112/ff. 47, 48, 50-51, 52-53; entries for 23 February, 5

March, 10 March, 17 March, 11 August 1684, proceedings of the duke's commissioners of revenue, BL, Add. MSS 24927, ff. 35, 36, 37, 40, 41. For the signing of the bill for the provincial legislature, see the memorandum in the New York entry book, CO 5/1112/ff. 50, 53.

44. Observations on the charter for New York, CO 1/66/f. 354; minutes of the Lords of Trade, 3 March 1684/5, CO 391/5/pp. 101–3.

Chapter 13

1. Fitzjohn Winthrop to Wait Winthrop, 5 April 1680, "Winthrop Papers," *MHSC,* 5th ser. 8:286; Fitzjohn Winthrop to [Andros], 22 November 1680, ibid., pp. 292–93; Andros to [Fitz]john Winthrop, 29 November 1680, ibid., 6th ser. 3:469.

2. Harris to Secretary Williamson, 26 April 1675, CO 1/34/f. 127; Harris to Fleetwood Shephard, 26 April 1675, CO 1/34/ff. 125–26.

3. Reply of Stoughton and Bulkeley to the complaint of the Warwick men, 30 July 1678, CO 1/42/ff. 297–98; reply of Holden and Greene, 30 July 1678, CO 1/42/ff. 299–300; minutes of the Committee for Plantations, 30 July 1678, CO 391/2/p. 261.

4. Order in council, 2 July 1679, PC 2/68/pp. 159–60 (also CO 5/903/pp. 346–51); Charles II to the governor and General Court of New Plymouth, 9 July 1679, CO 389/9/pp. 12–14.

5. For changes in the membership of the company, see Arnold, *The Records of the Proprietors of the Narragansett,* pp. 26–39; and the "Trumbull Papers," *MHSC,* 5th ser. 9:98, 111.

6. Printed advertisement, CO 1/42/f. 369; see also Trumbull and Hoadley, *Public Records of the Colony of Connecticut,* 2:544.

7. Governor Josiah Winslow to Charles II, 2 November 1679, CO 5/904/pp. 81–84; Governor John Cranston to Charles II, 6 January 1679/80, CO 1/44/f. 2; petition of the Atherton Associates, CO 1/42/f. 286.

8. Leete to Sunderland, 15 July 1680, CO 1/45/ff. 214, 223; Richard Wharton and John Saffin to Culpeper, 5 October 1680, CO 1/46/f. 50 with breviate, ff. 52–53; petition of Saffin and other Atherton Associates, CO 1/46/ff. 54–55; Wharton to Blathwayt, 10 June, 13 July, 4 October 1680, CW, Blathwayt Papers, vol. 6; John Allyn to Blathwayt, 22 September 1680, CW, Blathwayt Papers, vol. 4 (also in Connecticut Archives, Hartford, Foreign Correspondence, vol. 1, pt. 1, British government, 1663–1748, no. 23); Wharton to Fitzjohn Winthrop, 29 September 1680, "Winthrop Papers," *MHSC,* 6th ser. 3:466; Fitzjohn Winthrop to [Andros], 22 November 1680, "Winthrop Papers," *MHSC,* 5th ser. 8:292–93.

9. Blathwayt to Cranston, 11 June 1680, CW, Blathwayt Papers, vol. 11; Blathwayt to Southwell, 21 May, 15 June 1681, NUL, Portland MSS, PwV52; and Blathwayt to Richard Wharton, 21 October 1682, CW, Blathwayt Papers, vol. 6.

10. Minutes of the Committee for Plantation Affairs, 18 October 1681, CO 391/3/p. 292; "A State of the Narragansett Country," probably presented by

Culpeper, CO 1/43/ff. 366-67; Blathwayt to Richard Wharton, 22 October 1681, CW, Blathwayt Papers, vol. 6; and report of the Lords of Trade, n.d., 1682, CO 5/904/pp. 140-42.

11. Richard Wharton to Wait Winthrop, 16 July 1683, "Trumbull Papers," *MHSC,* 5th ser. 9:112-13; Coddington to the Lords of Trade, 15 September 1683, CO 1/52/f. 240; Randall Holden and John Greene to the king, 17 September 1683, CO 1/52/f. 242; Holden and Greene to [Blathwayt or Southwell], 29 September 1683, HL, Blathwayt Papers, BL287.

12. Cranfield to Leoline Jenkins, 19 October 1683, CO 1/53/f. 55; Cranfield to the Lords of Trade, 19 October 1683, CO 1/53/f. 70; Cranfield to Blathwayt, 27 September 1683, CW, Blathwayt Papers, vol. 12; Cranfield to Blathwayt, 5 October 1683, ibid., vol. 1.

13. Minutes of the Atherton partners, 11 October 1683, *The Records of the Proprietors of the Narragansett,* ed. Arnold, p. 38; report of the Cranfield commission, Boston, 20 October 1683, CO 1/56/ff. 177-81 (printed in *MSHC,* 1st ser. 5:235-43.

14. See the orders in council, 27 February 1683/4, CO 1/54/f. 87; and 24 March 1684/5, PC 2/71/p. 39.

15. Wharton to Blathwayt, 10 June 1680, CW, Blathwayt Papers, vol. 6.

16. John Crown's petition, n.d., CO 1/43/f. 13; Nathaniel Morton to Charles II, 13 July 1677, CO 1/41/f. 33; and Randall Holden and John Greene's claims in behalf of Rhode Island, 3 February 1678/9, CO 1/43/f. 18.

17. Governor and council of New Plymouth to Charles II, 1 July 1679, CO 1/43/ff. 144-45; certificate by Winslow, 22 August 1679, Connecticut Archives, Foreign Correspondence, vol. 1, pt. 1, British government, doc. no. 12b; commissioners of the New England Confederation to Sunderland, 25 August 1679, CO 1/43/ff. 195-96.

18. Report of the Lords of Trade, 4 December 1679, CO 1/43/ff. 308-11; Charles II to New Plymouth, 12 January 1679/80, CO 5/903/pp. 315-17.

19. Petition of the General Court of New Plymouth, 15 September 1680, CO 1/46/ff. 17-18; Winslow to the king, 2 July 1680, CO 1/45/f. 177; Blathwayt to Randolph, 20 August 1680, CW, Blathwayt Papers, vol. 1, no. 53: Blathwayt to Winslow, 29 February 1679/80; Winslow to Blathwayt, 2 July 1680; Winslow to Blathwayt, 15 September 1680; and Blathwayt to Richard Wharton, 26 May 1681, CW, Blathwayt Papers, vol. 6.

20. Richard Smith of the Narragansett country, having been ejected by the Rhode Islanders, had turned for aid to the General Court of New Plymouth (minutes of the Committee for Trade and Plantations, 16 April 1681, CO 391/3/p. 260; Hinckley to Blathwayt, 26 May 1682, "Hinckley Papers," *MHSC,* 4th ser. 5:65; Hinckley to Blathwayt, 18 November 1682, ibid., pp. 77-78).

21. Blathwayt to Hinckley, 27 September 1683, "Hinckley Papers," *MHSC,* 4th ser. 5:91-92.

22. Hinckley and the council of New Plymouth to the king, [? November 1683], CO 1/53/ff. 155-56. The endorsement on the colony's petition of 15 September 1680, CO 1/46/ff. 17-18, indicates that it was read on two occasions, once on 27 October 1681 and again on 17 November 1684.

23. Lord, "Politics and Social Structure of Portsmouth," pp. 186-210, 312-13.

24. Proposals of Gorges, Mason, and the earl of Stirling, n.d., CO 1/31/f. 72; petitions of Mason and Gorges and a statement of Mason's title, CO 1/34/ff. 3-4, 103-4; Collins to Leverett, 19 March 1674/5, *Original Papers,* comp. Hutchinson, pp. 472-73.

25. Minutes of the Committee for Trade and Plantations, 1, 2 December 1675, CO 1/35/ff. 268-70; order in council, 22 December 1675, PC 2/65/pp. 77-78 (also CO 5/903/pt. 2/pp. 79-82).

26. The answer of the Bay Colony and the instructions to Bulkeley and Stoughton are printed in Bouton, *New Hampshire Provincial Papers,* 1:326-33, 333-34.

27. Report of Raynsford and North, [17 July 1677], CO 1/41/ff. 51-53; order in council, 18 July 1677, PC 2/66/p. 75.

28. Mason to the Lords of Trade, 25 March 1678, CO 1/42/f. 84; Blathwayt to Bulkeley and Stoughton, enclosing the petition of Mason, 15 January 1678/9, CO 1/43/ff. 4, 5; Stoughton and Bulkeley to the Lords of Trade, 4 February 1678/9, CO 1/43/f. 19; and their reasons for deferring action, 12 March 1678/9, CO 1/43/ff. 48-49.

29. Order in council, 20 June 1679, CO 5/903/pp. 351-57; Mason's agreement with the crown, 1 July 1679, CO 5/940/pp. 2-3 (also CO 1/43/f. 142); order in council with the report of the committee, 2 July 1679, PC 2/68/pp. 169-71; Warren to Sir Robert Southwell, 7 July 1679, CO 1/43/f. 158; and the list of nominees, 7 July 1679, CO 1/43/f. 160.

30. Council to the king, 29 March 1680; and Cutt to the governor of Massachusetts, 25 May 1680, *Documents of New Hampshire,* ed. Bouton, 1:409-10, 410-11. See also Edward Randolph to Josiah Winslow, 29 January 1679 [1680], in Robert Noxon Toppan, *Edward Randolph: Including His Letters and Official Papers . . . with Other Documents,* 7 vols. (Boston, 1898-1909), 3:64; and the extracts of Randolph's letters prepared by Blathwayt, CO 1/44/ff. 75-80.

31. The laws of March 1680 are in Bouton, *Documents of New Hampshire,* 1:383-84.

32. See the proceedings of the council relating to Randolph and Barefoote, CO 1/56/ff. 134-35; Blathwayt to Randolph, 20 August 1680, CW, Blathwayt Papers, vol. 1, no. 52.

33. Council of New Hampshire to the king, 31 May 1681, CO 1/46/ff. 355-56; warrant for the apprehension of Mason, 18 May 1681, CO 1/46/f. 333; council to the Lords of Trade, 7 May 1681, CO 1/46/f. 289 with enclosures and the comments of the English attorney general on the New Hampshire statutes.

34. Representation of Nicholas Shapleigh, Francis Champernoun, Walter Barefoote, and William Bickham to the king, 17 May 1681, CO 1/46/f. 330; testimony of various witnesses as gathered by Mason, CO 1/46/ff. 251, 320, 332, CO 1/47/ff. 131-32; Chamberlain to Blathwayt, 14 May 1681, CO 1/46/f. 326; Chamberlain to the Lords of Trade, 16 May 1681, CO 1/46/ff. 328-29.

35. Articles against Waldron and Martin, 13 November 1681, CO 1/47/f. 215; petition of Mason to the Lords of Trade, [10 November 1681], CO 1/47/f.

210; Lords of Trade to the king, 13 January 1681/2, CO 5/940/pp. 30–31. Apparently Cranfield was extremely reluctant to take the position, later complaining bitterly that it was only Blathwayt's importuning that made him accept. So Robert Southwell recounted him as saying when Cranfield and Blathwayt had fallen out (Southwell to Blathwayt, 6 January 1685/6, CW, Blathwayt Papers, vol. 1, no. 37). Neither Blathwayt nor his patron, Southwell, seem to have had his own way in naming men for colonial posts. Southwell was particularly opposed by "a great Lord," possibly Rochester, Clarendon, or Sunderland, "whose design is to expose you as a supporter of fanaticks." Southwell perhaps tended to take a moderate position on New England, and Blathwayt thought Cranfield would answer his purpose (Blathwayt to Southwell, 2 November 1681, 5 April 1682, NUL, Portland MSS, PwV52).

36. Commission and instructions for Cranfield, CO 5/940/pp. 35–51, 51–62 (also in CO 389/8/pp. 129–43, 147–57); Cranfield to Leoline Jenkins, 14 May 1684, CO 1/54/f. 278; and John Yonge Akerman, ed., "Moneys Received and Paid for Secret Services of Charles II and James II from 30th March, 1679, to 25th Dec., 1688," Camden Society, *Publications,* 52 (London, 1851): 51.

37. Cranfield to the Lords of Trade, 1 December 1682, CO 5/940/pp. 77–83; Cranfield to Blathwayt, 23 October, 1 December 1682, CW, Blathwayt Papers, vol. 1, nos. 10, 17; Cranfield to [Sir Leoline Jenkins], n.d., but received at the end of January 1682/3, CO 1/50/f. 185. The petition from the inhabitants of Maine supporting a merger with New Hampshire (CO 1/50/f. 187) bears thirty-nine signatures, but all were written by three or four persons.

38. Cranfield to the Lords of Trade, 30 December 1682, CO 1/50/ff. 245–46; Randolph to the Lords of Trade, 30 December 1682, CO 1/50/f. 249.

39. Randolph's "Short Narrative," CO 1/53/f. 24; Mason to Blathwayt, 22 March 1682/3, CW, Blathwayt Papers, vol. 12; Hannah Gove's petition, CO 1/51/f. 95; and Gove's later statement, CO 1/58/f. 86b. The letter he wrote to the justices of the court of sessions on 29 January 1682/3 (Bouton, *Documents of New Hampshire,* 1:459) while in jail is not altogether coherent.

40. Richard Waldron's account of the trial of Gove, CO 1/51/f. 78; another report in CO 1/52/ff. 11–13; Cranfield to the Lords of Trade, 20 February 1682/3, CO 1/51/f. 88.

41. Cranfield to Secretary Jenkins, 20 February 1682/3, CO 1/51/ff. 76–77; Cranfield to the Lords of Trade, 10 January 1682/3, CO 1/51/f. 4–5; Cranfield to Blathwayt, 20 February 1682/3, CW, Blathwayt Papers, vol. 1, no. 24. See also Jacobsen, *William Blathwayt,* pp. 464–65.

42. The case of Barefoote against Wadleigh, 23 March 1682/3, CO 1/51/ff. 175–76; Walton's case, 23 March 1682/3, CO 1/51/f. 204; orders in council, 25 August, 24 October 1683, 23 January 1683/4, PC 2/70/pp. 34, 48, 107–8.

43. Barefoote to the Lords of Trade, ? March 1683, CO 1/51/f. 164; Cranfield to the Lords of Trade, 27 March 1683, CO 1/51/ff. 222–23; Cranfield to Jenkins, 19 June 1683, CO 1/52/f. 32; Cranfield to Blathwayt, 5 October 1683, CW, Blathwayt Papers, vol. 1, no. 28; Gove to Randolph, 11 June 1683, CO 1/52/f. 16; Gove's petition, n.d., SP, 29/435/no. 178; Gove to the Lords of Trade, 10 September 1684, CO 1/55/f. 97; Randolph to Sir Robert Southwell, 1

September 1685, in Toppan, *Randolph Letters,* 4:42; and James II to the president and council of New England, 13 April 1686, CO 389/9/p. 388.

44. See Vaughan's letter in the form of a journal sent to Weare from Portsmouth, 4 February 1683/4, *Documents of New Hampshire,* ed. Bouton, 1:527.

45. Cranfield to the Lords of Trade, 6 January, 16 January 1683/4, CO 1/57/f. 2, CO 1/54/ff. 13–14; the information against Moody and William Vaughan's journal, *Documents of New Hampshire,* ed. Bouton, 1:484–85, 520.

46. Cranfield to the Lords of Trade, 14 May 1684, CO 1/54/f. 268; Cranfield to Secretary Jenkins, 14 May 1684, CO 1/54/f. 278.

47. Order in council, 11 July 1684 and the petition by Weare, CO 1/55/ff. 11, 13–14.

48. Lords of Trade to Cranfield, 23 July 1684, CO 5/940/p. 109; Cranfield to the Lords of Trade, 16 October 1684, CO 1/55/ff. 176–77.

49. Order in council, 8 April 1685, PC 2/71/p. 65, approving a report of the Lords of Trade of 22 March 1684/5; two orders in council, 29 April 1685, PC 2/71/pp. 73, 74.

50. Navy Board to Samuel Pepys, 15 May 1686, PRO, Adm. I, 3555/p. 731.

51. Blathwayt to Sir Philip Musgrove, 12 December 1685, CW, Blathwayt Papers, vol. 1, no. 27; Sir Robert Southwell to Blathwayt, 6 January 1685/6, ibid., vol. 1, no. 28.

Chapter 14

1. See the discussion in Lewis and Webb, "Voting for the Massachusetts Council of Assistants," pp. 625–34.

2. Orders and laws of the General Court, 3 November 1675, *Records of Massachusetts Bay,* ed. Shurtleff, 5:59–63; Richard Wharton to John Winsley, 10 February 1675/6, CO 1/36/f. 40.

3. Martin to Bradstreet, 26 March 1683, Bradstreet to Martin, 27 March 1683, CO 1/51/ff. 217, 219.

4. Perry Miller, *The Puritan Mind: From Colony to Province* (Boston: Beacon Press, 1961), pp. 137–40.

5. See the analysis in Stephen Foster, *Their Solitary Way,* pp. 184–85.

6. See the notes by Joseph Williamson on New England trade and the analysis of Sir George Downing, 24 April 1676, CO 1/36/ff. 87–88; Customs Board to the Council for Plantations, 12 May 1675, CO 1/34/f. 156; Customs to the Treasury, 11 October 1675, CO 1/35/f. 237. For evidence that some New England shippers were conforming to the requirements to land enumerated produce before proceeding to Amsterdam and other European ports, see the reports from officials in the outports in *CSPD, Charles II, 1675–1676,* pp. 134, 181, 435; and SP 29/391/no. 119, SP 29/401/no. 140.

7. John Collins to Leverett, 10 April 1674, Thompson to Leverett, 3 August 1674, *Original Papers,* ed. Hutchinson, pp. 444, 462–63.

8. Petition of the English merchants, CO 1/36/f. 16; opinion of the at-

torney general, 8 February 1675/6, CO 5/903/pt. 2, p. 106; questions to be asked of the merchants trading to New England, 18 April 1676, CO 1/36/ff. 83–84; minutes of the Lords of Trade, 28 January, 24 April 1676, CO 5/903/pt. 2, pp. 85, 108–10.

9. Leverett to Thompson, 24 August 1674, *Original Papers,* comp. Hutchinson, p. 465; Gorges's proposals to Danby, 24 February 1675/6, Osborne-Danby Papers, BL, Add. MSS 28089, f. 1; Mason to Danby, 5 March 1675/6, BL, Egerton MSS 3340, f. 155; order in council, 22 December 1675 on the report of the committee, 20 December 1675, CO 389/3/pp. 30–32. See also Leverett to Anglesey, 6 September 1675, CO 1/35/f. 108.

10. Mason to the lord treasurer, 5 March 1675/6, BL, Egerton MSS 3340, f. 155; minutes of the Committee for Trade and Plantations, 2 December 1675, CO 5/903/pt. 2, pp. 61–63; Leverett to Williamson, 24 October 1677, CO 1/41/f. 232.

11. Royal letter, 10 March 1675/6, CO 324/2/pp. 82–83; and the points of inquiry given Randolph by the Committee for Plantations, 20 March 1675/6, CO 1/36/ff. 62–63.

12. Leverett to Secretary Coventry, 13 June 1676, CO 1/37/f. 13; Randolph to Coventry, 17 June 1676, CO 1/37/ff. 18–19 (copy in Danby's papers, Leeds Papers, 17, BL, Egerton 3340, f. 162.

13. Randolph's report, 20 September 1676, CO 1/37/ff. 191–92 (also in BL, Add. MSS 28,089, ff. 20–24); notes on New England trade 1 August 1676, Osborne-Danby Papers, BL, Add. MSS 28,089, f. 3; and Blathwayt to Southwell, 18 September 1676, NUL, Portland MSS, PwV51.

14. Randolph's report, 12 October 1676, CO 1/37/ff. 237–44 (also in Osborne-Danby Papers, BL, Add. MSS 28,089, ff. 7–20).

15. Shurtleff, *Records of Massachusetts,* 4:99–100, 106–16; Leverett to Coventry, 12 October 1676, Longleat House, Coventry MSS, vol. 77, f. 239; petition of Stoughton and Bulkeley, 13 December 1676, CO 1/38/ff. 248–49; Blathwayt to Southwell, 16 December 1676, NUL, Portland MSS, PwV51.

16. See the notes by Secretary Williamson, 7 February 1676/7, SP 29/366/ff. 149–50 and the report of Lord Justice Raynsford and Lord Justice North, CO 1/41/ff. 51–53.

17. Minutes of the Committee for Plantation Affairs, 19, 27 July 1677, CO 391/2/pp. 89, 95; the case of the governor and company of Massachusetts, n.d., CO 1/41/ff. 66–68; report of the Lords of Trade, 19 July 1677, CO 1/41/f. 65; order in council, 20 July 1677, CO 1/41/ff. 70–73; memoranda concerning New England, n.d., CO 1/41/ff. 74–76; memorandum on the abridgment of the charter of 1629, CO 1/41/ff. 77–82; narrative of the state of New England, CO 1/41/ff. 83–84; objections against the charter, CO 1/41/ff. 85–86; and brief of the prosecution against the charter, CO 1/41/ff. 87–88.

18. Minutes of the Lords of Trade, 2 August 1677, CO 391/2/p. 99; report of the law officers, CO 1/41/ff. 110, 111.

19. Minutes of the Committee for Plantations, 8 April 1678, CO 391/2/pp. 233–45; Randolph to the Lords of Trade, 18 April 1678, CO 1/42/ff. 116–17 (also CO 5/903/pp. 267–75); Sir Robert Southwell to the attorney general and solicitor general, 8 [18] April 1678, CO 1/42/f. 154 (also CO 5/903/pp. 265–66); report of the law officers, 16 May 1678, CO 1/42/f. 155.

20. Two sets of answers by Bulkeley and Stoughton, 28 June, 2 July 1678, CO 1/42/ff. 188-91.

21. Minutes of the Lords of Trade, 30 July 1678, CO 391/2/p. 261; Southwell to the duke of Ormonde, 27 August 1678, HMC, *Ormonde MSS,* n.s. 4:447; order in council, 31 July 1678, PC 2/66/p. 379. Following the Restoration Robert Mason had turned over to Lord Chancellor Clarendon the volume of proceedings of the old council of Plymouth held by his grandfather, John Mason. In the spring of 1678 the Lords of Trade wrote to Clarendon's son to return the book. Later records dating from the Restoration were so incomplete that Southwell was also forced to write to the younger Clarendon, hoping that some of the late lord chancellor's private papers might contain relevant documents (Lords of Trade to Clarendon, 24 May 1678, CO 1/42/f. 168; Southwell to Clarendon, 18 September 1678, CO 1/42/no. 127).

22. See the answers of the General Court to the objections raised by the crown law officers, 2 October 1678, and their letter to the provincial agents, 10 October 1678, *Records of Massachusetts Bay,* ed. Shurtleff, 5:198-201, 201-3.

23. Randolph's proposals, 15 January, 22 February 1678/9, CO 1/43/ff. 2, 33; Southwell's report to the Committee for Plantations, 8 March 1678/9, CO 1/43/f. 47; Lords of Trade to the Treasury, 10 March 1678/9, CO 5/903/pp. 343-44; order in council, 6 June 1679, CO 1/43/f. 123; Blathwayt to Southwell, 25 July 1679, NUL, Portland MSS, PwV51; Cranston to Southwell, 1 August 1679, Blathwayt to Cranston, 8 April 1680, CW, Blathwayt Papers, vol. 11.

24. Proposals by Stoughton and Bulkeley, 23 May 1679, CO 1/43/f. 110; draft memorandum of the Lords for Plantation Affairs, n.d., CO 1/43/ff. 37-38; order in council, 19 June 1679, with draft of letter from the crown, 20 June 1679, CO 5/903/pp. 351-57 (also PC 2/68/pp. 132-35).

25. Robert Holden to the Commissioners of Customs, 10 June 1679, CO 1/43/ff. 124-26.

26. See Barrow, *Trade and Empire,* pp. 31-33, as a corrective to Bailyn, *The New England Merchants in the Seventeenth Century,* p. 163.

27. Randolph to [Southwell], 12 March 1680, HL, BL 227.

28. William Andrew Polf, "Puritan Gentlemen: The Dudleys of Massachusetts, 1576-1686," (Ph.D. diss., Syracuse University, 1974), pp. 216-17; Lewis, "Massachusetts and the Glorious Revolution," p. 91.

29. Bradstreet to the Lords of Trade, 18 May 1680, CO 1/44/f. 407; replies of the General Court, CO 1/44/ff. 409-13; Bradstreet and the General Court to Sunderland, 22 May 1680, CO 1/44/f. 421; Bridgewater to Secretary Jenkins, 19 July 1680, SP 29/414/no. 28.

30. Blathwayt to Randolph, 20 August 1680, CW, Blathwayt Papers, vol. 1, no. 52; report of the Lords of Trade, 15 September 1680, CO 389/9/pp. 50-53; order in council, [1] 5 September 1680, PC 2/69/pp. 103-4.

31. Randolph to Sir Leoline Jenkins, 16, 30 April 1681, CO 1/46/ff. 258-59, 283-84; articles against Massachusetts, CO 1/46/f. 260; Randolph's petition to the king and his articles of high misdemeanor against Danforth, CO 1/46/ff. 243, 244.

32. Minutes of the Lords of Trade, 9, 16 April 1681, CO 391/3/pp. 256, 260.

33. Randolph's queries for the attorney general and Robert Sawyer's reply,

CO 5/904/pp. 120–22 (also in BL, Egerton MSS 2395, f. 595) and a second set of questions and replies, CO 1/46/ff. 353, 354.

34. Minutes of the Lords of Trade, 18 October 1681, CO 391/3/p. 292; Blathwayt to Randolph, 22 October 1681, in Toppan, *Randolph Letters,* 3:113; Blathwayt to Richard Wharton, 22 October 1681, CW, Blathwayt Papers, vol. 6; order in council, 21 October 1681 with the royal letter to Massachusetts, CO 1/47/ff. 181, 183; and Blathwayt to Southwell, 2 November 1681, NUL, Portland MSS, PwV52.

35. Answer of the elders, 4 January 1680/1, CO 1/46/f. 164.

36. Shurtleff, *Records of Massachusetts Bay,* 5:333, 339, 340; instructions to the agents, ibid., pp. 346–49.

37. Randolph to Jenkins, 11 April 1682, CO 1/48/f. 202; Randolph's articles against Danforth, 28 May 1682, CO 1/48/f. 265; Randolph to Jenkins, 29 May, 14 June, 7 August 1682, CO 1/48/ff. 267, 333–35, CO 1/49/ff. 96–97; Randolph to Bishop Compton, 29 May 1682, in Toppan, *Randolph Letters,* 3:145–46; Randolph to Rochester, 24 June 1682, ibid. 3:154–55.

38. Petition of the Governor and Company of Massachusetts, CO 1/49/f. 114; answer of the agents, 29 August 1682, CO 1/49/ff. 144–50 based on the instructions of the Massachusetts General Court of 15 February 1681/2; order in council, 20 September 1682, PC 2/69/pp. 545–46 (also CO 5/904/pp. 166–67; copies of the queries by Randolph and the opinion of the attorney general, CO 1/49/f. 233; and the list of laws of Massachusetts, CO 1/50/ff. 264–66; Richards to Mather, 12 December 1682, "Mather Papers," *MHSC,* 4th ser. 8:499; petition by Richards and Dudley, 24 January 1682/3, CO 5/904/p. 167.

39. Nowell to Richards, 9 November 1682, 28 March 1682/3, "Winthrop Papers," *MHSC,* 5th ser. 1:431–32; instructions and letter to the agents, 30 March 1683, *Records of Massachusetts Bay,* ed. Shurtleff, 5:389–92.

40. Address and directions for signing, CO 1/52/ff. 3, 4.

41. Randolph's articles against Massachusetts, CO 1/52/ff. 5–6, 22–23; minutes of the committee, 12 June 1683, CO 391/4/p. 167; memorandum of the committee, 12 June 1683, CO 5/904/pp. 166–67; order in council, 13 June 1683, PC 2/70/p. 1; and Normansell to the Governor and Company of Massachusetts Bay, 9 July 1683, CO 5/905/pp. 180–81; Blathwayt to Lord Conway, 16 June 1683, SP 29/425/no. 7.

42. Randolph to [the Lords of Trade], 11 July 1683, CO 1/52/f. 47; Blathwayt to the attorney general, 17 July 1683, CO 5/904/pp. 183–84; order in council, 20 July 1683, and royal declaration, 9 August 1683, CO 389/8/pp. 214, 215–16 (also CO 1/52/ff. 61, 63).

43. Randolph to Leoline Jenkins, 26 July, 3 August 1683, CO 1/52/ff. 71, 96; Randolph's particulars on the government of Massachusetts, HL, Blathwayt Papers, BL230; Randolph to Southwell, 19 August 1683, in Toppan, *Randolph Papers,* 3:262; Randolph to Blathwayt, 3 September 1683, CW, Blathwayt Papers, vol. 1, no. 27; Cranfield to Blathwayt, 5 October 1683, CW, Blathwayt Papers, vol. 1, no. 28.

44. Shurtleff, *Records of Massachusetts Bay,* 5:421, 423–25, 430–31, 439–41; Randolph's "Short Narrative," CO 1/54/ff. 101–3.

45. Dudley to Blathwayt, 1 December 1683, Bulkeley to Blathwayt, 7

December 1683, CW, Blathwayt Papers, vol. 4; Bradstreet and the majority of the magistrates to Secretary Jenkins, 7 December 1683, CO 1/53/f. 234.

46. [Richard Wharton?] to Randolph (extract), n.d., CO 1/54/f. 121; and the extracts of a paper probably by Increase Mather printed in Palfrey, *History of New England,* 3:383-85.

47. Dudley to Blathwayt, 4 May 1684, CW, Blathwayt Papers, vol. 4; Stoughton to Richard Streton, 5 May 1684, BL, Stowe MSS 746, f. 89.

48. Cranfield to Blathwayt, 16 January 1683/4, CW, Blathwayt Papers, vol. 1, no. 30; Randolph's "Narrative," CO 1/54/ff. 101-3; Randolph to Secretary Jenkins, 14 February 1683/4; and Bradstreet and others to Jenkins, endorsed as received on 22 March 1683/4, CO 1/54/f. 154.

49. The letter, variously dated 3 December and 9 December 1683, is printed in Toppan, *Randolph Papers,* 3:312-16 from a copy the younger Wharton turned over to Secretary Jenkins. See Randolph to Samuel Shrimpton, 18 July 1684; Randolph to Bradstreet, 4 September 1684, ibid., 3:310-11, 320-23; and the certificate by Jenkins, *CSPD, Charles II, 1683-1684,* p. 344. The letter is also printed in the *New England Historical and Genealogical Register* 49 (January 1885): 23-25 from a copy provided by G. D. Scull of Oxford. Scull may have used the version in the Bodl., MS Tanner 32 ff. 196-98.

50. Memorandum of the attorney general, 3 May 1684, CO 1/54/f. 228; orders in Chancery, 12, 14, 18, 21 June 1684, CO 1/54/ff. 250, 355, 360, 369.

51. Humphreys to Dudley, n.d., printed in Toppan, *Randolph Papers,* 3:240-41 from a copy in the Massachusetts Archives, CVI, 332; abstracts of letters from Bradstreet, Dudley, Stoughton, and Richard Wharton sent to Randolph, 8 December 1684, CO 1/56/ff. 197-98; and [Wharton?] to Randolph, 15 September 1684, CO 1/55/f. 108.

52. Notes of the arguments made in Chancery, CO 1/55/f. 237. Following the overthrow of James II some years later, agents for Massachusetts argued that the patent for the colony, like the charters of the English municipalities, had been illegally voided. Parliament failed to include the provincial charter in legislation for restoring the charters to the English boroughs. The action against the charter of Massachusetts stood.

53. See Ronald Dennis Cohen, "Colonial Leviathan: New England Foreign Affairs in the Seventeenth Century," (Ph.D. diss., University of Minnesota, 1967), pp. 393-95.

54. Order in council, 23 May 1682, CO 1/48/f. 254; Cranfield to Blathwayt, 23 October 1682, CW, Blathwayt Papers, vol. 1, no. 15; Cranfield to the Lords of Trade, 14 May 1684, CO 1/54/f. 268; and [Richard Wharton] (extract) to [?], 15 September 1684, CO 1/55/f. 108.

55. Minutes of the Lords of Trade, 8 November 1684, CO 391/5/p. 21. While it is tempting to conclude that military coercion was to be used to enforce royal authority, Blathwayt, who had now added the post of secretary at war to his other positions, at about this time wrote, "It cannot be to any purpose that H[is] M[ajesty] be at any charge (except for shipping and a small Honorary Guard for the Governor) for if the people be refractory the power of shipping will be much more effectual than 1,000 men in Pay which cannot cost less than £20,000 which H[is] M[ajesty] can expect no profitable returns from New

England" (draft, "Reflections on a Paper concerning America," HL Blathwayt Papers, BL416).

56. Minutes of the Lords of Trade, 22 November 1684, CO 391/5/p. 35; and Halifax's notes in Helen Charlotte Foxcraft, ed., *The Life and Letters of Sir George Savile, Bart., First Marquis of Halifax,* 2 vols. (London, 1898), 1:428–29; Lords of Trade to the lord president, 26 August 1685, CO 5/904/p. 251.

57. Randolph to Dudley, 9 January 1684/5, in Toppan, *Randolph Papers,* 4:12–13; Randolph to the bishop of Saint Asaph, ? March 1685, ibid., pp. 15–18; Randolph's memorial to the Lords of Trade with enclosures, 2 September 1685, CO 1/58/ff. 120, 121.

58. Blathwayt to Lord Howard of Effingham, 9 December 1684 (draft), CW, Blathwayt Papers, vol. 14; Blathwayt to Randolph, 20 August 1680, ibid., vol. 1, no. 52; Randolph to the [lord keeper], 3 December 1684, HL, Blathwayt Papers, BL232.

Epilogue

1. See Eugene L. Asher, *The Resistance in the Maritime Classes: The Survival of Feudalism in the France of Colbert* (Berkeley: University of California Press, 1960), pp. v, 94.

2. Chandaman, *English Public Revenue, 1660–1688,* pp. 33–35, 255–56.

3. For detailed treatments of this most complex subject, see Kenyon, *Robert Spencer, Earl of Sunderland,* pp. 124–200; and Godfrey Davies, "Tory Churchmen and James II," *Essays on the Later Stuarts* (San Marino, Calif.: Huntington Library, 1958), pp. 53–57. Jones, *Saw-Pit Wharton,* p. 257, thought it a moot point whether James really wanted only toleration and equality for all religions. He concluded that the weight of opinion was and remained that such equality would have led to the reestablishment of Catholicism, with diminishing hopes for toleration or even the survival of other Christian faiths. Illick, *William Penn, the Politician,* p. 77 was more emphatic: James's real policy was conversion of England to Roman Catholicism. Maurice Ashley, "King James II and the Revolution of 1688: Some Reflections on the Historiography," in *Historical Essays, 1600–1750: Presented to David Ogg* (New York: Barnes & Noble [1963]), pp. 201–2 pointed out that historians have repeated completely false accounts of the character of the king and his policies. Ashley's own conclusions were tentative, and while he doubted whether the king could ever be whitewashed, he found it difficult to believe that James was the tool of Sunderland, his priests, or the French king or that James was inconsistent in his attitude toward religious toleration. Miller, *Popery and Politics in England,* pp. 192–222, was convinced that James's primary aim was to improve the position of Catholicism in England by peaceful means. There was not the slightest possibility of imposing Popery by force. The king's actions, condemned as arbitrary and illegal by later Whiggish historians, were all directed toward the single end of allowing greater liberty and more civil rights to English Catholics and securing that freedom and those rights by parliamentary statute. The fallacy

in James's thinking lay in assuming that once Catholicism was allowed to compete, it could win out over Protestantism.

4. Boyer, *English Declarations of Indulgence*, pp. 68–71; Cranston, *John Locke*, p. 260; royal warrants, 9 March, 25 March 1686, SP 44/336/pp. 385–86, 391; order in council, 28 May 1687, PC 2/72/p. 461.

5. Newsletter for 12 April 1687, HMC, *Downshire Papers*, 4 vols. in 5 (London, 1924–40), 1(1):237; Marriett to Penn, n.d., BL, Add. MSS 34727, f. 157; Jones, *Saw-Pit Wharton*, pp. 257–58.

6. Maurice Ashley, *The Glorious Revolution of 1688* (London: Hodder Stoughton, 1966), pp. 59, 112; Davies, "Tory Churchmen and James II," pp. 76–84.

7. Unsigned newsletter in the hand of a clerk, dated Whitehall, 1 June 1686, in King William's Chest, SP 8/1/f. 74.

8. Philip S. Haffenden concluded a rather ambiguous essay by admitting that historians would never possess detailed knowledge of what James II intended, a purposeful conversion to Catholicism and abolition of assemblies or religious toleration and respect for the principle of representative government, but that, nonetheless, the scarcity of facts did not destroy the "central theme" ("The Crown and the Colonial Charters," p. 465). The conclusion of this present work suggests that there was no *central* theme, that Charles and James were in the main reacting to diverse developments and seeking several limited goals.

9. Blathwayt to Effingham, 6 March, 2 July 1685, CW, Blathwayt Papers, vol. 14.

10. Orders in council, 17 July 1685, CO 324/4/230–32 (also CO 5/723/pp. 102–3); order in council, 10 July 1685, PC 2/71/p. 115; Randolph to the Lords of Trade, 3, 18 August 1685, CO 1/58/ff. 52A, 71; minutes of the Lords of Trade, 3 August 1685, CO 5/904/pp. 249–50; order in council, 11 October 1685, PC 2/71/p. 143.

11. Randolph to Sir Robert Southwell, 1 August 1685, in Toppan, *Randolph Papers,* 4:29–30; Povey to Southwell, 1 April, 26 May 1686, NUL, Portland MSS, PwV60; Lords of Trade to the lord president of the council, 26 August 1685, CO 5/904/p. 251. On the role of Sunderland, see the discussion on Mather's source in Jacobsen, *William Blathwayt,* pp. 134–35.

12. Memorandum of the Lords of Trade, 21 April 1686, CO 324/4/pp. 232–33; order of the king in council, 30 April 1686, 324/4/pp. 233–34, also PC 2/71/p. 258; order in council, 30 May 1686, PC 2/71/p. 282; newsletter of 1 June 1686, Whitehall, in King William's Chest, SP 8/1/f. 74.

13. Sunderland to the attorney general, 6 June 1686, SP 44/56/p. 337.

14. Earl of Shaftesbury to the earl of Craven, 7 July 1686, CO 1/59/f. 390 (read to the king on 25 July 1686); Muschamp to the proprietors of Carolina, 11 April 1687 and attorney general Thomas Powis to the Lords of Trade, 7 July 1687, CO 1/62/f. 90; Commissioners of Customs to the Treasury, n.d., CO 5/288/f. 59; order in council, 30 July 1687, CO 324/5/p. 1 (also PC 2/72/p. 491).

15. Penn to the council of Pennsylvania, 25 September 1686, *PMHB*, 33, no. 3 (1909): 305; Kenyon, *Sunderland*, p. 175.

16. On this point see Jones, *The Revolution of 1688 in England,* pp. 176–77.

17. Randolph to [John Povey?] 27 June 1686, CW, Blathwayt Papers, vol. 1, no. 43; Randolph to Blathwayt, 28 July 1686, ibid., vol. 1, no. 49; and Dongan to Sunderland, 31 October 1687, CO 1/63/267–68.

18. Blathwayt to Southwell, 5 May 1688, NUL, Portland MSS, PwV53; Blathwayt to Randolph, 10 March 1687/8, in Toppan, *Randolph Papers,* 4:216.

19. Minutes of the council meeting, 18 June 1687, PC 2/72/p. 467; order in council, 23 March 1687/8, CO 1/64/no. 41; warrant dated 25 March 1688, CO 389/9/p. 467; and Sunderland to Dongan, 20 April 1688, CO 389/9/p. 469.

20. Minutes of the Lords of Trade, 26 April 1689, CO 391/6/p. 209.

21. Meeting of the General Court, 18 March 1684/5, *Records of Massachusetts Bay,* ed. Shurtleff, 5:469; entries for 21 July, 23 July 1685, in Samuel Sewall, *The Diary of Samuel Sewall,* ed. M. Halsey Thomas, 2 vols. (New York: Farrar, Straus, and Giroux, 1973), 1:71, 72.

22. William Dyer to Blathwayt, 16 November 1685, CW, Blathwayt Papers, vol. 4.

23. Sewall, *Diary,* 1:112, 113–17.

Index

Index

DATE DUE

GAYLORD   PRINTED IN U.S.A.